Scriptures of the Oral Torah

Sanctification and Salvation in the Sacred Books of Judaism

An Anthology
Edited and Translated by
JACOB NEUSNER

1817

Harper & Row, Publishers, San Francisco

Cambridge, Hagerstown, New York, Philadelphia, Washington
London, Mexico City, São Paulo, Singapore, Sydney

FIRST EDITION

Library of Congress Cataloging-in-Publication Data

Scriptures of the Oral Torah.

Bibliography: p.
Includes Index.
I. Neusner, Jacob, 1932–
BM497.2.N48   1987   296.1'205'21   87-45192
ISBN 0-06-066106-2

---

87 88 89 90 91 RRD 10 9 8 7 6 5 4 3 2 1

Contents

In memory of Frits C. Wieder, Jr.
Managing Director of E. J. Brill, Leiden

When, from 1960 to 1980, I was unable to publish a scholarly book or monograph in the U.S.A., he graciously accepted and published without subsidy every scholarly book I offered to him. In those same bleak years, he invited me to edit for Brill two academic monograph series, *Studies in Judaism in Late Antiquity* and *Studies in Judaism in Modern Times*. This he did not out of friendship but out of a sense of honor: respect for his own vocation, which was to secure for learning free exchange of ideas and open debate of even unthinkable possibilities, *sine ira et studio*. I offer in his memory my prayer that he receive the just reward reserved for all who risk error in quest of truth, who secure a fair hearing for persons and views subjected, whether for theological or political reasons, or merely because of envy, to bureaucratic excommunication. And that reward is great indeed because it is shared by only a few.

God rest his soul and bless him.

1. Process and Proposition, Sanctification and Salvation

This anthology presents scriptures of the oral Torah, with special reference, as I shall explain, to two matters, one of process, the other of proposition. The process displayed here shows how the oral Torah relates to the written Torah. The proposition that forms the centerpiece of this anthology concerns the matter of life after death for the individual and salvation at the end of time for Israel, the holy people of God. Through selections from the seven most important documents of the oral Torah brought to closure in late antiquity, from the second to the seventh century, we shall see how the framers of the oral Torah relate to the written Torah, or Scripture, their principal proposition concerning salvation and eternal life. In this way we shall see in rich detail how the characteristic and distinctive holy books of Judaism set forth on the foundations of God's revelation to Moses at Sinai doctrines central to the faith of Judaism as they proposed to teach that faith. Let us then begin with this notion of the oral Torah and consider its substance and sense.

DEFINING THE ORAL TORAH

When Moses received the Torah at Mount Sinai, God gave that Torah, or revelation in two media, the one in writing, the other formulated and trasmitted only orally, that is, in memory and not written down. The oral Torah—*Torah she-be-al-peh,* Torah that is memorized—is that half of the one whole Torah revealed by God to Moses at Mount Sinai that came down, from then to late antiquity, formulated and transmitted in memory alone. The oral Torah serves to complement and complete the written one—and vice versa. If we wish to understand Judaism, therefore, we first of all must ask how the Torah in two media, written, memorized, forms a single and cogent statement. Given the standing and authority of the Torah in Judaism, that is, God's full and exhaustive statement of God's will for the world and for holy Israel, God's first love, the issues are considerable. For the Judaism of the dual Torah, written and memorized, encompasses in its vision not Israel alone, but all of creation, to the outer reaches of uncharted space, and the entirety of humanity, traveling companions of all times on earth. All nations, all creatures through the revelation of the Torah come into relationship with God, creator of heaven and earth, ruler of the world, redeemer and savior of all being. When Israel speaks through the Torah, it addresses all being, and when God wishes to address the world, the Torah holds, God speaks through Moses in the Torah of the two media. This is an anthology of scriptures of that originally oral and memorized component of the Torah revealed by God to Moses at Mount Sinai: God's will for Israel and the world. Seven documents of the oral Torah contribute exemplary statements, in writing, of the memorized half of the one whole Torah of Moses, our master or rabbi.

All of these documents, each with its own style and points of special stress and emphasis, as I shall explain, reached written form in the language and categories of the sages of late antiquity, from the first through the seventh centuries of the Common Era. The statement alerts us to a paradox. Since these samples of the oral Torah are disparate and hardly uniform in style or in substance, since they come to us in writing, not orally, and since they furthermore reach the form in which we have them only long after the event of the revelation of the Torah to Moses at Sinai and not from the twelfth or thirteenth century Before the Common Era when, it is generally maintained, Israel made the Exodus from Egypt and reached Sinai, we have to notice a certain distance between the origin and authority of our documents, on the one side, and their form and particular point of entry into history, on the other. What God told Moses we hear for the first time in a variety of accents and modes of expression, in the name not of

God speaking to Moses in the wilderness of Sinai but of Yohanan ben Zakkai or Aqiba or Judah the Patriarch, all of whom lived in the Land of Israel nearly a thousand years after Moses, and the message comes in categories and circumstances deriving not from Israel in the wilderness but Jewry in what Israel called the Land of Israel but what the world knew as a Roman province, conquered Palestine, or in "exile" (in Israel's term) or in the satrapy of Babylonia in the Iranian Empire of the Parthian, then the Sasanian dynasty, as the world grasped matters. What Moses and the prophets and sages of old formulated and transmitted only in memory, orally, now reaches us in written form. The authorities, circumstances, and substance hardly conform to those of the first, the written Torah.

Clearly we face the task of sorting out facts of history and literature—what happened where and when, how we know about it, the traits of the writings that tell us—from fundamentals of faith. We have to sort things out the way the blind Isaac did when he gave his blessing to Jacob: the hand is the hand of Esau, the voice is the voice of Jacob. We live in the West, the modern and secular world of Esau. Finding our way in our blindness, from touch and feel we know that the hand that wrote the words was the hand of men* who lived in a particular place at a certain time. But the voice—that is another matter. For we hear in ways in which we do not feel and touch. The word not tangible, not in the storm and not in the fury, is the voice of silence, thin and sinewy. The voice is (not *was*) the voice of God, who speaks (not *spoke*) through Moses, *our* rabbi (not only theirs, long ago), who through time and today has spoken and now speaks through sages who have mastered and now stand for and exemplify God's Torah to Moses at Sinai. The Torah creates for holy Israel, the super-

---

I refer to "men" because all authors of the documents of the Judaism of the oral Torah were men. Women occur as authorities only very seldom indeed. In our own day, for the first time, women have found a place in the rabbinate as Reform, Reconstructionist, and Conservative rabbis and also serve as cantors. In addition, there are women who have joined in the scholarly enterprise of Judaism and have published important books.

natural entity, and eternal present, here and now as much as there and then. So has the Judaism of the dual Torah claimed from late antiquity to the present in its system of the sanctification of the here and now for the goal of salvation then and there, at the end of time.

The statements of a profound, theological truth with which I began therefore should not suffer reduction to a mere historical narrative. When we speak of Torah, God, and Moses, we address eternal verities to the current age. The when and where of our address locate themselves in historical time. But what we say, the words, come from beyond time and reach us out of eternity. When we speak of heaven and earth, creation, revelation and re-demption, holy Israel, God's people (not to be confused with the contemporary State of Israel, an altogether distinct category and entity of discourse), we therefore do not make use of historical language and we do not appeal to historical facts. And we cannot. For to the realm of being, in the reality of which we speak, history proves irrelevant and has nothing to say.

The reason is that history describes the order of events of a worldly character, drawing upon evidence of a secular order, and history explains those events by appeal to their order: this came first, therefore this stood before and caused that. Historical fact derives from historical evidence. Historical explanation rests upon this-worldly sequences of factual events. Historical narrative—us-ing the past tense to be sure—then forms a picture of reality based upon that selection and ordering of historical fact that rest upon the secular premise. An event is something that happens in the here and now and is to be documented in the completed past. And that is how it should be. History orders its world in precisely the way it must, telling the story of things humanity has been and done.

And so too does the Torah, or, in more general terms, religion. But the Torah, exemplifying religion, orders its world in its way, speaking of what God is and what God does. When, therefore, we open the Torah, or, in secular language, the sacred books of Judaism, we go in search not of an account of this-worldly events, their order and secular meaning, but supernatural happenings, their message and command. Still, we also live in the here and now of this world's order and ask questions about history and literature, not only about religion, the realm of the sacred and its—God's—reality. The Torah presents us with God's picture of ourselves. But the Torah speaks to us in historical time and out of historical circumstance. God spoke not only to humanity but through humanity, and the human being lives only in the here and now of a particular time and place, communicates solely in the language of historical time. That is the sole medium for communication to us, even though we are made in God's image, after God's likeness. We therefore affirm our humanity in God's image when, with all reverence and respect, we open the writings of the oral Torah by asking where, when, and why those words reached written form. The sages of the Mishnah and the Talmud and Midrash compilations, present what they, and all Israel from then for a long time with them, maintained were teachings that, in the language of their own place and time, contained the truth of Sinai. Writing down many of these teachings in the Mishnah, Talmuds, and Midrash compilations, sages shifted the oral part of the one whole Torah from one medium to the other, and that is why we can read them here.

WHERE, WHEN, AND WHY THE ORAL TORAH WAS WRITTEN DOWN

As a matter of historical fact, the oral Torah reached written form between the second and the seventh centuries, in a series of documents produced by the Judaic sages, or rabbis, of the Land of Israel and of Babylonia, beginning with the Mishnah and ending with the Talmud of Babylonia. The canon of rabbinical writings consists of exegeses of two principal documents, the Scriptures (the written Torah) and the Mishnah, a law code, ca. 200 C.E., which is the first document of the oral Torah. The explanations of the Mishnah begin with the Tosefta, a corpus of supplementary sayings, and continues with the Talmud of the Land of Israel, ca. 400 C.E., a systematic exegesis of the Mishnah, and the Talmud of Babylonia, also a systematic explanation of the Mishnah, ca. 500–600 C.E. A separate body of exegesis concentrates on Scripture, first of all, books of the Pentateuch, of Five Books attributed to Moses. These include Genesis Rabbah, on the book of Genesis, commonly regarded as a work of ca. 400, Leviticus Rabbah, on the book of Leviticus, ordinarily dated in ca. 450, and works on legal passages of Exodus, Leviticus, Numbers, and Deuteronomy, Sifra, on Leviticus, Sifré Numbers, and Sifré Deuteronomy; these are of indeterminate date, but probably of the later third or fourth century. (Yet another work, Mekhilta imputed to R. Ishmael, on Exodus, is generally held to derive from the same period, but some scholars place it in the Middle Ages, and the matter is still subject to debate.) There were various other writings of the same age, for instance, Pesiqta deRav Kahana, a collection of exegeses of verses of Scripture important on special occasions, following the style and conceptual program of Leviticus Rabbah; the Fathers According to Rabbi Nathan, an amplification of the Mishnah-tractate; the Fathers, in which stories about sages are told to enrich the Mishnah-tractate's account of sayings assigned to sages. All together, these and related contemporary writings constitute the oral Torah, as it had reached writing by the end of late antiquity, signified by the Muslim conquest of the Christian Middle East. It is, in writing, that is, that body of tradition assigned to the authority of God's revelation to Moses at Mount Sinai.

The oral Torah reached written form in two stages, the one marked in ca. 200 by the framing of the Mishnah and its closely associated documents, the Tosefta and tractate Avot, the other defined in ca. 400 by the Talmud of the Land of Israel and its friends, Genesis Rabbah and Leviticus Rabbah.

FROM THE FIRST CENTURY TO THE FOURTH IN JUDAISM

Two important events defined the history of the Jews in the Land of Israel from the first century to the fourth, the destruction of the Temple of Jerusalem in 70, and the catastrophic failure of the rebellion against Rome led by Bar Kokhba in 132–135. These two events formed, in reality, a single historical moment. For, in the mind of many, the first set in motion the expectations that led to the second. When the Temple was destroyed, Jews naturally looked to Scripture to find the meaning of what had happened and, more important, to learn what to expect. There they discovered that when the Temple had been destroyed earlier, a period of three generations—seventy years—intervened. Then, in the aftermath of atonement and reconciliation with God, Israel was restored to its Land, the Temple to Jerusalem, the priests to the service of the altar. So, many surmised, in three generations the same pattern will be reenacted, now with the Messiah at the head of the restoration. So people waited patiently and hopefully. But whether or not Bar Kokhba said he was the Messiah, he was to disappoint the hopes placed in him. The Jews, possessed of a mighty military tradition then as now, fought courageously but lost against overwhelming force. The result: Jerusalem was closed to the Jews, except on special occasions, and much Jewish settlement in the southern part of the country was wiped out. Deep disappointment settled over the people.

In ancient Israelite times the history of Israel defined the issues of faith, and the prophets in God's name interpreted events as statements of God's will to Israel. So it was perfectly natural that, in the period at hand, the Judaism that took shape should respond in a direct and immediate way to the momentous events of the day. In many ways Judaism, from age to age, forms God's commentary on the text that is formed by the events of the history of the Jewish people, and the holy books of Judaism contain that commentary. So too in the history of Judaism from the first to the fourth century. We work our way back from the books sages wrote to the Judaism that, through those books, they constructed in God's service. Of those books, the first and most important, the foundation for all else, the basis for Judaism from then to now, was the Mishnah. So let us consider the historical setting for that book and its message for the moment at which it came forth.

The Mishnah is a work of philosophy expressed through laws.

That is to say, it is a set of rules, phrased in the present tense: "one does this, one does not do that." But when we look closely at the issues worked out by those laws, time and again we find such profound essays on philosophical questions as being and becoming, the acorn and the oak, the potential and the actual. The topical program of the document, as distinct from the deep issues worked out through discussion of the topics, focuses upon the sanctification of the life of Israel, the Jewish people. Four of the six principal parts of the Mishnah deal with the cult and its officers. These are, first, Holy Things, which addresses the everyday conduct of the sacrificial cult; second, Purities, which takes up the protection of the cult from sources of uncleanness specified in the book of Leviticus (particularly Leviticus 12–15); third, Agriculture, which centers on the designation of portions of the crop for the use of the priesthood (and others in the same classification of a holy caste, such as the poor), and so provides for the support of the Temple staff; and, fourth, Appointed Times, the larger part of which concerns the conduct of the cult on such special occasions as the Day of Atonement, Passover, Tabernacles, and the like (and the rest of which concerns the conduct in the village on those same days, with the basic conception that what you do in the cult forms the mirror image of what you do in the village). Two further divisions of the document as a whole deal with everyday affairs, one, Damages, concerning civil law and government, the other, Women, taking up issues of family, home, and personal status. That, sum and substance, is the program of the Mishnah.

When did the document take shape, why did it endure, and what accounts for its importance? The document was completed—the consensus of scholarship holds—around the year 200. That is to say, approximately two long generations after the defeat of Bar Kokhba's armies, the Mishnah came forth. It lasted and proved influential because it served as the basic law book of the Jewish government of the Land of Israel, the authority of the patriarchate, as well as the Jewish government of the Jewish minority in Babylonia, a western province of the Iranian Empire. That empire allowed its many diverse ethnic groups to run internal affairs on their own, and the Jews' regime, in the hands of a "head of the exile," or exilarchate, employed sages who had mastered the Mishnah and therefore imposed the pertinent laws of the Mishnah within its administration and courts. So the Mishnah rapidly became not a work of speculative philosophy, in the form of legal propositions or rules, but a law code for the concrete and practical administration of the Jewish people in its autonomous life. Why was the Mishnah important? It was important because of two considerations, first, the political, but, second, the intellectual.

Before we speak of the Mishnah's future, as the foundation for Judaism from then to now, we have to take one last look backward, at the Mishnah's message on the recent past. If we were to ask the framers of the document to tell us where, in their writing, they speak of what has happened in their own century, they will direct our attention to a few episodic allusions to the destruction of the Temple, on the one side, and the repression after the war of 132–135, on the other. But if we were to ask them to give us their comment on the catastrophe—the radical turning—of their day, they will direct us to look not at bits and pieces, but at the whole of their document. For the Mishnah focuses upon the sanctification of Israel, the Jewish people, and its message is that the life of the people, like the life of the cult, bears the marks of holiness. One important aspect of how critical to the Mishnah is the dimension of holiness is the role of women.

The law of the Mishnah repeatedly uses the language of sanctification when it speaks of the relationship between man and woman, and it regards marriage as a critical dimension of the holiness of Israel, the Jewish people. Building on the scriptural rules, the sages point to the holiness of the marital bed, conducted as it is in accord with the laws of Leviticus 15, the holiness of the woman to the man, and of the man to the woman, as effected when a union between the two is sanctified under God's rule, the holiness of the table and the heart, where food that accords with the levitical requirements, e.g., of Leviticus 11, is served, and the holiness of the rhythm of time and circumstance, as a holy day comes to the home and transforms the home into the model of the Temple. In all these ways, therefore, the message of the Mishnah comes through: the holy Temple is destroyed, but holy Israel endures and will endure until, in God's time, the holy Temple is restored. That focus upon sanctification therefore imparts to the Mishnah remarkable relevance to the question on peoples' mind: if we have lost the Temple, have we also lost our tie to God? No, the Mishnah's authors reply, Israel remains God's holy people. The Mishnah then outlines the many areas of sanctification that endure: land and priesthood, in Agriculture; time, in Appointed Times; not to mention the record of the Temple, studied and restudied in the mind's reenactment of the cult. But, as we shall see, the Mishnah stressed sanctification, to the near omission of the other critical dimension of Israel's existence, salvation. Only later on would Scripture exegetes complete the structure of Judaism, a system resting on the twin foundations of sanctification in this world and salvation in time to come. But first we have to see what happened then, that is, why did the Mishnah make a difference?

We turn now to the future. Why did the Mishnah matter to generations to come? The Mishnah mattered, on the near term, because of its importance to the Jewish state(s) of the day. But it mattered on the long term because of its centrality in the intellectual life of the Jews' sages. These sages, many of them clerks in the Jewish governments, believed and persuaded many, that the Mishnah formed part of the Torah, God's will for Israel revealed to Moses at Sinai. So the Mishnah, originally not a work of religion in a narrow sense, attained the status of revelation. How did this happen? A look at the first great apologetic for the Mishnah, the Sayings of the Founders (Pirqé Avot) tells us the answer. It begins, "Moses received Torah on Sinai and handed it on to Joshua . . . ," and, as the chain of tradition goes on, the latest in the list turn out to be authorities of the generations who form the named authorities of the Mishnah itself. So what these authorities teach they have received in the chain of tradition from Sinai. And what they teach is Torah. Now the Mishnah, which is their teaching, enjoys its standing and authority because it comes from sages, and, it follows, sages' standing and authority come from God.

Such a claim imparted to the Mishnah and its teachers a position in the heart and mind of Israel, the Jewish people, that would insure the long-term influence of the document. What happened beyond 200 and before 400? Two processes, one of which generated the other. The first of the two was that the Mishnah was extensively stated, line by line, word by word. The modes of study were mainly three. First, the sages asked about the meanings of words and phrases. Then they worked on the comparison of one set of laws with another, finding the underlying principles of each, and comparing and harmonizing, those principles. So they formed of the rather episodic rules a tight and large fabric. Third, they moved beyond the narrow limits of the Mishnah into still broader and more speculative areas of thought. So, in all, the sages responsible to administer the law also expounded, and, willy-nilly, expanded the law. Ultimately, in both countries, the work of Mishnah-commentary developed into two large-scale documents, each called a Talmud. We have them as the Talmud of the Land of Israel, which I have translated into English, completed by about 400, and the Talmud of Babylonia, completed by about 600.

The second process—besides the work of Mishnah-commentary—drew attention back to Scripture. Once the work of reading the new code got under way, an important problem demanded attention. What is the relationship between the Mishnah and the established Scripture of Israel, the written Torah? The Mishnah only occasionally adduces texts of the Scriptures in support of its rules. Its framers worked out their own topical program, only part of which intersects with that of the laws of the Pentateuch. They followed their own principles of organization and development. They wrote in their own kind of Hebrew, which is quite different from biblical Hebrew. So the question naturally arose, Can we through sheer logic discover the law? Or must we tease laws out of Scripture through commentary, through legal exegesis? The Mishnah represented an extreme in this debate, since, as I said, so many of its topics to begin with do not derive from Scripture, and, further, a large part of its laws ignores Scripture's pertinent texts in that these texts are simply not cited. When, moreover, the framers of the Sayings of the Founders placed sages named in the Mishnah on the list of those who stand within the chain of tradition beginning at Sinai, they did not assign to those sages verses of Scripture, the written Torah (except in one or two instances). Rather, the Torah saying assigned to each of the named sages is not scriptural at all. So the sages enjoy an independent standing and authority on their own; they are not subordinate to Scripture, and their sayings enjoy equal standing with sentences of Scripture.

The work of exegesis of the Mishnah therefore drew attention, also, to the relationship of the Mishnah to Scripture. Consequently, important works of biblical commentary emerged in the third and fourth centuries. In these works, focused on such books as Leviticus (Sifra), Numbers (Sifré to Numbers) and Deuteronomy (Sifré to Deuteronomy), a paramount issue is whether law emerges solely on the basis of processes of reasoning, or whether only through looking in verses of Scripture are we able to uncover solid basis for the rules of the Mishnah. In that discourse we find the citation of a verse of Scripture followed by a verbatim citation of a passage of the Mishnah. Since this mode of reading Scripture is not apt to be familiar to many readers, let me give a concrete example of how the process of Mishnah-exegesis in relationship to Scripture exegesis was carried forward in the third and fourth centuries. What follows is from Sifré to Numbers:*

Pisqa **VI:II.1**

>   A. " . . . every man's holy thing shall be his; whatever any man gives to the priest shall be his" (Num. 5:10).
>   B. On the basis of this statement you draw the following rule:

---

*All translations in this book are mine, except as indicated otherwise.

C. If a priest on his own account makes a sacrificial offering, even though it falls into the week [during which] another priestly watch than his own [is in charge of the actual cult, making the offerings and receiving the dues], lo, that priest owns the priestly portions of the offering, and the right of offering it up belongs to him [and not to the priest ordinarily on duty at that time, who otherwise would retain the rights to certain portions of the animal]

[T. Men. 13:17].

What we have is simply a citation of the verse plus a law in a prior writing (in this case not the Mishnah, but the Tosefta, a compilation of supplements to the Mishnah's laws) which the verse is supposed to sustain. The formal traits require (1) citation of a verse, with or without comment, followed by (2) verbatim citation of a passage of the Mishnah or the Tosefta. What we have is a formal construction in which we simply juxtapose a verse, without or with intervening words of explanation, with a passage of the Mishnah or the Tosefta. So we see that, when sages proposed to provide for Scripture a counterpart, a commentary, to what they were even then creating for the Mishnah, they sought to build bridges from the Mishnah to Scripture. In doing so, they vastly articulated the theme of the Mishnah, the sanctification of Israel. But what of salvation? Where, when, and how did sages then shaping Judaism address that other and complementary category of Israel's existence? And, we further ask, is the work of linking the Mishnah to Scripture the only kind of scriptural commentary sages produced between the first and the fourth century? Not at all. Sages turned to Scripture to seek the laws of Israel's history, to ask the questions of salvation, of Israel's relationship to God, that, in the Mishnah and in the works of amplification of the Mishnah, they tended to neglect. When did they do so?

The answer to that question brings us to the fourth century. For that is when the sages produced the great works on Genesis, in Genesis Rabbah, and on Leviticus, in Leviticus Rabbah, which, as I shall explain, answered the questions of salvation, of the

meaning and end of Israel's history, that the Mishnah and its con-
tinuator-writings did not take up. Why in the fourth century?
Because, as I shall explain, the historical crisis precipitated by
Christianity's takeover of the Roman Empire and its government
demanded answers from Israel's sages: What does it mean? What
does history mean? Where are we to find guidance to the meaning
of our past—and our future? Sages looked, then, to Genesis,
maintaining that the story of the creation of the world and the
beginning of Israel would show the way toward the meaning of
history and the salvation of Israel. They further looked to Leviticus, and, in Leviticus Rabbah, they accomplished the link between the sanctification of Israel through its cult and priesthood,
which is the theme of the book of Leviticus, and the salvation of
Israel, which is the concern of the commentators to that book.
What they did was to place Israel, the people, at the center of the
story of Leviticus, applying to the life of the people of Israel those
rules of sanctification that, when observed, would prepare Israel,
holy Israel, for salvation. So, in a nutshell, the framers of Leviticus
Rabbah imparted to the book of Leviticus the message, in response
to the destruction of the Temple, that the authors of the Mishnah
had addressed two hundred years earlier: Israel's holiness endures.
Sanctifying the life of Israel now will lead to the salvation of Israel
in time to come: sanctification and salvation, the natural world
and the supernatural, the rules of society and the rules of history
all become one in the life of Israel.

But I have gotten ahead of my story. We take a step back. Let
me prepare the way for our consideration of Genesis Rabbah and
Leviticus Rabbah, works of the end of the fourth century, by
completing this picture of the principal work of sages, the main
kinds of books they wrote in the formation of Judaism in the
second, third, and, as we shall shortly see, fourth centuries. For
up to now I have omitted reference to a second sort of creative
effort. That concerns Scripture not in relationship to the Mishnah,
but on its own, and it further concerns that dimension of Israel's
life to which, in the aggregate, the Mishnah scarcely turns. You
will recall that I represented the Mishnah to you as an essentially

philosophical book, which rapidly came to serve other than spec-ulative purposes. But where is the other side to things, not the philosophy of life, the rules of natural and social existence, such as the Mishnah gives? Can we find the theology of life, the rules of supernatural and historical existence? Indeed we can and do, and they are in the other great area of commentary to Scripture. That other area required the reading of the books of Genesis and Leviticus in precisely the same way in which sages read the Mish-nah: same modes of exegesis, episodic and then generalizing. But the sages raised new questions, and, as we shall now see, it was an event as momentous as the destruction of the Temple that pre-cipitated and defined those questions. When Constantine declared Christianity a legal religion, then favored the Church, and finally converted, from 312 onward, and when his heirs and successors made Christianity the religion of the Roman Empire, sages and Israel in general had to negotiate a very difficult and critical mo-ment. The crisis was not so much political and legal, though it bore deep consequences in both politics and the Jews' standing in law, as it was spiritual. If the Messiah is yet to come, then how come Jesus, enthroned as Christ, now rules the world? Christians asked Israel that question, but, of greater consequence, Israel asked itself. And one more event of the fourth century, besides the triumph of Christianity, demands attention even as we turn to that critical age. In 362–363 a pagan, Julian, regained the throne and turned the empire away from Christianity. He further invited the Jews to rebuild the Temple. But the project proved a fiasco, and Julian was killed in battle against Iran. Consequently, the suc-ceeding emperors, Christians all, restored the throne to Christ (as they would put it) and secured for the church and Christianity the control of the state through law. So—and Chrysostom so argued in the aftermath of Julian's brief reign—the destruction of the Temple in 70 now has proved definitive. Three hundred years later, the Temple was supposed to be rebuilt, but God prevented it. What hope for Israel now—or ever? What meaning for Israel in history now—or at the end of time? The events of the day made urgent these essentially theological questions. So we come to the critical time, when Judaism as we know it reached the definition it would have for fifteen hundred years, and, in matters of politics and culture and the institutions of society, Christianity too would emerge as it would build the West.

THE FOURTH CENTURY AS THE FIRST CENTURY OF WESTERN CIVILIZATION

The West as we have known it from Constantine to the nineteenth century carried forward three principal elements of the heritage of antiquity and made of them one. These were, first, Roman law and institutions, second, the legacy of ancient Israel, the Hebrew Scriptures, and, third, Christianity as religion of the state and formative force in culture. The West was what it was because of Christianity. So the history of the West began when Christianity attained that position in politics and culture that it was to occupy for the history of the West, until nearly the present day.

The shift from pagan to Christian Rome took place in the fourth century, from the initial moment at which Constantine accorded to Christianity the status of licit, favored religion, at the outset, to the moment, by the end, at which Christianity became the official and governing religion of the state. Judaism and Christianity in late antiquity, we realize, present histories that mirror one another. When Christianity began, in the first century, Judaism was the dominant tradition in the Holy Land and framed its ideas within a political framework until the early fifth century. Christianity there was subordinate and had to work out against the background of a politically definitive Judaism. From the fourth century, the time of Constantine onward, matters reversed themselves. Now Christianity predominated, expressing its ideas in political and institutional terms. Judaism, by contrast, had lost its political foundations and faced the task of working out its self-understanding in terms of a world defined by Christianity, now everywhere triumphant and in charge of politics. The important shift came in the early fourth century, the West's first century. That was when the West began in the union of Christian religion and Roman rule. It also was when the Judaism that thrived in the

West reached the definition it was to exhibit for the next fifteen centuries, until, as I shall note at the end, our own time.

Historians of Judaism take as dogma the view that Christianity never made any difference to Judaism. Faith of a "people that dwells apart," Judaism went its splendid, solitary way, exploring paths untouched by Christians. Christianity—people hold—was born in the matrix of Judaism, but Judaism, beginning to now, officially ignored the new "daughter" religion and followed its majestic course in aristocratic isolation. But the Judaism expressed by the writings of the sages of the Land of Israel in the fourth century—the age of Constantine—not only responded to issues raised for Israel by the political triumph of Christianity but did so in a way that, intellectually at least, made possible the entire future history of Judaism in Europe and beyond.

The importance of the age of Constantine in the history of Judaism derives from a simple fact. It was at this time that important Judaic documents undertook to deal with agenda defined, for both Judaism and Christianity, by the triumph of Christianity. Important Christian thinkers reflected on issues presented by the political revolution in the status of Christianity. Issues of the rewriting of human history, the canonization of the Bible as the Old and New Testaments, the restatement of the challenge and claim of Christ the King as Messiah against the continuing "unbelief" of Israel (phrased from the Christian viewpoint; Jews would refer to their continuing belief in God's power to save the world at the end of time), the definition of who is Israel—these make their appearance in Christian writings of the day. And these issues derive from the common agenda of both Judaism and Christianity, namely, the Holy Scriptures of ancient Israel, received in Judaism as the written half of the one whole Torah of Moses, our Rabbi, and in Christianity as the Old Testament.

What in fact do the sages of the fourth century say to Israel? As I explained, they turned back to Scripture, rereading the two books that mattered, first, the one on the creation of the world and of the children of Israel, Genesis, second, the one on the sanctification of Israel. So they proposed to explain history by rereading the book of Genesis. There they found the lesson that what happened to the patriarchs in the beginning signals what would happen to their children later on. And Jacob then is Israel now, just as Esau then is Rome now. And Israel remains Israel: bearer of the blessing. They explain the status and authority of the traditions—now two hundred years old—of the Mishnah and related writings by assigning to them a place in the Torah. Specifically, in the canonical documents of the period at hand for the first time we find clear reference to the notion that when God revealed the Torah to Moses at Sinai, part of the Torah was in the medium of writing, the other part, in the medium of memory, hence oral. And, it would later be explained, the Mishnah (and much else) enjoyed the status of oral Torah. They explain the Messiah-claim of Israel in very simple terms. Israel indeed will receive the Messiah, but salvation at the end of time awaits the sanctification of Israel in the here and now. And that will take place through humble and obedient loyalty to the Torah. They counter the claim that there is a new Israel in place of the old, and this they do by rereading the book of Leviticus, with its message of sanctification of Israel, and finding in that book a typology of the great empires—Babylonia, Media, Greece, Rome. And the coming, the fifth and final sovereign, will be Israel's Messiah. So, in all, the points important to Christianity in the advent of Constantine and the Christian empire—history vindicates Christ, the New Testament explains the Old, the Messiah has come and his claim has now been proved truthful, and the Old Israel is done for and will not have a Messiah in the future—all those points were countered, for the Jews in a self-evidently valid manner, by the writings of the fourth-century sages. The rabbinic system, which laid stress on the priority of salvation over sanctification, on the dual media by which the Torah came forth from Sinai, on the messianic dimension of Israel's everyday life, and on the permanence of Israel's position as God's first love—that system came to first articulate expression in the Talmud of the Land of Israel and related writings—there, and not in the Mishnah and in its compansions. And the reason is clear: the system responded to a competing system, one heir of the ancient Israelite Scripture answering another heir and its claims. The siblings would struggle, like Esau and Jacob, for the common blessing. For the Jewish people, in any event, the system of the fourth-century sages would endure for millenia as self-evidently right and persuasive.

Christians had a great deal on their minds, much of which had no bearing at all on the public history of Christianity as worked out in the theories of history, Messiah, and Israel—topics so important to sages and to some of the great intellects of the church of the fourth century. The quest for a unifying creed, for example, absorbed the best efforts of generations of Christian theologians. But identifying these questions—the meaning of history, the identification of the Messiah, the definition of Israel, God's people— deriving from Scripture in particular, does not represent an act of anachronism. The questions at hand did demand attention and did receive it. And the shape of Judaism as laid forth in documents redacted in the fourth and early fifth century exhibits remarkable congruence to the contours of the same intellectual program. Specifically, in the Judaism of the sages of the Land of Israel who redacted the principal documents at hand both a doctrine and an apologetic remarkably relevant to the issues presented to both Christianity and Judaism by the crisis of Christianity's worldly triumph.

Jews and Christians alike believed in the Israelite Scriptures and so understood that major turnings in history carried a message from God. That message bore meaning for questions of salvation and the Messiah, the identification of God's will in Scripture, the determination of who is Israel and what it means to be Israel, and similar questions of a profoundly historical and social character. So it is no wonder that the enormous turning represented by the advent of a Christian empire should have precipitated deep thought on these issues, important as they are in the fourth-century thought of both Judaic sages and Christian theologians. The specification of the message at hand, of course, would produce long-term differences between the Christianity of the age and the Judaism of the time as well.

The success of the Judaism shaped in this place, in this time, is clear. Refined and vastly restated in the Talmud of Babylonia, two hundred years later, the system of Judaism worked out here and now enjoyed the status of self-evidence among Jews confronted with Christian governments and Christian populations over the next fifteen hundred years. So far as ideas matter in bonding a group—the success among the people of Israel in Europe, west and east alike, of the Judaism defined in the fourth-century writings of the sages of the Land of Israel derives from the power and persuasive effect of the ideas of that Judaism. Coming to the surface in the writings of the age, particularly the Talmud of the Land of Israel, Genesis Rabbah, and Leviticus Rabbah, that Judaism therefore secured for despairing Israel a long future of hope and confident endurance.

Prior to the time of Constantine, the documents of Judaism that evidently reached closure—the Mishnah, Pirqé Abot, the Tosefta—scarcely took cognizance of Christianity and did not deem the new faith to be much of a challenge. If the scarce and scattered allusions do mean to refer to Christianity at all, then sages regarded it as an irritant, an exasperating heresy among Jews who should have known better. But, then, neither Jews nor pagans took much interest in Christianity in the new faith's first century and a half. The authors of the Mishnah framed a system to which Christianity bore no relevance whatsoever; theirs were problems presented in an altogether different context. For their part, pagan writers were indifferent to Christianity, not mentioning it until about 160. Only when Christian evangelism enjoyed some solid success, toward the later part of that century, did pagans compose apologetic works attacking Christianity. Celsus stands at the start, followed by Porphyry in the third century. But by the fourth century, pagans and Jews alike knew that they faced a formidable, powerful enemy. Pagan writings speak explicitly and accessibly. The answers sages worked out for the intellectual challenge of the hour do not emerge equally explicitly and accessibly. But they are there, and, when we ask the right questions and establish the context of discourse, we hear the answers in the Talmud of the Land of Israel, Genesis Rabbah, and Leviticus Rabbah as clearly as we hear pagans' answers in the writings of Porphyry and Julian, not to mention the Christians' answers in the rich and diverse writings of the fourth-century fathers, such as Eusebius, Jerome, John Crysostom, and Aphrahat, to mention just four.

The Judaism of the sages of the Land of Israel who redacted the principal documents at hand therefore framed both a doctrine and an apologetic remarkably relevant to the issues presented to both Christianity and Judaism by the crisis of Christianity's worldly triumph. Why the common set of questions? Because, as I said, Jews and Christians alike believed in the Israelite Scriptures and so understood that major turnings in history carried a message from God. The specification of the message at hand, of course, would produce long-term differences between the Christianity of the age and the Judaism of the time as well. But the shared program brought the two religions into protracted confrontation on an intersecting set of questions. The struggle between the one and the other—a struggle that would continue until our own time—originated in the simple fact that, to begin with, both religions agreed on pretty much everything that mattered. They differed on little, so they made much of that little. Scripture taught them both that vast changes in the affairs of empires came about because of God's will. History proved principles of theology. In that same Torah prophets promised the coming of the Messiah, who would bring salvation. Who was, and is, that Messiah, and how shall we know? And that same Torah addressed a particular people, Israel, promising that people the expression of God's favor and love. But who is Israel, and who is not Israel? So Scripture defined the categories that were shared in common. Scripture filled those categories with deep meaning. That is why to begin with a kind of dialogue—made up, to be sure, of two monologues on the same topics—could commence. The dialogue continued for centuries because the conditions that to begin with precipitated it, specifically the rise to political dominance of Christianity and the subordination of Judaism, remained constant for fifteen hundred years.

That is not to suggest that only the three topics at hand dominated sages' thought and the consequent shape of their writings. I do not claim that all of Genesis Rabbah deals with the meaning of history, though much of it does; all of the Talmud of the Land of Israel takes up the messianic question, though important components do; or that all of Leviticus Rabbah asks about who is Israel, though the question is there. None, indeed, can presently claim to assess matters of proportion, importance, or therefore, predominance, in so sizable a canon as that of the sages before us. Characterizing so large and complex a corpus of writings as theirs poses problems of its own, which need not detain us. For we cannot readily settle to everyone's satisfaction the questions of taste and judgment involved in determination of proportion and identification of points of stress. That is why none can claim that just these questions took a paramount role in the documents I cite. Just as the formative figures of Christianity had more on their minds than the issues I lay out, so the creative and authoritative intellects of Judaism thought about many more things than those I take up.* But that is not the point. The point is simple. The topics before us, dictated by politics, did matter, and both sides did confront them. We know that is the fact, because we find in the writings of the age clear and important evidence that Judaic sages, as much as Christian theologians, answered these questions. Moreover, when they did address these questions, they defined the issues at hand in pretty much the same terms. So, sharing the premises that generated the questions and agreeing upon the source of facts that would settle them—Scripture in both cases—the two sets of intellectuals did agree as well on a common topic of argument. Having so much in common, they could differ, and the differences prove instructive. So Judaism and Christianity in the fourth century entered that initial confrontation that would define the terms for the next fifteen hundred years.

So we ask, when did people actually enter a confrontation on

---

*And that is not to ignore the vast internal agenda requiring discussion, questions of no interest whatsoever to the relationship between the two groups. The internal agenda in the writings of both parties to the debate surely predominated.

the same issues, defined in the same way? It was not in the first century. Christians and Jews in the first century did not argue with one another. Each set of groups—the family of Christianities, the family of Judaisms—went its way, focusing upon its own program. When Christianity came into being in the first century, one important strand of the Christian movement laid stress on issues of salvation, in the Gospels maintaining that Jesus was, and is, Christ, come to save the wrold and impose a radical change on history. At that same time, an important group within the diverse Judaic systems of the age, the Pharisees, emphasized issues of sanctification, maintaining that the task of Israel is to attain that holiness of which the Temple was a singular embodiment. When, in the Gospels, we find the record of the church placing Jesus into opposition with the Pharisees, we witness the confrontation of different people talking about different things to different people. But in the fourth century, by contrast, different people addressing different groups really did talk about exactly the same things. That is the point, therefore, at which the Judaic and Christian conflict reached the form in which, for fifteen hundred years, it would come to intellectual expression. People really did differ about the same issues. These issues—the meaning of history, the identity of the Messiah, and the definition of Israel, or of God's instrument for embodying in a social group God's will—would define the foundations of the dispute from then on. So we find for the first time a genuine confrontation: people differing about a shared agendum in exactly the same terms.

What about the moment at which Judaism in important documents did deal in a significant way with the existence of Christianity? Once more, I maintain, it was in the fourth century. How so? The issues presented to Jews by the triumph of Christianity do inform the documents shaped in the Land of Israel in the period of that triumph. The three largest writings, the great commentary to Genesis called Genesis Rabbah, the Talmud of the Land of Israel, and the commentary to Leviticus called Leviticus Rabbah, as I said, take up and systematically work out important components of the intellectual program of the age, once more: the meaning of history, the messianic crisis, the identification of Israel. These issues do not play an important role in prior components of the unfolding canon of Judaism, in particular, the Mishnah and the Tosefta and Sifré to Numbers, all of which, it is generally held, reached closure before the fourth century. So the contrast in each case suggests that a new set of issues has compelled attention, in documents of the age, to questions neglected in earlier compilations. And these issues proved pressing for other intellectuals, the Christian ones, of the same period. On the basis of the confluence of discourse on precisely the same questions, in precisely the same terms, I think we may fairly argue that the two groups talked about the same things at the same time and so engaged in whatever genuine debate proved possible. So, in all, in many ways the fourth century marks the point of intersection of trajectories of the history of the two religions, Judaic and Christian.

ORAL TORAH AND WRITTEN TORAH

The oral Torah stated in the circumstance and language of crisis the message of Sinai that, in written form, had come down from ancient times. Just as the exodus from Egypt and the revelation given to Moses precipitated a vast effort to write down and preserve the truth of that moment in the language and categories of that setting, so the events of late antiquity for Israel, the Jewish people, precipitated a vast and enduring work of preserving the revealed truth of the hour in the language and categories of that hour. The ancient rabbis looked out upon a world destroyed and still smoking in the aftermath of calamity, but they speak of rebirth and renewal. The holy Temple lay in ruins, but they asked about sanctification. The old history was over, but they look forward to future history. For their purposes they appealed to the truth of the written Torah, but they also wrote down and preserved as Torah from Sinai the truth their own day had received—from Sinai too. The task of holding together sanctification in the here and now and salvation at the end of time, the enormous challenge of finding warrant in the written Torah for the truth revealed in the oral Torah—these two challenges produced the response before us: the vast canon of the oral Torah worked out in relationship to the written one. Theirs, as we shall see, is a message that what is true and real is the opposite of what people perceive. God stands for paradox. Strength come through weakness, salvation through acceptance and obedience, sanctification through the ordinary and profane, which can be made holy. Israel's condition testifies to the deeper truth, the real structure of human life: sanctification outside of a temple, life out of the grave, eternity from death—all these paradoxes corresponded to the simple social fact that holy and supernatural Israel lived out its days as a conquered and subordinated people, among other peoples. So, we may say, social reality in the imagination of sages pointed to the deeper truth, for the deeper the truth, the richer the paradox! Israel's present condition presents a paradox, and, out of reflection on the social realities concealed by contemporary politics (as sages would have understood matters), sages penetrated into those revealed mysteries of the Torah—their Torah, the oral part—that would sustain Israel from then to now.

FROM SANCTIFICATION TO SALVATION

The oral Torah reached its first documentary statement with the Mishnah, which presents a system of sanctification focused on the holiness of the priesthood, the cultic festivals, the Temple and its sacrifices, as well as on the rules for protecting that holiness from levitical uncleanness—four of the six divisions of the Mishnah on a single theme. The Mishnah's system stresses the issue of sanctification, pure and simple. The Talmud of the Land of Israel is a document that reached closure approximately a century after the political triumph of Christianity. In the aftermath of the conversion of the Roman Empire to Christianity and the confirmation of the triumph of Christianity in the generation beyond Julian "the apostate," sages worked out in the pages of the Talmud of the Land of Israel and in the exegetical compilations of the age a Judaism intersecting with the Mishnah's but essentially asymmetrical with it. It was a system for salvation, focused on the salvific power of the sanctification of the holy people. Given the political changes of the age, with their implications for the meaning and end of history as Israel would experience it, the fresh emphasis on salvation, the introduction of the figure of the Messiah as a principal teleological force, the statement of an eschatological teleology for the system as a whole—these constitute answers to questions. The questions were raised by Christian theologians, the answers provided by the Judaic sages. The former held that the Christian triumph confirmed the Christhood of Jesus, the rejection of Israel, the end of Israel's hope for salvation at the end of time. The latter offered the Torah in its dual media, the affirmation of Israel as children of Abraham, Isaac, and Jacob, the coming of the Messiah at the end of time. The questions and answers fit the challenge of the age.

To understand when and why the issue of salvation became critical, not merely chronic, we have to recognize the full implications of the disappointment precipitated by the emperor Julian's promise of rebuilding the Temple, followed by the failure of that promise. Let us first turn back to the beginning of the fourth century and review the Christian challenge. With the triumph of Christianity through the conversion of Constantine in 312 and the favor of his successors in the West, Christianity's explicit claims, now validated in world-shaking events of the age, demanded a reply. The sages of the Talmud of the Land of Israel provided it. At those very specific points at which the Christian challenge met head-on old Israel's worldview, sages' doctrines responded. What did Israel's sages have to present as the Torah's answer to the cross? It was the Torah. This took three forms. The Torah was defined in the doctrine, first, of the status, as oral and memorized revelation, of the Mishnah, and, by implication, of other rabbinical writings. The Torah, moreover, was presented as the encompassing symbol of Israel's salvation. The Torah, finally, was embodied in the person of the Messiah who, of course, would be a rabbi. The Torah in all three modes confronted the cross, with its doctrine of the triumphant Christ, Messiah and king, ruler now of earth as of heaven.

To make matters more concrete, we return to those important changes, surveyed just now, that first emerged in the writings of sages of the Land of Israel that reached closure at the end of the fourth and the beginning of the fifth century. These changes, as we have now noticed, marked shifts in the symbolic system and structure of the Judaism then taking shape. The fact is not merely that things changed, but that things took the particular changes . they did because of a critical challenge. The symbolic system of Christianity, with Christ triumphant, with the cross as the now-regnant symbol, with the canon of Christianity now defined and recognized as authoritative, called forth from the sages of the Land of Israel a symbolic system strikingly responsive to the crisis. This would take the form of the symbolic power of the dual Torah, with its explicit claim that sages' authority here and now represented the will of God in heaven. The first change was doctrinal, involving the inclusion into the Mishnaic system of the belief, omitted in the teleological system of the Mishnah, in the coming of the Messiah. That belief now claimed a place as the teleology of the system of Judaism as sages defined that system. The second was the symbol of the Torah expanded to encompass the entirety of the sages' teachings, as much as the written Torah everyone acknowledged as authoritative.

The fourth century therefore marked the first century of Judaism and of Christianity, as the Judaism of the dual Torah would flourish in the West (as well as in the Islamic world), and as Christianity in its political formulation would define and govern the civilization of the West. When, in the aftermath of Constantine's legalization of Christianity in 312, Christianity became first the most favored religion, then the established one, and finally, by the end of the fourth century, triumphant, the condition of Israel changed in some ways but not in others. What remained the same was the politics and social circumstance of a defeated nation. What changed was the context of the religious system of Judaism. The worldly situation of Israel did not change. The setting of Judaism did. For while Israelites in the Land of Israel persisted as a subject people, Judaism confronted a world in which its principal components—hermeneutic, teleology, symbol—met an effective challenge in the corresponding components of the now triumphant faith in Christ. Specifically, the Hebrew Scriptures, the written Torah, now demanded a reading as the Old Testament, predicting the New. The reason, in the Christian view, was that history proved that Scripture's prophetic promises of a king-Messiah pointed toward Jesus, now Christ enthroned. Concomitantly, the teleology of the Israelite system of old, focused as it was on the coming of the Messiah, in the Christians' mind found confirmation and realization in the rule of Jesus, again, Christ enthroned. And the symbol of the whole—hermeneutics, teleology alike—rose in heaven's heights: the cross that had triumphed at the Milvian Bridge.

Why did the conversion of the empire to Christianity make a difference to Israel's sages, while they paid slight heed to Christianity in its prior apolitical condition? A move of the empire from reverence for Zeus to adoration of Mithra meant nothing; paganism was what it was, lacking all differentiation in the Jewish eye. Christianity was something else. It was like Judaism. Christians read the Torah and claimed to declare its meaning. Accordingly, the trend of sages' speculation cannot have avoided the issue of the place, within the Torah's messianic pattern, of the remarkable turn in world history represented by the triumph of Christianity. Since the Christians vociferously celebrated confirmation of their faith in Christ's messiahship and, at the moment, Jews were hardly prepared to concur, it falls surely within known patterns for us to suppose that Constantine's conversion would have been identified with some dark moment to prefigure the dawning of the messianic age.

If, now, we inquire into what in fact sages did at that time, the answer is clear. They composed the Talmud of the Land of Israel as we know it. They collected exegeses of Scripture and made them into systematic and sustained accounts of, initially, the meaning of the Pentateuch (assuming dates in these centuries, late third through early fifth, for Sifra, the two Sifrés, Genesis Rabbah, and Leviticus Rabbah). When we recall what Christians had to say to Israel, we may find entirely reasonable the view that compiling scriptural exegeses constituted part of a Jewish apologetic response. For one Christian message had been that Israel "after the flesh" had distorted and continually misunderstood the meaning of what had been its own Scripture. Failing to read the Old Testament in the light of the New, the prophetic promises in the perspective of Christ's fulfillment of those promises, Israel "after the flesh" had lost access to God's revelation to Moses at Sinai. If we were to propose a suitably powerful, yet appropriately proud, response, it would have two qualities. First, it would supply a complete account of what Scripture had meant, and always must mean, as Israel read it. Second, it would do so in such a way as not to dignify the position of the other side with the grace of an explicit reply at all. The compilations of exegeses and the Yerushalmi accomplished at this time assuredly take up the challenge of restating the meaning of the Torah revealed by God to Moses at Mount Sinai. This the sages did in a systematic and thorough way. At the same time, if the charges of the other side precipitated the work of compilation and composition, the consequent collections in no way suggest so. The issues of the documents are made always to emerge from the inner life not even of Israel in general, but of the sages' estate in particular. Scripture was thoroughly rabbinized, as earlier it had been Christianized. None of this suggests the other side had won a response for itself. Only the net effect—a complete picture of the whole, as Israel must perceive the whole of revelation—suggests the extraordinary utility for apologetics, outside as much as inside the faith, served by these same compilations.

It follows, I think, that the changes at the surface, in articulated doctrines of teleology, hermeneutics, and symbolism, respond to changes in the political condition of Israel as well as in the religious foundations of the politics of the day. Paganism had presented a different and simpler problem to sages. Christianity's explicit claims, validated in world-shaking events of the age, demanded a reply. The sages of the Talmud of the Land of Israel provided it. So it is at those very specific points at which the Christian challenge met head-on old Israel's worldview that sages' doctrines change from what they had been. What did Israel have to present to the cross? The Torah, in the doctrine, first, of the status, as oral and memorized revelation, of the Mishnah, and, by implication, of other rabbinical writings. The Torah, moreover, in the encompassing symbol of Israel's salvation. The Torah, finally, in the person of the Messiah who, of course, would be a rabbi. The Torah in all three modes confronted the cross, with its doctrine of the triumphant Christ, Messiah, and king, ruler now of earth as of heaven.

The documents of the oral Torah that reached conclusion in the fourth and fifth centuries beginning with the Talmud of the Land of Israel, encompassing also Genesis Rabbah and Leviticus Rabbah, completed the Mishnah. Specifically, those documents, as we shall see in the following anthology, presented doctrines of salvation to complement the doctrine of sanctification that the authorship of the Mishnah had worked out. The Mishnah, in ca. 200 C.E., described an orderly world, in which Israelite society was neatly divided among its castes, arranged in priority around the center that is the Temple, systematically engaged in a life of sanctification remote from the disorderly events of the day. The Talmud of the Land of Israel, in ca. 400 C.E., portrayed the chaos of Jews living among gentiles, governed by a diversity of authorities, lacking all order and arrangement, awaiting a time of salvation for which, through sanctification, they made themselves ready. The Mishnah's Israel in imagination is governed by an Israelite king, high priest, and sanhedrin. The Talmud of the Land of Israel's Jews lived under both rabbis near at hand, who settle everyday disputes of streets and households, and also distant archons of a nameless state, to be manipulated and placated on earth as in heaven. The Mishnah's Judaism breathes the pure air of public piazza and stoa, the Talmud of the Land of Israel's, the ripe stench of private alleyway and courtyard. The image of the Mishnah's Judaism is evoked by the majestic Parthenon, perfect in all its proportions, conceived in a single moment of pure rationality. The Talmud of the Land of Israel's Judaism is a scarcely choate cathedral in process, the labor of many generations, each of its parts the conception of diverse moments of devotion, all of them the culmination of an ongoing and evolving process of revelation in the here and now.

From the strict and formal classicism of the Mishnah, like Plato's *Republic* describing for no one in particular an ideal society never, in its day, to be seen, the Judaism described by the Talmud of the Land of Israel turned to the disorderly detail of the workaday world, taking the utopian Mishnah along. If Aristotle's *Politics* had been written as a gloss to Plato's *Republic*, amplifying and extending piece by piece the once whole but no longer cogent writing of Plato, we should have a rough analogy to what the Talmud of the Land of Israel does with the Mishnah of Judah the Patriarch (henceforward: Rabbi). If, further, many philosophers took up the fantastic account of the *Republic* and out of its materials, and other writings, worked out new *Republics,* so bringing diversity to what had been a single conception and book, we should find a possible precedent for what happened from 200 to 400 in the move, in Judaism, from the ancient to the medieval mode: theoretical to practical, monothetic to polythetic, uniform to diverse, cogent to chaotic, and system to tradition.

The doctrine of salvation, given mythic expression in the picture of the Messiah at the end of times, emerges in rich and full detail in particular in the Talmud of the Land of Israel. In the Talmud of the Land of Israel two historical contexts framed discussion of the Messiah, the destruction of the Temple and the messianic claim of Bar Kokhba.* Rome played a role in both, and the authors of the materials gathered in the Talmud made a place for Rome in the history of Israel. This they did, as we shall see when we come to Genesis Rabbah, in conformity to their larger theory of who is Israel, specifically by assigning to Rome a place in the family. As to the destruction of the Temple, we find a statement that the Messiah was born on the day that the Temple

---

*The Talmud of the Land of Israel totally ignores whatever messianic hopes and figures took part in the fiasco of Julian's projected rebuilding of the Temple.

was destroyed. The Talmud's doctrine of the Messiah therefore finds its place in its encompassing doctrine of history. What is fresh in the Talmud is the perception of Rome as an autonomous actor, as an entity with a point of origin (just as Israel has a point of origin) and a tradition of wisdom (just as Israel has such a tradition). So as Rome is Esau, so Esau is part of the family—a point to which we shall return—and therefore plays a role in history. And—yet another point of considerable importance—since Rome does play a role in history, Rome also finds a position in the eschatological drama. This sense of poised opposites, Israel and Rome, comes to expression in two ways. First, Israel's own history calls into being its counterpoint, the antihistory of Rome. Without Israel, there would be no Rome—a wonderful consolation to the defeated nation. For if Israel's sin created Rome's power, then Israel's repentance would bring Rome's downfall. The entire world and what happens in it enter into the framework of meaning established by Israel's Torah. So what the Romans do, their historical actions, can be explained in terms of Israel's conception of the world. The concept of two histories, balanced opposite one another, comes to particular expression, within the Talmud of the Land of Israel, in the balance of Israelite sage and Roman emperor. Just as Israel and Rome, God and no-gods, compete (with a foreordained conclusion), so do sage and emperor. In this age, it appears that the emperor has the power. God's Temple, by contrast to the great churches of the age, lies in ruins. But just as sages can overcome the emperor through their inherent supernatural power, so too will Israel and Israel's God in the coming age control the course of events. In the doctrine at hand, we see the true balance: sage as against emperor. In the age of the Christian emperors, the polemic acquires power. The sage, in his small claims court, weighs in the balance against the emperor in Constantinople—a rather considerable claim. So two stunning innovations appear: first, the notion of emperor and sage in mortal struggle; second, the idea of an age of idolatry and an age beyond idolatry. The world had to move into a new orbit indeed for Rome to enter into the historical context formerly defined wholly by what happened to Israel. How does all this relate to the messianic crisis at hand? The doctrine of sages, directly pertinent to the issue of the coming of the Messiah, holds that Israel can free itself of control by other nations only by humbly agreeing to accept God's rule. The nations—Rome, in the present instance—rest on one side of the balance, while God rests on the other. Isreal must then choose between them. There is no such thing for Israel as freedom from both God and the nations, total autonomy and independence. There is only a choice of masters, a ruler on earth or a ruler in heaven.

The doctrine of salvation, as expressed in the messianic framework, vastly transcends the familiar idea of the Messiah's claim to save Israel. What is important is the particular and distinctive doctrine that Israel will be saved through total submission, under the Messiah's gentle rule, to God's yoke and service. In the model of the sage, the Messiah will teach Israel the power of submission. So God is not to be manipulated through Israel's humoring heaven in rite and cult. The notion of keeping the commandments so as to please heaven and get God to do what Israel wants is totally incongruent to the text at hand. Keeping the commandments as a mark of submission, loyalty, humility before God is the rabbinic system of salvation. So Israel does not save itself. Israel never controls its own destiny, either on earth or in heaven. The only choice is whether to cast one's fate into the hands of cruel, deceitful men, or to trust in the living God of mercy and love. We now understand the stress on the centrality of hope. Hope signifies patient acceptance of God's rule, and as an attitude of mind and heart; it is something that Israel can sustain on its own as well, the ideal action. We shall now see how this critical position that Israel's task is humble acceptance of God's rule is spelled out in the setting of discourse about the Messiah in the Talmud of the Land of Israel. Bar Kokhba weighs in the balance against the sage, much as the Roman emperor weighs in the balance against the sage, and for the same reason. The one represents arrogance, the other, humility. Bar Kokhba, above all, exemplified arrogance against God. He lost the war because of that arrogance. In particular, he ignored the authority of sages—a point not to be missed, since it forms the point of critical tension of the tale:

Y. Taanit 4:5

XJ. Said R. Yohanan, "Upon orders of Caesar Hadrian, they killed eight hundred thousand in Betar."

K. Said R. Yohanan, "There were eighty thousand pairs of trumpeteers surrounding Betar. Each one was in charge of a number of troops. Ben Kozeba was there and he had two hundred thousand troops who, as a sign of loyalty, had cut off their little fingers.

L. "Sages sent word to him, 'How long are you going to turn Israel into a maimed people?'

M. "He said to them, 'How otherwise is it possible to test them?'

N. "They replied to him, 'Whoever cannot uproot a cedar of Lebanon while riding on his horse will not be inscribed on your military rolls.'

O. "So there were two hundred thousand who qualified in one way, and another two hundred thousand who qualified in another way."

P. When he would go forth to battle, he would say, "Lord of the world! Do not help and do not hinder us! 'Hast thou not rejected us, O God? Thou dost not go forth, O God, with our armies' " [Ps. 60:10].

Q. Three and a half years did Hadrian besiege Betar.

R. R. Eleazar of Modiin would sit on sackcloth and ashes and pray every day, saying, "Lord of the ages! Do not judge in accord with strict judgment this day! Do not judge in accord with strict judgment this day!"

S. Hadrian wanted to go to him. A Samaritan said to him, "Do not go to him until I see what he is doing, and so hand over the city [of Betar] to you. [Make peace . . . for you.]"

T. He got into the city through a drain pipe. He went and found R. Eleazar of Modiin standing and praying. He pretended to whisper something into his ear.

U. The townspeople saw [the Samaritan] do this and brought him to Ben Kozeba. They told him, "We saw this man having dealings with your friend."

V. [Bar Kokhba] said to him, "What did you say to him, and what did he say to you?"

W. He said to [the Samaritan], "If I tell you, then the king will kill me, and if I do not tell you, then you will kill me. It is better that the king kill me, and not you.

X. "[Eleazar] said to me, 'I should hand over my city.' ['I shall make peace. . . .']"

Y. He turned to R. Eleazar of Modiin. He said to him, "What did this Samaritan say to you?"

Z. He replied, "Nothing."

AA. He said to him, "What did you say to him?"

BB. He said to him, "Nothing."

CC. [Ben Kozeba] gave [Eleazar] one good kick and killed him.

DD. Forthwith an echo came forth and proclaimed the following verse:

EE. "Woe to my worthless shepherd, who deserts the flock! May the sword smite his arm and his right eye! Let his arm be wholly withered, his right eye utterly blinded! [Zech. 11:17].

FF. "You have murdered R. Eleazar of Modiin, the right arm of all Israel, and their right eye. Therefore may the right arm of that man wither, may his right eye be utterly blinded!"

GG. Forthwith Betar was taken, and Ben Kozeba was killed.

We notice two complementary themes. First, Bar Kokhba treats heaven with arrogance, asking God merely to keep out of the way. Second, he treats an especially revered sage with a parallel arrogance. The sage had the power to preserve Israel. Bar Kokhba destroyed Israel's one protection. The result was inevitable.

In the Talmud of the Land of Israel we witness, among the Mishnah's heirs, a striking reversion to biblical convictions about the centrality of history in the definition of Israel's reality. The heavy weight of prophecy, apocalyptic, and biblical historiography, with their emphasis upon salvation and on history as the indicator of Israel's salvation, stood against the Mishnah's quite separate thesis of what truly mattered. What, from sages' viewpoint, demanded description and analysis and required interpretation? It was the category of sanctification, for eternity. The true issue framed by history and apocalypse was how to move toward the foreordained end of salvation, how to act in time to reach salvation at the end of the time. The Mishnah's teleology beyond time and its capacity to posit an eschatology without a place for a historical Messiah take a position beyond that of the entire antecedent sacred literature of Israel. Only one strand, the priestly one, had ever taken so extreme a position of the centrality of sanctification and the peripheral nature of salvation. Wisdom had stood in between, with its own concerns, drawing attention both to what happened and to what endured. But to Wisdom what finally mattered was not nature or supernature, but rather abiding relationships in historical time.

But we should not conclude that the Talmud at hand has simply moved beyond the Mishnah's orbit. The opposite is the case. What the framers of the document have done is to assemble materials in which the eschatological, therefore messianic, teleology is absorbed within the ahistorical, therefore sagacious one. The Messiah turned into a sage is no longer the Messiah embodied in the figure of the arrogant Bar Kokhba (in the Talmud's representation of the figure). The reversion to the prophetic notion of learning history's lessons carried in its wake a reengagement with the Messiah myth. But the reengagement does not represent a change in the unfolding system. Why not? Because the climax comes in an explicit statement that the conduct required by the Torah will bring the coming Messiah. That explanation of the holy way of life focuses upon the end of time and the advent of the Messiah— both of which therefore depend upon the sanctification of Israel. So sanctification takes priority, salvation depends on it. The framers of the Mishnah had found it possible to construct a complete and encompassing teleology for their system with scarcely a single word about the Messiah's coming at that time when the system would be perfectly achieved.

Two things are happening here. First, the system of religious observance, including study of Torah, is explicitly invoked as having salvific power. Second, the persistent hope of the people for the coming of the Messiah is linked to the system of rabbinic observance and belief. In this way, the austere program of the

Mishnah develops in a different direction, with no trace of a promise that the Messiah will come if and when the system is fully realized. Here a teleology lacking all eschatological dimension gives way to an explicitly messianic statement that the purpose of the law is to attain Israel's salvation: "If you want it, God wants it too." The one thing Israel commands is its own heart; the power it yet exercises is the power to repent. These suffice. The entire history of humanity will respond to Israel's will, to what happens in Israel's heart and soul. With the Temple in ruins, repentance can take place only within the heart and mind. Israel may contribute to its own salvation by the right attitude and the right deed. But Israel bears responsibility for its present condition. So what Israel does makes history. Any account of the Messiah-doctrine of the Talmud of the Land of Israel must lay appropriate stress on that conviction: Israel makes its own history, therefore shapes its own destiny. This lesson, sages maintained, derives from the very condition of Israel even then, its suffering and its despair.

History taught moral lessons. Historical events entered into the construction of a teleology for the Talmud of the Land of Israel's system of Judaism as a whole. What the law demanded reflected the consequences of wrongful action on the part of Israel. So, again, Israel's own deeds defined the events of history. Rome's role, like Assyria's and Babylonia's, depended upon Israel's provoking divine wrath as it was executed by the great empire. The paradox of the Talmud of the Land of Israel's system of history and Messiah lies in the fact that Israel can free itself of control by other nations only by humbly agreeing to accept God's rule. The nations—Rome, in the present instance—rest on one side of the balance, while God rests on the other. Israel must then choose between them. In the Talmud's theory of salvation, therefore, the framers provided Israel with an account of how to overcome the unsatisfactory circumstances of an unredeemed present, so as to accomplish the movement from here to the much-desired future. When the Talmud's authorities present statements on the promise of the law for those who keep it, therefore, they provide glimpses of the goal of the system as a whole. These invoked the primacy of the rabbi and the legitimating power of the Torah, and in those two components of the system we find the principles of the messianic doctrine. And these bring us back to the argument with Christ triumphant, as the Christians perceived him.

SANCTIFICATION AND SALVATION: ONE CRITICAL PROPOSITION OF THE ORAL TORAH

Two critical issues, composed of an urgent question and a self-evidently true answer to that question, define the Judaism of the dual Torah, written and oral: sanctification in the here and now, and salvation in the life hereafter through the resurrection of the dead and eternal life. Two urgent questions—what will happen to me after I die? what will be the destiny of Israel, the Jewish people, in the time to come?—in the revelation written down in the oral Torah find self-evidently true answers. The individual and the nation, Israel, should live a holy life now, so that the person in particular, and all Israel in general, may gain life eternal after death (for the individual) and salvation in the age to come (for the nation). The complementary answers, one addressing the individual, the other the holy nation or community at large bear the single message of sanctification of this life, salvation in the hereafter. Together, they come to full and profound statement in the documents of the oral Torah.

But to the untutored eye, the written Torah does not present these answers to the questions at hand. For one thing, the written Torah, that is, Hebrew Scriptures or what the Christian world knows as the Old Testament, has its own doctrines on the same questions, and they prove asymmetrical to the doctrines of life after death, the resurrection of the dead, the last judgment, and Israel's salvation in the age to come, that for the Judaism of the dual Torah provide self-evidently true answers to the urgent question of the meaning and end of humanity and history. That the propositions that formed the foundation of Judaism as a way of sanctification and salvation may not turn up in the one whole

Torah of Moses, our rabbi, in both media, written and oral, presented an unthinkable possibility. To the framers of the components of the canon of Judaism we know as the oral Torah, the gap between contemporary conviction and the contents of Scripture posed a question, which I may state as follows: Do these same self-evidently true answers to our urgent question of what happens after death, on the one side, and in the future of the holy people, on the other, derive from the written Torah as much as from the oral Torah, and how does Torah in the one medium, oral, relate to Torah in the other, written?

If we wish to restate these same questions in the language of our own times, the relationship of the Torah in the one medium to the Torah in the other medium concerns the standing and authority of Scripture in the unfolding of the conviction of the faith. When we learn how the sages of the oral Torah addressed the written Torah, the way in which they sorted out the several available theories of the authority of Scripture in the encounter with the living faith of Israel, the Jewish people, we find remarkably contemporary choices. The answers to these questions of scriptural authority turn out to define the process, on the one side, and to form the propositional center of the system of the Judaism of the dual Torah, on the other. Process and proposition together have set the norm for Israel, the Jewish people, from antiquity to our own day. When we understand how the oral Torah relates to the written Torah so that the two form that one whole Torah of Moses, our rabbi, we grasp the dynamics of Judaism. So before us are the two central issues, process and proposition: how does the faith discover truth in revelation, and how do the sages of the Torah discover the particular truth about life after death and the salvation of the individual and of holy Israel?

In this anthology, therefore, I deal with a critical contemporary issue of religious life, that of Scriptural authority, and illustrate how Judaism worked out that issue in a very particular and central conviction, so using for a case study of the relationship of the oral to the written Torah the belief in the resurrection of the dead and the messianic age that, for Judaism, constituted the doctrine of the meaning and end of life, individual and community alike. In showing the method, I work on a particular matter of substance, and therefore I display those texts, drawn from the principal documents of the oral Torah, that address the twin issues of process and proposition, first, the *process* of relating beliefs expressed in Torah in one medium to the authority of the Torah in the other medium, oral and written, respectively; second, the *proposition* of salvation through the resurrection of the dead, which forms the test case for the study of the process of the Torah. Hence we analyze the standing and authority of the written Torah in relationship to the oral Torah by tracing the doctrine of salvation as it unfolds in the successive documents of the oral Torah, to which we now turn.

THE SELECTIONS

I present, in my own translation, the movement of the theme of salvation as it is spelled out in a single chapter, from the Mishnah through the Bavli.

MISHNAH AND ITS EXEGESIS

That is Mishnah-tractate Sanhedrin Chapter Ten, which begins, *All Israel has a portion in the world to come.* This is given in Chapter 2. Then in Chapter 3 I present the corresponding amplification of that same chapter in the Tosefta. Then we turn aside, in Chapter 4, to tractate Avot and consider how it treats the same theme, namely, life after death and the world to come. We see that the former theme focuses upon the individual, and the national-historical category of the world to come for Israel, the nation, scarcely enters discourse. Chapter 5 brings us to the amplification by the framers of the Talmud of the Land of Israel ("the Yerushalmi") of Mishnah-tractate Sanhedrin Chapter Ten.

SCRIPTURE AND ITS EXEGESIS

We next step outside of the exegesis of the Mishnah and turn to how two compilations of exegeses of Scripture ("midrashim") treat the same theme, namely, the history and salvation of Israel. This theme they read into the stories of Genesis, revised in the compilation, Genesis Rabbah, and the laws of Leviticus, reworked as typologies of Israel's historical salvation, in the compilation, Leviticus Rabbah.

THE BAVLI AS THE ORAL TORAH

Finally we turn to the summa and climax of the oral Torah, the Talmud of Babylonia ("Bavli"), and see how, in its vast amplification of the Mishnah-chapter with which we begin, that document states the whole and complete picture of the individual's hope for life after death and Israel's expectation of salvation at the end of time as these are portrayed by the oral Torah. Since in the community of Judaism the Bavli constitutes the single authoritative statement of the oral Torah, being the one document that learned Jews choose for their most concentrated and lifelong study, we must regard the Bavli as the oral Torah in its single full and cogent statement. We therefore consider the way in which, the theme of salvation, joined to sanctification, emerges in the treatment by the authorship of the Bavli of Mishnah-tractate Sanhedrin Chapter Ten (given in the Bavli as we now have it as Chapter Eleven).

In the suggestions for further reference, I have provided a full account of my own translations and studies of the documents anthologized here. Each of these studies contains a full bibliography for further reference.

Readers familiar with my book *The Oral Torah: The Sacred Books of Judaism; An Introduction* (San Francisco, 1986: Harper & Row) will note the following correspondences:

Oral Torah	Scriptures of the Oral Torah
No counterpart	Chapter 1
Chapters 1 and 2	Chapters 2 and 3
Chapter 3	Chapter 4
Chapter 4	Chapter 5
Chapter 5	Chapters 6 and 7

Chapter 6   Chapter 8
Chapters 7 and 8   No counterpart

As is clear, this book is meant to provide an ample set of abstracts of the oral Torah, to illustrate and amplify the introduction in *The Oral Torah*. But each of the two works stands on its own and makes its own point.

2. The Mishnah

Beyond Scripture, the written Torah, the Mishnah presents the entire topical program of the oral Torah. The sages who stand behind the document—authorities of the first and second centuries of the Common Era—worked out a complete and encompassing system for Israel's holy life. In the history of Judaism the Mishnah provides the single most extreme statement of the centrality of sanctification, the peripherality of the matter of salvation. The here and now of everyday life in the natural world forms the counterpart and opposite of the supernatural world of God in heaven, and the ordering and regularizing of the one in line with the main outlines of the other constitutes, for the system of the Mishnah, the labor of sanctification. In its quest for the rules of order and regularity, the authorship of the Mishnah classifies and compares, finding the right rule for each matter, each important situation, by determining whether one case is like another or not like another. If it is like another, it follows the rule governing that other, and if not, it follows the opposite of that rule. In this way an orderly and logical way to sort out chaos and discover the inner order of being generates the balanced and stable, secure world described by the Mishnah. Historical events, when they enter at all, lose their one-time and unprecedented character and are shown to follow, even to generate, a fixed rule; events therefore are the opposite of eventful. This age and the age to come, history and the end of history—these categories play little role. Even the figure of the Messiah serves as a classification, namely, designation or anointment distinguishes one priest from another. So, in all, the Mishnah's method—its process, in terms of this book—dictates the results of its authorship's thought on any given topic, including the one of salvation, which is the proposition before us.

First, let us survey the Mishnah's topical program as a whole, then turn to a brief survey of its components.

The system of philosphy expressed through concrete and detailed law presented by the Mishnah consists of coherent logic and topic, a cogent worldview and comprehensive way of living. It is a worldview that speaks of transcendent things, a way of life in response to the supernatural meaning of what is done, a heightened and deepened perception of the sanctification of Israel in deed and in deliberation. Sanctification thus means two things, first, distinguishing Israel in all its dimensions from the world in all its ways; second, establishing the stability, order, regularity, predictability, and reliability of Israel in the world of nature and supernature in particular at moments and in contexts of danger. Danger means instability, disorder, irregularity, uncertainty, and betrayal. Each topic of the system as a whole takes up a critical and indispensable moment or context of social being. Through what is said in regard to each of the Mishnah's principal topics, what the halakhic system as a whole wishes to declare is fully expressed. Yet if the parts severally and jointly give the message of the whole, the whole cannot exist without all of the parts, so well joined and carefully crafted are they all. This brings us to a rapid survey of the several parts of the system, the six divisions and their sixty-two tractates.

The Division of Agriculture treats two topics, first, producing crops in accord with the scriptural rules on the subject, second, paying the required offerings and tithes to the priests, Levites, and poor. The principal point of the Division is that the Land is holy, because God has a claim both on it and upon what it produces. God's claim must be honored by setting aside a portion of the produce for those for whom God has designated it. God's ownership must be acknowledged by observing the rules God has laid down for use of the Land. In sum, the Division is divided along these lines: (1) Rules for producing crops in a state of holiness—tractates Kilayim, Shebiit, Orlah; (2) Rules for disposing of crops in accord with the rules of holiness—tractates Peah, Demai, Terumot, Maaserot, Maaser Sheni, Hallah, Bikkurim, Berakhot.

The Division of Appointed Times forms a system in which the advent of a holy day, like the Sabbath of creation, sanctifies the life of the Israelite village through imposing on the village rules on the model of those of the Temple. The purpose of the system, therefore, is to bring into alignment the moment of sanctification of the village and the life of the home with the moment of sanctification of the Temple on those same occasions of appointed times. The underlying and generative theory of the system is that the village is the mirror image of the Temple. If things are done in one way in the Temple, they will be done in the opposite way in the village. Together the village and the Temple on the occasion of the holy day therefore form a single continuum, a completed creation, thus awaiting sanctification.

The village is made like the Temple in that on appointed times one may not freely cross the lines distinguishing the village from the rest of the world, just as one may not freely cross the lines distinguishing the Temple from the world. But the village is a mirror image of the Temple. The boundary lines prevent free entry into the Temple, so they restrict free egress from the village. On the holy day what one may do in the Temple is precisely what one may not do in the village. So the advent of the holy day affects the village by bringing it into sacred symmetry in such wise as to effect a system of opposites; each is holy, in a way precisely the opposite of the other. Because of the underlying conception of perfection attained through the union of opposites, the village is not represented as conforming to the model of the cult, but of constituting its antithesis. The world thus regains perfection when on the holy day heaven and earth are united, the whole completed and done: the heaven, the earth, and all their hosts. This moment of perfection renders the events of ordinary time, of "history," essentially irrelevant. For what really matters in time is that moment in which sacred time intervenes and effects the perfection formed of the union of heaven and earth, of Temple, in the model of the former, and Israel, its complement. It is not a return to a perfect time but a recovery of perfect being, a fulfillment of creation, which explains the essentially ahistorical character of the

Mishnah's Division of Appointed Times. Sanctification constitutes an ontological category and is effected by the creator.

This explains why the Division in its rich detail is composed of two quite distinct sets of materials. First, it addresses what one does in the sacred space of the Temple on the occasion of sacred time, as distinct from what one does in that same sacred space on ordinary, undifferentiated days, which is a subject worked out in Holy Things. Second, the Division defines how for the occasion of the holy day one creates a corresponding space in one's own circumstance, and what one does, within that space, during sacred time. The issue of the Temple and cult on the special occasion of festivals is treated in tractates Pesahim, Sheqalim, Yoma, Sukkah, and Hagigah. Three further tractates, Rosh Hashshanah, Taanit, and Megillah, are necessary to complete the discussion. The matter of the rigid definition of the outlines in the village, of a sacred space, delineated by the limits within which one may move on the Sabbath and festival, and of the specification of those things which one may not do within that space in sacred time, is in Shabbat, Erubin, Besah, and Moed Qatan. While the twelve tractates of the Division appear to fall into two distinct groups, joined merely by a common theme, in fact they relate through a shared, generative metaphor. It is, as I said, the comparison, in the context of sacred time, of the spatial life of the Temple to the spatial life of the village, with activities and restrictions to be specified for each, upon the common occasion of the Sabbath or festival. The Mishnah's purpose therefore is to correlate the sanctity of the Temple, as defined by the holy day, with the restrictions of space and of action which make the life of the village different and holy, as defined by the holy day.

The Division of Women defines the women in the social economy of Israel's supernatural and natural reality. Women acquire definition wholly in relationship to men, who impart form to the Israelite social economy. The status of women is effected through both supernatural and natural, this-worldly action. What man and woman do on earth provokes a response in heaven, and the correspondences are perfect. So women are defined and secured both in heaven and here on earth, and that position is always and invariably relative to men. The principal interest for the Mishnah is the point at which a woman becomes, and ceases to be, holy to a particular man, that is, enters and leaves the marital union. These transfers of women are the dangerous and disorderly points in the relationship of woman to man, therefore, the Mishnah states, to society as well.

The formation of the marriage comes under discussion in *Qiddushin* and *Ketubot,* as well as in *Yebamot.* The rules for the duration of the marriage are scattered throughout but derive especially from parts of *Ketubot, Nedarim,* and *Nazir,* on the one side, and the paramount unit of *Sotah,* on the other. The dissolution of the marriage is dealt with in *Gittin,* as well as in *Yebamot.* We see very clearly, therefore, that important overall are issues of the transfer of property, along with women, covered in *Ketubot* and to some measure in *Qiddushin,* and the proper documention of the transfer of women and property, treated in *Ketubot* and *Gittin.* The critical issues therefore turn upon legal documents—writs of divorce, for example—and legal recognition of changes in the ownership of property, for example, through the collection of the settlement of a marriage contract by a widow, through the provision of a dowry, or through the disposition of the property of a woman during the period in which she is married. Within this orderly world of documentary and procedural concerns a place is made for the disorderly conception of the marriage not formed by human volition but decreed in heaven, the levirate connection. *Yebamot* states that supernature sanctifies a woman to a man (under the conditions of the levirate connection). What it says by indirection is that man sanctifies too: man, like God, can sanctify that relationship between a man and a woman, and can also effect the cessation of the sanctity of that same relationship. Five of the seven tractates of the Division of Women are devoted to the formation and dissolution of the marital bond. Of them, three treat what is done by man here on earth, that is, formation of a marital bond through betrothal and marriage contract and dissolution through divorce and its consequences: *Qid-*

dushin, Ketubot, and *Gittin.* One of them is devoted to what is done by woman here on earth: *Sotah.* And *Yebamot,* greatest of the seven in size and in formal and substantive brilliance, deals with the corresponding heavenly intervention into the formation and end of a marriage: the effect of death upon both forming the marital bond and dissolving it through death. The other two tractates, *Nedarim* and *Nazir,* draw into one the two realms of reality, heaven and earth, as they work out the effects of vows, perhaps because vows taken by women and subject to the confirmation or abrogation of the father or husband make a deep impact upon the marital life of the woman who has taken them.

The Division and its system delineate the natural and supernatural character of the woman's role in the social economy framed by man: the beginning, end, and middle of the relationship. The whole constitutes a significant part of the Mishnah's encompassing system of sanctification, for the reasion that heaven confirms what men do on earth. A correctly prepared writ of divorce on earth changes the status of the woman to whom it is given, so that in heaven she is available for sanctification to some other man, while, without that same writ, in heaven's view, should she go to some other man, she would be liable to be put to death. The earthly deed and the heavenly perspective correlate. That is indeed very much part of larger system, which says the same thing over and over again. The system of Women thus focuses upon the two crucial stages in the transfer of women and of property from one domain to another, the leaving of the father's house in the formation of a marriage, and the return to the father's house at its dissolution through divorce or the husband's death. There is yet a third point of interest, though, as is clear, it is much less important than these first two stages: the duration of the marriage. Finally, included within the Division and at a few points relevant to women in particular are rules of vows and of the special vow to be a Nazir. The former is included because, in the scriptural treatment of the theme, the rights of the father or husband to annul the vows of a daughter or wife form the central problematic. The latter is included for no very clear reason except that it is a species of which the vow is the genus.

The Division of Damages comprises two subsystems, which fit together in a logical way. One part presents rules for the normal conduct of civil society. These cover commerce, trade, real estate, and other matters of everyday intercourse, as well as mishaps, such as damages by chattels and persons, fraud, overcharge, interest, and the like, in that same context of everyday social life. The other part describes the institutions governing the normal conduct of civil society, that is, courts of administration, and the penalties at the disposal of the government for the enforcement of the law. The two subjects form a single tight and systematic dissertation on the nature of Israelite society and its economic, social, and political relationships, as the Mishnah envisages them.

The main point of the first of the two parts of the Division is expressed in the sustained unfolding of the three *Babas, Baba Qamma, Baba Mesia,* and *Baba Batra.* It is that the task of society is to maintain perfect stasis, to preserve the prevailing situation, and to secure the stability of all relationships. To this end, in the interchanges of buying and selling, giving and taking, borrowing and lending, it is important that there be an essential equality of interchange. No party in the end should have more than what he had at the outset, and none should be the victim of a sizable shift in fortune and circumstance. All parties' rights to, and in, this stable and unchanging economy of society are to be preserved. When the condition of a person is violated, so far as possible the law will secure the restoration of the antecedent status.

An appropriate appendix to the *Babas* is at *Abodah Zarah,* which deals with the orderly governance of transactions and relationships between Israelite society and the outside world, the realm of idolatry, relationships that are subject to certain special considerations. These are generated by the fact that Israelites may not derive benefit (as through commercial transactions) from anything that has served in the worship of an idol. Consequently, commercial transactions suffer limitations on account of extrinsic considerations of cultic taboos. While these cover both special occasions, for instance, fairs and festivals of idolatry, and general matters, that is, what Israelites may buy and sell, the main practical illustrations of the principles of the matter pertain to wine. The Mishnah supposes that gentiles routinely make use, for a libation, of a drop of any sort of wine to which they have access. It therefore is taken for granted that wine over which gentiles have had control is forbidden for Israelite use, and also that such wine is prohibited for Israelites to buy and sell. This other matter—ordinary everyday relationships with the gentile world, with special reference to trade and commerce—concludes what the Mishnah has to say about all those matters of civil and criminal law, which together define everyday relationships within the Israelite nation and between that nation and all others in the world among whom, in Palestine as abroad, they lived side by side.

The other part of the Division describes the institutions of Israelite government and politics. This is in two main aspects, first, the description of the institutions and their jurisdiction, with reference to courts, conceived as both judicial and administrative agencies, and, second, the extensive discussion of criminal penalties. The penalties are three: death, banishment, and flogging. There are four ways by which a person convicted of a capital crime may be put to death. The Mishnah organizes a vast amount of information on what sorts of capital crimes are punishable by which of the four modes of execution. That information is alleged to derive from Scripture. But the facts are many, and the relevant verses few. What the Mishnah clearly contributes to this exercise is a first-rate piece of organization and elucidation of available facts. Where the facts come from we do not know. The Mishnah-tractate *Sanhedrin* further describes the way in which trials are conducted in both monetary and capital cases and pays attention to the possibilities of perjury. The matter of banishment brings the Mishnah to a rather routine restatement by flogging and application of that mode of punishment conclude the discussion. Our selection from the Mishnah derives from Mishnah-tractate *Sanhedrin,* because that is where the reward and punishment involved in eternal life, or life in the world to come, takes its place within the larger category of penalty for violating the law of the Torah.

The matters of court procedure, worked out at *Sanhedrin-Makkot*, are supplemented in two tractates, *Shebuot* and *Horayot*, both emerging from Scripture. Lev. 5 and 6 refer to various oaths which apply mainly, though not exclusively, in courts. Lev. 4 deals with errors of judgment inadvertently made and carried out by the high priest, the ruler, and the people; the Mishnah knows that these considerations apply to Israelite courts too. What for Leviticus draws the chapters together is their common interest in the guilt offering, which is owing for violation of the rather diverse matters under discussion. Now in tractates *Shebuot* and *Horayot* the materials of Lev. 5–6 and 4, respectively, are worked out. But here is it from the viewpoint of the oath or erroneous instruction, rather than the cultic penalty. In *Shebuot* the discussion in intellectually imaginative and thorough, in *Horayot*, routine. The relevance of both to the issues of *Sanhedrin* and *Makkot* is obvious. For the matter of oaths in the main enriches the discussion of the conduct of the courts. The possibility of error is principally in the courts and other political institutions. So the four tractates on institutions and their functioning form a remarkable unified and cogent set.

The goal of the system of civil law is the recovery of the prevailing order and balance, the preservation of the established wholeness of the social economy. This idea is powerfully expressed in the organization of the three *Babas*, which treat first abnormal and then normal transactions. The framers deal with damages done by chattels and by human beings, thefts and other sorts of malfeasance against the property of others. The *Babas* in both aspects pay closest attention to how the property and person of the injured party so far as possible are restored to their prior condition, that is, a state of normality. So attention to torts focuses upon penalties paid by the malefactor to the victim, rather than upon penalties inflicted by the court on the malefactor for what he has done. When speaking of damages, the Mishnah thus takes as its principal concern the restoration of the fortune of victims of assault or robbery. Then the framers take up the complementary and corresponding set of topics, the regulation of normal transactions. When we rapidly survey the kinds of transactions of special interest, we see from the topics selected for discussion what we have already uncovered in the deepest structure of organization and articulation of the basic theme.

The other half of this same unit of three tractates presents laws governing normal and routine transactions, many of them of the same sort as those dealt with in the first half. Bailments, for example, occur in both wings of the triple tractate, first, bailments subjected to misappropriation, or accusation therof, by the bailiff, then, bailments transacted under normal circumstances. Under the rubric of routine transactions are those of workers and householders, that is, the purchase and sale of labor; rentals and bailments; real estate transactions; and inheritances and estates. Of the lot, the one involving real estate transactions is the most fully articulated and covers the widest range of problems and topics. The *Babas* all together thus provide a complete account of the orderly governance of balanced transactions and unchanging civil relationships within Israelite society under ordinary conditions.

The character and interests of the Division of Damages present probative evidence of the larger program of the philosophers of the Mishnah. Their intention is to create nothing less than a full-scale Israelite government, subject to the administration of sages. This government is fully supplied with a constitution and bylaws (*Sanhedrin, Makkot*). It makes provision for a court system and procedures (*Shebuot, Sanhedrin, Makkot*), as well as a full set of laws governing civil society (*Baba Qamma, Baba Mesia, Baba Batra*) and criminal justice (*Sanhedrin, Makkot*). This government, moreover, mediates between its own community and the outside ("pagan") world. Through its system of laws it expresses its judgment of the others and at the same time defines, protects, and defends its own society and social frontiers (*Abodah Zarah*). It even makes provision for procedures of remission, to expiate its own errors (*Horayot*).

The (then nonexistent) Israelite government imagined by the

second-century philosophers centers upon the (then nonexistent) Temple, and the (then forbidden) city, Jerusalem. For the Temple is one principal focus. There the highest court is in session; there the high priest reigns. The penalties for law infringement are of three kinds, one of which involves sacrifice in the Temple. (The others are compensation, physical punishment, and death.) The basic conception of punishment, moreover, is that unintentional infringement of the rules of society, whether "religious" or otherwise, is not penalized but rather expiated through an offering in the Temple. If a member of the people of Israel intentionally infringes against the law, to be sure, that one must be removed from society and is put to death. And if there is a claim of one member of the people against another, that must be righted, so that the prior, prevailing status may be restored. So offerings in the Temple are given up to appease heaven and restore a whole bond between heaven and Israel, specifically on those occasions on which without malice or ill will an Israelite has disturbed the relationship. Israelite civil society without a Temple is not stable or normal, and not to be imagined. And the Mishnah is above all an act of imagination in defiance of reality.

The plan for the government involves a clear-cut philosophy of society, a philosophy that defines the purpose of the government and ensures that its task is not merely to perpetuate its own power. What the Israelite government, within the Mishnaic fantasy, is supposed to do is to preserve that state of perfection that, within the same fantasy, the society to begin everywhere attains and expresses. This is in at least five aspects. First of all, one of the ongoing principles of the law, expressed in one tractate after another, is that people are to follow and maintain the prevailing practice of their locale. Second, the purpose of civil penalties, as we have noted, is to restore the injured party to his or her prior condition, so far as this is possible, rather than merely to penalize the aggressor. Third, there is the conception of true value, meaning that a given object has an intrinsic worth, which, in the course of a transaction, must be paid. In this way the seller does not leave the transaction any richer than when he entered it, or the buyer any poorer (parallel to penalties for damages). Fourth, there can be no usury, a biblical prohibition adopted and vastly enriched in the Mishnaic thought, for money ("coins") is what it is. Any pretense that it has become more than what it was violates, in its way, the conception of true value. Fifth, when real estate is divided, it must be done with full attention to the rights of all concerned, so that, once more, one party does not gain at the expense of the other. In these and many other aspects the law expresses its obsession with the perfect stasis of Israelite society. Its paramount purpose is in preserving and ensuring that that perfection of the division of this world is kept involate or restored to its true status when violated.

The Division of Holy Things presents a system of sacrifice and sanctuary: matters concerning the praxis of the altar and maintenance of the sanctuary. The praxis of the altar, specifically, involves sacrifice and things set aside for sacrifice and so deemed consecrated. The topic covers these among the eleven tractates of the present Division: *Zebahim* and part of *Hullin*, *Menahot*, *Temurah*, *Keritot*, part of *Meilah*, *Tamid*, *and Qinnim*. The maintenance of the sanctuary (inclusive of the personnel) in dealt with in *Bekhorot*, *Arakhin*, part of *Meilah*, *Middot*, and part of *Hullin*. Viewed from a distance, therefore, the Mishnah's tractates divide themselves up into the following groups (in parentheses are tractates containing relevant materials): (1) Rules for the altar and the praxis of the cult—*Zebahim Menahot*, *Hullin*, *Keritot*, *Tamid*, *Qinnim* (*Bekhorot*, *Meliah*); (2) Rules for the altar and the animals set aside for the cult—*Arakhin*, *Temurah*, *Meilah* (*Bekhorot*); and (3) Rules for the altar and support of the Temple staff and buildings—*Bekhorot*, *Middot* (*Hullin*, *Arakhin*, *Meilah*, *Tamid*). In a word, this Division speaks of the sacrificial cult and the sanctuary in which the cult is conducted. The law pays special attention to the matter of the status of the property of the altar and of the sanctuary, both materials to be utilized in the actual sacrificial rites, and property the value of which supports the cult and sanctuary in general. Both are deemed to be sanctified, that is, "holy things."

The Division of Holy Things centers upon the everyday and rules always applicable to the cult: the daily whole offering, the sin offering and guilt offering which one may bring any time under ordinary circumstances; the right sequence of diverse offerings; the way in which the rites of the whole, sin, and guilt offerings are carried out; what sorts of animals are acceptable; the accompanying cereal offerings; the support and provision of animals for the cult and of meat for the priesthood; the support and material maintenance of the cult and its building. We have a system before us: the system of the cult of the Jerusalem Temple, seen as an ordinary and everyday affair, a continuing and routine operation. That is why special rules for the cult, both in respect to the altar and in regard to the maintenance of the buildings, personnel, and even the holy city, will be elsewhere—in Appointed Times and Agriculture. But from the perspective of Holy Things, those Divisions intersect by supplying special rules and raising extraordinary (Agriculture: land-bound; Appointed Times: time-bound) considerations for that theme which Holy Things claims to set forth in its most general and unexceptional way: the cult as something permanent and everyday.

The Division of Holy Things thus in a concrete way maps out the cosmology of the sanctuary and its sacrificial system, that is, the world of the Temple, which had been the cosmic center of Israelite life. A later saying states matters as follows: "Just as the navel is found at the center of a human being, so the Land of Israel is found at the center of the world . . . and it is the foundation of the world. Jerusalem is at the center of the Land of Israel, the Temple is at the center of Jerusalem, the Holy of Holies is at the center of the Temple, the Ark is at the center of the Holy of Holies, and the Foundation Stone is in front of the Ark, which spot is the foundation of the world" (*Tanhuma Qedoshim* 10).

The Division of Purities presents a very simple system of three principal parts: sources of uncleanness, objects and substances susceptible to uncleanness, and modes of purification from uncleanness. So it tells the story of what makes a given sort of object unclean and what makes it clean. The tractates on these several topics are as follows: (1) sources of uncleanness—*Ohalot, Negaim, Niddah, Makhshirin, Zabim, Tebul Yom;* (2) objects and substances susceptible to uncleanness—*Kelim, Tohorot, Uqsin;* and (3) modes of purification—*Parah, Miqvaot, Yadayim.* Viewed as a whole, the Division of Purities treats the interplay of persons, food, and liquids. Dry inanimate objects or food are not susceptible to uncleanness. What is wet is susceptible. So liquids activate the system. What is unclean, moreover, emerges from uncleanness through the operation of liquids, specifically, through immersion in fit water of requisite volume and in natural condition. Liquids thus deactivate the system. That is, water in its natural condition is what concludes the process by removing uncleanness. Water in its unnatural condition, that is, deliberately affected by human agency, is what imparts susceptibility to uncleanness to begin with. The uncleanness of persons, furthermore, is signified by body liquids or flux in the case of the menstruating woman (*Niddah*) and the *zab* (*Zabim*). Corpse uncleanness is conceived to be a kind of effluent, a viscous gas, which flows like liquid. Utensils for their part receive uncleanness when they form receptacles able to contain liquid. In sum, we have a system in which the invisible flow of fluidlike substances or powers serve to put food, drink, and receptacles into the status of uncleanness and to remove those things from that status. Whether or not we call the system "metaphysical," it certainly has no material base but is conditioned upon highly abstract notions. Thus in material terms, the effect of liquid is upon food, drink, utensils, and people. The consequence has to do with who may eat and drink what food and liquid, and what food and drink may be consumed in which pots and pans. These loci are specified by tractates on utensils (*Kelim*) and on food and drink (*Tohorot* and *Uqsin*).

The human being is ambivalent. Persons fall in the middle, between sources and loci of uncleanness, because they are both. They serve as sources of uncleanness. They also become unclean. The *zab*, suffering the uncleanness described in Leviticus Chapter 15, the menstruating woman, the woman after childbirth, and the person afflicted with the skin ailment described in Leviticus Chapters

13 and 14—all are sources of uncleanness. But being unclean, they fall within the system's loci, its program of consequences. So they make other things unclean and are subject to penalties because they are unclean. Unambiguous sources of uncleanness never also constitute loci affected by uncleanness. They always are unclean and never can become clean: the corpse, the dead creeping thing, and things like them. Inanimate sources of uncleanness and inanimate objects are affected by uncleanness. Systemically unique, humans and liquids have the capacity to inaugurate the processes of uncleanness (as sources) and also are subject to those same processes (as objects of uncleanness). The Division of Purities, which presents the basically simple system just now described, is not only the oldest in the Mishnah. It also is the largest and contains by far the most complex laws and ideas.

Let us now stand back and characterize the system as a whole. Overall, its stress lies on sanctification, understood as the correct arrangement of all things, each in its proper category, each called by its rightful name, just as at the creation: everything having been given its proper name, God called the natural world very good and God sanctified it. For the Mishnah makes a statement of philosophy, concerning the order of the natural world in its correspondence with the supernatural world. Later on, the Midrash-compilations and the Talmud of the Land of Israel would make a statement of theology, concerning the historical order of society in its progression from creation through salvation at the end of time. Judaism in the dual Torah then constitutes a complete statement about philosophy and nature, theology and history, the one in the oral, the other in the written Torah. All together the two components would constitute that "one whole Torah of Moses, our rabbi."

The selection before us, given in italics as are all citations of passages of the Mishnah in this anthology, addresses the issue of salvation. It makes one point, which is that salvation consists of a share in the world to come. Precisely what is meant by *the world to come* is not made clear. We look in vain for a definition, since, once the basic point is made that everyone of Israel has a share, we proceed to list the exceptions. These are the ones who deny (1) that the principle of the resurrection of the dead rests upon the authority of the written Torah, (2) that the Torah comes from God in heaven, and (3) an Israelite who is philosophically an Epicurean. The first two items are of special interest to us. The former represents our proposition, the latter, the issue of process. The Mishnah's sages insist that the dogma at hand derives from the written Torah; that of course indicates that the framer of this passage takes for granted that when we speak of the Torah, we mean what is now meant by the written Torah, in contradistinction to the oral one. The proposition, as I said, is remarkably inarticulate. The world to come of M. San. 11:1A seems to form the counterpart to the resurrection of the dead in M. 11:1D. If that is the case, then it follows that when M. 11:1A states, "All Israelites have a share in the world to come," the framer of the passage means that all Israelites will rise from the dead. As we note, the rest of our chapter simply catalogues those who do not share in the world to come. I have divided the remainder of the chapter in line with its division in the Talmud of Babylonia, even though our selection of the Talmud's treatment of our chapter is limited, by reason of size, only to its amplification of M. 11:1–2. But, as we shall see, that is the important part, because of the Bavli's authorship's stress on the matter of how the written Torah proves that the dead will be raised.

11:1–2

A. *All Israelites have a share in the world to come,*

B. *as it is said, "your people also shall be all righteous, they shall inherit the land forever; the branch of my planting, the work of my hands, that I may be glorified" (Is. 60:21).*

C. *And these are the ones who have no portion in the world to come;*

D. *He who says, the resurrection of the dead is a teaching which does not derive from the Torah, and the Torah does not come from Heaven; and an Epicurean.*

E. R. Aqiba says, "Also: He who reads in heretical books,

F. "and he who whispers over a wound and says, 'I will put none of the diseases upon you which I have put on the Egyptians, for I am the Lord who heals you' (Ex. 15:26)."

G. Abba Saul says, "Also: He who pronounces the divine Name as it is spelled out."

M. Sanhedrin 11:1

A. Three kings and four ordinary folk have no portion in the world to come.

B. Three kings: Jeroboam, Ahab, and Manasseh.

C. R. Judah says, "Manasseh has a portion in the world to come,

D. "since it is said, 'And he prayed to him and he was entreated of him and heard his supplication and brought him again to Jerusalem into his kingdom' (2 Chr. 33:13)."

E. They said to him, "To his kingdom he brought him back, but to the life of the world to come he did not bring him back."

F. Four ordinary folk: Balaam, Doeg, Ahitophel, and Gehazi.

M. 11:2

11:3A–CC

A. The generation of the flood has no share in the world to come,

B. and they shall not stand in the judgment,

C. since it is written, "My spirit shall not judge with man forever" (Gen. 6:3)

D. neither judgment nor spirit.

E. The generation of the dispersion has no share in the world to come,

F. since it is said, "So the Lord scattered them abroad from there upon the face of the whole earth" (Gen. 11:8)

G. "So the Lord scattered them abroad"—in this world,

H. "and the Lord scattered them from there"—in the world to come.

I. The men of Sodom have no portion in the world to come,

J. since it is said, "Now the men of Sodom were wicked and sinners against the Lord exceedingly" (Gen. 13:13).

K. "Wicked"—in this world,

L. "and sinners"—in the world to come.

M. *But they will stand in judgment.*

N. *R. Nehemiah says, "Both these and those will not stand in judgment,*

O. *"for it is said, 'Therefore the wicked shall not stand in judgment [108A], nor sinners in the congregation of the righteous' (Ps. 1:5).*

P. *" 'Therefore the wicked shall not stand in judgment'—this refers to the generation of the flood.*

Q. *" 'Nor sinners in the congregation of the righteous'—this refers to the men of Sodom."*

R. *They said to him, "They will not stand in the congregation of the righteous, but they will stand in the congregation of the sinners."*

S. *The spies have no portion in the world to come,*

T. *as it is said, "Even those men who brought up an evil report of the land died by the plague before the Lord" (Num. 14:37).*

U. *"Died"—in this world.*

V. *"By the plague"—in the world to come.*

W. *"The generation of the wilderness has no portion in the world to come and will not stand in judgment,*

X. *"for it is written, 'In this wilderness they shall be consumed and there they shall die' (Num. 14:35)," the words of R. Aqiba.*

Y. *R. Eliezer says, "Concerning them it says, 'Gather my saints together to me, those that have made a covenant with me by sacrifice' (Ps. 50:5)."*

Z. *"The party of Korah is not destined to rise up,*

AA. *"for it is written, 'And the earth closed upon them'—in this world.*

BB. *"And they perished from among the assembly'—in the world to come," the words of R. Aqiba.*

CC. *And R. Eliezer says, "Concerning them it says, 'The Lord kills and resurrects, brings down to Sheol and brings up again' (1 Sam. 2:6)."*

11:3DD–FF

DD. *"The ten tribes are not destined to return,*

EE. *"since it is said, 'And he cast them into another land, as on this day' (Deut. 29:28). Just as the day passes and does not return,*

*so they have gone their way and will not return," the words of
R. Aqiba.*

FF.   *R. Eliezer says, "Just as this day is dark and then grows light,
so the ten tribes for whom it now is dark—thus in the future it
is destined to grow light for them."*

M. 11:3

A.   *The townsfolk of an apostate town have no portion in the world
to come,*

B.   *as it is said, "Certain base fellows [sons of Belial] have gone
out from the midst of thee and have drawn away the inhabitants
of their city" (Deut. 13:14).*

C.   *And they are not put to death unless those who misled the [town]
come from that same town and from that same tribe,*

D.   *and unless the majority is misled,*

E.   *and unless men did the misleading.*

F.   *[If] women or children misled them,*

G.   *of if a minority of the town was misled,*

H.   *or if those who misled the town came from outside of it,*

I.   *lo, they are treated as individuals [and not as a whole town],*

J.   *and they [thus] require stimony against them] by two witnesses,
and a statement of warning, for each and every one of them.*

K.   *This rule is more strict for individuals than for the community:*

L.   *for individuals are put to death by stoning.*

M.   *Therefore their property is saved.*

N.   *But the community is put to death by the sword,*

O.   *therefore their property is lost.*

M. 11:4

A.   *"And you shall surely smite the inhabitants of the city with the
edge of the sword" (Deut. 13:15).*

B.   *Ass-drivers, camel-drivers, and people passing from place to
place—lo these have the power to save it,*

C.   *as, it is said, "Destroying it utterly and all that is therein and
the cattle thereof, with the edge of the sword" (Deut. 13:17).*

D.   *On this basis they said, The property of righteous folk which
happens to be located in it is lost. But that which is outside of
it is saved.*

E. *And as to that of evil folk, whether it is in the town or outside of it, lo, it is lost.*

M. 11:5

A. *[As it is said,] "And you shall gather all the spoil of it into the midst of the wide place thereof" (Deut. 13:17).*
B. *If it has no wide place, they make a wide place for it.*
C. *[If] its wide place is outside of it, they bring it inside.*
D. *"And you will burn with fire the city and all the spoil thereof, (ever whit, unto the Lord your God)" (Deut. 13:17).*
E. *"The spoil thereof"—but not the spoil which belongs to heaven.*
F. *On this basis they have said:*
G. *Things which have been consecrated which are in it are to be redeeemed; heave-offering left therein is allowed to rot; second tithe and sacred scrolls are hidden away.*
H. *"Every whit unto the Lord your God":*
I. *Said R. Simeon, "Said the Holy One, blessed be he: 'If you enter into judgment in the case of an apostate city, I give credit to you as if you had offered a whole burnt-offering before me."*
J. *"And it shall be a heap forever, it shall not be built again."*
K. *"It should not be made even into vegetable patches or orchards," the words of R. Yose the Galilean.*
L. *R. Aqiba says, " 'It shall not be built again'—as it was it may not be rebuilt, but it may be made into vegetable patches and orchards."*
M. *"And there shall cleave nought of the devoted things to your hand [that the Lord may turn from the fierceness of his anger and show you mercy and have compassion upon you and multiply you]" (Deut. 13:18).*
N. *for so long as evil people are in the world, fierce anger is in the world.*
O. *When the evil people have perished from the world, fierce anger departs from the world.*

M. 11:6

3. The Tosefta

The Tosefta is a corpus of complementary or supplementary materials for the Mishnah, following the plan and order of the Mishnah and citing the same authorities as occur in the Mishnah, in the language and syntax of the Mishnah. Since the Tosefta contains numerous verbatim citations of the Mishnah, the document as a whole certainly comes later than the Mishnah, ca. 200 C.E., and since its materials, for their part, are cited in the Talmud of the Land of Israel, ca. 400 C.E., the closure of the Tosefta should fall some time between those two estimated dates. A guess of ca. 300 seems justified. But while the date of the document is indeterminate, its place in the order of the unfolding of the documentary components of the oral Torah is not. It is, as we see, midway between the Mishnah and the first of the two Talmuds.

The Tosefta is made up of three types of distinct statements. The first cites and then glosses a sentence of the Mishnah. The second refers to a principle given in the Mishnah but does not cite it verbatim; this second type cannot be fully understood without reference to the Mishnah. The third sort stands completely separate from the Mishnah and contributes a rule on a topic found in the Mishnah but in no way relates to, or intersects with, a rule on the same topic given by the Mishnah. The materials of the Tosefta, relating in order to the topical program of the Mishnah, tend to follow a plan by which first comes citation of the Mishnah's rule, then comes amplification, finally are given those autonomous and freestanding statements that are essentially supplementary to the Mishnah's treatment of a given subject.

We turn first to the issue of process, namely, the relationship of the oral Torah to the written Torah. The theory of the authorship of the Tosefta concerning the relationship of the Mishnah to Scripture may be stated in one sentence. Each sentence of the

Mishnah demands its supporting text of Scripture. The implicit premise is that the Mishnah in no way stands as an autonomous source of revelation, of the Torah of Moses at Sinai, but forms a secondary and derivative amplification of what is in writing. The Mishnah's authority, therefore, depends wholly upon that of the written Torah. We know that that premise pervades the document, because at every occasion at which a prooftext may be introduced in support of a statement of the Mishnah, the Tosefta's authorship will provide such a statement. The authorship of the Talmud of the Land of Israel and the Talmud of Babylonia follows suit, as we shall see.

The matter of proposition requires no discussion whatsoever. The authorship of the Tosefta restates the proposition supplied by the Mishnah, which is that salvation comes to all Israel and consists in the resurrection of the dead: supernature succeeding and complementing nature. There is no doctrine of national salvation nor theory of this age and the age to come at the end of time, nor do the figure of the Messiah and the eschatological teleology of the system as a whole play a role in the Tosefta's propositional program.

I give the entire selection in boldface type, and when the Tosefta is cited in later chapters, the citations occur in boldface type as well.

13:1

> A. **"Minors, children of the wicked of the Land [of Israel] have no portion in the world to come, as it is said, 'Behold, the day is coming, burning like a furnace, and all the proud, and all who do wickedly, shall be as stubble' (Mal. 1:1)," the words of Rabban Gamaliel.**
>
> B. **R. Joshua says, "They come into the world to come. For later it says, 'The Lord preserves the simple' (Ps. 116:6), and further, 'Hew down the tree and destroy it, nevertheless, leave the stump of the roots thereof in the earth' (Dan. 4:23)."**
>
> C. **Said Rabban Gamaliel to [Joshua], "How shall I interpret, 'He shall leave them to neither root nor branch'?"**

D. [Joshua] said to [Gamaliel], "That the Omnipresent will not leave for them [the merit of a single] religious duty or the remnant of a religious duty, or for their fathers, for ever."

13:2

A. Another matter:

B. "Root"—this refers to the soul.

C. "And branch"—this refers to the body.

D. And the children of the wicked among the heathen will not live [in the world to come] nor be judged.

E. R. Eliezer says, "None of the gentiles has a portion in the world to come,

F. "as it is said, 'The wicked shall return to Sheol, all the gentiles who forget' God (Ps. 9:17).

G. "*The wicked shall return to Sheol*—these are the wicked Israelites."

H. [Supply: "*And all the gentiles who forget God*—these are the nations."]

I. Said to him R. Joshua, "If it had been written, '*The wicked shall return to Sheol—all the gentiles*' and then said nothing further, I should have maintained as you do.

J. "Now that it is in fact written, *All the gentiles who forget God*, it indicates that there also are righteous people among the nations of the world, who do have a portion in the world to come."

13:3

A. The House of Shammai says, "There are three groups, one for eternal life, one *for shame and everlasting contempt* (Dan. 12:2)—these are those who are completely evil.

B. "An intermediate group go down Gehenna and scream and come up again and are healed,

C. "as it is said, 'I will bring the third part through fire and will refine them as silver is refined and will test them as gold is tested, and they shall call on my name and I will be their God' (Zech. 13:9).

D. "And concerning them did Hannah say, 'The Lord kills and brings to life, brings down to Sheol and brings up' (I Sam. 2:6)."

E. And the House of Hillel says, "*Great in mercy* (Ex. 34:6)— He inclines the decision toward mercy,

F. "and concerning them David said, 'I am happy that the Lord has heard the sound of my prayer' (Ps. 116:1),

G. "and concerning them is said the entire passage."

13:4

A. The Israelites who sinned with their bodies and gentiles who sinned with their bodies go down to Gehenna and are judged there for twelve months.

B. And after twelve months their souls perish, their bodies are burned, Gehenna absorbs them, and they are turned into dirt.

C. And the wind blows them and scatters them under the feet of the righteous,

D. as it is written, "And you shall tread down the wicked, for they shall be dust under the soles of the feet of the righteous in the day that I do this, says the Lord of Hosts" (Mal. 4:3).

13:5

A. But heretics, apostates, traitors, Epicureans, those who deny the Torah, those who separate from the ways of the community, those who deny the resurrection of the dead, and whoever both sinned and caused the public to sin—

B. for example, Jeroboam and Ahab,

C. and those who sent their arrows against the land of the living and stretched out their hands against the "lofty habitation" [the Temple],

D. Gehenna is locked behind them, and they are judged therein for all generations,

E. since it is said, "And they shall go forth and look at the corpses of the men who were transgressors against me. For their worm dies not, and their fire is not quenched. And they shall be an abhorring unto all flesh" (Is. 66:24).

F. Sheol will waste away, but they will not waste away,

G. for it is written, ". . . and their form shall cause Sheol to waste away" (Ps. 49:14).

H. What made this happen to them? Because they stretched out their hand against the "lofty habitation,"

I. as it is said, "Because of his lofty habitation," and lofty habitation refers only to the Temple, as it is said, "I have surely built you as a lofty habitation, a place for you to dwell in forever" (I Kings 8:13).

13:6

A. "The generation of the Flood has no share in the world to come" [M. San. 10:3a],

B. nor will they live in the world to come,

C. as it is said, "And he destroyed every living thing that was upon the face of the earth" (Gen. 7:23)—in this world;

D. and they perished from the earth—in the world to come.

E. R. Judah b. Betera says, " 'And the Lord said, My spirit shall not contend with man forever' (Gen. 6:3)—

F. "it will not contend, nor will my spirit be in them forever."

G. Another matter: "And the Lord said, My spirit shall not contend"—Said the Omnipresent, "I shall give them back their spirit as a gift."

H. R. Menahem b. R. Yos says, "It will not contend—

I. "Said the Omnipresent, 'I shall not contend with them when I pay the good reward which is coming to the righteous.'

J. "But the spirit of the evil is harder for them than that of all the others,

K. "as it is written, 'Their spirit is a fire consuming them' (Is. 33:11)."

13:7

A. The generation of the Tower of Babylon have no portion in the world to come [M. San. 10:3E], and will not live in the world to come,

B. as it is said, "Then the Lord scattered them abroad from thence upon the face of the whole earth" (Gen. 11:8)—in this world;

C. And they ceased to build the city—in the world to come.

13:8

A. The men of Sodom have no portion in the world to come [M. San. 10:31],

B. and they will not live in the world to come.

C. since it is said, "And the men of Sodom were wicked and sinners [against the Lord exceedingly]" (Gen. 13:13)—in this world;

D. against the Lord exceedingly—in the world to come.

E. Another matter: Wicked—each person against his fellow;

F. and sinners—in fornication;

G. against the Lord—through idolatry;

H. exceedingly—in bloodshed.

13:9

A. The spies have no portion in the world to come [M. San. 10:3S],

B. as it is said, "Nor shall any of them that despised me see it" (Num. 14:23).

C. "Korach and his company have no portion in the world to come and will not live in the world to come,

D. "since it is said, 'And the earth closed upon them' (Num. 16:33)—In this world.

E. " 'And they perished from among the assembly'—in the world to come," the words of R. Aqiba [M. San. 10:3Z–BB].

F. R. Judah b. Petera says, "They will come to the world to come.

G. "For concerning them it is written, 'I have gone astray like a perishing sheep; seek your servant' (Ps. 119:176).

H. "Perishing is said here, and in the matter of Korah and his company, perishing also is said.

I. "Just as perishing spoken of later on refers to that which is being sought, so perishing spoken of here refers to that which is being sought."

13:10

A. "The generation of the wilderness has no portion in the world to come [M. San. 10:3W],

B. "and will not live in the world to come,

C. "for it is written, 'In this wilderness they shall be consumed and there they shall die' (Num. 14:35):

D. "In this wilderness they shall be consumed—in this world,

E. "and there they will die, in the world to come.

F. "And it says, 'Of them I swore in my wrath that they should not enter into my rest' (Ps. 95:11)," the words of R. Aqiba.

G. R. Eliezer says, "They will come into the world to come,

H. "for concerning them it is said, 'Gather my saints together to me, those that have made a covenant with me by sacrifices' (Ps. 50:51)" [M. San. 10:3Y].

13:11

A. What does Scripture mean, "I swore in my wrath"?

B. In my wrath I swore, but I retract it.

C. R. Joshua b. Qorha says, "These things were spoken only regarding generations to come,

D. "as it is said, 'Gather my saints together to me'—because they did deeds of loving-kindness to me.

E. " 'Those that have made a covenant with me'—because they were cut for my sake.

F. "By sacrifice—because they exalted me and were sacrificed in my behalf.

G. R. Simeon b. Menassia says, "They will come [into the world to come],

H. "and concerning them it is said, 'And the redeemed of the Lord shall return and come to Zion with gladness' (Is. 35:10)."

13:12

A. The ten tribes have no portion in the world to come and will not live in the world to come,

B. as it is said, "And the Lord drove them out of their land with anger and heat and great wrath" (Deut. 29:28)—in this world;

C. "and cast them forth into another land" (Deut. 29:28)—in the world to come.

D. R. Simeon b. Judah of Kefar Akkum says, "Scripture said, 'As at this day—'

E. "If their deeds remain as they are this day, this will [not] reach it."

4. The Fathers (Pirqé Avot)

Unlike the Tosefta, which depends upon the Mishnah for its structure and organization, its topical program and its purpose, Mishnah-tractate Avot stands separate from the Mishnah, although it conventionally is included with that document. Formally, rhetorically, and topically, tractate Avot must be regarded as singular and distinct. For one thing, its authorship appeals to a later layer of authorities. Since the last-named authorities in the document are generally supposed to have flourished in the generation beyond Judah the Patriarch, sponsor of the Mishnah, the document is conventionally given the date of ca. 250. Not only so, but the tractate stands outside of the Mishnah and addresses a principal problem of that document. Specifically, its authorship provides the Mishnah's first and most extreme apologetic, treating the Mishnah as part of the revelation, the Torah, of Sinai.

This brings us, first, to the former of our two ongoing concerns, the matter of process. The position of the authorship of tractate Avot on the issue of process—the relationship of the oral Torah to the written Torah—is stated implicitly. Specifically, the authorship of the tractate listed as its authorities Moses, Joshua, prophets, and onward, in a chain of tradition. What makes the chain a statement of an extreme position is the compositors' inclusion of the names, within the tradition of Sinai, of authorities of the Mishnah itself. That fact indicates the whole of their polemic: the Mishnah's rules derive from authorities who stand in a direct line to Sinai. Then the Mishnah enjoys the standing and authority of God's revelation to Moses at Sinai and forms part of the Torah of Sinai. Later on, as we shall see, in the Talmud of the Land of Israel or the Yerushalmi, the process by which this component of the Torah reached the sages of the first and second centuries would be spelled out. It would be described as a process of oral formulation and oral transmission through the memories of sages, hence the oral Torah.

We shall understand the position of the framers of Avot when we recognize the problem that confronted them. As soon as the Mishnah made its appearance, the vast labor of explaining its meaning and justifying its authority got under way. The Mishnah presented one striking problem in particular. It rarely cited scriptural authority for its rules. Omitting scriptural prooftexts bore the implicit claim to an authority independent of Scripture, and in that striking fact the document set a new course for itself and raised problems for those who would apply its law to Israel's life. For from the formation of ancient Israelite Scripture into a holy book in Judaism, as the aftermath of the return to Zion and the creation of the Torah-book in Ezra's time (ca. 450 B.C.E.) as the established canon of revelation (whatever its contents), coming generations routinely set their ideas into relationship with Scripture. This they did by citing prooftexts alongside their own rules. Otherwise, in the setting of Israelite culture, the new writings could find no ready hearing.

Over the six hundred years from the formation of the Torah of "Moses" in the time of Ezra, from ca. 450 B.C.E. to ca. 200 C.E., four conventional ways to accommodate new writings—new "tradition"—to the established canon of received Scripture had come to the fore.

First and simplest, a writer would sign a famous name to his book, attributing his ideas to Enoch, Adam, Jacob's sons, Jeremiah, Baruch, and any number of others, down to Ezra. But the Mishnah bore no such attribution, e.g., to Moses. Implicitly, to be sure, the statement of M. Avot 1:1, "Moses received Torah from Sinai" carried the further notion that sayings of people on the list of authorities from Moses to nearly their own day derived from God's revelation at Sinai. But no one made that premise explicit before the time of the Talmud of the Land of Israel.

Second, an authorship might also imitate the style of biblical Hebrew and so try to creep into the canon by adopting the cloak of Scripture. But the Mishnah's authorship ignores biblical syntax and style.

Third, an author would surely claim his work was inspired by God, a new revelation for an open canon. But, as we realize, that claim makes no explicit impact on the Mishnah.

Fourth, at the very least, someone would link his opinions to biblical verses through the exegesis of the latter in line with the former so Scripture would validate his views. The authorship of the Mishnah did so only occasionally, but far more commonly stated on its own authority whatever rules it proposed to lay down.

The Hebrew of the Mishnah complicated the problem, because it is totally different from the Hebrew of the Hebrew Scriptures. Its verb, for instance, makes provision for more than completed or continuing action, for which the biblical Hebrew verb allows, but also for past and future times, subjunctive and indicative voices, and much else. The syntax is Indo-European, in that we can translate the word order of the Mishnah into any Indo-European language and come up with perfect sense. None of that crabbed imitation of biblical Hebrew, which makes the Dead Sea scrolls an embarrassment to read, characterizes the Hebrew of the Mishnah. Mishnaic style is elegant, subtle, exquisite in its sensitivity to word order and repetition, balance, pattern.

The solution to the problem of the authority of the Mishnah, that is to say, its relationship to Scripture, was worked out in the period after the closure of the Mishnah. Since no one now could credibly claim to sign the name of Ezra or Adam to a book of this kind, and since biblical Hebrew had provided no apologetic aesthetics whatever, the only options lay elsewhere. The two were, first, provide a myth of the origin of the contents of the Mishnah, and, second, link each allegation of the Mishnah, through processes of biblical (not Mishnaic) exegesis, to verses of the Scriptures. These two procedures, together, would establish for the Mishnah that standing that the uses to which the document was to be put demanded for it: a place in the canon of Israel, a legitimate relationship to the Torah of Moses. There were several ways in which the work went forward. These are represented by diverse documents that succeeded and dealt with the Mishnah. Let me now state the three principal possibilities.

(1) The Mishnah required no systematic support through exegesis of Scripture in light of Mishnaic laws. That is the position of tractate Avot.

(2) The Mishnah by itself provided no reliable information and all of its propositions demanded linkage to Scripture, to which the Mishnah must be shown to be subordinate and secondary. The authorship of the two Talmuds implicitly adopts that position, by making every effort to show, sentence by sentence, how every rule, including those of the Mishnah, rests upon a phrase or word of Scripture.

(3) The Mishnah is an autonomous document, but closely correlated with Scripture. That is the position of the authorship of the Tosefta, as we have seen. But the distance between position (2) and position (3) is not great.

The first extreme is represented by the Abot, ca. 250 C.E., which represents the authority of the sages cited in Abot as autonomous of Scripture. Those authorities in Abot do not cite verses of Scripture but what they say does constitute a statement of the Torah. There can be no clearer way of saying that what these authorities present in and of itself falls into the classification of the Torah. The authorship of the Tosefta, ca. 300, takes the middle position. It very commonly cites a passage of the Mishnah and then adds to that passage an appropriate prooftext. That is a quite common mode of supplementing the Mishnah. The mediating view is further taken by the Talmud of the Land of Israel, ca. 400, among the various documents produced by the Jewish sages of the Land of Israel between the end of the second century and the sixth.

The Talmud of the Land of Israel ("Palestinian Talmud of the Land of Israel," "Yerushalmi"), like the one made up at the same period, in the third and fourth centuries, in Babylonia, was organized around the Mishnah. It provided a line-by-line or paragraph-by-paragraph exegesis and amplification of the Mishnah.

Produced in schools in Tiberias, Sepphoris, Lud (Lydda), and Caesarea, the Talmud of the Land of Israel developed a well-crafted
theory of the Mishnah and its relationship to Scripture. The far
extreme—everything in the Mishnah makes sense only as a
(re)statement of Scripture or upon Scripture's authority—is taken
by the Sifra, a post-Mishnaic compilation of exegeses on Leviticus,
redacted at an indeterminate point, perhaps about 300 C.E. The
Sifra systematically challenges reason (= the Mishnah), unaided by
revelation (that is, exegesis of Scripture), to sustain positions taken
by the Mishnah, which is cited verbatim, and everywhere proves
that it cannot be done.

From process, we turn to the matter of proposition. We ask
about the matter of sanctification and salvation. Neither category
plays a role in our document. The systemic teleology of the authorship of tractate Avot appeals to this life and the life to come.
Salvation as a national and historical category plays no part. When
we survey the entirety of tractate Avot, we shall look in vain for
the conception of a national entity, Israel, that all together and all
at once will enjoy a single history, now, and destiny at the end
of time. When the authorship at hand speaks of the purpose and
goal of life and of the system under exposition, the categories are
this life and the life to come, rather than this age and the age to
come. The point of distinction is not linguistic but substantive.
Reference is repeatedly made to the individual and his or her existence beyond death, but the conception that the nation, Israel,
has a history that is divided between now and then, this age and
the coming age, and that the purpose of keeping the Torah is to
secure for the nation salvation, that is, entry into the coming
age—these propositions play no role whatsoever. When in the two
Talmuds and Genesis Rabbah and Leviticus Rabbah we pursue the
same inquiry into propositions of salvation, we shall see a stunning contrast. The categorical construction before us rests upon
the individual. The purpose of studying the Torah and keeping
its rules now is to secure the afterlife.

What I offer is not an argument from silence, but a case that
rests upon what the document says, as well as what it does not

invoke as its teleology. The teleology of tractate Avot in no way invokes historical and eschatological considerations and in no way speaks to the nation as its prime entity. Rather, it invokes the dimensions of the natural life leading toward supernatural being and addresses the individual and his or her life now and then. To appreciate the power of the salvific doctrine before us, we shall review the entirety of the tractate, even though only at some passages the proposition of special concern to us comes up for discussion.

THE SAYINGS OF THE FATHERS

CHAPTER ONE

1:1.   Moses received the Torah at Sinai and handed it on to Joshua, Joshua to elders, and elders to prophets. And prophets handed it on to the men of the great assembly. They said three things: Be prudent in judgment. Raise up many disciples. Make a fence for the Torah.

1:2.   Simeon the Righteous was one of the last survivors of the great assembly. He would say, "On three things does the world stand: On the Torah, and on the Temple service, and on deeds of loving kindness."

1:3   Antigonus of Sokho received [the Torah] from Simeon the Righteous. He would say: "Do not be like servants who serve the master on condition of receiving a reward, but [be] like servants who serve the master not on condition of receiving a reward. And let the fear of Heaven be upon you."

1:4   Yosé b. Yoezer of Zeredah and Yosé b. Yohanan of Jerusalem received [the Torah] from them. Yosé ben Yoezer says: "Let your house be a gathering place for sages. And wallow in the dust of their feet, and drink in their words with gusto."

1:5.   Yosé b. Yohanan of Jerusalem says: "Let your house be open wide. And seat the poor at your table ["make the poor members of your household"]. And don't talk too much with women. (He referred to a man's wife, all the more so is the rule to be applied to the wife of one's fellow. In this regard did sages say: So long as a man talks too much with a woman, he brings trouble on himself, wastes time better spent on studying the Torah, and ends up an heir of Gehenna.)"

1:6. Joshua b. Perahyah and Nittai the Arbelite received [the Torah] from them. Joshua ben Perahyah says: "Set up a master for yourself. And get yourself a companion-disciple. And give everybody the benefit of the doubt."

1:7. Nittai the Arbelite says: "Keep away from a bad neighbor. And don't get involved with a bad person. And don't give up hope of retribution."

1:8A. Judah ben Tabbai and Simeon ben Shetah received [the Torah] from them.

1:8B. Judah b. Tabbai says: "Don't make yourself like one of those who advocate before judges [while you yourself are judging a case]. And when the litigants stand before you, regard them as guilty. But when they leave you, regard them as acquitted (when they have accepted your judgment)."

1:9. Simeon b. Shetah says: "Examine the witnesses with great care. And watch what you say, lest they learn from what you say how to lie."

1:10. Shemaiah and Avtalyon received [the Torah] from them. Shemaiah says: "Love work. Hate authority. Don't get friendly with the government."

1:11. Avtalyon says: "Sages, watch what you say, lest you become liable to the punishment of exile, and go into exile to a place of bad water, and disciples who follow you drink bad water and die, and the name of Heaven be thereby profaned."

1:12. Hillel and Shammai received [the Torah] from them. Hillel says: "Be disciples of Aaron, loving peace and pursuing grace, loving people and drawing them near to the Torah."

1:13A. He would say [in Aramaic]: "A name made great is a name destroyed, and one who does not add, subtracts.

1:13B. "And who does not learn is liable to death. And the one who uses the crown, passes away."

1:14. He would say: "If I am not for myself, who is for me? And when I am for myself, what am I? And if not now, when?"

1:15. Shammai says: "Make your learning of the Torah a fixed obligation. Say little and do much. Greet everybody cheerfully."

1:16. Rabban Gamaliel says: "Set up a master for yourself. Avoid doubt. Don't tithe by too much guesswork."

1:17. Simeon his son says: "All my life I grew up among the sages, and I found nothing better for a person [the body] than silence. And not the learning is the thing, but the doing. And whoever talks too much causes sin."

1:18. Rabban Simeon ben Gamaliel says: "On three things does the world stand: on justice, on truth, and on peace. As it is said, 'Execute the judgment of truth and peace in your gates' (Zech 8:16)."

CHAPTER TWO

2:1. Rabbi says: "What is the straight path which a person should choose for himself? Whatever is an ornament to the one who follows it, and an ornament in the view of others. Be meticulous in a small religious duty as in a large one, for you do not know what sort of reward is coming for any of the various religious duties. And reckon with the loss [required] in carrying out a religious duty against the reward for doing it; and the reward for committing a transgression against the loss for doing it. And keep your eye on three things, so you will not come into the clutches of transgression. Know what is above you. An eye which sees, and an ear which hears, and all your actions are written down in a book."

2:2. Rabban Gamaliel, a son of Rabbi Judah the Patriarch says: "Fitting is learning in the Torah along with a craft, for the labor put into the two of them makes one forget sin. And all learning of the Torah which is not joined with labor is destined to be null and causes sin. And all who work with the community—let them work with them [the community] for the sake of Heaven. For the merit of the fathers strengthens them, and the righteousness which they do stands forever. And, as for you, I credit you with a great reward, as if you had done [all the work required by the community].

2:3. "Be wary of the government, for they get friendly with a person only for their own convenience. They look like friends when it is to their benefit, but they do not stand by a person when he is in need."

2:4. He would say: "Make His wishes into your own wishes, so that He will make your wishes into His wishes. Put aside your wishes on account of His wishes, so that He will put aside the wishes of other people in favor of your wishes." Hillel says: "Do not walk out on the community. And do not have confidence in yourself until the day you die. And do not judge your companion until you are in his place. And do not say anything which cannot be heard, for in the end it will be heard. And do not say: When I have time I shall study, for your may never have time."

2:5. He would say: "A coarse person will never fear sin, nor will an *am ha-Aretz* (a boor) ever be pious, nor will a shy person learn, nor will an ignorant person teach, nor will anyone too occupied in business get wise. In a place where there are no individuals, try to be an individual."

2:6. Also, he saw a skull floating on the water and said to it [in Aramaic]: "Because you drowned others, they drowned you, and in the end those who drowned you will be drowned."

2:7. He would say: "Lots of meat, lots of worms; lots of property, lots of worries; lots of women, lots of witchcrafts; lots of slave girls, lots of lust; lots of slave boys, lots of robbery. Lots of the Torah, lots of life; lots of discipleship, lots of wisdom; lots of counsel, lots of understanding; lots of righteousness, lots of peace. [If] one has gotten a good name, he has gotten it for himself. [If] he has gotten teachings of the Torah, he has gotten himself life eternal."

2:8A.   Rabban Yohanan b. Zakkai received [the Torah] from Hillel and Shammai. He would say: "If you have learned much Torah, do not puff yourself up on that account, for it was that purpose that you were created. He had five disciples, and these are they: Rabbi Eliezer b. Hyrcanus, Rabbi Joshua b. Hananiah, Rabbi Yosé the Priest, Rabbi Simeon b. Nethanel, and Rabbi Eleazar b. Arakh.

2:8B.   He would list their good qualities: Rabbi Eliezer b Hyrcanus—a plastered well, which does not lose a drop of water. Rabbi Joshua—happy is the one who gave birth to him. Rabbi Yosé—a pious man. Rabbi Simeon b Nethanel—a man who fears sin, and Rabbi Eleazar ben Arakh—a surging spring.

2:8C.   He would say: "If all the sages of Israel were on one side of the scale, and Rabbi Eliezer b Hyrcanus were on the other, he would outweigh all of them."

2:8D.   Abba Saul says in his name: "If all of the sages of Israel were on one side of the scale, and Rabbi Eliezer b Hyrcanus was also with them, and Rabbi Eleazar [ben Arakh] were on the other side, he would outweigh all of them."

2:9A.   He said to them: "Go and see what is the straight path to which someone should stick."

2:9B.   Rabbi Eliezer says: "A generous spirit." Rabbi Joshua says: "A good friend." Rabbi Yosé says: "A good neighbor." Rabbi Simeon says: "Foresight." Rabbi Eleazar says: "Good will."

2:9C.   He said to them: "I prefer the opinion of Rabbi Eleazar ben Arakh, because in what he says is included everything you say."

2:9D.   He said to them: "Go out and see what is the bad road, which someone should avoid." Rabbi Eliezer says: "Envy." Rabbi Joshua says: "A bad friend." Rabbi Yosé says: "A bad neighbor." Rabbi Simeon says: "A loan." (All the same is a loan owed to a human being and a loan owed to the Omnipresent, the blessed, as it is said, "The wicked borrows and does not pay back, but the righteous person deals graciously and hands over [what is owed].)" Ps. 37:21.

2:9E.   Rabbi Eleazar says: "Ill will."

2:9F.   He said to them: "I prefer the opinion of Rabbi Eleazar ben Arakh, because in what he says is included everything you say."

2:10A.   They [each] said three things.

2:10B.   Rabbi Eliezer says: "Let the respect owing to your companion be as precious to you as the respect owing to yourself. And don't be easy to anger. And repent one day before you die. And warm yourself by the fire of the sages, but be careful of their coals, so you don't get burned—for their bite is the bite of a fox, and their sting is the sting of a scorpion, and their hiss is like the hiss of a snake, and everything they say is like fiery coals."

2:11.   Rabbi Joshua says: "Envy, desire of bad things, and hatred for people push a person out of the world."

2:12.   Rabbi Yosé says: "Let your companion's money be as precious to you as yoru own. And get yourself ready to learn the Torah, for it does not come as an inheritance to you. And may everything you do be for the sake of Heaven."

2:13.   Rabbi Simeon says: "Be meticulous about the recitation of the Shema and the Prayer. And when you pray, don't treat your praying as a matter of routine; but let it be a [plea for] mercy and supplicaton before the Omnipresent, the blessed, as it is said, "For He is gracious and full of compassion, slow to anger and full of mercy, and repents of the evil" (Joel 2:13). And never be evil in your own eyes."

2:14.   Rabbi Eleazar says: "Be constant in learning of the Torah; and know what to reply to an Epicurean; and know before whom you work, for your employer can be depended upon to pay your wages for what you do."

2:15.   Rabbi Tarfon says: "The day is short, the work formidable, the workers lazy, the wages high, the employer impatient."

2:16. He would say: "It's not your job to finish the work, but you are not free to walk away from it. If you have learned must Torah, they will give you a good reward. And your employer can be depended upon to pay your wages for what you do. And know what sort of reward is going to be given to the righteous in the coming time."

CHAPTER THREE

3:1A. Aqabiah b. Mehallalel says, "Reflect upon three things and you will not fall into the clutches of transgression: "Know (1) from whence you come, (2) whither you are going, and (3) before whom you are going to have to give a full account of yourself.

3:1B. "From whence do you come? From a putrid drop. Whither are you going? To a place of dust, worms, and maggots.

3:1C. "And before whom are you are going to give a full account of yourself? Before the King of kings, of kings, the Holy One, blessed be he."

3:2A. R. Hananiah, Prefect of the Priests, says, "Pray for the welfare of the government. For if it were not for fear of it, one man would swallow his fellow alive."

3:2B. R. Hananiah b. Teradion says, "[If] two sit together and between them do not pass teachings of the Torah, lo, this is a seat of the scornful, as it is said, 'Nor sits in the seat of the scornful' (Ps. 1:1). But two who are sitting, and words of the Torah do pass between them—the Presence is with them, as it is said, 'Then they that feared that Lord spoke with one another, and the Lord hearkened and heard, and a book of remembrance was written before him, for them that feared the Lord and gave thought to his name' (Mal. 3:16).' I know that this applies to two. How do I know that even if a single person sits and works on the Torah, the Holy One, blessed be He, set aside a reward for him? As it is said, 'Let him sit alone and keep silent, because he has laid it upon him' (Lam. 3:28)."

3:3. R. Simeon says, "Three who ate at a single table and did not talk about teachings of the Torah while at that table are as though they ate from dead sacrifices (Ps. 106:28), as it is said, 'For all tables are full of vomit and filthiness [if they are] without God' (Ps. 106:28). But three who ate at a single table and did talk about teachings of the Torah while at that table are as if they ate at the table of the Omnipresent, blessed is he, as it is said, 'And he said to me, This is the table that is before the Lord' (Ez. 41:22)."

3:4. R. Hananiah b. Hakhinai says, "(1) He who gets up at night, and (2) he who walks around by himself, and (3) he who turns his desire to emptiness—lo, this person is liable for his life."

3:5. R. Nehunia b. Haqqaneh says, "From whoever accepts upon himself the yoke of the Torah do they remove the yoke of the state and the yoke of hard labor. And upon whoever removes from himself the yoke of the Torah do they lay the yoke of the state and the yoke of hard labor."

3:6. R. Halafta of Kefar Hananiah says, "Among ten who sit and work hard on the Torah the Presence comes to rest, as it is said, 'God stands in the congregation of the mighty' (Ps. 82:1). And how do we now that the same is so even of five? For it is said, 'And he has founded his group upon the earth' (Amos 9:6). And how do we know that this is so even of three? Since it is said, 'And he judges among the judges' (Ps. 82:1). And how do we know that this is so even of two? Because it is said, 'Then they that feared the Lord spoke with one another, and the Lord hearkened and heard' (Mal. 3:16). And how do we know that this is so even of one? Since it is said, 'In every place where I record my name I will come to you and I will bless you' (Ex. 20:24)."

3:7A. R. Eleazar of Bartota says, "Give him what is his, for you and yours are his. For so does it say about David, 'For all things come of you, and of your own have we given you' (1 Chron. 29:14)."

3:7B. R. Simeon says, "He who is going along the way and repeating [his Torah-tradition] but interrupts his repetition and says, How beautiful is that tree! How beautiful is that ploughed field!—Scripture reckons it to him as if he has become liable for his life."

3:8. R. Dosetai b. R. Yannai in the name of R. Meir says, 'Whoever forgets a single thing from what he has learned—Scripture reckons it to him as it he has become liable for his life, as it is said, 'Only take heed to yourself and keep your soul diligently, lest you forget the words which your eyes saw' (Deut. 4:9). It is possible that this is so even if his learning became too much for him? Scripture says, 'Lest they depart from your heart all the days of your life.' Thus he becomes liable for his life only when he will sit down and actually remove [his learning] from his own heart."

3:9A. R. Haninah b. Dosa says, "For anyone whose fear of sin takes precedence over his wisdom, his wisdom will endure. And for anyone whose wisdom takes precedence over his fear of sin, wisdom will not endure."

3:9B. He would say, "Anyone whose deeds are more than his wisdom—his wisdom will endure. And anyone whose wisdom is more than his deeds—his wisdom will not endure."

3:10A. He would say, "Anyone from whom people take pleasure—the Omnipresent takes pleasure. And anyone from whom people do not take pleasure, the Omnipresent does not take pleasure."

3:10B. R. Dosa b. Harkinas says, "(1) Sleeping late in the morning, (2) drinking wine at noon, (3) chatting with children, and (4) attending the synagogues of the ignorant drive a man out of the world."

3:11. R. Eleazar the Modite says, "(1) He who treats Holy Things as secular, and (2) he who despises the appointed times, (3) he who humiliates his fellow in public, (4) he who removes the signs of the covenant of Abraham, our father, (may he rest in peace), and (5) he who exposes aspects of the Torah not in accord with the law, even though he has in hand learning in the Torah and good deeds, will have no share in the world to come."

3:12. R. Ishmael says, "(1) Be quick [in service] to a superior,

(2) efficient in service [to the state], and (3) receive everybody with joy."

3:13. R. Aqiba says, "(1) Laughter and lightheadedness turn lewdness into a habit. (2) Tradition is a fence for the Torah. (3) Tithes are a fence for wealth. (4) Vows are a fence for abstinence. (5) A fence for wisdom is silence."

31:14A. He would say, "Precious is the human being, who was created in the image [of God]. It was an act of still greater love that it was made known to him that he was created in the image [of God]. As it is said, 'For in the image of God he made man' (Gen. 9:6).

31:4B. "Precious are Israelites, who are called children to the Omnipresent. It was an act of still greater love that it was made known to them that they were called children to the Omnipresent, as it is said, 'You are the children of the Lord your God' (Deut. 14:1).

3:14C. "Precious are Israelites, to whom was given the precious thing. It was an act of still greater love that it was made known to them that to them was given that precious thing with which the world was made, as it is said, 'For I give you a good doctrine. Do not forsake my Torah' (Prov. 4:2).

3:15. "Everything is foreseen, and free choice is given. In goodness the world is judged. And all is in accord with the abundance of deed[s]."

3:16A. He would say, "(1) All is handed over as a pledge, (2) And a net is cast over all the living. (3) The store is open, (4) the storekeeper gives credit. (5) The account-book is open. And (6) the hand is writing.

3:16B. "Whoever wants to borrow may come and borrow. (2) The charity collectors go around every day and collect from man whether he knows it or not. (3) And they have grounds for what they do. (4) And the judgment is a true judgment. (5) And everything is ready for the meal."

3:17A.   R. Eleazar b. Azariah says, "If there is no learning of the Torah, there is no proper conduct. If there is no proper conduct, there is no learning in the Torah. If there is no wisdom, there is no reverence. If there is no reverence, there is no wisdom. If there is no understanding, there is no knowledge. If there is no knowledge, there is no understanding. If there is no sustenance, there is no Torah-learning. If there is no Torah-learning, there is no sustenance."

3:17B.   He would say, "Anyone whose wisdom is greater than his deeds—to what is he to be likened? To a tree with abundant foliage, but few roots. When the winds come, they will uproot it and blow it down. As it is said, 'He shall be like a tamarisk in the desert and shall not see when good comes, but shall inhabit the parched places in the wilderness' (Jer. 17:6). But anyone whose deeds are greater than his wisdom—to what is he to be likened? To a tree with little foliage but abundant roots. For even if all the winds in the world were to come and blast at it, they will not move it from its place, as it is said, 'He shall be as a tree planted by the waters, and that spreads out its roots by the river, and shall not fear when heat comes, and his leaf shall be green, and shall not be careful in the year of drought, neither shall cease from yielding fruit' (Jer. 17:8)."

3:18.   R. Eleazar Hisma says, "The laws of bird-offerings and of the beginning of the menstrual period—they are indeed the essentials of the Torah. Calculation of the equinoxes and reckoning the numerical value of letters are the savories of wisdom."

CHAPTER FOUR

4:1   Ben Zoma says, "Who is a sage? He who learns from everybody, as it is said, 'From all my teachers I have gotten understanding' (Ps. 119:99). Who is strong? He who overcomes his desire, as it is said, 'He who is slow to anger is better than the mighty, and he who rules his spirit than he who takes a city' (Prov. 16:32). Who is rich? He who is happy in what he has, as it is said, 'When you eat the labor of your hands, happy will you be, and it will go well with you' (Ps. 128:2). ('Happy will you be—in this world, and it will go well with you—in the world to come.') Who is honored? He who honors everybody, as it is said, 'For those who honor me I shall honor, and they who despise me will be treated as of no account' (1 Sam. 2:30)."

4:2. Ben Azzai says, "Run after the most minor religious duty as after the most important, and flee from transgression. For doing one religious duty draws in its wake doing yet another, and doing one transgression draws in its wake doing yet another. For the reward of doing a religious duty is a religious duty, and the reward of doing a transgression in a transgression."

4:3. He would say, "Do not despise anybody and do not treat anything as unlikely. For you have no one who does not have his time, and you have nothing which does not have its place."

4:4A. R. Levitas of Yavneh says, "Be exceedingly humble, for the future of humanity is the worm."

4:4B. R. Yohanan b. Beroqa says, "Whoever secretly treats the Name of Heaven as profane publicly pays the price. All the same are the one who does so inadvertently and the one who does so deliberately, when it comes to treating the name of Heaven as profane."

4:5A. R. Ishmael, his son, says, "He who learns so as to teach— they give him a chance to learn and to teach. He who learns so as to carry out his teachings—they give him a chance to learn, to teach, to keep, and to do."

4:5B. R. Sadoq says, "Do not make [Torah-teachings] a crown in which to glorify yourself or a spade with which to dig. So did Hillel say, 'He who uses the crown perishes.' Thus have you learned: Whoever derives worldly benefit from teachings of the Torah takes his life out of this world."

4:6. R. Yosé says, "Whoever honors the Torah himself is honored by people. And whoever disgraces the Torah himself is disgraced by people."

4:7.   R. Ishmael, his son, says, "He who avoids serving as a judge avoids the power of enmity, robbery, and false swearing. And he who is arrogant about making decisions is a fool, evil, and prideful."

4:8.   He would say, "Do not serve as a judge by yourself, for there is only One who serves as a judge all alone. And do not say, 'Accept my opinion,' For they have the choice in the matter, not you."

4:9.   R. Jonathan says, "Whoever keeps the Torah when poor will in the end keep it in wealth. And whoever treats the Torah as nothing when he is wealthy in the end will treat it as nothing in poverty."

4:10.   R. Meir says, "Keep your business to a minimum and make your business the Torah. And be humble before everybody. And if you treat the Torah as nothing, you will have many treating you as nothing. And if you have labored in the Torah, [the Torah] has a great reward to give you."

4:11A.   R. Eleazar b. Jacob says, "He who does even a single religious duty gets himself a good advocate. He who does even a single transgression gets himself a powerful prosecutor. Penitence and good deeds are like a shield against punishment."

4:11B.   R. Yohanan Hassandelar says, "Any gathering which is for the sake of Heaven is going to endure. And any which is not for the sake of Heaven is not going to endure."

4:12.   R. Eleazar b. Shammua says, "The honor owing to your disciple should be as precious to you as yours. And the honor owing to your fellow should be like the reverence owing to your master. And the reverence owing to your master should be like the awe owing to Heaven."

4:13A.   R. Judah says, "Be meticulous about learning, for error in learning leads to deliberate [violation of the Torah]."

4:13B.   R. Simeon says, "There are three crowns: the crown of the Torah, the crown of priesthood, and the crown of sovereignty. But the crown of a good name is best of them all."

4:14. R. Nehorai says, "Go into exile to a place of the Torah, and do not suppose that it will come to you. For your fellow-disciples will make it solid in your hand. And on your own understanding do not rely."

4:15A. R. Yannai says, "We do not have in hand [an explanation] either for the prosperity of the wicked or for the suffering of the righteous."

4:15B. R. Matya b. Harash says, "Greet everybody first, and be a tail to lions. But do not be a head of foxes."

4:16. R. Jacob says, "This world is like an antechamber before the world to come. Get ready in the antechamber, so you can go into the great hall."

4:17. He would say, "Better is a single moment spent in penitence and good deeds in this world than the whole of the world to come. And better is a single moment of inner peace in the world to come than the whole of a lifetime spent in this world."

4:18. R. Simeon b. Eleazar says, "(1) Do not try to make amends with your fellow when he is angry, or (2) comfort him when the corpse of his beloved is lying before him, or (3) seek to find absolution for him at the moment at which he takes a vow, or (4) attempt to see him when he is humiliated."

4:19. Samuel the Small says, " 'Rejoice not when your enemy falls, and let not your heart be glad when he is overthrown, lest the Lord see it and it displease him, and he turn away his wrath from him' (Prov. 24:17)."

4:20. Elisha b. Abuyah says, "He who learns when a child—what is he like? Ink put down on a clean piece of paper. And he who learns when an old man—what is he like? Ink put down on a paper full of erasures."

4:21A. R. Yośe b. R. Judah of Kefar Habbabli says, "He who learns from children—what is he like? One who eats sour grapes and drinks fresh wine. And he who learns from old men—what is he like? He who eats ripe grapes and drinks vintage wine."

4:21B.   Rabbi says, "Do not look at the bottle but at what is in it. You can have a new bottle of old wine, and an old bottle which has not got even new wine."

4:22A.   R. Eleazar Haqqappar says, "Jealousy, lust, and ambition drive a person out of this world."

4:22B.   He would say, "Those who are born are [destined] to die, and those who die are [destined] for resurrection. And the living are [destined] to be judged—so as to know, to make known, and to confirm that (1) he is God, (2) he is the one who forms, (3) he is the one who creates, (4) he is the one who understands, (5) he is the one who judges, (6) he is the one who gives evidence, (7) he is the one who brings suit, (8) and he is the one who is going to make the ultimate judgment.

4:22C.   "Blessed be he, for before him are no (1) guile, (2) forgetfulness, (3) respect for persons, or (4) bribe-taking, for everything is his. And know that everything is subject to reckoning. And do not let your evil impulse persuade you that Sheol is a place of refuge for you. For (1) despite your wishes were formed, (2) despite your wishes were you born, (3) despite your wishes do you live, (4) despite your wishes do you die, and (5) despite your wishes are you going to give a full accounting before the King of kings of kings, the Holy One blessed be he."

CHAPTER FIVE

5:1.   By ten acts of speech was the world made. And what does Scripture mean [by having God say say ten times]? But it is to exact punishment from the wicked, who destroy a world which was created through ten acts of speech, and to secure a good reward for the righteous, who sustain a world which created through ten acts of speech.

5:2.   There are ten generations from Adam to Noah, to show you how long-suffering is [God]. For all those generations went along spiting him until he brought the water of the flood upon them. There are ten generations from Noah to Abraham, to show you how long-suffering is [God]. For all those generations went along spiting him, until Abraham came along and took the reward which had been meant for all of them.

5:3. Ten trials were inflicted upon Abraham, our father, may he rest in peace, and he withstood all of them, to show you how great is His love for Abraham, our father, may he rest in peace.

5:4. Ten wonders were done for our fathers in Egypt, and ten at the Sea. Ten blows did the holy One, blessed be he, bring upon the Egyptians in Egypt, and ten at the Sea. Ten trials did our fathers inflict upon the Omnipresent, blessed be he, in the Wilderness, as it is said, "Yet they have tempted me these ten times and have not listened to my voice" (Num. 14:22).

5:5. Ten wonders were done for our fathers in the Temple: (1) A woman never miscarried on account of the stench of the meat of Holy Things. (2) And the meat of the Holy Things never turned rotten. (3) A fly never made an appearance in the slaughter house. (4) A high priest never suffered a nocturnal emission on the eve of the Day of Atonement. (5) The rain never quenched the fire on the altar. (6) No wind ever blew away the pillar of smoke. (7) An invalidating factor never affected the 'omer, the Two Loaves, or the show bread. (8) When the people are standing, they are jammed together. When they go down and prostrate themselves, they have plenty of room. (9) A snake and a scorpion never bit anybody in Jerusalem. (10) And no one ever said to his fellow, "The place is too crowded for me" (Is. 49:20) to stay in Jerusalem.

5:6A. Ten things were created on the eve of the Sabbath [Friday] at twilight, and these are they: (1) the mouth of the earth [Num. 16:32]; (2) the mouth of the well [Num. 21:16–18]; (3) the mouth of the ass [Num. 22:38]; (4) the rainbow [Gen. 9:13]; (5) the manna [Ex. 16:15]; (6) the rod [Ex. 4:17]; (7) the Shamir; (8) letters; (9) writing; (10) and the tables of stone [of the ten commandments, Ex. 32:15f.].

5:6B. And some say, Also the destroyers, the grave of Moses, and the tamarisk of Abraham, our father.

5:6C. And some say, Also the tongs made with tongs [with which the first tongs were made].

5:7. There are seven traits to an unformed clod, and seven to a sage. (1) A sage does not speak before someone greater than he in wisdom. (2) And he does not interrupt his fellow. (3) And he is not at a loss for an answer. (4) He asks a relevant question and answers properly. (5) And he addresses each matter in its proper sequence, first, then second. (6) And concerning something he has not heard, he says, "I have not heard the answer." (7) And he concedes the truth [when the other party demonstrates it]. And the opposite of these traits apply to a clod.

5:8. There are seven forms of punishment which come upon the world for seven kinds of transgression. (1) [If] some people give tithes and some people do not give tithes, there is a famine from drought. So some people are hungry and some have enough. (2) [If] everyone decided not to tithe, there is famine of unrest and drought. (3) [If all decided] not to remove dough offering, there is a famine of totality. (4) Pestilence comes to the world on account of the death penalties which are listed in the Torah but which are not in the hands of the court [to inflict]; and because of the produce of the Seventh Year [which people buy and sell]. (5) A sword comes into the world because of the delaying of justice and perversion of justice, and because of those who teach the Torah not in accord with the law.

5:9A. (6) A plague of wild animals comes into the world because of vain oaths and desecration of the Divine Name. (7) Exile comes into the world because of those who worship idols, because of fornication, and because of bloodshed, and because of the neglect of the release of the Land [in the year of release].

5:9B. At four turnings in the year pestilence increases: in the fourth year, in the seventh year, in the year after the seventh year, and at the end of the Festival [of Tabernacles] every year: (1) in the fourth year, because of the poorman's tithe of the third year [which people have neglected to hand over to the poor]; (2) in the seventh year, because of the poorman's tithe of the sixth year; (3)

in the year after the seventh year, because of the dealing in produce of the seventh year; and (4) at the end of the Festival every year, because of the thievery of the dues [gleanings and the like] owing to the poor [not left for them in the antecedent harvest].

5:10.   There are four sorts of people: (1) he who says, "What's mine is mine and what's yours is yours"—this is the average sort (and some say, "This is the sort of Sodom"); (2) "What's mine is yours and what's yours is mine"—this is a boor; (3) "What's mine is yours and what's yours is yours"—this is a truly pious man; (4) "What's mine is mine and what's yours is mine"—this is a truly wicked man.

5:11.   There are four sorts of personality: (1) easily angered, easily calmed—he loses what he gains; (2) hard to anger, hard to calm— what he loses he gains; (3) hard to anger and easy to calm—a truly pious man; (4) easy to anger and hard to calm—a truly wicked man.

5:12.   There are four types of disciples: (1) quick to grasp, quick to forget—he loses what he gains; (2) slow to grasp, slow to for-get—what he loses he gains; (3) quick to grasp, slow to forget— a sage; (4) slow to grasp, quick to forget—a bad lot indeed.

5:13.   There are four traits among people who give charity: (1) he who wants to give, but does not want others to give—he be-grudges what belongs to others; (2) he wants others to give, but he does not want to give—he begrudges what belongs to himself; (3) he will give and he wants others to give—he is truly pious; (4) he will not give and he does not want others to give—he is truly wicked.

5:14.   There are four sorts among those who go to the study-house: (1) he who goes but does not carry out [what he learns]— he has at least the reward for the going; (2) he who practices but does not go [to study]—he has at least the reward for the doing; (3) he who both goes and practices—he is truly pious; (4) he who neither goes nor practices—he is truly wicked.

5:15.   There are four traits among those who sit before the sages:

a sponge, a funnel, a strainer, and a sifter: (1) a sponge—because he sponges everything up; (2) a funnel—because he takes in on one side and lets out on the other; (3) a strainer—for he lets out the wine and keeps the lees; (4) and a sifter—for he lets out the flour and keeps in the finest flour.

5:16. [In] any loving relationship which depends upon something, [when] that thing is gone, the love is gone. But any which does not depend upon something will never come to an end. What is a loving relationship which depends upon something? That is the love of Amnon and Tamar [2 Sam. 13:15]. And one which does not depend upon something: that is the love of David and Jonathan.

5:17. Any dispute which is for the sake of Heaven will in the end yield results, and any which is not for the sake of Heaven will in the end not yield results. What is a dispute for the sake of Heaven? This is the sort of dispute between Hillel and Shammai. And what is one which is not for the sake of Heaven? It is the dispute of Korach and all his party.

5:18. He who brings merit to the community never causes sin. And he who causes the community to sin—they never give him a sufficient chance to attain penitence. Moses attained merit and bestowed merit on the community. So the merit of the community is assigned to his [credit], as it is said, "He executed the justice of the Lord and his judgments with Israel" (Deut. 33:21). Jeroboam sinned and caused the community of the Israelites to sin. So the sin of the community is assigned to his [debit], as it said, "For the sins of Jeroboam which he committed and wherewith he made Israel to sin" (1 Kings 15:30).

5:19. Anyone in whom are these three traits is one of the disciples of Abraham, our father; but [if he bears] three other traits, he is one of the disciples of Balaam, the wicked; (1) a generous spirit, (2) a modest men, and (3) a humble soul—he is one of the disciples of Abraham, our father. He who exhibits (1) a grudging spirit, (2) an arrogant mien, and (3) a proud soul—he is one of the disciples of Balaam, the wicked. What is the difference between the disciples of Abraham our father and the disciples of Balaam the wicked? The disciples of Abraham our father enjoy the benefit [of their learning] in this world and yet inherit the world to come, as it is said, "That I may cause those who love me to inherit substance, and so that I may fill their treasures" (Prov. 8:21). The disciples of Balaam the wicked inherit Gehenna and go down to the Pit of Destruction, as it is said, "But you, O God, shall bring them down into the pit of destruction; bloodthirsty and deceitful men shall not live out half their days" (Ps. 55:24).

5:20A.   Judah b. Tema says, "Be strong as a leopard, fast as an eagle, fleet as a gazelle, and grave as a lion, to carry out the will of your Father who is in heaven."

5:20B.   He would say, "The shameless go to Gehenna, and the diffident to the garden of Eden.

5:20C.   "May it be found pleasing before you, O Lord our God, that you rebuild your city quickly in our day and set our portion in your Torah."

5:21.   He would say, "(1) At five to Scripture, (2) ten to Mishnah, (3) thirteen to religious duties, (4) fifteen to Talmud, (5) eighteen to the wedding canopy, (6) twenty to responsibility for providing for a family, (7) thirty to fullness of strength, (8) forty to understanding, (9) fifty to counsel, (10) sixty to old age, (11) seventy to ripe old age, (12) eighty to remarkable strength, (13) ninety to a bowed back, and (14) at a hundred—he is like a corpse who is already passed and gone from this world."

5:22.   Ben Bag Bag says [in Aramaic], "Turn it over and over because everything is in it. And reflect upon it now, grow old and worn in it, and do not leave it, [in Hebrew], for you have no better lot than that."

5:23.   Ben He He says, "In accord with the effort is the reward."

5. The Yerushalmi

Let us return to the consideration of process, that is, the way in which the authorship of the documents of the oral Torah related their work to the written Torah. The final and normative solution to the problem of the authority of the Mishnah worked out in the third and fourth centuries produced the myth of the dual Torah, oral and written, which formed the indicative and definitive trait of the Judaism that emerged from late antiquity. Tracing the unfolding of that myth leads us deep into the processes by which that Judaism took shape. The Yerushalmi knows the theory that there is a tradition separate from, and in addition to, the written Torah. This tradition it knows as "the teachings of scribes." The Mishnah is not identified as the collection of those teachings. An ample instantiation of the Yerushalmi's recognition of this other, separate tradition is contained in the following unit of discourse. What is interesting is that, if these discussions take for granted the availability to Israel of authoritative teachings in addition to those of Scripture, they do not then claim those teachings are contained, uniquely or even partially, in the Mishnah in particular. Indeed, the discussion is remarkable in its supposition that extra-Scriptural teachings are associated with the views of "scribes," perhaps legitimately called sages, but not in a book to be venerated or memorized as a deed of ritual-learning.

Y. Abodah Zarah 2:7:

III. A. Associates in the name of R. Yohanan: "The words of scribes are more beloved than the words of Torah and more cherished than words of Torah: 'Your palate is like the best wine' (Song 7:9)."

    B. Simeon bar Ba in the name of R. Yohanan: "The words of scribes are more beloved than the words of Torah and more cherished than words of Torah: 'For your love is better than wine' (Song 1:2)."

D. R. Ishmael repeated the following: "The words of Torah are subject to prohibition, and they are subject to remission; they are subject to lenient rulings, and they are subject to strict rulings. But words of scribes all are subject only to strict interpretation, for we have learned there: He who rules, 'There is no requirement to wear phylacteries,' in order to transgress the teachings of the Torah, is exempt. But if he said, 'There are five partitions in the phylactery, instead of four,' in order to add to what the scribes have taught, he is liable' [M. San. 11:3]."

E. R. Haninah in the name of R. Idi in the name of R. Tanhum b. R. Hiyya: "More stringent are the words of the elders than the words of the prophets. For it is written, 'Do not preach'— thus they preach—'one should not preach of such things' (Micah 2:6). And it is written, '[If a man should go about and utter wind and lies, saying,] "I will preach to you of wine and strong drink," he would be the preacher for this people!' (Micah 2:11).

F. "A prophet and an elder—to what are they comparable? To a king who sent two senators of his to a certain province. Concerning one of them he wrote, 'If he does not show you my seal and signet, do not believe him.' But concerning the other one he wrote, 'Even though he does not show you my seal and signet, believe him.' So in the case of the prophet, he has had to write, 'If a prophet arises among you . . . and gives you a sign or a wonder . . .' (Deut. 13:1). But here [with regard to an elder:] '. . . according to the instructions which they give you . . .' (Deut. 17:11) [without a sign or a wonder]."

What is important in the foregoing anthology is the distinction between teachings contained in the Torah and teachings in the name or authority of "scribes." These latter teachings are associated with quite specific details of the law and are indicated in the Mishnah's rule itself. Further, at E we have "elders" (that is, sages) as against prophets.

What conclusion is to be drawn from this mixture of word choices that all together clearly refer to a law or tradition in addition to that of Scripture? The commonplace view, maintained in diverse forms of ancient Judaism, that Israel had access to a tradition beyond Scripture, clearly was well known to the framers of the Yerushalmi. The question of how, in that context, these framers viewed the Mishnah, however, is not to be settled by that fact. As I said, I cannot point to a single passage in which explicit judgment upon the character and status of the Mishnah as a complete document is laid down. Nor is the Mishnah treated as a symbol or called "the oral Torah." But there is ample evidence, once again implicit in what happens to the Mishnah in the Talmud of the Land of Israel, to allow a reliable description of how the Talmud of the Land of Israel's founders viewed the Mishnah. That view may be stated very simply. The Mishnah rarely cites verses of Scripture in support of its propositions. The Talmud of the Land of Israel routinely adduces scriptural bases for the Mishnah's laws. The Mishnah seldom undertakes the exegesis of verses of Scripture for any purpose. The Talmud of the Land of Israel consistently investigates the meaning of verses of Scripture, and does so for a variety of purposes. Accordingly, the Talmud of the Land of Israel, subordinate as it is to the Mishnah, regards the Mishnah as subordinate to, and contingent upon, Scripture. That is why, in the Talmud of the Land of Israel's view, Mishnah requires the support of prooftexts of Scripture. Let me state the upshot with the necessary emphasis: *that fact can mean only that, by itself, the Mishnah exercises no autonomous authority and enjoys no independent standing or norm-setting status.*

What is important in the following abstract, which forms a bridge from the matter of process to the particular proposition concerning salvation, is that the search for prooftexts in Scripture sustains not only propositions of the Mishnah, but also of the Tosefta as well as those of the Talmud of the Land of Israel's own *sages.* This is a stunning fact. It indicates that the search of Scriptures is primary, the source of propositions or texts to be supported by those Scriptures, secondary. There is no limit, indeed, to the purposes for which scriptural texts will be found relevant. Here we see how the oral Torah's authorship links its principles to those of Scripture.

Y. Sanhedrin 10:4:

II. A. *The party of Korach has no portion in the world to come and will not live in the word to come,* [M. San. 10:4].

     B. What is the scriptural basis for this view?

     C. *"[So they and all that belonged to them went down alive into Sheol;] and the earth closed over them, and they perished from the midst of the assembly"* (Num. 16:33).

     D. *"The earth closed over them"*—in this world.

     E. *"And they perished from the midst of the assembly"*—in the world to come [M. San. 10:4D–F].

     F. It was taught: R. Judah b. Batera says, "[The contrary view] is to be derived from the implication of the following verse:

     G. " 'I have gone astray like a lost sheep: seek thy servant [and do not forget thy commandments]' (Ps. 119:176).

     H. "Just as the lost object which is mentioned later on in the end is going to be searched for, so the lost object which is stated herein is destined to be searched for" [T. San. 13:9].

     I. Who will pray for them?

     J. R. Samuel bar Nahman said, "Moses will pray for them:

     K. " 'Let Reuben live, and not die, [nor let his men be few]' (Deut. 33:6)."

     L. R. Joshua b. Levi said, "Hannah will pray for them."

     M. This is the view of R. Joshua b. Levi, for R. Joshua b. Levi said, "Thus did the party of Korach sink ever downward, until Hannah went and prayed for them and said, 'The Lord kills and brings to life; he brings down to Sheol and raises up' (I Sam. 2:6)."

We have a striking sequence of prooftexts, serving, one by one, the cited statement of the Mishnah, A–C, then an opinion of a rabbi in the Tosefta, F–H, then the position of a Talmudic rabbi, J–K, L–M. The process of providing the prooftexts therefore is central, the differentiation among the passages requiring the prooftexts, a matter of indifference. The search for appropriate verses of Scripture vastly transcended the purpose of study of the Mishnah, exegesis of its rules, and provision of adequate authority for the document and its laws. In fact, any proposition to be taken seriously will elicit interest in scriptural support, whether one in the Mishnah, in the Tosefta, or in the mouth of a Talmudic sage himself. So the main thing is that the Scripture is at the center and focus. A verse of Scripture settles all pertinent questions, wherever they are located, whatever their source. That is the Talmud of the Land of Israel's position. We know full well that it is not the Mishnah's position.

This fact shows us in a detail a part of a broad shift that was taking place in the generations that received the Mishnah, that is, over the third and fourth centuries. If the sages of the second century, who made the Mishnah as we know it, spoke in their own name and in the name of the logic of their own minds, those who followed, certainly the ones who flourished in the later fourth century, took a quite different view. Reverting to ancient authority like others of the age, they turned back to Scripture, deeming it the source of certainty about truth. Unlike their masters in the Mishnah, theirs was a quest for a higher authority than the logic of their own minds. The shift from age to age then is clear. The second-century masters took commonplaces of Scripture, well-known facts, and stated them wholly in their own language and context. Fourth-century masters phrased commonplaces of the Mishnah or banalities of worldly wisdom, so far as they could, in the language of Scripture and its context.

The real issue turns out to have been not the Mishnah at all, not even its diverse sayings vindicated one by one. Once what a sage says, not merely a rule for the Mishnah, is made to refer to Scripture for proof, it must follow that, in the natural course of things, a rule of the Mishnah and of the Tosefta will likewise be asked to refer also to Scripture. The fact that the living sage validates what he says through Scripture explains why the sage also validates through verses of Scripture what the ancient sages of the Mishnah and Tosefta say. It is one undivided phenomenon. The reception of the Mishnah constitutes merely one, though massive, testimony to a prevalent attitude of mind, important for the age of the Talmud of the Land of Israel, the third and fourth centuries, not solely for the Mishnah. The stated issue was the standing of the Mishnah. But the heart of the matter turns out to have been the authority of the sage himself, who identified with the authors of the Mishnah and claimed authoritatively to interpret the Mishnah and much else, specifically including Scripture. The appeal to Scripture in behalf of the Mishnah represents simply one more expression of what proved critical in the formative age of Judaism: the person of the holy man himself, this new man, this incarnate Torah. When revelation—Torah—became flesh, Judaism was born.

We turn now to the treatment of our Mishnah-chapter by the authorities of the Talmud of the Land of Israel. Mishnah passages are given in italics, those deriving from the Tosefta in boldface type.

Yerushalmi Sanhedrin

CHAPTER TEN

10:1

A. [27C]. *All Israelites have a share in the world to come, as it is said, "Your people also shall be all righteous; they shall inherit the land forever, the branch of my planting, the work of my hands, that I may be glorified" (Is 60:21).*

B. *And these are the ones who have no portion in the world to come:*
(1) He who says, the resurrection of the dead is a teaching which does not derive from the Torah, (2) and the Torah does not come from Heaven; and (3) an Epicurean.

C. *R. Aquiba says, "Also: He who reads in heretical books, and he who whispers over a wound and says, 'I will put none of the diseases upon you which I have put on the Egyptians; for I am the Lord who heals you' " (Ex. 15:26).*

D. *Abba Saul says, "Also: He who pronounces the divine Name as it is spelled out."*

I. A. **They added to the list of those [who have no portion in the world to come (M. San. 10:1)]:**

  B. **he who breaks the yoke, violates the covenant, deals arrogantly with the Torah** *pronounces the Divine Name as it is spelled out (M. 10:1G)—*

  C. **they have no portion in the world to come [T. San. 12:9].**

  D. "He who breaks the yoke"—this is he who says, "There is a Torah, but I do not accept it."

  E. "He who violates the covenant" is he who extends the foreskin [to hide the mark of circumcision].

  F. "He who deals arrogantly with the Torah" is he who says, "The Torah does not come from Heaven."

  G. Now you have not already learned this item: *". . . and the Torah does not come from Heaven" [M. San. 10:1D(2)]?*

  H. R. Haninah of Antonia *('ntwny)* taught before R. Mana, "This is one who violates the rules of the Torah in public,

  I. "for example, Jehoiakim son of Josiah, king of Judah, and his followers."

II. A. As to idolatry and fornication,

  B. R. Jonah and R. Yosah—

  C. One of them said, "These are among the lesser violations of the law [which are punished in this world only]."

  D. The other of them said, "They are among the greater violations of the law [which are punished in the world to come]." [This is clarified shortly.]

  E. How shall we interpret this matter?

  F. If it concerns repentance, nothing stands before those who repent.

  G. But this is how we must interpret the matter: concerning one who did not repent and died through extirpation.

  H. If the greater part of his record consisted of honorable deeds, and the smaller part, transgressions, they exact punishment from him [in this world, as at C].

  I. If the smaller part of the transgressions which he has done are of the lesser character, [he is punished] in this world so as to pay him his full and complete reward in the world to come.

  J. If the greater part of his record consisted of transgressions and the lesser part of honorable deeds, they pay him off with the reward of the religious deeds which he has done entirely in this world, so as to exact punishment from him in a whole and complete way in the world to come.

K. If the greater part of his record consisted of honorable deeds, he will inherit the Garden of Eden. If the greater part consisted of transgressions, he will inherit Gehenna.

L. [If the record] was evenly balanced—

M. Said R. Yosé b. Haninah, " '. . . forgives sins . . .,' is not written here, but rather, '. . . forgives [a] sin' (Num 14:18). That is to say, the Holy One, blessed be he, tears up one bond [recorded] among the transgressions, so that the honorable deeds then will outweigh the others."

N. Said R. Eleazar, " 'And that to thee, O Lord, belongs steadfast love. For thou dost requite a man according to his work' (Ps. 62:13). 'His deed' is not written here, but '*like* his deed'—if he has none, you give him one of yours."

O. That is the view of R. Eleazar. R. Eleazar said, " '[The Lord passed before him, and proclaimed, The Lord, the Lord, a God merciful and gracious, slow to anger,] and abounding in steadfast love [and faithfulness]' (Ex. 34:6). He tips the scale in favor of mercy."

P. R. Jeremiah said that R. Samuel bar R. Isaac asked about the following: " 'Righteousness guards him whose way is upright, but sin overthrows the wicked' (Prov. 3:6). 'Misfortune pursues sinners, but prosperity rewards the righteous' (Prov. 13:21). 'Toward the scorner he is scornful, but to the humble he shows favor' (Prov. 3:34). 'He will guard the feet of his faithful ones; but the wicked shall be cut off in darkness; [for not by might shall a man prevail]' (1 Sam. 2:9). 'The wise will inherit honor, but fools get disgrace' (Prov. 3:35).

Q. "Now do they build a fence and lock the doors? And thus indeed is the way, that they do build a fence and lock the doors, [as we shall now see that God makes it possible for the righteous to do righteous deeds and confirms the wicked in their way too]."

R. R. Jeremiah in the name of R. Samuel bar R. Isaac: "[If] a man keeps himself from transgression once, twice, and three times, from that time forth, the Holy One, blessed be he, keeps him from it."

S. What is the scriptural basis for this statement?

T. " 'Behold, God does all these things, twice, three times, with a man' " (Job 33:29).

U. Said R. Zeira, "And that is on condition that the man not revert [to his evil deeds]."

V. What is the scriptural basis for this statement?

W. " 'A threefold cord is *never* broken' is not written, but rather:

X. " '[And though a man might prevail against one who is alone, two will withstand him.] A threefold cord is not quickly broken' " (Qoh. 4:12).

Y. For if one lays stress on it, indeed it will snap.

Z. R. Huna in the name of R. Abbahu: "The Holy One, blessed be he—before him there is no forgetting, as it were.

AA. "But in behalf of Israel he turns absentminded."

BB. What is the scriptural basis for this statement?

CC. "[Who is a God like thee,] pardoning iniquity [and passing over transgression for the remnant of his inheritance]?" (Mic. 7:18)

DD. And so did David say, "Thou didst forgive the iniquity of thy people; thou didst pardon all their sin" (Ps. 85:2).

III. A. R. Mattia b. Heresh raised the question in session before R. Eleazar b. Azariah, saying to him, "Have you heard the four distinctions among kinds of atonement which R. Ishmael expounded?"

B. He said to him, "They are three, outside of repentance."

C. One verse in Scripture says, "Return, O faithless children, [says the Lord; for I am your master; I will take you, one from a city and two from a family, and I will bring you to Zion]" (Jer. 3:14).

D. And another verse in Scripture says, "For on this day shall atonement be made for you, to cleanse you; [from all your sins you shall be clean before the Lord]" (Lev. 16:30).

E. And one verse in Scripture says, "Then I will punish their transgression with the rod and their iniquity with scourges" (Ps. 89:33).

F. And another verse in Scripture says, "[The Lord of hosts has revealed himself in my ears:] 'Surely this iniquity will not be forgiven you till you die,' [says the Lord God of Hosts]" (Is. 22:14).

G. [Supply: **R. Ishmael says,**] **"There are four kinds of atonement.**

H. "[If] one has violated a positive commandment but repented, he hardly moves from his place before the Holy One, blessed be he, forgives him.

I. "And in this case it is said, 'Return backsliding children. I will heal your backsliding' (Jer. 3:22) [T. Yoma 4:6].

J. "[If] he has violated a negative commandment but repented, repentance suspends the punishment, and the Day of Atonement effects atonement.

K. "And in this case it is said, 'For that day will effect atonement for you' (Lev. 16:30) [T. Yoma 4:7].

L. "[If] he has deliberately violated [a rule for which the punishment is] extirpation or death at the hands of an earthly court, but repented, repentance and the Day of Atonement atone for half [of the punishment], and suffering on other days of the year wipes away the other half.

M. "And in this case it says, 'Then will I visit their transgression with a rod' (Ps. 89:32).

N. "But he through whom the Name of Heaven is profaned deliberately (but who repented)—repentance does not have power to suspend [the punishment], nor the Day of Atonement to atone.

O. "But repentance and the Day of Atonement atone for a third, suffering atones for a third, and death wipes away the sin [27d], with suffering.

P. "And in this case it is said, 'Surely this iniquity shall not be purged from you until you die' " (Is. 22:14) [T. Yoma 4:8].

Q. "Thus we learn that death wipes away sin."

R. Said R. Yohanan, "This is the opinion of R. Eleazar b. Azariah, R. Ishmael, and R. Aqiba.

S. "But in the view of sages, the scapegoat effects atonement."

T. How does it effect atonement?

U. R. Zeira said, "Step by step."

V. R. Haninah said, "At the end [only]."

W. What is the difference between these two views?

X. If one died suddenly.

Y. In the opinion of R. Zeira, the scapegoat already has effected atonement for him.

Z. In the opinion of R. Haninah, the scapegoat has not effected atonement for him.

AA. Said R. Hanina, "A Tannaitic teaching supports the position of R. Zeira."

BB. **R. Eleazar b. R. Simeon says, "A strict rule applies to the goat which does not apply to the Day of Atonement,**

CC. **"and to the Day of Atonement which does not apply to the goat:**

DD. **"for the Day of Atonement effects atonement [even if] no goat [is offered].**

EE. **"But the goat effects atonement only along with the Day of Atonement [T. Yoma 4:16].**

FF. **"A more strict rule applied to the goat:**

GG. **"For the goat['s sacrifice takes effect] immediately,**

HH. **"but the Day of Atonement [takes effect only] at dusk" [T. Yoma 4:17].**

II. Said R. Huna, "I was sitting before R. Jeremiah, and he said, 'Interpret the saying to apply to a case in which they intended to bring yet another goat but did not bring it.' "

JJ. Said R. Yosah b. Yosah, "But does the Holy One, blessed be he, not see what is to happen? Let the goat then effect atonement forthwith."

IV. A. It is written, "Because he has despised the word of the Lord, [and has broken his commandment, that person shall be utterly cut off; his iniquity shall be upon him]" (Num. 15:31).

B. I know that this applies only when he despised the teaching of Torah [entirely.]

C. How do I know that [this applies] if he denied even a single word of Scripture, a single verse of Targum, a single argument *a fortiori?*

D. Scripture says, "[Because he has despised the word of the Lord,] and has broken his commandment, [that person shall be utterly cut off; his iniquity shall be upon him]" (Num. 15:31).

E. As to a single verse of Scripture: "[The sons of Lotan were Hori and Heman;] and Lotan's sister was Timna" (Gen. 36:22).

F. As to a single verse of Targum: "Laban called it Jegarsahadutha: [but Jacob called it Galeed]" (Gen. 31:47).

G. As to a single argument *a fortiori:* "If Cain is avenged sevenfold, [truly Lamech seventy-sevenfold]" (Gen. 4:24).

H. Another interpretation: "For he has despised the word of the Lord" (Num. 15:31)—this refers to one who makes mention of teachings of Torah in a filthy place.

I. This teaching is illustrated in the following: R. Ila and the associates were sitting before an inn at evening [so not realizing where they were]. They said, "What is the law as to expressing a teaching of Torah?"

J. They said, "Now, since if it were day, we should see what is before us, but under these conditions, it is forbidden."

V. A. Bar Kappara said, "Ahaz and all of the evil kings of Israel have no portion in the world to come."

B. What is the scriptural basis for this statement?

C. "[All of them are hot as an oven, and they devour their rulers.] All their kings have fallen; and none of them calls upon me" (Hos. 7:7).

D. They objected to him, "And lo, he is numbered in the era of the kings:

E. " '[The vision of Isaiah the son of Amoz, which he saw concerning Judah and Jerusalem] in the days of Uzziah, Jotham, Ahaz, and Hezekiah, kings of Judah' " (Is. 1:1).

F. He said to them, "Because he was subject to shame."

G. What sort of shame applied to him?

H. R. Aha in the name of R. Eleazar, R. Yosé in the name of R. Joshua b. Levi: "You find that when the prophet came to indict him, he fled to an unclean place and hid his face in an unclean place, as if to say that the Presence of God does not dwell in an unclean place."

I. This is in line with that which is written: "And the Lord said to Isaiah, 'Go forth to meet Ahaz, you and Shear-jashub your son, at the end of the conduit of the upper pool on the highway to the Fuller's Field' "(Is. 7:3).

J. Do not read "The Fuller's (KWBS) Field" but "The Field of the one who hides his face," for he hid his face and fled from him.

K. Lo, how is this so?

L. When the prophet came to indict him, he fled to an unclean place and hid his face in an unclean place.

M. R. Judah says, "It was because he was punished through the suffering of his firstborn son."

N. What is the scriptural basis for this statement?

O. "And Zichri, a mighty man of Ephraim, slew (Maaseiah the king's son and Azrikam the commander of the palace and Elkanah the next in authority to the king]" (2 Chron. 28:7).

P. R. Hoshaiah the Great said, "It was because his father [Jotham b. Uzziah] was a righteous man."

Q. As to Manassah, was his father not a righteous man?

R. Manassah's father was a righteous man, but his son was evil.

S. And Hezekiah—his father was an evil man, and his son was evil.

T. For Hezekiah says, " 'Lo, it was for my welfare that I had great bitterness; [but thou hast held back my life from the pit of destruction, for thou hast cast all my sins behind my back]' " (Is. 38:17).

U. "It was bitter for me on the count of my predecessor, Ahaz, and it was bitter for me on the count of my successor, Manassah."

V. As to Ahaz, his father was a righteous man and his son was a righteous man.

W. This is in line with the following verse of Scripture:

X. "Be assured, an evil man will not go unpunished, but those who are righteous will be delivered" (Prov. 11:21).

Y. "He who is righteous" is not written, but rather, "Those who are righteous will be delivered."

Z. "He who is located between two righteous men [Jotham and Hezekiah] will be delivered."

AA. Another interpretation as to, "Be assured, an evil man will not go unpunished."

BB. Said R. Phineas, "This refers to him who does a righteous deed and wants to take the reward for it right away."

CC. Said R. Simon, "It is like a man who says, 'Here is the sack, here is the sela, here is the seah measure—get up and measure out [wheat].' "

DD. And you should know that that is the case, for lo, the fathers of the world, if they had wanted to take the reward for the commandments which they did in this world—how would the merit of their deeds have remained for their children after them?

EE. That is the meaning of that which Moses said to Israel, "Then I will remember my covenant with Jacob, [and I will remember my covenant with Isaac and my covenant with Abraham, and I will remember the land]" (Lev. 26:42).

VI. A. How long did the merit of the patriarchs endure [to protect Israel]?

B. R. Tanhuma said in the name of R. Hiyya the Elder, Bar Nahman stated in the name of R. Berekiah, R. Helbo in the name of R. Ba bar Zabeda: "Down to Joahaz.

C. " 'But the Lord has gracious to them and had compassion on them, [because of his covenant with Abraham, Isaac, and Jacob, and would not destroy them; nor has he cast them from his presence until now' (2 Kings 13:23).

D. "Up to that time the merit of the patriarchs endured."

E. Samuel said, "Down to Hosea.

F. " 'Now I will uncover the lewdness in the sight of her lovers, and no man shall rescue her out of my hand' (Hos. 2:12).

G. "Now 'man' can refer only to Abraham, as you say, 'Now then restore the man's wife; for he is a prophet, [and he will pray for you, and you shall live. But if you do not restore her, know that you will surely die, you, and all that are yours]' (Gen. 20:7).

H. "And 'man' can refer only to Isaac, as you say, '[Rebekah said to the servant,] "Who is the man yonder, walking in the field to meet us?" [The servant said, "It is my master." So she took her veil and covered herself]' (Gen. 24:65).

I. "And 'man' can refer only to Jacob, as you say, '[When the boys grew up, Esau was a skillful hunter, a man of the field,] while Jacob was a quiet man, [dwelling in tents]' " (Gen. 25:27).

J. R. Joshua b. Levi said, "It was down to Elijah.

K. " 'And at the time of the offering of the oblation, Elijah the prophet came near and said, 'O Lord, God of Abraham, Isaac, and Israel, let it be known this day that thou art God in Israel, and that I am thy servant, [and that I have done all these things at thy word]' " (1 Kgs. 18:36).

L. R. Yudan said, "It was down to Hezekiah.

M. " 'Of the increase of his government and of peace there will be no end, [upon the throne of David, and over his kingdom, to establish it, and to uphold it with justice and with righteousness from this time forth and for evermore. The zeal of the Lord of hosts will do this]" (Is. 9:6).

N. Said R. Aha, "The merit of the patriarchs endures forever [to protect Israel].

O. "For the Lord your God is a merciful God; [he will not fail you or destroy you or forget the covenant with your fathers which he swore to them]' (Deut. 4:31).

P. "This teaches that the covenant is made with the tribes."

Q. R. Yudan bar Hanan in the name of R. Berekiah: "Said the Holy One, blessed be he, to Israel, 'My children, if you see the merit of the patriarchs declining, and the merit of the matriarchs growing feeble, go and cleave unto the trait of steadfast love."

R. What is the scriptural basis for this statement?

S. "For the mountains may depart and the hills be removed, [but my steadfast love shall not depart from you, and my covenant of peace shall not be removed, says the Lord, who has compassion on you" (Is. 54:10).

T. "For the mountains may depart"—this refers to the merit of the patriarchs.

U. "And the hills be removed"—this refers to the merit of the matriarchs.

V. Henceforth: "But my steadfast love shall not depart from you, and my covenant of peace shall not be removed, says the Lord, who has compassion on you."

VII. A. *An Epicurean [M. San. 10:1D(3)].*

B. R. Yohanan and R. Eleazar—

C. One said, "It is a priest who said, 'Now is *that* a scribe?!' "

D. The other said, "It is a priest who said, 'Now are *those* rabbis?!' "

E. R. Eleazar and R. Samuel bar Nahman—

F. One said, "It [unbelief] is comparable to a pile of stones. Once one of them shifts, all of them tumble down."

G. And the other said, "It is comparable to a storehouse full of straw. Even though you take out all of the straw which is in the storehouse, there still is straw which eventually will weaken the walls."

H. Rah said, "Korach was very rich. [The location of] Pharaoh's treasures was revealed to him, between Migdol and the sea." [This item breaks off here.]

I. Rab said, "Korach was an Epicurean. What did he do? He went and made a prayer shawl which was entirely purple [although the law is that only the fringe was to be purple]."

J. He went to Moses, saying to him, "Moses, our rabbi: A prayer shawl which is entirely purple, what is the law as to its being liable to show fringes?"

K. He said to him, "It is liable, for it is written, 'You shall make yourself tassels [on the four corners of your cloak with which you cover yourself]' " (Deut. 22:12).

L. [Korah continued,] "A house which is entirely filled with holy books, what is the law as to its being liable for a *mezuzah* [containing sacred Scripture, on the doorpost]?"

M. He said to him, "It is liable for a *mezuzah,* for it is written, 'And you shall write them on the doorposts of your house [and upon your gates]' " (Deut. 6:9).

N. He said to him, "A bright spot the size of a bean—what is the law [as to whether it is a sign of uncleanness in line with Lev. 13:2ff.]?"

O. He said to him, "It is a sign of uncleanness."

P. "And if it spread over the whole of the man's body?"

Q. He said to him, "It is a sign of cleanness."

R. [28a] At that moment Korach said, "The Torah does not come from Heaven, Moses is no prophet, and Aaron is not a high priest."

S. Then did Moses say, "Lord of all worlds, if from creation the earth was formed with a mouth, well and good, and if not, then make it now!"

T. "But if the Lord creates [something new, and the ground opens its mouth, and swallows them up, with all that belongs to them, and they go down alive to Sheol, then you shall know that these men have despised the Lord]" (Num. 16:30).

U. Said R. Simeon b. Laqish, "Three denied their prophetic gift on account of the baseness [with which they were treated].

V. "And these are they: Moses, Elijah, and Micah."

W. Moses said, "If these men die the common death of all men, [or if they are visited by the fate of all men, then the Lord has not sent me]" (Num. 16:29).

X. Elijah said, "Answer me, O Lord, answer me, [that this people may know that thou, O Lord, art God, and that thou hast turned their hearts back]" (1 Kings 18:37).

Y. Micah said, "[And Micaiah said,] 'If you return in peace, the Lord has not spoken to me.' [And he said, 'Hear all you peoples!']" (1 Kings 22:28).

Z. "So they and all that belonged to them went down alive into Sheol; [and the earth closed over them, and they perished from the midst of the assembly]" (Num. 16:33).

AA. R. Berekiah in the name of R. Helbo: "Even the mention of their names flew off the pages of the record books [of bonds and documents] containing them."

BB. Said R. Yosé bar Haninah, "Even a needle belonging to them which had been lent to an Israelite by them was swallowed up with them,

CC. "as it is written, 'So they and all that belonged to them went down alive into Sheol' " (Num. 16:33).

DD. And who prayed in their behalf?

EE. R. Samuel bar Nahman said, "Moses prayed in their behalf: 'Let Reuben live and not die, [nor let his men be few]' " (Deut. 33:6).

FF. R. Joshua b. Levi said, "Hannah prayed in their behalf."

GG. That indeed is the view of R. Joshua b. Levi, for R. Joshua b. Levi said in the name of R. Yosé. "So did the band of Korach sink and fall, until Hannah went and prayed for them.

HH. "She said, 'The Lord kills and brings to life; he brings down to Sheol and raises up' " (1 Sam. 2:6).

VIII. A. *R. Aqiba says, "Also: He who reads in heretical books" [M. San. 10:1E].*

B. These are, for example, the books of Ben Sira and the books of Ben Laanah.

C. But as to the books of Homer and all books written hence forward—he who reads in them is tantamount to one who [merely] reads a letter.

D. What is the scriptural basis for that statement?

E. "My son beware of anything beyond these. [Of making many books there is no end, and much study is weariness of the flesh]" (Qoh. 12:12).

F. They are permitted for speculation, they are not permitted for serious work.

G. "The sayings of the wise are like goads, [and like nails firmly fixed are the collected sayings which are given by one Shepherd]" (Qoh. 12:11).

H. R. Huna said, "Like lovely pearls."

I. There they call a pearl "dirah."

J. "Like goads" (KDRBNWT)—

K. That is, like this ball for little girls (KDR BNWT).

L. Just as this ball falls from hand to hand, but in the end comes out in yet some other hand, *so did Moses receive Torah from Sinai and hand it on to Joshua, Joshua to elders, elders to prophets, and prophets handed it on to the men of the Great Assembly [M. Abot. 1:1].*

M. Another interpretation: "Like goads"—the same object bears three names, staff, goad, and lead.

N. Staff (*mardea*), because it shows the way for a cow.

O. Goad—because it imparts knowledge to a cow.

P. Lead—for it leads the cow to plough so as to give life to its owner.

Q. Said R. Hama bar Haninah, "Now if for a cow a man makes a goad, for his impulse to do evil, which leads him from the life of this world and from the life of the world to come, how much the more so [should he make a goad]!"

R. "[The sayings of the wise are like goads,] and like nails firmly fixed [are the collected sayings which are given by one Shepherd]" (Qoh. 12:11).

S. Now why did he not say, "And like nails permanently knocked in," and "like trees firmly fixed"?

T. They chose [to compare] them to iron, and [also] praised them as the [pole] which is planted firmly.

U. Another matter: "And like nails firmly fixed"—Now just as in the case of a nail, if you fix it firmly, then even if fire should come and take the nail away from its place, the place in which it had been located still is to be discerned,

V. so against whomever the sages have stretched forth their hands [for the purpose of excommunication], even though they went and drew him near again, in the end he will take what is his from their hands [that is to say, he will ultimately be punished].

W. Another matter: "Like nails firmly fixed"—nails is written not with *samekh* but with a *sin*. This represents an allusion to the twenty-four [nails used in a sandal], and so to the twenty-four cohorts [watches of the Temple].

X. And how many nails may there be in a sandal [for the person to be permitted to go about in it on the Sabbath without violating the law of M. Shab. 6:2: *A man may not go out with a nail-studded sandal]?*

Y. Yohanan said, "Five, for the five books of the Torah."

Z. Hanina said, "In seven, '[Your bars shall be iron and bronze;] and as your days, so shall your strength be'" (Deut. 33:25).

AA. R. Aha expounded in the name of R. Haninah, "Nine."

BB. Rabbi would put eleven on this one and thirteen on the other, that is, the number of priestly cohorts.

CC. R. Yosé b. Haninah said, "The shoemaker's pegging is not counted as one of the nails."

DD. R. Ba bar Zabeda raised the question before R. Zeira: "What is the law as to putting all of them on one shoe?"

EE. He said to him, "It is permitted."

FF. He said to him, "What is the law as to putting all of them on one sandal?"

GG. He said to him, "It is permitted."

HH. It was taught: They do not scrape off sandals and old shoes, but they do anoint and wash them off [to make them fit for wear on the Sabbath].

II. R. Qerispai in the name of R. Yohanan, a disciple of R. Hiyya the Elder says, "The former authorities would say, 'They do scrape them off.' The later authorities would say, 'They do not scrape them off.' "

JJ. They asked Rabbi, who said to them, "They do not scrape them off."

KK. Said R. Zeira, "[Rabbi was one of the earlier authorities, yet he said they do not scrape them off]. Thus is to be discounted one of the disciples of R. Hiyya the Elder.

LL. "R. Hiyya bar Ashi said, 'We would be accustomed to sit before Rab and anoint and rinse off [our shoes], but we did not scrape them.' "

MM. It was taught: A person should not put on new shoes or sandals unless he walked about in them while it was still day [prior to the Sabbath].

NN. And how much should he have walked about in them?

OO. The members of the household of Bar Qappara say, "From the schoolhouse of Bar Qappara to the schoolhouse of R. Hoshaiah."

PP. The men of Sepphoris say, "From the synagogue of the Babylonians to the courtyard of R. Hama bar Haninah."

QQ. The men of Tiberias say, "From the great school to the shop of R. Hoshaiah."

RR. It was taught: A person should not anoint shoes and new sandals [on the Sabbath]. A person should not anoint his foot with oil while it is in a shoe, or his foot when it is in a sandal. But he may anoint his foot with oil and then put it into a shoe, or his foot with oil and put it into a sandal. A man may anoint his body with oil and roll about on new leather [on the Sabbath] and need not scruple on that account. **But he should not put [oil] on a marble table in order to roll about it on it [T. Shab. 16:14].** Rabban Simeon b. Gamaliel permits doing so.

SS. Another interpretation: "And like nails firmly fixed"—when teachings of Torah go forth in a proper way from the mouth of the one who presents them, they are a pleasure to the ones who hear them, like nails firmly fixed.

TT. And when they go forth in a garbled way, they are as bitter to the ones who hear them as nails.

IX. A. "Collected sayings"—the reference to "collections" refers only to the *Sanhedrin,*

B. as you say, "[And the Lord said to Moses,] collect for me seventy men of the elders of Israel, [whom you know to be the elders of the people and officers over them; and bring them to the tent of meeting, and let them take their stand there with you]" (Num. 11:16).

C. Another interpretation: "Collected sayings"—sayings which are stated at an assembly.

D. Said R. Simeon b. Laqish, "If someone should tell me that [there are traditions concerning] the Book of Chronicles in Babylonia, lo, I should make the trip and bring [them] back from there. And now, if all of our rabbis should gather together, they will be unable to bring them back from there [because they are so numerous and weighty]."

E. "Given by one shepherd"—

F. Said the Holy One, blessed be he, "If you hear a teaching from an Israelite minor, and it gave pleasure to you, let it not be in your sight as if one has heard it from a minor, but as if one has heard it from an adult,

G. "and let it not be as if one has heard it from an adult, but as if one has heard it from a sage,

H. "and let it not be as if one has heard it from a sage, but as if one has heard it from a prophet,

I. "and let it not be as if one has heard it from a prophet, but as if one has heard it from the shepherd,

J. "and there is as a shepherd only Moses, in line with the following passage: 'Then he remembered the days of old, of Moses his servant. Where is he who brought out of the sea the shepherds of his flock? Where is he who put in the midst of them his holy Spirit?' (Is. 63:11).

K. "It is not as if one has heard it from the shepherd but as if one has heard it from the Almighty."

L. "Given by one Shepherd"—and there is only One who is the Holy One, blessed be he, in line with that which you read in Scripture: "Hear, O Israel: the Lord our God is one Lord" (Deut. 6:4).

X. A. *He who whispers over a wound and says, "I will put none of the diseases upon you which [28b] I have put on the Egyptians; for I am the Lord who heals you" (Ex. 15:26).*

B. Rab said, "But this [statement is prohibited] only if the one who says it then spits."

C. R. Joshua b. Levi said, "Even if one has said, 'When a man has on the skin of his body a swelling or an eruption or a spot, and it turns into a leprous disease on the skin of his body' (Lev. 13:2), and then has spat—he has no portion in the world to come."

XI. A. *Abba Saul says, "Also: he who pronounces the divine Name as it is spelled out" [M. San. 10:1G].*

B. R. Mana said, "For example, the Cutheans, who take an oath thereby."

C. R. Jacob bar Aha said, "It is written YH[WH] and pronounced AD[onai]."

Unit **I** takes up the exposition of materials closely relevant to Mishnah. The absence of the items at **II**.A requires comment, since, in general, one would have expected those items to be on the list at M. 10:1D. That discussion draws in its wake the matter of atonement and repentance, on which basis, I assume, unit **III** is inserted, nearly whole, and, in its wake, the remainder of unit **III**'s materials. Unit **IV** carries forward the same concern, namely, atonement for sin; but this is in general relevant to M. 10:1D, namely, dishonoring the Torah. Unit **V** is entirely out of the range of M. 10:1, and perhaps would be more appropriately located in the repertoire of materials thematically relevant to M. 10:2. Unit **VI** carries forward a minor theme of unit **V**. Unit **VII** provides a rich repertoire of materials to define the Epicurean, or nonbe-

liever, using Korach as the example. There are some inserted materials, **VII**.U–Z, but on the whole unit **VII** is unitary and well
put together. The same cannot be said of unit **VII,** because of the
elaborate insertion, whole and complete, of **VIII**.W–QQ. Without that insertion, we have a systematic account of the exegesis
of Qoh. 12:11–12. None of this has very much to do with the
cited lemma of Mishnah. Unit **IX** contains the exegesis of the
same verses but moves on to different elements thereof. Units **X**
and **XI,** finally, briefly complement Mishnah as cited. In all we
have a vastly expanded anthology, only partly relevant to the
Mishnah.

10:2

    A. *Three kings and four ordinary folk have no portion in the world
to come.*

    B. *Three kings: Jeroboam, Ahab, and Manasseh.*

    C. *R. Judah says, "Manasseh has a portion in the world to come,*

    D. *"since it is said, 'And he prayed to him and he was entreated
of him and heard his supplication and brought him again to
Jerusalem into his kingdom' " (2 Chron. 33:13).*

    E. *They said to him, "To his kingdom he brought him back, but
to the life of the world to come he did not bring him back."*

    F. *Four ordinary folk: Balaam, Doeg, Ahithophel, and Gahazi.*

I.   A. And all of [the three kings] invented new kinds of transgression.

    B. Now what did Jeroboam do?

    C. It was because he made two golden calves.

    D. And is it not so that the Israelites had made any number of
golden calves [so what was new about this]?

    E. R. Simeon b. Yohai taught, "Thirteen golden calves did the
Israelites make, and there was one which was common property
for all of them."

    F. What is the scriptural basis for this statement?

    G. "[And he received the gold at their hand, and fashioned it with
a graving tool, and made a molten calf; and they said,] 'These
are your gods, O Israel, [who brought you up out of the land
of Egypt]' " (Ex. 32:4).

H. Lo, they were for the twelve tribes.

I. "[Even when they had made for themselves a molten calf and said,] 'This is your God [who brought you up out of Egypt,]' and had committed great blasphemies" (Neh. 9:18).

J. [The reference to "this is your god"] indicates the one which was common property for all.

II. A. Now what did Ahab do?

B. It is written, "And as if it had been a light thing for him to walk in the sins of Jeroboam the son of Nebat, [he took for wife Jezebel the daughter of Ethbaal king of the Sidonians, and went and served Baal, and worshiped him]" (1 Kgs. 16:31).

C. And is it not so that the minor peccadilloes of Ahab are like the major crimes of Jeroboam?

D. So why was Jeroboam listed first of all?

E. It is because he is the one who began first the process of the ruin [of Israel].

F. What did Ahab do?

G. He would adorn himself every day and get up before Hiel, commander of his army (1 Kgs. 16:34), and he would say to him, "How much am I worth today?" And he would say to him, "Thus and so." Then he would take the amount [that he was said to be worth] and set it apart for an idol.

H. That is in line with the following:

I. [Ahab said to Elijah, "Have you found me, O my enemy?" He answered, "I have found you,] because you have sold yourself to do what is evil in the sight of the Lord" (1 Kgs. 21:20).

J. For six months R. Levi would interpret the following verse of Scripture in a negative sense:

K. "There was none who sold himself to do what was evil in the sight of the Lord like Ahab, [whom Jezebel his wife incited]" (1 Kgs. 21:25).

L. Then [Ahab] came to him by night and said to him, "What made you take this view, and how have I sinned in your sight? You take account of the beginning of the verse, but you ignore the end of it: 'whom Jezebel his wife incited'!"

M. So for six months Levi went and interpreted the matter in a positive way, "There was none who sold himself to do what was evil in the sight of the Lord like Ahab, whom Jezebel his wife incited" (1 Kgs. 21:25).

III. A. It is written, "In his days Hiel of Bethel built Jericho; he laid its foundation at the cost of Abiram his firstborn, and set up its gates at the cost of his youngest son, Segub, [according to the word of the Lord, which he spoke by Joshua the son of Nun]" (1 Kgs. 16:34).

B. Hiel came from Jehoshaphat. Jericho is in the territory of Benjamin.

C. But they assign more credit to the one who is creditable, and they assign more blame to the one who is blameworthy.

D. And that is in line with the following: "He laid its foundation at the cost of Abiram, his firstborn, and set up its gates at the cost of his youngest son, Segub."

E. Now in the case of Abiram, the firstborn, he had none whence to learn, but in the case of Segub, the youngest son, that evil man surely had whence to learn.

F. [They did as they did] because they wanted to make money, so the curse fell upon them, and they [the walls and gates] went and trembled, in line with the following verse: "[In his days Hiel of Bethel built Jericho; he laid its foundation at the cost of Abiram his firstborn, and set up its gates at the cost of his youngest son, Segub,] according to the word of the Lord, which he spoke by Joshua the son of Nun" (1 Kgs. 16:34) [T. San. 14:7-0].

G. It is written, "Now Elijah the Tishbite, of Tishbe in Gilead, said to Ahab, 'As the Lord the God of Israel lives, before whom I stand, there shall be neither dew nor rain these years, except by my word'" (1 Kgs. 17:1).

H. Now what has one thing to do with the other [that the matter of Hiel is joined to the matter of the drought]?

I. But the Holy One, blessed be he, said to Elijah, "This Hiel is a great man. Go and see him [because his sons have died]."

J. He said to him, "I am not going to see him."

K. He said to him, "Why?"

L. He said to him, "For if I go and they say things which will outrage you, I shall not be able to bear it."

M. He said to him, "Then if they say things which outrage me, then whatever you decree against them I shall carry out."

N. He came and found them occupied with the following verse: "Joshua laid an oath upon them at that time, saying, 'Cursed before the Lord be the man that rises up and rebuilds this city, Jericho. At the cost of his firstborn shall he lay its foundation, and at the cost of his youngest son shall he set up its gates" (Josh. 6:26).

O. He said, "Blessed be the God of the righteous, for he carries out the words of righteous men."

P. Now Ahab was there. Ahab said to him, "Now who is greater than whom—Moses or Joshua?"

Q. They said to him, "Moses."

R. He said to him, "In the Torah of Moses it is written, 'Take heed lest your heart be deceived, and you turn aside and serve other gods and worship them' (Deut. 11:16).

S. "Now what is written thereafter? 'And he will be angry with you and shut up the heaven that there be no rain' (Deut. 11:16f.).

T. "Now I have not left a single idol in the world, which I have not worshiped. And yet every sort of good and consolation which there are in the world have come in my generation.

U. "Thus what Moses taught has not come about, while what Joshua taught did come about [in the death of the two sons]."

V. Elijah then said to him, "And the Lord God of Israel lives, before whom I stand, there shall not be dew or rain these years, but according to my word" (1 Kgs. 17:1).

W. When he heard this, he began to cry.

X. That is in line with the following verse of Scripture: "And when Ahab head those words, he rent his clothes, and put sackcloth upon his flesh, and lay in sackcloth, and went about dejectedly" (1 Kgs. 21:27).

Y. How long did he afflict himself? It was in periods of three hours. [That is to say,] if he was accustomed to eat at three hours, he ate at six. If it was at six, he ate at nine.

Z. "And he went about dejectedly?"

AA. What is the meaning of "dejectedly"?

BB. R. Joshua b. Levi said, "that he went about barefooted."

CC. It is written, "And the word of the Lord came to Elijah the Tishbite, saying, 'Have you seen how Ahab has humbled himself before me? [I will not bring the evil in his days; but in his son's days I will bring the evil upon his house]' " (1 Kgs. 21:28–29).

DD. Said the Holy One, blessed be he, to Elijah. "Now see the good lot which I have given in my world. If a man sins before me in much but repents, I accept him back."

EE. This is in line with the following verse of Scripture: "Have you seen how Ahab has humbled himself before me?" (1 Kgs. 21:28).

FF. Do you see how Ahab has repented?

GG. "Because he has humbled himself before me, 'I shall not bring the evil in his days; but in his son's days, I will bring the evil upon his house' " (1 Kgs. 21:20).

IV. A. Now what did Ahaz do?

B. It was because he built a throne in the courtyard of the Temple.

C. This is in line with the following verse of Scripture: "And on the eighth day of the month they came to the vestibule of the Lord" (2 Chron. 29:17).

D. R. Honiah in the name of R. Eleazar: "Why is he called 'Ahaz' [seize]?"

E. "Because he seized the synagogues and schools."

F. To what is Ahaz to be compared?

G. To a king who had a son, who handed him over to a governor. He wanted to kill him. He said, "If I kill him, I shall be declared liable ot death. But lo, I'll take his wet-nurse from him, and he'll die on his own."

H. So did Ahaz say, "If there are no lambs, there will be no sheep; if there are no sheep, there will be no flock; if there is no flock, there will be no shepherd; if there is no shepherd, there will be no world; if there is no world—as it were . . ."

I. So did Ahaz reckon, saying, "If there are no children, there will be no adults; if there are no adults, there will be no sages; if there are no sages, there will be no prophets; if there are no prophets, there will be no Holy Spirit; if there is no Holy Spirit, there will be no synagogues or schoolhouses—as it were . . . In that case, as it were, the Holy One, blessed be he, will not let his Presence rest upon Israel."

J. R. Jacob bar Abayye in the name of R. Aha brings proof of the same proposition from the following verse of Scripture: "I will wait for the Lord, who is hiding his face from the house of Jacob, and I will hope in him" (Is. 8:17).

K. There was never a more difficult hour for the world than that hour at which the Holy One, blessed be he, said to Moses, "And I will surely hide my face in that day [on account of all the evil which they have done, because they have turned to other gods]" (Deut. 31:18).

L. At that hour: "I will wait for the Lord," for thus did he say to him at Sinai, "[And when many evils and troubles have come upon them, this song shall comfort them as a witness,] for it will live unforgotten in the months of their descendants; [for I know the purposes which they are already forming, before I have brought them into the land that I swore to give]" (Deut. 31:21).

M. And to what end?

N. "Behold, I and the children whom the Lord has given me [are signs and the portents in Israel from the Lord of hosts, who dwells on Mount Sinai]" (Is. 8:18).

O. Now were they really his children? And were they not his disciples?

P. But it teaches that they were as precious to him as his children, so he called them, "My children."

V. A. Now what did Manasseh do?

B. It is written, "In those days Hezekiah became sick and was at the point of death. [And Isaiah the prophet and son of Amoz came to him, and said to him, 'Thus says the Lord: Set your house in order; for you shall die, you shall not recover]' " (Is. 38:1).

C. "For [28c] you shall die, and you shall not recover"—

D. "You shall die" in this world, "And you shall not recover" in the world to come.

E. He said to him, "Why?"

F. He said to him, "Because you did not want to raise up children."

G. He said to him, "And why did you not want to raise up children?"

H. He said to him, "Because I saw that I would produce an evil son. On that account, I did not want to raise up children."

I. He said to him, "Take my daughter. Perhaps on my account and on your account she will produce a good man."

J. Even so, only a bad person came forth.

K. That is in line with the following verse of Scripture: "The knaveries of the knave are evil; [he devises wicked devices to ruin the poor with lying words, even when the plea of the needy is right]" (Is. 32:7).

L. He said to him, "I am not going to listen to you. I am going to follow only that which my elder said to me, 'If you see bad dreams or bad visions, seek three things and you will be saved, and these are they: prayer, charity, and repentance.' "

M. And three of them are to be derived from a single verse of Scripture:

N. "If my people who are called by my name humble themselves, and pray and seek my face, and turn from their wicked ways, then I will hear from heaven, and will forgive their sin and heal their land" (2 Chron. 7:14).

O. "Pray"—this refers to prayer.

P. "And seek my face"—this refers to charity,

Q. as you say, "As for me, I shall behold thy face in righteousness; when I awake, I shall be satisfied with beholding thy form" (Ps. 17:15).

R. "And turn from their wicked ways"—this refers to repentance.

S. Now if they do these things, what is written concerning them?

T. "Then I will hear from heaven and will forgive their sin and heal their land."

U. Forthwith, "And he turned . . .," as it is written, "Then Hezekiah turned his face to the wall, and prayed to the Lord" (Is. 38:2).

VI. A. To which wall did he turn?

B. R. Joshua b. Levi, "It was to the wall of Rahab that he turned: '[Then she let them down by a rope through the window,] for her house was built into the city wall, so that she dwelt in the wall' " (Josh. 2:15).

C. He said to him, "Lord of all worlds, Rahab saved two souls for you, and see how many souls you saved for her!"

D. That is in line with the following verse which is written: "So the young men who had been spies went in, and brought out Rahab, and her father and mother and brothers and all who belonged to her; and they brought all her kindred, and set them outside the camp of Israel" (Josh. 6:23).

E. R. Simeon b. Yohai taught, "Even if there were in her families two hundred men, who went and married into two hundred families, all the two hundred families were saved on her account.

F. "Now my forefathers, who brought near to you all these proselytes, how much the more so should you give me back my life!"

G. R. Samuel b. Nahman said, "He looked toward the wall of the Shunamite: 'Let us make a small roof chamber with walls, and put there for him a bed, a table, a chair, and a lamp, [so that whenever he comes to us, he can go in there]' " (2 Kings 4:10).

H. He said to him, "Lord of all worlds, the Shunamite made a single wall for Elisha, and you saved the life of her son. My forefathers, who made all this glory for you—how much the more so that you should give me back my life?"

I. R. Hinnena bar Papa said, "It was to the walls of the Temple that he turned."

J. "By setting their threshold against my threshold and their door-post against my doorpost, with only a wall between me and them. [They have defiled my holy name by their abominations which they have committed, so I have consumed them in my anger]" (Ez. 43:8).

K. "They were great men and could not go up and pray whenever at any time, and they would pray in their houses. The Holy One, blessed be he, credited it to them as if they had prayed in the Temple. Now my fathers, who gave such glory to you— how much the more so that you should give me back my life."

L. And rabbis say, "It was to the walls of his heart that he turned."

M. "My anguish, my anguish! I writhe in pain! Oh, the walls of my heart! My heart is beating wildly; I cannot keep silent; [for I hear the sound of the trumpet, the alarm of war]" (Jer. 4:19).

N. He said before him, "Lord of all worlds, I have gone over the two hundred and forty-eight limbs which you have given me, and I have not found that I ever angered you in any one of them. How much the more so, then, that my life should be given back to me?"

O. It is written, "Then the word of the Lord came to Isaiah: 'Go and say to Hezekiah, Thus says the Lord, the God of David your father: I have heard your prayer, I have seen your tears; behold I will add fifteen years to your life' " (Is. 38:4–5).

P. [Isaiah] said to him, "Thus I've already told him, and how thus do I say to him?

Q. "He is a man occupied with great affairs, and he will not believe me."

R. [God] said to him, "He is a very humble man, and he will be-lieve you. And not only so, but as yet the rumor has not yet gone forth in the city."

S. "And before Isaiah had gone out of the middle court, [the word of the Lord came to him]" (2 Kgs. 20:4).

T. When Manasseh arose, he pursued Isaiah, wanting to kill him. [Isaiah] fled from before him. He fled to a cedar, which swallowed him up, except for the show fringes [of his cloak], which revealed where he was.

U. They came and told him. He said to them, "Go and cut the cedar down." They cut the cedar down, and blood showed [indicating that Isaiah had been sawed too].

V. "[And also for the innocent blood that he had shed; for he filled Jerusalem with innocent blood,] and the Lord would not pardon" (2 Kgs. 24:4).

W. It is on this basis that he has no portion in the world to come.

VII. A. [Challenging the view of Judah, M. 10:2C,] And lo, it is written, "[Surely this came upon Judah at the command of the Lord, to remove them out of his sight,] for the sins of Manasseh, [according to all that he had done]" (2 Kgs. 24:3).

B. Shall we say that this was before he repented [so he did inherit the world to come after all]?

C. "On account of all the wrath whereby Manasseh had caused him to be wrathful"—

D. Shall we say that this was before he repented?

E. And lo, it is written, "[And he did not humble himself before the Lord, as Manasseh his father had humbled himself,] but this Amon incurred guilt more and more" (2 Chron. 33:23).

F. He did not add [to the sins], he made entirely new [and unprecedented ones].

G. And is it not written, "Moreoever Manasseh shed very much innocent blood, till he had filled Jerusalem from one end to another, [besides the sin which he made Judah to sin so that they did what was evil in the sight of the Lord]" (2 Kgs. 21:16).

H. Now is it possible for human beings to fill up the whole of Jerusalem with innocent blood from one end to the other?

I. But he killed Isaiah, who was equal to Moses, as it is written concerning him, "With him I speak mouth to mouth, [clearly, and not in dark speech; and he beholds the form of the Lord]. [Why then were you not afraid to speak against my servant Moses?]" (Num. 12:8).

J. And it is written, "The Lord spoke to Manasseh and his people, but they gave no heed. Therefore the Lord brought upon them the commanders of the army of the kind [of Assyria], who took Manasseh with hooks [and bound him with fetters of bronze and brought him to Babylon]" (2 Chron. 33:10–11).

K. What is "with hooks?"

L. [They took him] with handcuffs.

M. Said R. Levi, "They made him a mule of bronze, and they put him in it, and they made a fire under it. When he began to feel pain, he left not a single idol in the world, on the name of which he did not call.

N. "When he realized that it did him no good, he said, 'I remember that my father would read to me this verse in the synagogue: "When you are in tribulation, and all these things come upon you in the latter days, you will return to the Lord your God and obey his voice, for the Lord your God is a merciful God; he will not fail you or destroy you or forget the covenant with your fathers which he swore to them" (Deut. 4:30–31).

O. 'Lo, I shall call upon him. If he answers me, well and good, and if not, lo, all ways are the same [and no good]."

P. Now all the ministering angels went and closed the windows, so that the prayer of Manasseh should not reach upward to the Holy One, blessed be he.

Q. The ministering angels were saying before the Holy One, blessed be he, "Lord of the world, a man who worshiped idols and put up an image in the Temple—are you going to accept him back as a penitent?"

R. He said to them, "If I do not accept him back as a penitent, lo, I shall lock the door before all penitents."

S. What did the Holy One, blessed be he, do? He made an opening [through the heavens] under his throne of glory and listened to his supplication.

T. That is in line with the following verse of Scripture: "He prayed to him, and God received his entreaty and heard his supplication and brought him again [to Jerusalem into his kingdom]. [Then Manasseh knew that the Lord was God]" (2 Chron. 33:13).

U. Said R. Eleazar b. R. Simeon, "In Arabia that they call 'breaking through (HTRTH) 'supplication' (TRTH).'"

V. "And they brought him again to Jerusalem into his kingdom" (2 Chron. 33:13).

W. With what did they bring him back?

X. Samuel bar Buna in the name of R. Aha: "They brought him back with the wind."

Y. This is in line with that which you say, "He brings back the wind."

Z. "And Manasseh knew that the Lord [28d] was God" (2 Chron. 33:13).

AA. At that moment Manasseh said, "There is justice and there is a judge."

VIII. A. Now what did the evil Balaam do [to warrant losing his portion in the world to come]?

B. It was because he gave advice to Balak son of Zippor on how to cause Israel's downfall by the sword.

C. He said to him, "The God of this nation hates fornication. So put up your daughters for fornication, and you will rule over them."

D. He said to him, "And will [the Moabites] listen to me [when I tell them to turn their daughters into whores]?"

E. He said to him, "Put up your own daughter first, and they will see and then accept what you say to them."

F. That is in line with the following verse of Scripture: "[And the name of the Midianite woman who was slain was Cozbi the daughter of Zur,] who was the head of the people of a father's house in Midian" (Num. 25:15).

G. What did they do? They built for themselves temples from Beth HaJeshimmon to the Snowy Mountain, and they set in them women selling various kinds of sweets. They put the old lady outside, and the young girl inside.

H. Now the Israelites would then eat and drink, and one of them would go out to walk in the marketplace, and he would buy something from a stallkeeper. The old lady then would sell him the thing for whatever it was worth, and the young girl would say, "Come on in and take it for still less." So it was on the first day, the second day, and the third day. And then, she would say to him, "From now on, you belong here. Come on in and choose whatever you like."

I. When he came in [he found there] a flagon of wine, Ammonite wine, which is very strong. And it serves as an aphrodisiac to the body, and its scent was enticing. (Now up to this time the wine of gentiles had not been prohibited for Israelite use by reason of its being libation wine.)

J. Now the girl would say to him, "Do you want to drink a cup of wine," and he would reply to her, "Yes." So she gave him a cup of wine, and he drank it.

K. When he drank it, the wine would burn in him like the venom of a snake. Then he would say to her, "Surrender yourself [sexually] to me." She would say to him, "Do you want me to 'surrender' myself to you?" And he would say "Yes." Then she took out an image of Peor from her bosom, and she said to him, "Bow down to this, and I'll surrender myself to you." And he would say to her, "Now am I going to bow down to an idol?" And she would say to him, "You don't really bow down to it, but you expose yourself to it."

L. This is in line with that which sages have said, "He who exposes himself to Baal Peor—this is the appropriate manner of worshiping it; and he who tosses a stone at Merkolis—this is the appropriate manner of worshiping it."

M. [When he came in, he found] there a flagon full of wine, Ammonite wine, which is very strong. And it serves as an aphrodisiac to incite the body to passion, and its scent was enticing. (Now up to this time the wine of gentiles had not been prohibited for Israelite use by reason of its being libation wine.) Now the girl would say to him, "Do you want to drink a cup of wine," and he would reply to her, "Yes." So she gave him a cup of wine, and he drank it. When he drank it, the wine would burn in him like the venom of a snake. Then he would say to her, "Surrender yourself to me."

N. And she would say to him, "Separate yourself from the Torah of Moses, and I shall 'surrender' myself to you."

O. That is in line with the following verse of Scripture: "[Like grapes in the wilderness, I found Israel. Like the first fruits on the fig tree, in its first season, I saw your fathers.] But they came to Baal Peor, and consecrated themselves to Baal, and became detestable like the thing they loved" (Hos. 9:10).

P. They became detested until they became detestable to their Father who is in heaven.

Q. Said R. Eleazar, "Just as this nail—one cannot separate it from the door without a piece of wood, so it is not possible to separate from Peor without [the loss of] souls."

R. M'SH B: "Subetah from Ulam hired out his ass to a gentile woman, [to take her] to bow down to Peor. Whey they got to Peor's house, she said to him, "Wait for me here, while I go in and worship Peor." When she came out, he said to her, "Wait for me here, until I go in and do just what you did." What did he do? He went in and took a shit, and he wiped his ass on the nose of Peor. Everyone present praised him, and said to him, "No one ever did it the way this one did it!"

S. M'SH B: Menahem of Gypta Ary was moving jugs. The chief of Peor came to him by night. What did he do? He took the spit and stood up against him, and [the chief] fled from him. He came to him the next night. Menahem said to him, "How are you going to curse me? You are afraid of me!" And he said to him, "I'm not going to curse you anymore."

T. M'SH B: An officer came from overseas to bow down to Peor. He said to them, "bring me an ox, a ram, a sheep, to worship Peor." They said to him, "You don't have to go to all that trouble. All you have to do is expose yourself to it." What did he do? He called up his troops, who beat them and broke their skulls with staves, and he said to them, "Woe for you and for this big 'mistake' of yours!"

U. It is written: "And the Lord was angry at Israel, and the Lord said to Moses, 'Take all the chiefs of the people, and hang them in the sun before the Lord, [that the fierce anger of the Lord may turn away from Israel]' " (Num. 25:4).

V. He said to him, "Appoint their heads as judges over them, and let them put the sinners to death toward the sun."

W. This is in line with the following verse of Scripture: "And Moses said to the judges of Israel, 'Everyone of you slay his men who have yoked themselves to Baal Peor' " (Num. 25:5).

X. And how many are the judges of Israel? They are 78,600 [calculation as follows]:

Y. Heads of thousands are six hundred.

Z. Heads of hundreds are six thousand.

AA. Heads of troops of fifty are twelve thousand.

BB. Heads of troops of ten are sixty thousand.

CC. It thus turns out that the judges of Israel [heads of all units] are 78,600.

DD. He said to them, "Each one of you kill two." So 157,200 turned out to be put to death.

EE. "And behold, one of the people of Israel came and brought a Midianite woman to his family, in the sight of Moses [and in the sight of the whole congregation of the people of Israel, while they were weeping at the door of the tent of meeting]" (Num. 25:6).

FF. What is the meaning of, "In the sight of Moses"?

GG. It was like someone who says, "Here—right in your eye!"

HH. He said [to Moses] "Is your Zipporah not Midianite, and are not her feet cloven? [Is she not clean for you, fit to be your wife?] This one [Zipporah] is clean but that one [my woman] is unclean?!"

II. Now Phineas was there. He said, "Is there no man here who will kill him even at the expense of his life?"

JJ. "Where are the lions?"

KK. "Judah is a lion's whelp; [from the prey, my son, you have gone up. He stooped down, he couched as a lion, and as a lioness who dares to rouse him?]" (Gen. 49:9).

LL. "[And of Dan he said,] 'Dan is a lion's whelp, [that leaps forth from Bashan]' " (Deut. 33:22).

MM. "Benjamin is a ravenous wolf, [in the morning devouring the prey, and at evening dividing the spoil]" (Gen. 49:27).

NN. When he [Phineas] saw that no Israelite did a thing, forthwith, Phineas stood up from his Sanhedrin seat and took a spear in his hand and put the iron head of it under his *fascia*. He leaned on the wood [of the spear so concealing its purpose] until he reached his door. When he came to his door, [the occupant] said to him, "Whence and whither, Phineas?"

OO. He said to them, "Do you not agree with me that the tribe of Levi is near the tribe of Simeon under all circumstances?"

PP. They said to him, "Leave him [me] alone. Maybe the separatists have permitted this matter [after all]!"

QQ. When he got in, the Holy One, blessed be he, did six miracles.

RR. The first miracle: It is the usual way [after intercourse] to separate from one another, but the angel of the Lord kept them stuck together.

SS. The second miracle: He aimed the spear directly into the belly of the woman, so that the man's penis would stick out of her belly.

TT. And this was on account of the nitpickers, so that they should not go around saying, "He too shouldered his way in and did what came naturally."

UU. The third miracle: The angel sealed their lips, so that they could not cry out.

VV. The fourth miracle: They did not slip off the spear but remained in place. [Phineas lifted them up on the spear.]

WW. The fifth miracle: The angel raised the lintel [so that he could carry the two of them on the spear], so that both of them could go out on his shoulder.

XX. The sixth miracle: When he went out and saw the plague [29a] afflicting the people, what did he do? He threw them down to the ground and stood and prayed.

YY. This is in line with the following verse of Scripture: "Then Phineas stood up and interposed, and the plague was stayed" (Ps. 106:30).

ZZ. Now when the Israelites came to take vengeance against Midian, they found Balaam ben Beor there.

AAA. Now what had he come to do?

BBB. He had come to collect his salary for the twenty-four thousand Israelites who had died in Shittim on his account.

CCC. Phineas said to him, "You did not do what you said, and you also did not do Balak's bidding.

DDD. "You did not do what you said, for He said to you, 'You shall not go with the messengers of Balak,' but you went along with them.

EEE. "And you did not do what Balak said, for he said to you, 'Go and curse Israel,' but you blessed them.

FFF. "So, for my part, I'm not going to withhold your salary!"

GGG. That is in line with that which is written in Scripture: "Balaam also, the son of Beor, the soothsayer, the people of Israel killed with the sword among the rest of their slain" (Josh. 13:22).

HHH. What is the meaning of "among the rest of their slain"?

III. That he was equal to all the other slain put together.

JJJ. Another interpretation: "Among the rest of their slain"—Just as their slain no longer have substance, so he was of no substance.

KKK. Another interpretation: "Among the rest of their slain"—for he hovered [in the air] over their slain, and Phineas showed him the [priestly] frontlet, and he fell down [to earth].

IX. A. Another interpretation: "Among the rest of their slain"—this teaches that the Israelites paid him his salary in full and did not hold it back.

B. Doeg was a great man in learning of Torah.

C. The Israelites came and asked David, "In regard to the showbread, what is the law as to its overriding the restrictions of the Sabbath?"

D. Now Doeg was there, and he said, "Who is this one who comes to teach in my presence?"

E. They told him, "It is David, son of Jesse."

F. Forthwith, he went and gave advice to Saul, king of Israel, to kill Nob, the city of the priests.

G. This is in line with the following statement of Scripture: "And the king said to the guard who stood about him, 'Turn and kill the priests of the Lord; because their hand is also with David, [and they knew that he had fled, and did not disclose it to me].' [But the servants of the king would not put forth their hand to fall upon the priests of the Lord]" (1 Sam. 22:17). Who were they?

H. Said R. Samuel bar R. Isaac, "They were Abner and Amasa."

I. They said to him, "Now do you have any claim against us except for this belt and this cloak? Lo, they are thrown down before you!"

J. "[And the king said to the guard who stood about him, 'Turn and kill the priests of the Lord; because their hand is also with David, and they knew that he had fled, and did not disclose it to me.'] But the servants of the king would not put forth their hands to fall upon the priests of the Lord" (1 Sam. 22:17).

K. "And the king said to Doeg . . ."

L. Said R. Judah bar Pazzi, "It is written, 'to Du-eg' (DWYYG)."

M. He said to him, "You are trapped like a fish, you have done a great thing.

N. "[Then the king said to Doeg], 'You turn and fall upon the priests' And Doeg the Edomite turned and fell upon the priests, [and he killed that day eighty-five persons who wore the linen ephod]" (1 Sam. 22:18).

O. Now did not R. Hiyya teach, "They do not appoint two high priests at the same time"? [How could there be many?]

P. But this teaches that all of them were worthy of the high priests.

Q. How was he [shown to be ultimately] set apart?

R. R. Haninah and R. Joshua b. Levi—

S. One of them said, "Fire burst forth from the house of the Holy of Holies and licked round about him."

T. And the other one said, "His old students got together with him, and they were studying, but he forgot [his learning].

U. "[This fulfills the verse which says, 'He swallows down riches and vomits them up again; God casts them out of his belly' (Job 20:25). [That was a sign of his excommunication; and the students killed him.]"

X. A. Ahithopel was a man mighty in Torah learning.

B. It is written, "David again gathered all the chosen men of Israel, thirty thousand. [And David arose and went with all the people who were with him . . . to bring up from there the ark of the Lord]" (2 Sam. 6:1–2).

C. R. Berekiah in the name of R. Abba bar Kahana: "Ninety thousand elders did David appoint on a single day, but he did not appoint Ahithophel among them."

D. This is in line with that which is written in Scripture: "David again gathered all the chosen men of Israel, thirty thousand. . . ." That is, "And he added" means "thirty." And "again" means "thirty." The Scripture explicitly speaks of thirty. Lo, there are then ninety in all.

E. You find that when David came to bear the ark of the covenant of the Lord, he did not bear it in accord with the Torah:

F. "And they carried the Ark of God on a new cart, [and brought it out of the house of Abinadab which was on the hill; and Uzzah and Ahio, the sons of Abinadab, were driving the new cart]" (2 Sam. 6:3). [That is, the Torah requires that the priests carry it, but they carried it in a cart instead.]

G. Now the ark carried the priests on high, but let them fall down; the ark carried the priests on high, but let them fall down to the ground?

H. David sent and brought Ahithophel. He said to him, "Will you not tell me what is with this ark, which raises the priests up high and casts them down to the ground, raises the priests on high and casts them down to the ground?"

I. He said to him, "Send and ask those wise men whom you appointed!"

J. Said David, "One who knows how to make the ark stop and does not do so in the end is going to be put to death through strangulation."

K. He said to him, "Make a sacrifice before [the ark], and it will stop."

L. This is in line with the following verse which is written in Scripture: "And when those who bore the ark of the Lord had gone six paces, he sacrificed an ox and a fatling" (2 Sam. 6:13).

M. R. Haninah and R. Mana—

N. One of them said, "At every step an ox and a fatling, and at the end, seven oxen and seven rams."

O. And the other said, "At every step seven oxen and seven rams, and at the end, an ox and a fatling."

P. Said the Holy One, blessed be he, to Ahithophel, "A teaching which children say every day in the school you did not report to him!

Q. " 'But to the sons of Kohath gave none, because they were charged with the care of the holy things *which had to be carried on the shoulder*' (Num. 7:9).

R. "And this [to sacrifice] you told him!"

S. And so you find that when David came to dig the foundations of the Temple, he dug fifteen hundred cubits and did not reach the nethermost void. In the end he found one clay pot, and he wanted to remove it.

T. It said to him, "You cannot do so."

U. He said to it, "Why not?"

V. It said to him, "For I here am the cover over the great deep."

W. He said to it, "And how long have you been here?"

X. It said to him, "From the time that I heard the voice of the All-Merciful at Sinai: 'I am the Lord your God, [who brought you out of the land of Egypt, out of the house of bondage]' (Ex. 20:2), the earth shook and trembled.

Y. "And I am set here to seal the great deep."

Z. Even so, [David] did not listen to it.

AA. When he removed the clay pot, the great deep surged upward to flood the world.

BB. And Ahithophel was standing there. He said, "Thus will David be strangled [in the flood] and I shall become king."

CC. Said David, "He who is a sage, knowing how to stop up the matter, and does not stop it, will in the end be put to death through strangulation."

DD. [Ahithophel] said what he said and stopped up [the flood].

EE. David began to say a psalm, "A song of ascents. [In my distress I cry to the Lord, that he may answer me]" (Ps. 120:1).

FF. "A song of ascents" *(maalot)* is a song for a hundred *(meah)* whole offerings *(olot)*.

GG. At every hundred cubits he would say a psalm.

HH. Even so, in the end [Ahithophel] was strangled to death.

II. Said R. Yosé, "This is in line with what the proverb says: A person has to scruple about a curse of a great master, even if it was for nought."

JJ. R. Jeremiah in the name of R. Samuel bar Isaac, "A scroll which Samuel handed over to David did Ahithophel recite by means of the Holy Spirit."

KK. What did Ahithophel do?

LL. When someone came to him for advice, he would say to him, "Go and do thus and so, and if you don't believe me, then go and ask the Urim and Thummim."

MM. And the man would go and ask and find out that indeed that was how matters were.

NN. This is in line with that which is written in Scripture: "Now in those days the counsel which Ahithophel gave was as if one consulted [the oracle of God; so was the counsel of Ahithophel esteemed, both by David and by Absalom]" (2 Sam. 16:23).

OO. You read "Man"; it is not written thus, for the Scripture could not call him a [mere] man.

PP. How was he set apart?

QQ. When Ahithophel saw that his counsel was not followed, he saddled his ass [and went off home to his own city]. [And he set his house in order, and hanged himself; and he died, and was buried in the tomb of his father]" (2 Sam. 17:23).

RR. Three things did Ahithophel command his sons, saying to them:

SS. "Do not rebel against the royal house of David, for we shall find that the Holy One, blessed be he, shows favor to them even in public.

TT. "And do not have business [29b] dealings with someone on whom the hour smiles.

UU. "And if the day of Pentecost is bright, sow the best quality of wheat."

VV. But they did not know whether it means "bright" in dew or "bright" in dry heat.

XI. A. Gehazi was a man powerful in learning of Torah.

B. But he had three bad traits: niggardliness, womanizing, and denying the resurrection of the dead.

C. Niggardliness: When Elisha was sitting in his learning session, Gehazi would be in session at the door, and his disciples looked to him, and they said, "Gehazi did not enter, so shall we enter?"

D. So [Elisha] would be repeating his traditions, but no one derived any benefits from them.

E. Once [Gehazi] was separated, what is written there?

F. "Now the sons of the prophets said to Elisha, 'See, [the place where we dwell under your charge is too small for us]' (2 Kgs. 6:1).

G. "It cannot contain the crowd of disciples who are there."

H. And he was licentious: for lo, the Shunamite said to her husband, "[And she said to her husband,] 'Behold now, I perceive that this is a holy man of God, who is continuously passing our way'" (2 Kgs. 4:9).

I. Said R. Jonah, "*He* was a holy man—but his disciple was no saint."

J. Said R. Abin, "The fact was that [Elisha] never in his life laid eyes on her."

K. And rabbis of Caesarea say, "The reason was that he never produced a drop of semen on his garments in his entire life."

L. The serving girl of R. Samuel bar R. Isaac said, "I would wash the clothing of my master. In my whole life I never saw any sort of bad thing on the garments of my master."

M. It is written, "[And when she came to the mountain to the man of God, she caught hold of his feet.] And Gehazi came to thrust her away. [But the man of God said, 'Let her alone, for she is in bitter distress; and the Lord has hidden it from me, and has not told me]' " (2 Kgs. 4:27).

N. What is the meaning of "to thrust her away"?

O. Said R. Yosé b. Hanina, "He put his hand on the cleavage between her breasts."

P. Nor did he believe in the resurrection of the dead:

Q. You find that when Elisha came to resurrect the son of the Shunamite, he said to him, "[He said to Gehazi,] 'Gird up your loins, and take my staff in your hand, and go. If you meet anyone, do not salute him; and if anyone salutes you, do not reply; [and lay my staff on the face of the child]' " (2 Kgs. 4:29).

R. But he did not do so. Rahter, when someone met him, he said to him, "Whence and whither, Gehazi?"

S. And he said to him, "*I* am going to raise the dead."

T. And he said to him, "There is none who raises the dead except for the Holy One, blessed be he, as it is written in Scripture concerning him, 'The Lord kills and brings to life; he brings down to Sheol and raises up' " (1 Sam. 2:6).

U. He went his way and did nothing whatsoever.

V. He returned to [Elisha], who said to him, "I know that if he was asleep, he would not be awakened through you [because you did not carry out my instructions]."

W. You find that when Naaman the general of the army of the king of Aram came to Elisha, he came to him on his horse and with his chariot [2 Kgs. 5:9].

X. Said R. Yohanan, " 'With his *horse*' [singular] is written."

Y. He wanted to give to him gold and silver, robes and garments, precious jewels and pearls, but he would not accept them from him.

Z. This is in line with the following verse in Scripture: "[But he said, 'As the Lord lives, whom I serve, I will receive none.'] And he urged him to take it, but he refused" (2 Kgs. 5:16).

AA. Gehazi came along and said, "[Gehazi, the servant of Elisha the man of God, said, 'See, my master has spared Naaman the Syrian, in not accepting from his hand what he brought.] As the Lord lives, I will run after him, and get something from him' " (2 Kgs. 5:20).

BB. For "something (MWMH)" "blemish" (MWMH) is written.

CC. He went and found him and took what he took and put it in his upper room.

DD. He came to Elisha who said to him, "Whence and wither, Gehazi?

EE. "You have refused to give the reward which is owing to the righteous."

FF. He said to him, "[He went in, and stood before his master, and Elisha said to him, 'Where have you been, Gehazi?' And he said,] 'Your servant went nowhere' " (2 Kgs. 5:25).

GG. And he said to him, "Did I not go with you in spirit when the man turned from his chariot to meet you? Was it a time to accept money and garments, olive orchards and vineyards, sheep and oxen, menservants and maidservants?" (2 Kgs. 5:26).

HH. "Therefore the leprosy of Naaman shall cleave to you and to your descendants forever. So he went out from his presence a leper, as white as snow" (2 Kgs. 5:27).

II. And it is written in Scripture: "Now there were four men who were lepers at the entrance to the gate; [and they said to one another, 'Why do we sit here till we die?']" (2 Kgs. 7:3).

JJ. Who were they?

KK. R. Judah in the name of Rab: "They were Gehazi and his three sons."

LL. It is written, "Now Elisha came to Damascus. Benhadad the king of Syria was sick; [and when it was told him, 'The man of God has come here,' the king said to Hazael, 'Take a present with you and meet the man of God, and inquire of the Lord through him saying, "Shall I recover from this sickness?" ']" (2 Kgs. 8:7–8).

MM. Why did [Elisha] go there? He wanted to do something there. He went, hoping to bring Gehazi back. He found him a certified [leper].

NN. On his basis we learn that they push away [a sinner] with the left hand, but draw him near with the right hand.

OO. R. Yohanan said, " 'The sojourner has not lodged in the street; I have opened my doors to the wayfarer' (Job 31:32). On the basis of this verse [we learn] that they push away with the left hand and draw near with the right."

PP. And this is not as did Elisha, who drove away Gehazi with both hands.

QQ. There were two ailments which Elisha suffered: one from normal causes, the other in regard to his driving away Gehazi.

XII. A. R. Hananiah and R. Joshua b. Levi: "When they voted and decided, *Three kings and four ordinary folk have no portion in the world [M. San. 10:2A],* an echo came forth and said, 'Will he then make requital to suit you, because you reject it? For you most choose and not I; therefore declare what you know' (Job 34:33).

B. "They proposed to include Solomon with them.

C. "David came along and prostrated himself before them,

D. "and there is he who says that a fire went forth from the house of the Holy of Holies and licked round about them.

E. "Hadar-Ila was learned in praying and fasting. When Solomon was counted with them, [Hadar-Ila] prayed but was not answered."

F. Those who interpret signs said, "All of them have a portion in the world to come."

G. What is the scriptural basis for this position?

H. "Gilead is mine; Manasseh is mine; Ephraim is my helmet; Judah is my scepter. Moab is my washbasin; upon Edon I cast my shoe; over Philistia I shout in triumph [HTRWY]" (Ps. 60:7–8).

I. "Gilead is mine;—this refers to Ahab, king of Israel, who fell on the heights of Gilead.

J. "Manasseh is mine" means what is says.

K. "Ephraim is my helmet"—this is Jeroboam ben Nabat of Ephraim.

L. "Judah is my scepter" refers to Ahithophel.

M. "Moab is my washbasin"—this refers to Gehazi.

N. "Upon Edom I cast my shoe"—this refers to Doeg the Edomite.

O. The Israelites said before the Holy One, blessed be he, "Lord of all worlds, what shall we do when David, king of Israel, is cursing them?

P. " 'Men of blood and treachery shall no live out half their days' " (Ps. 55:23).

Q. He said to them, "It is my task to make them friends (RYYM) again with one another:

R. " 'Over Philistia I shout in triumph' (TRW) (Ps. 108:9).

S. " 'Over Philistia I should in triumph' (HTRWY) (Ps. 60:8).

T. "It is my task to seek out (PLS) for them good deeds, to make them friends (RYYM) once more with one another."

The first seven units deal with the materials of M. San. 10:2A–E. The Talmud unfolds fairly systematically, with Jeroboam, unit **I**, Ahab, units **II–III**, and Manasseh, units **V–VII**, with Judah's view, M. San. 10:2C, dealt with at **VII**. I am not sure why Ahaz is included at unit **IV**. The introduction **IV**.A is consistent with **I**.A, **II**.A, and **V**.A., as if to indicate that Ahaz is in the same list as the others. I separate unit **VI** from unit **V** because it seems to me an essentially independent unit, but of course, the opposite view is reasonable. The ordinary folk begin at unit **VIII** and run to the end. We notice that units **IX, X,** and **XI** open with the same theme, that the villain was the master of Torah and none-theless so grievously sinned that he lost the world to come. But I see no important patterns in the formation of the subsequent constructions, which exhibit the expected character of an anthology. Unit **VIII** bears a number of inserted tales about the worship of Peor, **VIII**.R, S, T, and it also has some minor literary problems, e.g., of repetition. But in the main the story unfolds smoothly and makes its points clearly.

10:3

    A. *The generation of the flood has no share in the world to come,*

    B. *and they shall not stand in the judgment,*

    C. *since it is written, "My spirit shall not judge with man forever" (Gen. 6:3)—*

    D. *[neither judgment nor spirit].*

    E. *The generation of the dispersion has no share in the world to come,*

    F. *since it is said, "So the Lord scattered them abroad from there upon the face of the whole earth" (Gen. 11:8).*

    G. *"So the Lord scattered them abroad"—in this world,*

    H. *"and the Lord scattered them from there"—in the world to come.*

    I. *The men of Sodom have no portion in the world to come,*

    J. *since it is said, "Now the men of Sodom were wicked and sinners against the Lord exceedingly (Gen. 13:13)—*

    K. *"Wicked"—in this world.*

    L. *"And sinners"—in the world to come.*

M. *But they will stand in judgment.*

N. *R. Nehemiah says, "Both these and those will not stand in judgment,*

O. *"for it is said, 'Therefore the wicked shall not stand in judgment, nor sinners in the congregation of the righteous' (Ps. 1:5)—*

P. *" 'Therefore the wicked shall not stand in judgment'—this refers to the generation of the flood.*

Q. *" 'Nor sinners in the congregation of the righteous'—this refers to the men of Sodom."*

R. *They said to him, "They will not stand in the congregation of the righteous, but they will stand in the congregation of the sinners."*

S. *[The spies have no portion in the world to come,*

T. *as it is said, "Even those men who brought up an evil report of the land died by the plague before the Lord" (Num. 14:37)—*

U. *"Died"—in this world.*

V. *"By the plague"—in the world to come].*

I.   A. *[The generation of the flood (M. San. 10:3A)] will not live in the world to come.*

B. What is the scriptural basis for this statement?

C. "He blotted out every living thing that was on the face of the ground [man and animals and creeping things and birds of the air; they were blotted out of the earth]" (Gen. 7:23).

D. "[He blotted out every living thing that was on the face of the ground, man and animals and creeping things and birds of the air;] they were blotted out of the earth" (Gen. 7:23).

E. **"And he blotted out every living thing"—in this world.**

F. **"And they were blotted out of the earth"—in the world to come [T. San. 13:6].**

G. It was taught: R. Nehemiah says, "It is implied by the following verse of Scripture: '[Then the Lord said,] "My spirit shall not abide in man for ever, [for he is flesh, but his days shall be a hundred and twenty years"]' " (Gen. 6:3).

H. R. Judah says, "My spirit will not abide with him, for I shall not place my spirit on mankind."

I. R. Simeon says, "My spirit will not abide with them, for I shall not put my spirit in them when I pay the reward which is coming to the righteous."

J. Others says, "My spirit will not abide with them, for I shall not bring back their souls to their cases [bodies]."

K. R. Joshua b. Levi said, "Their destruction by scalding water was final [so there is no resurrection for them]."

L. What is the scriptural basis for this statement?

M. "In time of heat they disappear; when it is hot they vanish from their place" (Job 6:17).

N. What is the meaning of "when it is hot"?

O. "When they are scalded."

P. Said R. Yohanan, "Every single drop which the Holy One, blessed be he, brought down on them, did he boil in Gehenna, and then he brought it down on them."

Q. This is in line with the following verse of Scripture:

R. "When it is hot they vanish from their place" (Job 6:17).

S. Judah b. R. Hezekiah and Rabbi say, "The Holy One, blessed be he, judges the wicked in Gehenna for twelve months. At the outset he puts a hook into them, and then he hangs them in fire, and they say, 'Woe, woe!' Then he hangs them into snow, and they say, 'Oh, oh!' "

T. What is the scriptural basis for this statement?

U. "He drew me up from the desolate pit, out of the miry bog, and set my feet upon a rock, making my steps secure]" (Ps. 40:3).

V. What is the meaning of "the miry bog (HYWN)"?

W. A place in which they say, "Oh (HWY)!"

X. And let them receive their punishment [29c] and then receive a portion in the world to come?

Y. [That is not possible,] in line with the following verse of Scripture: "[A wise son hears his father's instruction,] but a scoffer does not listen to rebuke" (Prov. 13:1).

II. A. *The men of Sodom have no portion in the world to come (M. San. 10:31),*

B. and they will not live in the world to come.

C. What is the scriptural basis for that statement?

D. "Now the men of Sodom were wicked, great sinners against the Lord" (Gen. 13:13).

E. **"Wicked and sinners"—in this world.**

F. **"Against the Lord exceedingly"—in the world to come.**

G. **Another interpretation: "Evil"—to one another.**

H. **"And sinning"—in fornication.**

I. **"Against the Lord"—in idolatry.**

J. **"Exceedingly"—in murder [T. San. 13:8].**

The Talmud treats the generation of the flood at unit **I,** the men of Sodom at unit **II.** No materials on the other topics are included.

10:4

A. *"The generation of the wilderness has no portion in the world to come and will not stand in judgment,*

B. *"for it is written, 'In this wilderness they shall be consumed and there they shall die' (Num. 14:35)," the words of R. Aqiba.*

C. *R. Eliezer says, "Concerning them it says, 'Gather my saints together to me, those that have made a covenant with me by sacrifice' " (Ps. 50:5).*

D. *"The party of Korah is not destined to rise up,*

E. *"for it is written, 'And the earth closed upon them' (Num. 16:33) [—in this world].*

F. *" 'And they perished from among the assembly' [—in the world to come]," the words of R. Aqiba.*

G. *And R. Eliezer says, "Concerning them it says, 'The Lord kills and resurrects, brings down to Sheol and brings up again' " (1 Sam. 2:6).*

I. A. **"The generation of the wilderness has no portion in the world to come and will not live in the world to come,**

B. **"as it is said, 'In this wilderness they shall be consumed, and there they shall die.'**

C. **" 'They shall be consumed'—in this world.**

D. **" 'And there they will die'—in the world to come.**

E. **"And so it says, 'Therefore I swore in my anger that they should not enter my rest' " (Ps. 95:11), the words of R. Aqiba.**

F. **R. Eliezer says, "Concerning them it is said, 'Gather my saints together to me, those that have made a covenant with me by sacrifice' " (Ps. 50:5) [T. San. 13:10].**

G. R. Joshua says, " 'I have sworn an oath and confirmed it' (Ps. 119:106).

H. Hananiah nephew of R. Joshua says, **"It is written, 'Therefore I swore in my anger . . .' (Ps. 95:11)—**

I. "In my anger did I swear, but I retract it" [T. San. 13:11].

J. It was taught, **R. Simeon b. Menassia says,** "Concerning them does Scripture state, 'Gather to me my faithful ones, who made a covenant with me by sacrifice!' (Ps. 50:5).

K. " 'My faithful ones'—who acted faithfully with me.

L. " 'Who have made a covenant with me'—who are cut in my behalf.

M. " 'With me by sacrifice'—who exalted me and are sacrificed in my name"

N. It was taught: **R. Joshua b. Qorha says,** "Concerning these generations, Scripture states, 'And then the ransomed of the Lord shall return, [and come singing to Zion]' " (Is. 35:10) [T. San. 13:11].

O. Rabbi says, "Both these and those do have a portion in the world to come."

P. What is the scriptural basis for this viewpoint?

Q. "And in that day a great trumpet will be blown, and those who were lost in the land of Assyria [and those who were driven out to the land of Egypt will come and worship the Lord on the holy mountain at Jerusalem]" (Is. 27:13).

R. "In the land of Assyria"—these are the ten tribes.

S. "And those who were driven out to the land of Egypt"—this is the generation of the wilderness.

T. These and those "will come and worship the Lord on the holy mountain at Jerusalem."

II. A. *The party of Korach has no portion in the world to come and will not live in the world to come.*

B. What is the scriptural basis for this view?

C. "[So they and all that belonged to them went down alive into Sheol'] and the earth closed over them, and they perished from the midst of the assembly" (Num. 16:33).

D. *"The earth closed over them"—in this world.*

E. *"And they perished from the midst of the assembly"—in the world to come [M. San. 10:4D–F].*

F. It was taught: **R. Judah b. Batera says,** "[The contrary view] is to be derived from the implication of the following verse:

G. " 'I have gone astray like a lost sheep; seek they servant [and do not forget thy commandments]' (Ps. 119:176).

H. **"Just as the lost object which is mentioned later on in the end is going to be searched for, so the lost object which is stated herein is destined to be searched for"** [T. San. 13:9].

I. Who will pray for them?

J. R. Samuel bar Nahman said, "Moses will pray for them."

K. "Let Reuben live, and not die, [nor let his men be few]" (Deut. 33:6).

L. R. Joshua b. Levi said, "Hannah will pray for them."

M. This is the view of R. Joshua b. Levi, for R. Joshua b. Levi said, "Thus did the party of Korach sink ever downward, until Hannah went and prayed for them and said, 'The Lord kills and brings to life; he brings down to Sheol and raises up' " (1 Sam. 2:6).

The Talmud presents no surprises, once more drawing on Tosefta's materials and lightly augmenting them.

10:5

A. *"The ten tribes are not destined to return,*

B. *"since it is said, 'And he cast them into another land, as on this day' (Deut. 29:28). Just as the day passes and does not return, so they have gone their way and will not return," the words of R. Aqiba.*

C. *R. Eliezer says, "Just as this day is dark and then grows light, so the ten ribes for whom it now is dark—thus in the future it is destined to grow light for them."*

I. A. *"The ten tribes have no portion in the world to come and will not live in the world to come, since it is said, 'And he cast them into another land, as on this day' (Deut. 29:28). Just as the day passes and does not return, so they have gone their way and will not return," the words of R. Aqiba [M. San. 10:5A–B].*

B. **R. Simeon b. Judah of Kefar Akkum says in the name of R. Simeon, "[Scripture said, 'As at this day']—**

C. **"if their deeds remain as they are on this day, they will [not] return, and if not, they will (not) return"** [T. San. 13:12].

II. A. R. Hezekiah, R. Abbahu in the name of R. Eleazar, "If the righteous proselytes come to the world to come, Antolinus will come at the head of all of them."

B. There are those who maintain that Antolinus did not convert, and there are those who maintain that Antolinus did convert.

C. What implication do you derive from that statement?

D. They saw him going out in a damaged shoe on the Day of Atonement.

E. So you derive from that fact that even those who fear heaven go out in such wise.

F. Antolinus came to Rabbi. He said to him, "Do you foresee that I shall eat from Leviathan in the world to come?"

G. He said to him, "Yes."

H. He said to him, "Now you did not let me eat from the Passover lamb in this world, and yet will you give me Leviathan's flesh to eat in the coming world?"

I. He said to him, "And what can we do for you? Concerning the Passover lamb it is written, '[And when a stranger shall sojourn with you and would keep the Passover to the Lord, Let all his males be circumcised, then he shall come near and keep it; he shall be as a native of the land.] But no uncircumcised person shall eat of it' " (Ex. 12:48).

J. (That is to say, Antolinus did not convert.)

K. When he heard this, he went and converted. He came to Rabbi, saying to him, "Now look at the mark of my circumcision!"

L. He said to him, "In my whole life I never looked at mine! Am I supposed to look at yours!"

M. (That is to say that Antolinus did convert.)

N. Now why was he called, "Our Holy Rabbi"? Because in his entire life he never looked at the mark of circumcision on his penis.

O. And why is Nahum called, "The Most Holy Man"? Because he never in his entire life looked at the face of a coin [on which a human figure was incised].

P. Antolinus came to Rabbi. He said to him, "Pray for me."

Q. He said to him, "May He protect you from cold, as it is written, '[He casts forth ice like morsels,] who can stand before his cold?' " (Ps. 147:17).

R. He said to him, "Rabbi, this prayer is not much. If you cover yourself, lo, the cold goes away."

S. He said to him, "May he spare you from the hot winds which blow through the world."

T. He said to him, "Now that is a fitting prayer. May your prayer be heard,

U. "for it is written, '[Its rising from the end of the heavens, and its circuit to the end of them.] And there is nothing hid from its heat' " (Ps. 19:7).

III. A. R. Yohanan said, "The party of Yohanan b. Korach has no portion in the world to come."

B. What is the scriptural basis for this view?

C. "They have dealt faithlessly with the Lord; for they have borne alien children. Now the new moon shall devour them with their fields" (Hos. 5:7).

IV. A. R. Eleazar and R. Judah—

B. One said, "They did not go into exile until they had become uncircumcised."

C. And the other said, "They did not go into exile until they had become *mamzerim*."

D. The one who said, "Uncircumcised" refers the verse to circumcision and practice of religious duties, and the one who said, "*mamzerim*" refers the verse to the doings of the fathers [which caused the calamity].

E. Said R. Yohanan, "Israel did not go into exile until it had turned into twenty-four parties of heretics."

F. What is the scriptural basis for that statement?

G. "[and he said to me,] 'Son of man, I send you to the people of Isreal, to a nation of rebels, who have rebelled against me; [and I heard him speaking to me]' " (Ez. 2:3).

H. "To a nation which rebels" is not written here but, rather, "to rebellious nations which have rebelled against me."

I. They and their fathers have transgressed against me until this very day.

J. R. Berekiah and R. Helbo in the name of R. Samuel bar Nahman: "The Israelites went into three different lands of exile, one beyond the Sambatyon River, one to Daphne at Antioch, and one on which the cloud descended, and which the cloud covered."

K. Just as they went into three different exiles, so the tribe of Reuben, Gad, and the half tribe of Manasseh went into three different exiles.

L. What is the scriptural basis for that statement?

M. "You have gone the way of your sister; therefore I will give her cup into your hand" (Ex. 23:31).

N. And when they come back, they will come back from all three exiles.

O. What is the scriptural basis for that statement?

P. "Saying to the prisoners, 'Come forth' to those who appear in darkness, 'Appear.' They shall feed along the ways, on all bare heights shall be their pasture" (Is. 49:9).

Q. "Saying to the prisoners, 'Come forth' "—this refers to those who went into exile on the other side of the Sambatyon River.

R. "To those who appear in darkness, 'Apprear' "—these are those on whom the cloud descended and whom it covered.

S. "They shall feed along the way, on all the bare heights shall be their pastures"—these are those who went into exile in Daphne at Antioch.

Only unit I follows the pattern established earlier. Reference to the redemption presumably accounts for the topic of unit II. Unit III serves M. 10:4. Unit IV deals with the Israelite exile and answers the question of whether the exile was because of the deeds of that generation or the accumulation of wickedness of the fathers.

10:6

A. *The townsfolk of an apostate town [have no portion in the world to come,*

B. *as it is said,] "Certain base fellows have come out from the midst of thee and have drawn away the inhabitants of their city" (Deut. 13:14).*

C. *Lo, they are not put to death unless those who misled the [town] come from that same town and from that same tribe,*

D. *and unless the majority is misled,*

E. *and unless men did the misleading.*

F. *[If] women or children misled them,*

G. *or if a minority of the town was misled,*

H. *or if those who misled the town came from outside of it,*

I. *lo, they are treated as individuals [and not as a whole town],*

J. *[and they thus] require testimony against them] by two witnesses, and a statement of warning, for each and every one of the [residents].*

K. *This rule is more strict for individuals than for the community:*

L. *for individuals are put to death by stoning.*

M. *Therefore their property is saved.*

N. *But the community is put to death by the sword.*

O. *Therefore their property is lost.*

I. A. "A town" (Deut. 13:14)—not a village.

B. "A town"—not a city.

C. "And that is to say there should be from five to ten [men]," the words of R. Meir.

D. R. Judah says, "From a hundred to as much as the majority of the whole tribe."

II. A. Two who misled two [that is, those who misled the apostate city are two in number; in this case, they misled only two, while the others in the town were misled by outsiders]—

B. those two who misled two—what is the law as to applying to them the rule governing those who misled [or] the rule governing those who are misled? [Are those who misled the town treated as guilty and culpable by stoning? Or are they deemed part of the ones who are misled, others being involved? They misled only two people, and so along with the rest are subject to the law of punishment through decapitation.]

C. If there were in the apostate town proselytes and resident aliens—what is the law as to their completing the number to make the required majority?

D. If there were in the town vivaria for wild beasts and birds [29d] and fish—

E. a bird flying above the town by more than ten cubits—

F. what is the law [governing their falling into the category of the possessions to be put to death]?

III. A. R. Simeon says, "The mode of execution through burning is more severe than the mode of execution through stoning."

B. And rabbis say, "The mode of execution through stoning is more severe than the mode of execution through burning."

C. R. Simeon says, "The mode of execution through strangulation is more severe than the mode of execution through decapitation."

D. And rabbis say, "The mode of execution through decapitation is more severe than the mode of execution through strangulation."

What is interesting are the several questions, not answered, in unit **II**. The rest is standard. Why unit **III** is appended I cannot say.

10:7

A. *"And you shall surely smite the inhabitants of the city with the edge of the sword" (Deut. 13:15)—*

B. *A caravan of ass drivers or camel rivers passing from place to place—lo, these have the power to save it.*

C. *"Destroying it utterly and all that is therein and the cattle thereof, with the edge of the sword" (Deut. 13:17)—*

D. *On this basis they said, The property of righteous folk which happens to be located in it is lost. But that which is outside of it is saved.*

E. *And as to that of evil folk, whether it is in the town or outside of it, lo, it is lost. But that which is outside of it is saved.*

I.   A. **R. Simeon says, " 'Its cattle,'—excluding firstling and tithe of cattle in it.**

B. **" 'And its spoils'—excluding money which has been consecrated, and money which has taken on the status of second tithe in it"** [T. San. 14:5].

C. R. Yose b. Haninah raised the question: "The hair [wigs] belonging top the righteous women which are in the town—what is the law? [Is this deemed in the status of the property of the righteous, which is lost, or in the status of their clothing, which is saved, in line with M. 10:7D?]

D. Let us derive the rule from the following: **R. Simeon says, " 'Its cattle'—excluding firstlings and title of cattle in it. 'And its spoil'—excluding money which has been consecrated and money which has taken on the status of second tithe in it."** [Similarly, the wigs of righteous women are not in the same status as ordinary property, just as firstlings are not in the same status as ordinary cattle.]

II. A. As to the consecrated beasts located in an apostate city—

B. R. Yohanan says, "The laws of sacrilege do not apply to them."

C. And R. Simeon b. Laqish said, "The laws of sacrilege do apply to them."

D. R. Yohanan raised the following objection to R. Simeon b. Laqish: "In your opinion, in holding that the laws of sacrilege do apply to them, we should also speak of six animals consecrated as sin offerings which are left to die, rather than merely five [as we find at M. Tem. 4:1, since these beasts too will retain the status of consecration and are left to die]."

E. He said to him, "But in fact even an animal consecrated as a whole offering in the apostate city is left to die."

F. R. Hela in the name of R. Simeon b. Laqish: "The laws of sacrilege apply to them, because the animals are in the status of beast declared consecrated by an apostate to idolatry, [and the laws of sacrilege do apply to such beasts, since the apostate retains the power of sanctification inherent in the Israelite]."

G. [And why should they be left to die?] Let them be offered on the altar.

H. [This is not done, by reason of] the following verse: "The sacrifice of the wicked is an abomination" (Prov. 21:27).

I. Said R. Uqba, "Also in the following do they differ:

J. " 'An ox which is going forth to be stoned when the witnesses against are are proved to be perjurers'—

K. "R. Yohanan said 'Whoever seizes possession of it first wins out.'

L. "And R. Simeon b. Laqish said, 'It is a case of the owner's having given up ownership by reason of despair [but having done so only] in error [and the owner retains ownership].'

M. "And so in the case of a slave being taken forth to be executed, when the witnesses against him are proved to be perjurers,

N. "R. Yohanan said, 'He acquires ownership of himself.'

O. "And R. Simeon b. Laqish said, 'It is a case of the owner's having given up ownership by reason of despair, [but having done so] only in error [so the original owner retains possession].' "

Unit **I** augments Mishnah's interest in the disposition of the property, M. 10:7C. Unit **II** then carries forward the same theme, namely consecrated property. In place of **II.I–O** in the argument's construction is not clear to me; it appears tacked on.

10:8

A. "*And you shall gather all the spoil of it into the midst of the wide place thereof*" (Deut. 13:16).

B. *If it has no wide place, they make a wide place for it.*

C. *[If] its wide place is outside of it, they bring it inside, as it is said,*" . . . *into the midst of the wide place thereof."*

D. "*And you will burn with fire the city and all the spoil thereof, every whit, unto the Lord your God*" (Deut. 13:16).

E. "*The spoil thereof*"—*but not the spoil which belongs to heaven.*

F. *On this basis they have said:*

G. *Things which had been consecrated which are in it are to be redeemed; heave offering left therein is allowed to rot; second tithe and sacred scrolls are hidden away.*

H. "*Every whit unto the Lord your God*"—

I. *Said R. Simeon, "Said the Holy One, blessed be he: 'If you enter into judgment in the case of an apostate city, I give credit to you as if you had offered a whole burnt offering before me.'*"

J. "*And it shall be a heap forever, it shall not be built again*"—

K. "*It should not be made even into vegetable patches or orchards,*" *the words of R. Yosé the Galilean.*

L. *R. Aqiba says,* "'*It shall not be built again*'—*as it was it may not be rebuilt, but it may be made into vegetable patches and orchards.*"

M. "*And there shall cleave nought of the devoted thing to your hand [that the Lord may turn from the fierceness of his anger and show you mercy and have compassion upon you and multiply you]*" (Deut. 13:17).

N. *For so long as evil people are in the world, fierce anger is in the world.*

O. *When the evil people have perished from the world, fierce anger departs from the world.*

I. A. Said R. Simeon, "This [disposition of the property of the righteous, M. 10:7D] yields an argument *a fortiori.*

B. "Now if regarding property, which has no knowledge of either good or evil, because it caused righteous people to make their dwelling with evil ones, the Torah has said that [such property] is to be burned—

C. "he who has the intention of misleading his fellow and actually does mislead him from the good way to the evil way—how much the more so [will he be punished]!"

D. Said R. Eleazar, "Proof for that proposition is found in the case of Lot, who dwelled in Sodom only on account of his property.

E. "He too got out with his skin."

F. That is in line with the following verse of Scripture:

G. "Make haste, escape there" (Gen. 19:22).

H. It is enough for you that you escape with your life.

I. It is written, **"In his days did Hiel the Bethelite build Jericho"** (1 Kgs. 16:34).

J. **And did not Hiel belong to Jehoshaphat, and Jericho to the district of Benjamin?**

K. [And why was the matter blamed on Ahab?]

L. **It teaches that they hang guilt on one who already is guilty [T. San. 14:7].**

M. [And so it says,] **"With the loss of Abiram his firstborn, he laid the foundation thereof, and with the loss of Segub his youngest son he set up the gates thereof"** (1 Kgs. 16:34).

N. **In the instance of Abiram, he had no [example] from which to learn.**

O. **But in the case of Segub, that wicked man had [an example] from which to learn!**

P. **They wanted to increase their money.**

Q. **Why? Because a curse had affected them and their funds simply continued to decline.**

R. **This supports Scripture, which says, "According to the word of the Lord, which he spoke by the hand of Joshua the son of Nun, 'Every whit unto the Lord your God . . . And there shall cleave nought of the devoted thing to your hand.' "** (1 Kgs. 16:34) [T. San. 14:9].

S. It was taught. **R. Simeon b. Eleazar says, "That [Jericho] he did not build, but he built another one. And when it was built, you are permitted to live in it. For it is said, 'And the sons of the prophets which in Jericho drew near to Elisha' "** (2 Kgs. 2:5) [T. San. 14:10].

T. **R. Yosé and R. Joshua b. Qorha say, "Why does Scripture say, ['Cursed is the man before the Lord who will rise and] build this city, Jericho' [Josh. 6:26]?**

U. "[Now don't we know that it is called Jericho?]

V. "[But the meaning is that] one may not rebuild it and call it by the name of some other town, and that one may not build some other town and call it Jericho" [T. San. 14:6].

W. And so it says, "You shall never return (SWB) that way again" (Deut. 17:16).

X. For the purposes of making a permanent settlement (YSYBH) you may not return, but you may return to do business, to engage in commerce and to conquer the land.

The homilies, serving M. 10:7 as indicated, include I.Iff., solely because of I.Q. That is, concern for making money caused the catastrophe. Then the entire construction, from I.I–X onward, is inserted whole on account of that one detail.

6. Genesis Rabbah

We move from our interest in process to our concern for the proposition of the oral Torah as it concerns the salvation of Israel. Genesis Rabbah in the aggregate responds to the question of the meaning of history, in particular, the history of Israel confronted by the triumph of its sibling-enemy. To find that meaning at the end, sages turned to the picture of creation in the beginning. That is why, in the book of Genesis, as the sages who composed Genesis Rabbah saw things, God set forth to Moses the entire scope and meaning of Israel's history among the nations and salvation at the end of days. They read Genesis not as a set of individual verses, one by one, but as a single and coherent statement, whole and complete. In a few words let me restate the conviction of the framers of Genesis Rabbah about the message and meaning of the book of Genesis:

We now know what will be in the future. How do we know it? Just as Jacob had told his sons what would happen in time to come, just as Moses told the tribes their future, so we may understand the laws of history if we study the Torah. And in the Torah, we turn to beginnings: the rules as they were laid out at the very start of human history. These we find in the book of Genesis, the story of the origins of the world and of Israel.

The Torah tells us not only what happened but why. The Torah permits us to discover the laws of history. Once we know those laws, we may also peer into the future and come to an assessment of what is going to happen to us—and, especially, of how we shall be saved from our present existence. Because everything exists under the aspect of a timeless will, God's will, and all things express one thing, God's program and plan, in the Torah we uncover the workings of God's will. Our task as Israel is to accept, endure, submit, and celebrate.

To the rabbis who created Genesis Rabbah, the book of Genesis told the story of Israel, the Jewish people, in the here and now. The principle was that what happened to the patriarchs and matriarchs signals what will happen to their descendants: the model of the ancestors sends a message for the children. So the importance of Genesis, as the sages of Genesis Rabbah read the book, derives not from its lessons about the past but its message for Israel's present—and, especially, future. Their conviction was that what Abraham, Isaac, and Jacob did shaped the future history of Israel. Sages maintained in line with the Mishnah's view that the world reveals not chaos but order, and God's will works itself out not once but again and again. Bringing to the stories of Genesis that conviction that the book of Genesis told not only the story of yesterday but also the tale of tomorrow, the sages transformed a picture of the past into a prophecy for a near tomorrow.

At the turn of the fifth century sages entertained deep forebodings about Israel's prospects. In Genesis Rabbah every word of Genesis is read against the background of the world-historical change that had taken place in the time of the formation of the document. The people who compiled the materials made a statement through what they selected and arranged. Let me give one concrete example of how in Genesis Rabbah sages responded. Rome now claimed to be Israel, that is, Christian and heir to the testament of the founders. To sages Genesis talked about the here and now, "about us, Israel, and about *our sibling,* Rome." That concession—Rome is a sibling, a close relative of Israel—represents an implicit recognition of Christianity's claim to share the patrimony of Judaism, to be descended from Abraham and Isaac. To deal with the glory and the power of our brother, Esau, and to assess today the future history of Israel, the salvation of God's first, best love, sages took the simple tack of restating matters already clear in Scripture. That is, it was not by denying Rome's claim but by evaluating it.

Sages in Genesis Rabbah represent Rome as Israel's brother, counterpart, and nemesis, Rome as the one thing standing in the way of Israel's and the world's ultimate salvation. It is not a political Rome but a messianic Rome that is at issue: Rome as surrogate for Israel, Rome as obstacle to Israel. The reason of course is that Rome now confronted Israel with a crisis, and Genesis Rabbah constitutes a response to that crisis. Rome in the fourth century became Christian. Sages respond by facing that fact quite squarely and saying, "Indeed, it is as you say, a kind of Israel, an heir of Abraham as your texts explicitly claim. But we remain the sole legitimate Israel, the bearer of the birthright—we and not you. So you are our brother: Esau, Ishmael, Edom." By rereading the story of the beginnings, sages discovered the answer and the secret of the end. Rome claimed to be Israel, and, indeed, sages conceded, Rome shared the patrimony of Israel. That claim took the form of the Christians' appropriation of the Torah as "the Old Testament," so sages acknowledged a simple fact in acceding to the notion that, in some way, Rome too formed part of Israel. But it was the rejected part, the Ishmael, the Esau, not the Isaac, not the Jacob. The advent of Christian Rome precipitated the sustained, polemical, and, I think, rigorous and well-argued rereading of beginnings in light of the end. Rome then marked the conclusion of human history as Israel had known it. Beyond lay the coming of the true Messiah, the redemption of Israel, the salvation of the world, the end of time.

Let us consider a simple example of how ubiquitous is the shadow of Ishmael/Esau/Edom/Rome. Wherever sages reflect on future history, their minds turn to their own day. They found the hour difficult, because Rome, now Christian, claimed that very birthright and blessing that they understood to be theirs alone. Christian Rome posed a threat without precedent. Now another dominion, besides Israel's, claimed the rights and blessings that sustained Israel. Wherever in Scripture they turned, sages found comfort in the iteration that the birthright, the blessing, the Torah, and the hope—all belonged to them and to none other. Here is a striking statement of that constant proposition.

Genesis Rabbah LIII:XII.

1.   A.   "[So she said to Abraham, 'Cast out this slave woman with her son, for the son of this slave woman shall not be heir with my son Isaac.'] And the thing was very displeasing to Abraham on account of his son" (Gen. 21:11):

B. That is in line with this verse: "And shuts his eyes from looking upon evil" (Is. 33:15). [Freedman, p. 471, n. 1: He shut his eyes from Ishmael's evil ways and was reluctant to send him away.]

2. A. "But God said to Abraham, 'Be not displeased because of the lad and because of your slave woman; whatever Sarah says to you, do as she tells you, for through Isaac shall your descendants be named' " (Gen. 21:12):

B. Said R. Yudan bar Shillum, "What is written is not 'Isaac' but 'through Isaac.' [The matter is limited, not through all of Isaac's descendants but only through some of them, thus excluding Esau.]"

Among the descendants of Isaac will be found Abraham's heirs, but not all the descendants of Isaac will be heirs of Abraham. No. 2 explicitly excludes Esau, that is Rome. As the several antagonists of Israel stand for Rome in particular, so the traits of Rome, as sages perceived them, characterized the biblical heroes. Esau provided a favorite target. From the womb Israel and Rome contended. Specifically, Esau hated Israel even while he was still in the womb. Jacob, for his part, revealed from the womb those virtues that would characterize him later on, eager to serve God as Esau was eager to worship idols. The ambiguous status of Rome as Christian brought sages to compare Rome to the swine, which, in one trait, appeared to be acceptable, but in reality was unacceptable.

LXV:I.

1. A. "When Esau was forty years old, he took to wife Judith, the daughter of Beeri, the Hittite, and Basemath the daughter of Elon the Hittite; and they made life bitter for Isaac and Rebecca" (Gen. 26:34–35):

B. "The swine out of the wood ravages it, that which moves in the fields feeds on it" (Ps. 80:14).

C. R. Phineas and R. Hilqiah in the name of R. Simon: "Among all of the prophets, only two of them spelled out in public [the true character of Rome, represented by the swine], Asaf and Moses.

D. "Asaf: 'The swine out of the wood ravages it.'

E. "Moses: 'And the swine, because he parts the hoof' (Deut. 14:8).

F. "Why does Moses compare Rome to the swine? Just as the swine, when it crouches, puts forth its hoofs as if to say, 'I am clean,' so the wicked kingdom steals and grabs, while pretending to be setting up courts of justice.

G. "So Esau, for all forty years, hunted married women, ravished them, and when he reached the age of forty, he presented himself to his father, saying, 'Just as father got married at the age of forty, so I shall marry a wife at the age of forty.'

H. " 'When Esau was forty years old, he took to wife Judith, the daughter of Beeri, the Hittite, and Basemath the daughter of Elon the Hittite.' "

The exegesis of course once more identifies Esau with Rome. The roundabout route linking the fact at hand, Esau's taking a wife, passes through the territory of Roman duplicity. Whatever the government does, it claims to do in the general interest. But it really has no public interest at all. Esau for his part spent forty years pillaging women and then, at the age of forty, pretended, to his father, to be upright. That, at any rate, is the parallel clearly intended by this obviously unitary composition. The issue of the selection of the intersecting verse does not present an obvious solution to me; it seems to me only the identification of Rome with the swine accounts for the choice.

Identifying Rome as Esau was a fresh idea. In the Mishnah, two hundred years earlier, Rome appears as a place, not as a symbol. But in Genesis Rabbah Rome is symbolized by Esau. Why Esau in particular? Because Esau is sibling: relations, competitor, enemy, brother. In choosing Rome as the counterpart to Israel, sages simply opened Genesis and found there Israel, that is Jacob, and his brother, his enemy, Esau. So why not understand the obvious: Esau stands for Rome, Jacob for Israel, and their relationship represents then what Israel and Rome would work out even now, in the fourth century, the first century of Christian rule. So Esau rules now, but Jacob possesses the birthright. Esau/Rome is the last of the four great empires (Persia, Media, Greece, Rome). On the other side of Rome? Israel's age of glory. And why is Rome now brother? Because, after all, the Christians do claim a common patrimony in the Hebrew Scriptures and do claim to form part of Israel. That claim was not ignored, it was answered: yes, part of Israel, the rejected part. Jacob bears the blessing and transmits the blessing to humanity, Esau does not. Such a message bore meaning only in the present context.

Sages read Genesis as the history of the world with emphasis on Israel. So the lives portrayed, the domestic quarrels and petty conflicts with the neighbors, all serve to yield insight into what was to be. While many times up to this point we have come across that simple truth, we now turn to a detailed examination of how sages spelled out the historical law at hand. For, as we have seen, just as the deeds of the patriarchs taught lessons on how the children were to act, so the lives of the patriarchs signaled the history of Israel. These propositions really laid down the same judgment, one for the individual and the family, the other for the community and the nation. Every detail of the narrative therefore served to prefigure what was to be, and Israel found itself, time and again, in the revealed facts of the history of the creation of the world, the decline of humanity down to the time of Noah, and, finally, its ascent to Abraham, Isaac, and Israel. The following picture of the way in which facts of Scripture settled claims of living enemies makes the matter clear. To sages Genesis reported what really happened. But, as we see throughout, Genesis also spelled out the meanings and truth of what happened.

LXI:VII.

1. A. "But to the sons of his concubines, Abraham gave gifts, and while he was still living, he sent them away from his son Isaac, eastward to the east country" (Gen. 25:6).

    B. In the time of Alexander of Macedonia the sons of Ishmael came to dispute with Israel about the birthright, and with them came two wicked families, the Canaanites and the Egyptians.

C. They said, "Who will go and engage in a disputation with them?"

D. Gebiah b. Qosem [the enchanter] said, "I shall go and engage in a disputation with them?"

E. They said to him, "Be careful not to let the Land of Israel fall into their possession."

F. He said to them, "I shall go and engage in a disputation with them. If I win over them, well and good. And if not, you may say, 'Who is this hunchback to represent us.?' "

G. He went and engaged in a disputation with them. Said to them Alexander of Macedonia, "Who lays claim against whom?"

H. The Ishmaelites said, "We lay claim, and we bring our evidence from their own Torah: 'But he shall acknowledge the firstborn, the son of the hated' (Deut. 21:17). Now Ishmael was the firstborn. [We therefore claim the land as heirs of the fistborn of Abraham.]"

I. Said to him Gebiah b. Qosem, "My royal lord, does a man not do whatever he likes with his sons?"

J. He said to him, "Indeed so."

K. "And lo, it is written, 'Abraham gave all that he had to Isaac' (Gen. 25:2)."

L. [Alexander asked,] "Then where is the deed of gift to the other sons?"

M. He said to him, "But to the sons of his concubines, Abraham gave gifts, [and while he was still living, he sent them away from his son Isaac, eastward to the east country]' (Gen. 25:6)."

N. [The Ishmaelites had no claim on the land.] They abandoned the field in shame.

O. The Canaanites said, "We lay claim, and we bring our evidence from their own Torah. Throughout their Torah it is written, 'the land of Canaan.' So let them give us back our land."

P. Said to him Gebiah b. Qosem, "My royal lord, does a man not do whatever he likes with his slave?"

Q. He said to him, "Indeed so."

R. He said to him, "And lo, it is written, 'A slave of slaves shall Canaan be to his brothers' (Gen. 9:25). So they are really our slaves."

S. [The Canaanites had no claim to the land and in fact should be serving Israel.] They abandoned the field in shame.

T. The Egyptians said, "We lay claim, and we bring our evidence from their own Torah. Six hundred thousand of them left us, taking away our silver and gold utensils: 'They despoiled the Egytians' (Ex. 12:36). Let them give them back to us."

U. Gebiah b. Qosem said, "My royal lord, six hundred thousand men worked for them for two hundred and ten years, some as silversmiths and some as goldsmiths. Let them pay us our salary at the rate of a *denar* a day."

V. The mathematicians went and added up what was owing, and they had not reached the sum covering a century before the Egyptians had to forfeit what they had claimed. They abandoned the field in shame.

W. [Alexander] wanted to go up to Jerusalem. The Samaritans said to him, "Be careful. They will not permit you to enter their most holy sanctuary."

X. When Gebiah b. Qosem found out about this, he went and made for himself two felt shoes, with two precious stones worth twenty thousand pieces of silver set in them. When he got to the mountain of the house [of the Temple], he said to him, "My royal lord, take off your shoes and put on these two felt slippers, for the floor is slippery, and you should not slip and fall."

Y. When they came to the most holy sanctuary, he said to him, "Up to this point, we have the right to enter. From this point onward, we do not have the right to enter."

Z. He said to him, "When we get out of here, I'm going to even out your hump."

AA. He said to him, "You will be called a great surgeon and get a big fee."

2. A. "[But to the sons of his concubines, Abraham gave gifts, and while he was still living,] he sent them away from his son Isaac, eastward to the east country]" (Gen. 25:6).

B. He said to them, "Go as far to the east as you can, so as not to be burned by the flaming coal of Isaac."

C. But because Esau came to make war with Jacob, he took his appropriate share on his account: "Is this your joyous city, whose feet in antiquity, in ancient days, carried her afar off to sojourn? Who has devised this against Tyre, the crowning city?" (Is. 23:7).

D. Said R. Eleazar, "Whenever the name of Tyre is written in Scripture, if it is written out [with all of the letters], then it refers to the province of Tyre. Where it is written without all of its letters [and so appears identical to the word for enemy], the reference of Scripture is to Rome. [So the sense of the verse is that Rome will receive its appropriate reward.]"

E. [As to the sense of the word for] "the crowning city,"

F. R. Abba bar Kahana said, "It means that they surrounded the city like a crown."

G. R. Yannai, son of R. Simeon b. R. Yannai, said, "They surrounded it with a fence of thorns."

No. 1 is deposited here because of the case of the Ishmaelites, Abraham's children, deprived as they were of their inheritance. That issue pressed on the consciousness of the exegete-composition. No. 2 carries forward the eschatological reading of the incident. Israel's later history is prefigured in the gift to Isaac and the rejection of the other sons. The self-evidence that Esau's reward will be recompense for his evil indicates that the passage draws upon sarcasm to make its point. Sages essentially looked in the facts of history for the laws of history. We may compare them to social scientists or social philosophers, trying to turn anecdotes into insight and to demonstrate how we may know the difference between impressions and truths. Genesis provided facts. Careful sifting of those facts will yield the laws that dictated why things happened one way, rather than some other. The language, as much as the substance, of the narrative provided facts demanding careful study. We understand why sages thought so if we call to mind their basic understanding of the Torah. To them (as to many today, myself included) the Torah came from God and in every detail contained revelation of God's truth. Accordingly, just as we study nature and derive facts demanding explanation and yielding law, so we study Scripture and find facts susceptible of explanation and yielding truth, a matter to which we shall return when we come to Leviticus Rabbah.

Let us begin with an exemplary case of how sages discovered social laws of history in the facts of Scripture. What Abraham did corresponds to what Balaam did, and the same law of social history derives proof from each of the two contrasting figures.

LV:VIII.

1. A. "And Abraham rose early in the morning, [saddled his ass, and took two of his young men with him, and his son Isaac, and he cut the wood for the burnt offering and arose and went to the place which God had told him]" (Gen. 22:3):

   B. Said. R. Simeon b. Yohai, "Love disrupts the natural order of things, and hatred disrupts the natural order of things.

   C. "Love disrupts the natural order of things we learn from the case of Abraham: '. . . he saddled his ass.' But did he not have any number of servants? But that proves love disrupts the natural order of things.

   D. "Hatred disrupts the natural order of things we learn from the case of Balaam: 'And Balaam rose up early in the morning and saddled his ass' (Num. 22:21). But did he not have any number of servants? But that proves hatred disrupts the natural order of things.

   E. "Love disrupts the natural order of things we learn from the case of Joseph: 'And Joseph made his chariot ready' (Gen. 46:29). But did he not have any number of servants? But that proves love disrupts the natural order of things.

   F. 'Hatred disrupts the natural order of things we learn from the case of Pharoah: 'And he made his chariot ready' (Ex. 14:6). But did he not have any number of servants? But that proves hatred disrupts the natural order of things."

2. A. Said R. Simeon b. Yohai, "Let one act of saddling an ass come and counteract another act of saddling the ass. May the act of saddling the ass done by our father Abraham, so as to go and carry out the will of him who spoke and brought the world into being counteract the act of saddling that was carried out by Balaam when he went to curse Israel.

B. "Let one act of preparing counteract another act of preparing. Let Joseph's act of preparing his chariot so as to meet his father serve to counteract Phararoh's act of preparing to go and pursue Israel."

C. R. Ishmael taught on Tannaite authority, "Let the sword held in the hand serve to counteract the sword held in the hand.

D. "Let the sword held in the hand of Abraham, as it is said, 'Then Abraham put forth his hand and took the knife to slay his son' (Gen. 22:10) serve to counteract the sword taken by Pharaoh in hand: 'I will draw my sword, my hand shall destroy them' (Ex. 15:9)."

We see that the narrative is carefully culled for probative facts, yielding laws. One fact is that there are laws of history. The other is that laws may be set aside, by either love or hatred. Yet another law of history applies in particular to Israel, as distinct from the foregoing, deriving from the life of both Israel and the nations, Abraham and Balaam. Here is an example of how the language of Scripture yields laws of history.

XLII:III.

1. A. R. Tanhuma and R. Hiyya the Elder state the following matter, as does R. Berekhiah in the name of R. Eleazar [the Modite], "The following exegetical principle came up in our possession from the exile.

B. "Any passage in which the words, "And it came to pass' appear is a passage that relates misfortune."

C. Said R. Samuel bar Nahman, "There are five such passages marked by the words, 'and it came to pass,' that bear the present meaning.

D. " 'And it came to pass in the days of Amraphel, king of Shinar . . . these kings made war with Bera, king of Sodom' (Gen. 14:1).

E. "The matter [of Abram's defending the local rulers] may be compared to the ally of a king who came to live in a province. On his account the king felt obligated to protect that entire province. Barbarians came and attacked him. Now when the barbarians came and attacked him, the people said, 'Woe, the king is not going to want to protect the province the way he used to [since it has caused him trouble]. That is in line with the following verse of Scripture, 'And they turned back and came to En Mishpat [source of justice], that is Kadesh [holy] [and subdued all the country of the Amalekites]' (Gen. 14:7)." [This concludes the first of the five illustrations.] [Lev. R. XI:VII.2E adds: So too, Abraham was the ally of the King, the Holy One, blessed be he, and in his regard it is written, 'And in you shall all the families of the earth be blessed' (Gen. 12:4). So it was on his account that the Holy One, blessed be he, felt obligated to protect the entire world.]

F. Said R. Aha, "They sought only to attack the orb of the eye of the world. The eye that had sought to exercise the attribute of justice in the world did they seek to blind: 'That is Kadesh' (Gen. 14:7)."

G. Said R. Aha, "It is written, 'that is . . . ,' meaning, that is the particular one who has sanctified the name of the Holy One, blessed be he, by going down into the fiery furnace."

H. [Reverting to the discourse suspended at the end of E:] When the barbarians came and attacked, they began to cry, "Woe, woe!"

I. "And it came to pass in the days of Amraphel" (Gen. 14:1).

2. A. "And it came to pass in the days of Ahaz" (Is. 7:1):

B. "The Aramaeans on the east and the Philistines on the west devour Israel with open mouth" (Is. 9:12):

C. The matter [of Israel's position] may be compared to the case of a king who handed over his son to a tutor, who hated the son. The tutor thought, "If I kill him now, I shall turn out to be liable to the death penalty before the king. So what I'll do is take away his wet-nurse, and he will die on his own."

D. So thought Ahaz, "If there are no kids, there will be no he-goats. If there are no he-goats, there will be no flock. If there is no flock, there will be no Shepherd, if there is no Shepherd, there will be no world."

E. So did Ahaz, plan, "If there are no children, there will be no adults. If there are no adults, there will be no disciples. If there are no disciples, there will be no sages. If there are no sages, there will be no prophets. If there are no prophets, the Holy One, blessed be he, will not allow his presence to come to rest in the world." [Lev. R.: . . . Torah. If there is no Torah, there will be no synagogues and schools. If there are no synagogues and schools, then the Holy One, blessed be he, will not allow his presence to come to rest in the world.]

F. That is in line with the following verse of Scripture: "Bind up the testimony, seal the Torah among my disciples" (Is. 8:16).

G. R. Huna in the name of R. Eleazar: "Why was he called Ahaz? Because he seized (*ahaz*) synagogues and schools."

H. R. Jacob in the name of R. Aha: "Isaiah said, 'I will wait for the Lord, who is hiding his face from the house of Jacob, and I will hope in him' (Is. 8:17). You have no more trying hour than that moment concerning which it is written, 'And I shall surely hide my face on that day' (Deut. 31:18).

I. "From that hour: 'I will hope in him' (Is. 8:17). For he has said, 'For it will not be forgotten from the mouth of his seed' (Deut. 31:21).

J. "What good did hoping do for Isaiah?

K. " 'Behold I and the children whom the Lord has given me are signs and portents in Israel from the Lord of host who dwells on Mount Zion' (Is. 8:18). Now were they his children? Were they not his disciples? But this teaches that they were precious to him so that he regarded them as his children."

L. [Reverting to G:] Now since everyone saw that Ahaz had seized the synagogues and schools, they began to cry out, "Woe, woe!' Thus: "And it came to pass [marking the woe] in the days of Ahaz" (Is. 7:1).

3. A. "And it came to pass in the days of Jehoiakim, son of Josiah" (Jer. 1:3).

B. "I look on the earth and lo, it was waste and void" (Jer. 4:23).

C. The matter may be compared to the case of royal edicts which came into a province. What did the people do? They took the document, tore it up, and burned the bits in fire. That is in line with the following verse of Scripture: "And it came to pass, as Jehudi read three or four columns, that is, three or four verses, the king would cut them off with a penknife and throw them into the fire in the brazier until the entire scroll was consumed in the fire that was in the brazier" (Jer. 36:23).

D. When the people saw all this, they began to cry out, "Woe, woe."

E. "And it came to pass in the days of Jehoiakim" (Jer. 1:3).

4. A. **"And it came to pass in the days in which the judges ruled" (Ruth 1:1). "There was a famine in the land" (Ruth 1:1).**

B. The matter may be compared to a province which owed taxes in arrears to the king, so the king sent a revenuer to collect. What did the inhabitants of the province do? They went and hung him, hit him, and robbed him. They said, "Woe is us, when the kings get word of these thing. What the king's representative wanted to do to us, we have done to him."

C. So too, woe to the generation that has judged its judges.

D. "And it came to pass in the days in which the judges themselves were judged" (Ruth 1:1).

5. A. "And it came to pass in the days of Ahasuerus" (Est. 1:1): "Haman undertook to destroy, to slay, and to annihilate all the Jews, young and old, women and children, in one day" (Est. 3:13).

B. The matter may be compared to the case of a king who had a vineyard, and three of his enemies attacked it. One of them began to clip off the small branches, the next began to take the pendants off the grapeclusters, and the last of them began to uproot the vines altogether.

C. Pharaoh [began by clipping off the small branches]: "Every son that is born will you throw into the river" (Ex. 1:22).

D. Nebuchadnezzar [began to clip off the pendants of the grapeclusters,] deporting the people: "And he carried away captive the craftsmen and smiths, a thousand" (2 Kgs. 24:16).

E. R. Berekhiah in the name of R. Judah and rabbis:

F. R. Berekhiah in the name of R. Judah: "There were a thousand craftsmen and a thousand smiths."

G. Rabbis say, "This group and that group all together added up to a thousand."

H. The wicked Haman began to uproot the vines altogether. He uprooted Israel from its roots: "To destroy, to slay, and to annihilate all the Jews" (Esther 3:13).

I.   When everybody saw that [Ahasuerus had sold and Haman had bought the Jews], they began to cry, "Woe, woe."

J.   "And it came to pass in the days of Ahasuerus" (Esther 1:1).

6.   A.   R. Simeon b. Abba in the name of R. Yohanan: "Any context in which the words, 'And it came to pass . . .,' appear serves to signify either misfortune or good fortune. If it is a case of misfortune, it is misfortune without parallel. If it is a case of good fortune, it is good fortune without parallel."

B.   R. Samuel b. Nahman came and introduced this distinction: "Any context in which the words, 'And it came to pass . . .' occur signifies misfortune, and any context in which the words, 'And it shall come to pass . . .' are used signifies good fortune."

C.   They objected [to this claim], "And God said, 'Let there be light,' and it came to pass that there was light" (Gen. 1:3).

D.   He said to them, "This too does not represent good fortune, for in the end the world did not enjoy the merit of actually making use of that light."

E.   R. Judah [b. R. Simeon] said, "With the light that the Holy One, blessed be he, created on the first day of creation, a person could look and see from one side of the world to the other. When the Holy One, blessed be he, foresaw that there would be wicked people, he hid it away for the [exclusive use of the] righteous. 'But the path of the righteous is as the light of the dawn that shines more and more to the perfect day' (Prov. 4:18)."

F.   They further objected, "And it came to pass that there was evening and morning, one day" (Gen. 1:5).

G.   He said to them, "This too does not signify good fortune. For whatever God created on the first day of creation is destined to be wiped out. That is in line with the following verse of Scripture: 'For the heaven shall vanish away like smoke, and the earth shall wax old like a garment' (Is. 51:6)."

H.   They further objected, "And it came to pass that there was evening and it came to pass that there was morning, a second day . . ., a third day . . ., a fourth day . . ., a fifth day . . ., a sixth day . . .," (Gen. 1:8, 13, 19, 23, 31).

I.   He said to them, "This too does not signify good fortune. For everything which God created on the six days of creation was incomplete and would require further processing. Wheat has to be milled, mustard to be sweetened, [lupine to impart sweetness]."

J. They further objected, "And it came to pass that the Lord was with Joseph, and Joseph was a prosperous man" (Gen. 39:2).

K. He said to them, "This too does not signify good fortune, for on this account that she-bear [Potiphar's wife] came his way."

L. They further objected, "And it came to pass on the eighth day that Moses called Aaron and his sons for consecration in the priesthood" (Lev. 9:1).

M. He said to them, "This too does not signify good fortune, for on that same day Nadab and Abihu died."

N. They further objected, "And it came to pass on the day on which Moses made an end of setting up the tabernacle" (Num. 7:1).

O. He said to them, "This too does not signify good fortune. For on the day on which the Temple was built, the tabernacle was hidden away."

P. They further objected, "And it came to pass that the Lord was with Joshua and his fame was in all the land" (Joshua 6:27).

Q. He said to them, "This too does not signify good fortune, for he still had to tear his garments [on account of the defeat at Ai, Joshua 7:6]."

R. They further objected, "And it came to pass that the king dwelt in his palace, and the Lord gave him rest round about" (2 Sam. 7:1).

S. He said to them, "This too does not signify good fortune. On that very day Nathan the prophet came to him and said, "You will not build the house' (1 Kgs. 8:19)."

T. They said to him, "We have given our objections, now you give your proofs about good fortune."

U. He said to them, " 'And it shall come to pass in that day that living waters shall go out of Jerusalem' (Zech. 14:8). 'And it shall come to pass in that day that a great horn shall be blown' (Is. 27:13). 'And it shall come to pass in that day that a man shall rear a youngling' (Is. 7:21). 'And it shall come to pass in that day that the Lord will set his hand again a second time to recover the remnant of his people' (Is. 11:11). 'And it shall come to pass in that day that the mountains shall drop down sweet wine' (Joel 4:18). [All of these represent good fortune without parallel.]"

V. They said to him, "And it shall come to pass on the day on which Jerusalem is taken . . .' (Jer. 38:28).'"

W. He said to them, "This too does not signify misfortune but good fortune [without parallel], for on that day the Israelites received a full pardon for all their sins.

X. "That is in line with what R. Samuel b. Nahman said, "The Israelites received a full pardon for all their sins on the day on which the Temple was destroyed. That is in line with the following verse of Scripture, 'The punishment of your iniquity is completed, daughter of Zion, and he will no more take you away into exile (Lam. 4:22).' "

The fundamental syllogism, not stated at all, is that Israel's history follows rules that can be learned in Scripture. Nothing is random, all things are connected, and fundamental laws of history dictate the sense and meaning of what happens. These laws are stated in the very language of Scripture. The long discussion obviously is constructed independent of any of the verses used as prooftexts. It serves equally well in any number of contexts, not only here but also at Lev. R. XI:VII, as indicated. The differences in the versions of Gen. R. and Lev. R. are minor and signify nothing of consequence. The sole point of intersection is at No. 1. When we turn to the biography of Abraham, we expect to find the history of Israel, detail by detail, and so we do.

XLII:IV.

1. A. "And it came to pass in the days of Amraphael" (Gen. 14:1):

   B. He had three names, Kush, Nimrod, and Amraphael.

   C. Kush, because he was in fact a Kushite.

   D. Nimrod, because he made the world rebel (MRD).

   E. Amraphael, for he [Freedman:] made a declaration (*amar imrah*), "I will cast down."

   F. [Freedman translates the words that follow in this way:] [Another interpretation is] that he made sport of the world, also that he made sport of Abraham, again, that he ordered Abraham to be thrown into the furnace. [Freedman, p. 346, n. 3: "The translation is conjectural. Neither the text nor its meaning is certain."]

2. A. "Arioch, king of Ellasar" (Gen. 14:1):

   B. Said R. Yose of Milhayya, "How come hazel nuts are called *elsarin?* Because they come from Ellasar."

3. A. "Chedorlaomer king of Elam and Tidal king of Goiim" (Gen. 14:1):

   B. Said R. Levi, "There is a place there which in Latin bears that name. The people took a man and made him king over them."

   C. Said R. Yohanan, " 'Tidal' was his name."

4. A. Another matter: "And it came to pass in the days of Amraphael, king of Shinar" (Gen. 14:1) refers to Babylonia.

   B. "Arioch, king of Ellasar" (Gen. 14:1) refers to Greece.

   C. "Chedorlaomer, king of Elam" (Gen. 14:1) refers to Media.

   D. "And Tidal, king of Goiim [nations]" (Gen. 14:1) refers to the wicked government [Rome], which conscripts troops from all the nations of the world.

   E. Said R. Eleazar bar Abina, "If you see that the nations contend with one another, look for the footsteps of the King-Messiah. You may know that that is the case, for lo, in the time of Abraham, because the kings struggled with one another, a position of greatness came to Abraham."

Obviously, No. 4 presents the most important reading of Gen. 14:1, since it links the events of the life of Abraham to the history of Israel and even ties the whole to the messianic expectation. I suppose that any list of four kings will provoke inquiry into the relationship of the entries of that list to the four kingdoms among which history, in Israel's experience, is divided. The process of history flows in both directions. Just as what Abraham did prefigured the future history of Israel, so what the Israelites later on were to do imposed limitations on Abraham.

Time and again events in the lives of the patriarchs prefigure the four monarchies, among which, of course, the fourth, last, and most intolerable was Rome. Here is another such exercise in the recurrent proof of a single proposition.

XLIV:XVII.

4. A. "[And it came to pass, as the sun was going down,] lo, a deep sleep fell on Abram, and lo, a dread and great darkness fell upon him" (Gen. 15:12):

   B. "Lo, a dread" refers to Babylonia, as it is written, "Then was Nebuchadnezzar filled with fury" (Gen. 3:19).

   C. "And darkness" refers to Media, which darkened the eyes of Israel by making it necessary for the Israelites to fast and conduct public mourning.

   D. "Great" refers to Greece.

   E. R. Simon said, "The kingdom of Greece set up one hundred and twenty commanders, one hundred and twenty hyparchs, and one hundred and twenty generals."

   F. Rabbis said, "It was sixty of each, as it is written, 'Serpents, fiery serpents, and scorpions' (Gen. 8:15). Just as the scorpion produces sixty eggs at a time, so the kingdom of Greece set up sixty at a time."

   G. "Fell upon him" refers to Edom, as it is written, "The earth quakes at the noise of their fall" (Jer. 49:21).

   H. Some reverse matters:

   I. "Fell upon him" refers to Babylonia, since it is written, "Fallen, fallen is Babylonia" (Is. 21:9).

   J. "Great" refers to Media, in line with this verse: "King Ahasuerus did make great" (Est. 3:1).

   K. "And darkness" refers to Greece, which darkened the eyes of Israel by its harsh decrees.

   L. "Lo, a dread" refers to Edom, as it is written, "After this I saw . . . a fourth beast, dreadful and terrible" (Dan. 7:7).

No. 4 successfully links the cited passage once more to the history of Israel. Israel's history falls under God's dominion. Whatever will happen carries out God's plan. The fourth kingdom is part of that plan, which we can discover by carefully studying Abraham's life and God's word to him.

XLIV:XVIII.

1. A. "Then the Lord said to Abram, "Know of a surety [that your descendants will be sojourners in a land that is not theirs, and they will be slaves there, and they will be oppressed for four hundred years; but I will bring judgment on the nation which they serve, and afterward they shall come out with great possessions']" (Gen. 15:13–14).

    B. "Know" that I shall scatter them.

    C. "Of a certainty" that I shall bring them back together again.

    D. "Know" that I shall put them out as a pledge [in expiation of their sins].

    E. "Of a certainty" that I shall redeem them.

    F. "Know" that I shall make them slaves.

    G. "Of a certainty" that I shall free them.

2. A. "That your descendants will be sojourners in a land that is not theirs and they will be slaves there, and they will be oppressed for four hundred years."

    B. It is four hundred years from the point at which you will produce a descendant. [The Israelites will not serve as slaves for four hundred years, but that figure refers to the passage of time from Isaac's birth.]

    C. Said R. Yudan, "The condition of being outsiders, the servitude, the oppression in a land that was not theirs all together would last for four hundred years, that was the requisite term."

No. 1 parses the cited verse and joins within its simple formula the entire history of Israel, punishment and forgiveness alike. No. 2 parses the verse to follow, trying to bring it into line with the chronology of Israel's later history. Ishmael, standing now for Christian Rome, claims God's blessing, but Isaac gets it, as Jacob will take it from Esau.

XLVII:V.

1. A. "God said, 'No, but Sarah your wife [shall bear you a son, and you shall call his name Isaac. I will establish my covenant with him as an everlasting covenant for his descendants after him.] As for Ishmael, I have heard you. Behold, I will bless him and make him fruitful and multiply him exceedingly. He shall be the father of twelve princes, and I will make him a great nation]' " (Gen. 17:19–20).

B. R. Yohanan in the name of R. Joshua b. Hananiah, "In this case the son of the servant woman might learn from what was said concerning the son of the mistress of the household:

C. " 'Behold, I will bless him' refers to Isaac.

D. " 'And make him fruitful' refers to Isaac.

E. " 'And multiply him exceedingly' refers to Isaac.

F. " 'As for Ishmael, I have informed you' through the angel. [The point is, Freedman, p. 401, n. 4, explains, Ishmael could be sure that his blessing too would be fulfilled.]"

G. R. Abba bar Kahana in the name of R. Birai: "Here the son of the mistress of the household might learn from the son of the handmaiden:

H. " 'Behold, I will bless him' refers to Ishmael.

I. " 'And make him fruitful' refers to Ishmael.

J. " 'And multiply him exceedingly' refers to Ishmael.

K. "And by an argument *a fortiori:* 'But I will establish my covenant with Isaac' (Gen. 17:21)."

2. A. Said R. Isaac, "It is written, 'All these are the twelve tribes of Israel' (Gen. 49:28). These were the descendants of the mistress [Sarah].

B. "But did Ishmael not establish twelve?

C. "The reference to those twelve is to princes, in line with the following verse: 'As princes and wind' (Prov. 25:14). [But the word for *prince* also stands for the word *vapor,* and hence the glory of the sons of Ishmael would be transient (Freedman, p. 402, n. 2).]

D. "But as to these tribes [descended from Isaac], they are in line with this verse: 'Sworn are the tribes of the word, selah' (Hab. 3:9). [Freedman, p. 402, n. 3: The word for *tribe* and for *staff* or *rod,* in the cited verse, are synonyms, both meaning tribes, both meaning rods, and so these tribes would endure like rods that are planted.]"

Nos. 1 and 2 take up the problem of the rather fulsome blessing assigned to Ishmael. One authority reads the blessing to refer to Isaac, the other maintains that the blessing refers indeed to Ishmael, and Isaac will gain that much more. No. 2 goes over the same issue, now with the insistence that the glory of Ishmael will pass like vapor, while the tribes of Isaac will endure as well-planted rods. The polemic against Edom-Rome, with its transient glory, is familiar. We should not limit sages' powers of interpretation to the exposition of lines of structure of whole stories. Details, as much as the main point, yielded laws of history. Here is how sages take up the detail of Rebecca's provision of a bit of water, showing what that act had to do with the history of Israel later on.

XLVIII:X.

2. A. "Let a little water be brought" (Gen. 18:4):

   B. Said to him the Holy One, blessed be he, "You have said, 'Let a little water be brought' (Gen. 18:4). By your life, I shall pay your descendants back for this: 'Then sang Israel this song, "Spring up O well, sing you to it" ' (Num. 21:7)."

   C. That recompense took place in the wilderness. Where do we find that it took place in the Land of Israel as well?

   D. "A land of brooks of water" (Deut. 8:7).

   E. And where do we find that it will take place in the age to come?

   F. "And it shall come to pass in that day that living waters shall go out of Jerusalem" (Zech. 14:8).

   G. ["And wash your feet" (Gen. 18:4)]: [Said to him the Holy One, blessed be he,] "You have said, 'And wash your feet.' By your life, I shall pay your descendants back for this: 'Then I washed you in water' (Ez. 16:9)."

   H. That recompense took place in the wilderness. Where do we find that it took place in the Land of Israel as well?

   I. "Wash you, make you clean" (Is. 1:16).

   J. And where do we find that it will take place in the age to come?

   K. "When the Lord will have washed away the filth of the daughters of Zion" (Is. 4:4).

   L. [Said to him the Holy One, blessed be he,] "You have said, 'And rest yourselves under the tree' (Gen. 18:4). By your life, I shall pay your descendants back for this: 'He spread a cloud for a screen' (Ps. 105:39)."

   M. That recompense took place in the wilderness. Where do we find that it took place in the Land of Israel as well?

   N. "You shall dwell in booths for seven days" (Lev. 23:42).

O. And where do we find that it will take place in the age to come?

P. "And there shall be a pavilion for a shadow in the daytime from the heat" (Is. 4:6).

Q. [Said to him the Holy One, blessed be he,] "You have said, 'While I fetch a morsel of bread that you may refresh yourself' (Gen. 18:5). By your life, I shall pay your descendants back for this: 'Behold I will cause to rain bread from heaven for you' (Ex. 16:45)."

R. That recompense took place in the wilderness. Where do we find that it took place in the Land of Israel as well?

S. "A land of wheat and barley" (Deut. 8:8).

T. And where do we find that it will take place in the age to come?

U. "He will be as a rich cornfield in the land" (Ps. 82:16).

V. [Said to him the Holy One, blessed be he,] "You ran after the herd ['And Abraham ran to the herd' (Gen. 18:7)]. By your life, I shall pay your descendants back for this: 'And there went forth a wind from the Lord and brought across quails from the sea' (Num. 11:27)."

W. That recompense took place in the wilderness. Where do we find that it took place in the Land of Israel as well?

X. "Now the children of Reuben and the children of Gad had a very great multitude of cattle" (Num. 32:1).

Y. And where do we find that it will take place in the age to come?

Z. "And it will come to pass in that day that a man shall rear a young cow and two sheep" (Is. 7:21).

AA. [Said to him the Holy One, blessed be he,] "You stood by them: 'And he stood by them under the tree while they ate' (Gen. 18:8). By your life, I shall pay your descendants back for this: 'And the Lord went before them' (Ex. 13:21)."

BB. That recompense took place in the wilderness. Where do we find that it took place in the Land of Israel as well?

CC. "God stands in the congregation of God" (Ps. 82:1).

DD. And where do we find that it will take place in the age to come?

EE. "The breaker is gone up before them . . . and the Lord at the head of them" (Mic. 2:13).

No. 2 presents a sizable and beautifully disciplined construction, making one point again and again. Everything that Abraham did brought a reward to his descendants. The enormous emphasis on the way in which Abraham's deeds prefigured the history of Israel, both in the wilderness, and in the Land, and, finally, in the age to come, provokes us to wonder who held that there were children of Abraham beside Israel. The answer then is clear. We note that there are five statements of the same proposition, each drawing upon a clause in the base verse. The extended statement, moreover, serves as a sustained introduction to the treatment of the individual clauses that now follow, item by item. Obviously, it is the merit of the ancestors that connects the living Israel to the lives of the patriarchs and matriarchs of old.

XLVIII:XII.

3. A. R. Jonah and R. Levi in the name of R. Hama b. R. Hanina: "The wilderness of Sin [Ex. 16:1ff.] and the wilderness of Alush [Num. 33:13] are the same place.

    B. "On account of what merit did the Israelites merit having manna given to them? It was because of the statement, 'knead it and make cakes.' [The word for knead is *lushi,* hence because of the kneading of the dough by Sarah, the later Israelites had the merit of receiving mana in the wilderness of Alush which is the same as the wilderness of Sin, where, in the biblical account, the mana came down, so Ex. 16:1ff.]"

The important contribution is at No. 3, at which the merit of Sarah's action stands for the later Israelites. The point-for-point emphasis on that theme presents no surprises. The reciprocity of the process of interpreting Israel's history in light of the founders' lives and the founders' lives through the later history of Israel infuses the explanation of the debate over Sodom. Never far from sages' minds is the entire sweep and scope of Israel's long history.

The later events in the history of Israel are drawn together to make the point that Israel's history takes place in eternity. Considerations of what comes first and what happens later—that is, priority and order—do not apply. That notion opens many passages to deep and nuanced interpretation, as in what follows.

LIII:V.

1. A. "Who has kept with your servant, David my father" (1 Kgs. 8:24):

   B. This refers to Abraham [even though it speaks of David].

   C. "That which you did promise him" (1 Kgs. 8:24). "At the set time I will return to you" (Gen. 18:14).

   D. "Yes, you spoke with your mouth and have fulfilled it with your hand as it is this day" (1 Kgs. 8:24).

   E. "And the Lord remembered Sarah" (Gen. 21:1).

2. A. "Who makes the barren woman dwell in her house" (Ps. 113:9).

   B. That verse refers to Sarah: "And Sarai was barren" (Gen. 11:30).

   C. "As a joyful mother of children" (Ps. 113:9).

   D. "Sarah has given children suck" (Gen. 21:7).

3. A. "And the Lord remembered Sarah as he had said" (Gen. 21:1):

   B. R. Judah said, " 'And the Lord remembered Sarah as he had said' (Gen. 21:1) refers to what he had stated to her by an act of saying, while 'And he did to Sarah as he had spoken' (Gen. 21:1) alludes to statements that he made to her with an act of speaking."

   C. R. Nehemiah said, " 'And the Lord remembered Sarah as he had said' (Gen. 21:1) refers to what he had stated to her through an angel, while 'And he did to Sarah as he had spoken' (Gen. 21:1) alludes to statements that he made to her himself."

4. A. R. Judah says, "And the Lord remembered Sarah' (Gen. 21:1) by giving her a son, 'and the Lord did to Sarah as he had promised' (Gen. 21:1) by giving her the blessing of milk."

   B. Said to him R. Nehemiah, "And had she already been informed about the matter of milk? But this teaches that the Holy One, blessed be he, restored her youth to her."

5. A. R. Abbahu [in the name of R. Yose b. R. Hanina]: "I shall place fear of her over all the nations of the world, so that they will not abuse her by calling her barren."

   B. R. Yudan [in the name of R. Simeon b. Laqish]: "She had no ovary, so the Holy One, blessed be he, formed an ovary for her."

6. A. "The Lord remembered Sarah" (Gen. 21:1):

   B. Said R. Aha, "The Holy One, blessed be he, takes care of [and remembers' bailments. Amalek entrusted to the Holy One bundles of thorns, so he returned him bundles of thorns: 'I remember what Amalek did to Israel' (1 Sam. 15:2).

C. "Sarah entrusted to the Holy One, blessed be he, the religious duties and good deeds that she had performed, and he returned to her the reward of doing religious duties and good deeds: 'The Lord remembered Sarah' (Gen. 21:1)."

Nos. 1 and 2 interweavings of verses, making points in an elegant way. No. 3 then reads the base verse in terms of its broader meaning. Judah wants to distinguish things God has said from those that he has spoken, and Nehemiah finds his own distinction for the same terms. What follows, however, has no place here. It has been revised from its original appearance, XLVII:II, at which point it made sense. No. 5 makes that certain, since it is completely irrelevant to the present context. We therefore see what the framers were willing to do to revise what they had received—and what they were not willing to do. Overall they simply inserted whole compositions, even though only small parts of those compositions had a place. But where they did make changes, as here, we can readily discern what was original and what has emerged as the revised version. No. 6 draws its own contrast, resting on the usages of the word *remember* of Amalek and Sarah. It produces the effect of linking the life of Sarah to the history of Israel. The lives of the patriarchs and matriarchs therefore prefigure the life of Israel, as we have seen throughout.

The reciprocal flow of merit found its counterpart in the two-way exchange of penalty as well. When Abraham erred, his descendants would pay the price.

LIV:IV.

1. A. "Abraham set seven ewe lambs of the flock apart" (Gen. 21:28):

   B. Said the Holy One, blessed be he, to him, "You have given him seven ewe lambs. By your life I shall postpone the joy of your descendants for seven generations.

C. "You have given him seven ewe lambs. By your life matching them his descendants [the Philstines] will kill seven righteous men among your descendants, and these are they: Hofni, Phineas, Samson, Saul, and his three sons.

D. "You have given him seven ewe lambs. By your life, matching them the seven sanctuaries of your descendants will be destroyed, namely, the tent of meeting, the altars of Gilgal, Nob, Gibeon, Shiloh, and the two eternal houses of the sanctuary.

E. "You have given him seven ewe lambs. [By your life, matching them] my ark will spend seven months in the fields of the Philistines."

2. A. R. Jeremiah in the name of R. Samuel bar R. Isaac: "If the mere chicken of one of them had been lost, would he not have gone looking for it by knocking on doors, so as to get it back, but my ark spent seven months in the field and you pay not mind to it. I on my own will take care of it: 'His right hand and his holy arm have wrought salvation for him' (Ps. 98:1).

B. "That is in line with this verse: 'And the kine took the straight way' (1 Sam. 6:12). They went straight forward, turning their faces to the ark and [since the word for *straight forward* contains the consonants for the word *song*] singing."

C. And what song did they sing?

D. R. Meir said, "The song of the sea. Here it is said, 'They went along . . . lowing as they went' (1 Sam. 6:12), and in that connection: 'For he is highly exalted' (Ex. 15:1). [The word for *lowing* and the word for *exalted* share the same consonants.]"

E. R. Yohanan said, " 'O sing to the Lord a new song' (Ps. 98:1)."

F. R. Eleazar said, " 'O Give thanks to the Lord, call upon his name' (Ps. 105:1)."

G. Rabbis said, " 'The Lord reigns, let the earth rejoice' (Ps. 97:1)."

H. R. Jeremiah said, "The three: 'O sing to the Lord a new song, sing to the Lord, all the earth' (Ps. 96:1). 'The Lord reigns, let the peoples tremble' (Ps. 99:1)."

I. Elijah taught, "[Freedman:] 'Rise, rise, you acacia, soar, soar, in your abundant glory, beautiful in your gold embroidery, extolled in the innermost shrine of the sanctuary, encased between the two cherubim.' "

J. Said R. Samuel bar R. Isaac, "How much did [Moses], son of Amram labor so as to teach the art of song to the Levites. But you beasts are able to sing such a song on your own, without instruction. All power to you!"

No. 1 reverts to the theme of indignation at Abraham's coming to an agreement with Abimelech, forcefully imposing the theme of the later history of Israel upon the story at hand. No. 2 is tacked on because of the concluding reference to No. 1. The binding of Isaac, critical in sages' reading of lessons taught by Abraham's deeds of their descendants, formed the centerpiece of their quest for the laws of history as well. At each point, in each detail, they discovered not only what we going to happen but also why.

The single most important paradigm for history therefore emerged from the deed at Moriah.

LVI:I.

1. A. "On the third day Abraham lifted up his eyes and saw the place afar off" (Gen. 22:4):

   B. "After two days he will revive us, on the third day he will raise us up, that we may live in his presence" (Hos. 16:2).

   C. On the third day of the tribes: "And Joseph said to them on the third day, 'This do and live' " (Gen. 42:18).

   D. On the third day of the giving of the Torah: "And it came to pass on the third day when it was morning" (Ex. 19:16).

   E. On the third day of the spies: "And hide yourselves there for three days" (Joshua 2:16).

   F. On the third day of Jonah: "And Jonah was in the belly of the fish three days and three nights" (Jon. 2:1).

   G. On the third day of the return from the Exile: "And we abode there three days" (Ezra 8:32).

   H. On the third day of the resurrection of the dead: "After two days he will revive us, on the third day he will raise us up, that we may live in his presence" (Hos. 16:2).

   I. On the third day of Esther: "Now it came to pass on the third day that Esther put on her royal apparel" (Est. 5:1).

J.   She put on the monarchy of the house of her fathers.

K.   On account of what sort of merit?

L.   Rabbis say, "On account of the third day of the giving of the Torah."

M.   R. Levi said, "It is on account of the merit of the third day of Abraham: 'On the third day Abraham lifted up his eyes and saw the place afar off' (Gen. 22:4)."

2.   A.   "Lifted up his eyes and saw the place afar off" (Gen. 22:4):

B.   What did he see? He saw a cloud attached to the mountain. He said, "It would appear that that is the place concerning which the Holy One, blessed be he, told me to offer up my son."

The third day marks the fulfillment of the promise, at the end of time of the resurrection of the dead, and, at appropriate moments, of Israel's redemption. The reference to the third day at Gen. 22:2 then invokes the entire panoply of Israel's history. The relevance of the composition emerges at the end. Prior to the concluding segment, the passage forms a kind of litany and falls into the category of a liturgy. Still, the recurrent hermeneutic that teaches that the stories of the patriarchs prefigure the history of Israel certainly makes its appearance.

LVI:II.

1.   A.   He said, "Isaac, my son, do you see what I see?"

B.   He said to him, "Yes."

C.   He said to the two lads, "Do you see what I see?"

D.   They said to him, "No."

E.   He said, "Since you do not see, 'Stay here with the ass' (Gen. 22:5), for you are like an ass."

F.   On the basis of this passage we learn that slaves are in the category of asses.

G.   Rabbis derive proof from the matter of the giving of the Torah: "Six days you shall labor and do all your work, you . . . your daughter, your man-servant, your maid-servant, your cattle" (Ex. 20:10).

2.   A.   Said R. Isaac, "Will this place [the Temple mount] ever be distant from its owner [God]? Never, for Scripture says, 'This is my resting place for ever; here I will dwell, for I have desired it' (Ps. 132:14).

B. "It will be when the one comes concerning whom it is written, 'Lowly and riding upon an ass' (Zech. 1:9)."

3. A. "I and the lad will go thus far [and worship and come again to you]" (Gen. 22:5):

B. Said R. Joshua b. Levi, "[He said,] 'We shall go and see what will be the end of "thus." ' " [Freedman, p. 492, n. 5: God had said, "Thus shall your seed be" (Gen. 15:5). So the sense is, "We will see how that can be fulfilled, now that I am to lose my son."]

4. A. "And we will worship [through an act of prostration] and come again to you" (Gen. 22:5):

B. He thereby told him that he would come back from Mount Moriah whole and in peace [for he said that *we* shall come back].

5. A. Said R. Isaac, "And all was on account of the merit attained by the act of prostration.

B. "Abraham returned in peace from Mount Moriah only on account of the merit owing to the act of prostration: '. . . and we will worship [through an act of prostration] and come [then, on that account] again to you' (Gen. 22:5).

C. "The Israelites were redeemed only on account of the merit owing to the act of prostration: And the people believed . . . then they bowed their heads and prostrated themselves' (Ex. 4:31).

D. "The Torah was given only on account of the merit owing to the act of prostration: 'And worship [prostrate themselves] you afar off' (Ex. 24:1).

E. "Hannah was remembered only on account of the merit owing to the act of prostration: 'And they worshiped before the Lord' (1 Sam. 1:19).

F. "The exiles will be brought back only on account of the merit owing to the act of prostration: 'And it shall come to pass in that day that a great horn shall be blown and they shall come that were lost . . . and that were dispersed . . . and they shall worship the Lord in the holy mountain at Jerusalem' (Is. 27:13).

G. "The Temple was built only on account of the merit owing to the act of prostration: 'Exalt you the Lord our God and worship at his holy hill' (Ps. 99:9).

H. "The dead will live only on account of the merit owing to the act of prostration: 'Come let us worship and bend the knee, let us kneel before the Lord our maker' (Ps. 95:6)."

No. 1 explains both how Abraham knew it was the place and also why he left the lads behind. No. 2 then takes up the language of "seeing the place from afar," and by a play on the words, asks whether this place will ever be made far from its owner, that is, God. The answer is that it will not. No. 3 draws a lesson from the use of *thus* in the cited verses. The sizable construction at No. 4 makes a simple point, to which our base verse provides its modest contribution. But its polemic is hardly simple. The entire history of Israel flows from its acts of worship ("prostration") and is unified by a single law. Every sort of advantage Israel has ever gained came about through worship. Hence what is besought, in the elegant survey, is the law of history. The Scripture then supplies those facts from which the governing law is derived.

LVI:IX.

1. A. "And Abraham lifted up his eyes and looked, and behold, behind him was a ram, [caught in a thicket by his horns. And Abraham went and took the ram and offered it up as a burnt offering instead of his son]" (Gen. 22:13):

   B. What is the meaning of the word for "behind"?

   C. Said R. Yudan, " 'Behind' in the sense of 'after,' that is, after all that happens, Israel nonetheless will be embroiled in transgressions and perplexed by sorrows. But in the end, they will be redeemed by the horns of a ram: 'And the Lord will blow the horn' (Zech. 9:14)."

   D. Said R. Judah bar Simon, " 'After' all generations Israel nonetheless will be embroiled in transgressions and perplexed by sorrows. But in the end, they will be redeemed by the horns of a ram: 'And the Lord God will blow the horn' (Zech. 9:14)."

   E. Said R. Hinena bar Isaac, "All through the days of the year Israelites are embroiled in transgressions and perplexed by sorrows. But on the New Year they take the ram's horn and sound it, so in the end, they will be redeemed by the horns of a ram: 'And the Lord God will blow the horn' (Zech. 9:14)."

   F. R. Abba bar R. Pappi, R. Joshua of Siknin in the name of R. Levi: "Since our father, Abraham, saw the ram get himself out of one thicket only to be trapped in another, the Holy One, blessed be he, said to him, 'So your descendants will be entangled in one kingdom after another, struggling from Babylonia to Media, from Media to Greece, from Greece to Edom. But in the end, they will be redeemed by the horns of a ram: 'And the Lord God will blow the horn . . . the Lord of Hosts will defend them' (Zech. 9:14–5)."

2. A. "And Abraham went and took the ram and offered it up as a burnt offering instead of his son]" (Gen. 22:13):

B. R. Yudan in the name of R. Benaiah: "He said before him, 'Lord of all ages, regard the blood of this ram as though it were the blood of Isaac, my son, its innards as though they were the innards of Isaac my son.' "

C. That [explanation of the word *instead*] accords with what we have learned in the Mishnah: "**Lo, this is instead of that, this is in exchange for that, this is in place of that"—lo, such is an act of exchanging [one beast for another in the sacrificial rite, and both beasts then are held to be sanctified] [M. Tem. 5:5].**

D. R. Phineas in the name of R. Benaiah: "He said before him, 'Lord of all ages, regard it as though I had offered up my son, Isaac, first, and afterward had offered up the ram in his place.' "

E. That [sense of the word *instead*] is in line with this verse: "And Jothan his son reigned in his stead" (2 Kgs. 15:7).

F. That accords with what we have learned in the Mishnah: **[If one says, "I vow a sacrifice] like the lamb," or "like the animals of the Temple stalls" [it is a valid vow] [M. Ned. 1:3].**

G. R. Yohanan said, "That is in the sense of 'like the lamb of the daily whole offering.' " [One who made such a statement has vowed to bring a lamb.]

H. R. Simeon b. Laqish said, " 'like the ram of Abraham, our father.' " [One who has made such a statement has vowed to bring a ram.]

I. There they say, " 'like the offspring of a sin-offering.' "

J. Bar Qappra taught on Tannaite authority, " 'like a lamb which has never given suck [thus, a ram].'"

The power of No. 1 is to link the life of the private person, affected by transgression, and the history of the nation, troubled by its wandering among the kingdoms. From the perspective of the Land of Israel, the issue is not Exile but the rule of foreigners. In both cases the power of the ram's horn to redeem the individual and the nation finds its origin in the binding of Isaac. The exegetical thrust, linking the lives of the patriarchs to the life of the nation, thus brings the narrative back to the paradigm of individual being, so from patriarch to nation to person. The path leads in both directions, of course, in a fluid movement of meaning. No. 2 works on the language of "instead," a technical term in the cult, and so links the binding of Isaac to the Temple cult.

LVI:XI.

1. A. "And the angel of the Lord called to Abraham a second time from heaven and said, 'By myself I have sworn, [says the Lord, because you have done this thing, and have not withheld your son, your only son, I will indeed bless you and I will multiply your descendants as the stars of heaven and as the sand which is on the seashore. And your descendants shall possess the gate of their enemies, and by your descendants shall all the nations of the earth bless themselves, because you have obeyed my voice']" (Gen. 22:15–17):
   B. What need was there for taking such an oath?
   C. He said to him, "Take an oath to me that you will never again test me or Isaac my son."
2. A. What need was there for taking such an oath?
   B. R. Levi in the name of R. Hama bar Hanina, "He said to him, 'Take an oath to me that you will never again test me.'
   C. "The matter may be compared to the case of a king who was married to a noble lady. She produced a first son from him, and then he divorced her, [remarried her, so she produced] a second son, and he divorced her again, a third son, and he divorced her again. When she had produced a tenth son, all of them got together and said to him, 'Take an oath to us that you will never again divorce our mother.'
   D. "So when Abraham had been tested for the tenth time, he said to him, 'Take an oath to me that you will never again test me.' "

3. A. Said R. Hanan, " 'because you have done this thing'! It was the tenth trial and he refers to it as 'this [one] thing'? But this also is the last, since it outweighs all the rest.

   B. "For if he had not accepted this last trial, he would have lost the merit of all that he had already done."

4. A. ". . . I will indeed bless you [and I will multiply your descendants as the stars of heaven and as the sand which is on the seashore. And your descendants shall possess the gate of their enemies, and by your descendants shall all the nations of the earth bless themselves, because you have obeyed my voice]" (Gen. 22:17):

   B. [Since the Hebrew makes use of the verb *bless* two times, translated "indeed bless," we explain the duplicated verb to mean] a blessing for the father, a blessing for the son.

   C. [Similarly, the duplicated verb for "multiply" means] myriads for the father and myriads for the son.

5. A. "And your descendants shall possess the gate of their enemies."

   B. Rabbi said, "This refers to Palmyra. Happy is he who will witness the fall of Palmyra, since it participated in both destructions of the Temple."

   C. R. Yudan and R. Hanina:

   D. One of them said, "At the destruction of the first Temple it provided eighty thousand archers."

   E. The other said, "At the destruction of the Temple it supplied eight thousand archers."

6. A. "So Abraham returned to his young men [and they arose and went together to Beersheba and Abraham dwelt at Beersheba]" (Gen. 22:19):

   B. And where was Isaac?

   C. R. Berekhiah in the name of Rabbis over there [in Babylonia]: "He had sent him to Shem to study Torah with him. [Why the emphasis on Torah-study?]

   D. "The matter may be compared to the case of a woman who got rich from her spinning. She said, 'Since it is from this spindle that I got rich, it will never leave my hand.' "

   E. R. Yose bar Haninah said, "He sent him away by night, on account of the evil eye."

   F. For from the moment that Hananiah, Mishael, and Azariah came up out of the fiery furnace, their names are not mentioned again in the narrative. So where had they gone?

G. R. Eleazar said, "They died in spit."

H. R. Yose bar Haninah said, "They died on account of the evil eye."

I. R. Joshua b. Levi said, "They changed their residence and went to Joshua b. Yehosedeq to study Torah, in line with this verse: 'Hear now, O Joshua the high priest, you and your fellows that sit before you, for they are men that are a sign' (Zech. 3:8)."

J. R. Tanhum bar Abina in the name of R. Hinena: "It was on that stipulation that Hananiah, Mishael, and Azariah descended to the fiery furnace."

No. 1 spells out the matter of the oath, which is an unusual and weighty procedure. No. 2 then carries forward a statement made in No. 1, though it has no bearing upon the larger issue. No. 4 and No. 5 gloss the base verse. No. 6 answers a basic question left open by the narrative. F–J were included in the composition before the whole was inserted here, and hence the syllogism preceded the exegesis.

While Abraham founded Israel, Isaac and Jacob carried forth the birthright and the blessing. This they did through the process of selection, ending in the assignment of the birthright to Jacob alone. The lives of all three patriarchs flowed together, each being identified with the other as a single long life. This immediately produces the proposition that the historical life of Israel, the nation, continued the individual lives of the patriarchs. The theory of who is Israel, therefore, rested on genealogy: Israel is one extended family, all being children of the same fathers and mothers, the patriarchs and matriarchs of Genesis. This theory of Israelite society, and of the Jewish people in the time of the sages of Genesis Rabbah, made of the people a family, and of genealogy, a kind of ecclesiology. The importance of that proposition in countering the Christian claim to be a new Israel cannot escape notice. Israel, sages maintained, is Israel after the flesh, and that in a most literal sense. But the basic claim, for its part, depended upon the facts of Scripture, not upon the logical requirements of theological dispute. Here is how those facts emerged in the case of Jacob. Specifically, we deal with the blessing that was bestowed upon Jacob by Isaac, who foresaw the entire history of Israel.

LXV:XXIII.

1. A. ["See the smell of my son is as the smell of a field which the Lord has blessed" (Gen. 27:27):] Another matter: this teaches that the Holy One, blessed be he, showed him the house of the sanctuary as it was built, wiped out, and built once more.

   B. "See the smell of my son:" This refers to the Temple in all its beauty, in line with this verse: "A sweet smell to me shall you observe" (Num. 28:2).

   C. "Is as the smell of a field:" This refers to the Temple as it was wiped out, thus: "Zion shall be plowed as a field" (Mic. 3:12).

   D. "which the Lord has blessed:" This speaks of the Temple as it was restored once more in the age to come, as it is said, "For there the Lord commanded the blessing, even life for ever" (Ps. 133:3).

The conclusion explicitly links the blessing of Jacob to the Temple throughout its history. The concluding prooftext presumably justifies the entire identification of the blessing at hand with what was to come.

LXVI:II.

1. A. R. Berekhiah opened [discourse by citing the following verse:] " 'Return, return, O Shulamite, return, return that we may look upon you' (Song 7:1):

   B. "The verse at hand refers to 'return' four times, corresponding to the four kingdoms in which Israel enters in peace and from which Israel comes forth in peace.

   C. " 'O Shulamite:' the word refers to the nation who every day is blessed with a blessing ending with peace [which shares the consonants of the word at hand], as it is said, 'And may he give you peace' (Num. 7:26).

   D. "It is the nation in the midst of which dwells the Peace of the ages, as it is said, 'And let them make me a sanctuary that I may dwell among them' (Ex. 25:8).

   E. "It is the nation to which I am destined to give peace: 'And I will give peace in the land' (Lev. 26:6).

F. "It is the nation over which I am destined to spread peace: 'Behold, I will extend peace to her like a river' (Is. 66:12)."

G. R. Samuel bar Tanhum, R. Hanan bar Berekiah in the name of R. Idi: "It is the nation that makes peace between me and my world. For if it were not for that nation, I would destroy my world."

H. R. Hana in the name of R. Aha: " 'When the earth and all the inhabitants thereof are dissolved' (Ps. 75:4), as in the statement, 'All the inhabitants of Canaan are melted away' (Ex. 15:15).

I. " 'I' (Ps. 75:4), that is, when they accepted upon themselves [the Ten Commandments, beginning,] 'I am the Lord your God' (Ex. 20:2), 'I established the pillars of it' (Ps. 75:4), and the world was set on a solid foundation."

J. Said R. Eleazar bar Merom, "This nation preserves [makes whole] the stability of the world, both in this age and in the age to come."

K. R. Joshua of Sikhnin in the name of R. Levi: "This is the nation on account of the merit of which whatever good that comes into the world is bestowed. Rain comes down only for their sake, that is, 'to you' [as in the base verse], and the dew comes down only 'to you.'

L. "May God give you of the dew of heaven."

The point of this rather sizable composition comes at the end, but the intersecting verse is worked out in its own terms. We have a philosophy of Israel among the nations, stating in one place every component. We begin with a reference to the four kingdoms, but then we move out of that item to the name of the Shulamite, and, third, we proceed to work on the theme of Israel as the nation of peace. Once the praise of Israel forms the focus, we leave behind the issue of peace and deal with the blessings that come to the world on Israel's account. Only at that point does the base verse prove relevant. I could not begin to speculate on the origins of this complex composition—unitary or incremental. What is important to us is the reason for its selection and inclusion on the part of those responsible for the document before us, and their interest is self-evident. But whether they took existing materials and tacked on their point, or whether the composition existed in this form prior to its selection and inclusion, we cannot now know. Whatever future history finds adumbration in the life of Jacob derives from the struggle with Esau. Israel and Rome— these two contend for the world. Still, Isaac plays his part in the matter. Rome does have a legitimate claim, and that claim demands recognition—an amazing, if grudging concession on the part of sages that Christian Rome at least is Esau. Jacob serves as a model and paradigm of Israel's history. For example, his dream of the ladder to heaven encompassed all of Israel's history, with stress not on Esau but on Sinai.

LXVIII:XII.

3. A. Bar Qappara taught on Tannaite authority, "There is no dream without a proper interpretation.

    B. " 'That there was a ladder': refers to the ramp to the altar.

    C. " 'Set up on the earth': that is the altar, 'An altar of dirt you will make for me' (Ex. 20:24).

    D. " 'And the top of it reached to heaven': these are the offerings, for their fragrance goes up to heaven.

    E. " 'And behold, the angels of God': these are the high priests.

    F. " 'Were ascending and descending on it': for they go up and go down on the ramp.

    G. " 'And behold, the Lord stood above it': 'I saw the Lord standing by the altar' (Amos 9:1)."

4. A. Rabbis interpreted the matter to prefigure Sinai: " 'And he dreamed:

    B. " 'That there was a ladder': this refers to Sinai.

    C. " 'Set up on the earth': 'And they stood at the lower part of the mountain' (Ex. 19:17).

    D. " 'And the top of it reached to heaven': 'And the mountain burned with fire into the heart of heaven' (Deut. 4:11).

    E. " 'And behold, the angels of God': these are Moses and Aaron.

    F. " 'Were ascending': 'And Moses went up to God' (Ex. 19:3).

    G. " 'And descending on it': 'And Moses went down from the mount' (Ex. 19:14).

    H. " 'And behold, the Lord stood above it': 'And the Lord came down upon Mount Sinai' (Ex. 19:20)."

5. A. Salomaini in the name of R. Simeon b. Laqish: "He showed him a throne with three legs."

    B. R. Joshua of Sikhnin in the name of R. Levi: " 'And you are the third of the three legs.' "

    C. That accords with the view of R. Joshua in the name of R. Levi: " 'For the portion of the Lord is his people, Jacob the cord of his inheritance' (Deut. 32:9): as a cord cannot be made of less than three strands [so there were three patriarchs, and hence he told Jacob that he would be the third of the three]."

    D. R. Berekhiah said, "He showed him a world and a third of the world.

    E. " 'Ascending' [in the plural] speaks of at least two angels, and 'descending' speaks of two, and each angel in size is a third of the world [thus a world and a third].

    F. "And how do we know that an angel is the size of a third of the world? 'His body also was like the beryl and his face as the appearance of lightning' (Dan. 10:6)."

6. A. R. Hiyya the Elder and R. Yannai:

    B. One of them said, " 'They were going up and coming down' on the ladder."

    C. The other said, " 'They were going up and coming down' on Jacob."

    D. The one who says, " 'They were going up and coming down' on the ladder," has no problems.

    E. As to the one who says, " 'They were going up and coming down' on Jacob," the meaning is that they were raising him up and dragging him down, dancing on him, leaping on him, abusing him.

    F. For it is said, "Israel, in whom I will be glorified" (Is. 49:3).

    G. [So said the angels,] "Are you the one whose visage is incised above?" They would then go up and look at his features and go down and examine him sleeping.

    H. The matter may be compared to the case of a king who was in session and judging cases in a judgment chamber. So people go up to the basilica and find him asleep. They go down to the judgment chamber and find him judging cases.

    I. Above whoever speaks in favor of Israel rises up, and whoever condemns Israel does down. Below, whoever speaks in his favor goes down, and whoever condemns him goes up.

7. A. The angels who accompany a person in the Land do not accompany him outside of the Land.

    B. "Ascending" are the ones who accompanied him in the land, and "descending" are the ones who will accompany him outside of the land.

8. A. R. Levi in the name of R. Samuel: "Because the ministering angels revealed the mystery of the Holy One, blessed be he, [telling Lot what he was about to do], they were sent into exile from their appropriate dwelling for a hundred and thirty-eight years."

    B. R. Tanhuma stated it in the word for "stalk," which contains the letters of a numerical value adding up to 138.

    C. Said. R. Hama bar Hanina, "It was because they puffed themselves up, saying, 'for *we* are about to destroy this place' (Gen. 19:13)."

    D. When did they return? Here: "ascending" and only then "descending." [Freedman, p. 627, n. 3: The banished angels were now permitted to reascend to heaven and then bidden to descend to accompany Jacob.]

No. 3 reads the dream in terms of the Temple cult, and No. 4 in terms of the revelation of the Torah at Sinai, and No. 5 has the dream refer to the patriarchs. At LXVIII:XII we complete the repertoire of parabolic interpretations of the base verse. No. 5 bears a sizable addendum, 5.D–F. No. 6 then goes over the matter of the ascent and the descent of the angels. It presents a number of separate themes, first the notion that the angels were curious about this Jacob, so they came down to see him. The other theme is the link from Jacob to Israel's condition, with the rueful observations at 6.I to make the point. I find the composite somewhat confusing, and I may have erred in not further dividing it. No. 7 works over the same issue, namely, the identification of the angels and their purpose in going up and down the ladder. No. 8 connects these angels to the ones who brought Lot out of Sodom.

LXX:VI.

1. A. "So that I come again to my father's house in peace, then the Lord shall be my God" (Gen. 28:20–22):

   B. R. Joshua of Sikhnin in the name of R. Levi: "The Holy One, blessed be he, took the language used by the patriarchs and turned it into a key to the redemption of their descendants.

   C. "Said the Holy One, blessed be he, to Jacob, 'You have said, "Then the Lord shall be my God." By your life, all of the acts of goodness, blessing, and consolation which I am going to carry out for your descendants I shall bestow only by using the same language:

   D. " 'Then in that day, living waters shall go out from Jerusalem' (Zech. 14:8). 'Then in that day a man shall rear a young cow and two sheep' (Is. 7:21). 'Then, in that day, the Lord will set his hand again the second time to recover the remnant of his people' (Is. 11:11). 'Then, in that day, the mountains shall drop down sweet wine' (Joel 4:18). 'Then, in that day, a great horn shall be blown and they shall come who were lost in the land of Assyria" (Is. 27:13).' "

The union of Jacob's biography and Israel's history yields the passage at hand. It is important only because it says once again what we have now heard throughout our survey of Genesis Rabbah—but makes the statement as explicit as one can imagine.

LXX:X.

1. A. "Jacob said to them, 'My brothers, where do you come from?' They said, 'We are from Haran' " (Gen. 29:40):

   B. R. Yose bar Haninah interpreted the verse at hand with reference to the Exile.

   C. " 'Jacob said to them, "My brothers, where do you come from?" They said, "We are from Haran": that is, "We are flying from the wrath of the Holy One, blessed be he." [Here there is a play on the words for *Haran* and *wrath,* which share the same consonants.]

   D. " 'He said to them, "Do you know Laban the son of Nahor?" ' The sense is this, 'Do you know him who is destined to bleach your sins as white as snow?' [Here there is a play on the words for *Laban* and *bleach,* which share the same consonants.]

E. " 'They said, "We know him." He said to them, "Is it well with him?" They said, "It is well." ' On account of what sort of merit?

F. [Yose continues his interpretation:] " '[The brothers go on,] " . . . and see, Rachel his daughter is coming with the sheep" ' " (Gen. 29:6–7).

G. "That is in line with this verse: 'Thus says the Lord, "A voice is heard in Ramah, lamentation and bitter weeping, Rachel weeping for her children. She refuses to be comforted." Thus says the Lord, "Refrain your voice from weeping . . . and there is hope for your future," says the Lord, "and your children shall return to their own border" ' " (Jer. 31:15–16).

Now the history of the redemption of Israel is located in the colloquy between Jacob and Laban's sons. Much that he said serves to illuminate Israel's future history.

LXXVIII:XIII.

1. A. "[Then Esau said, 'Let us journey on our way, and I will go before you.'] But Jacob said to him, 'My Lord knows [that the children are frail, and that the flocks and herds giving suck are a care to me; and if they are overdriven for one day, all the flocks will die. Let my lord pass on before his servant, and I will lead on slowly, according to the pace of the cattle which are before me and according to the pace of the children, until I come to my lord in Seir']" (Gen. 33:12–14):

   B. Said R. Berekhiah, " 'My lord knows that the children are frail' refers to Moses and Aaron.

   C. " 'And that the flocks and herds giving suck are a care to me' speaks of Israel: 'And you, my flock, the flock of my pasture, are men' (Ez. 34:31)."

   D. R. Huna in the name of R. Aha: "If it were not for the tender mercies of the Holy One, blessed be he, 'and if they are overdriven for one day, all the flocks will die' in the time of Hadrian."

E. R. Berekhiah in the name of R. Levi: " 'My lord knows that the children are frail' speaks of David and Solomon.

F. " 'The flocks and herds' refers to Israel: 'And you, my flock, the flock of my pasture, are men' " (Ez. 34:31).

G. Said R. Huna in the name of R. Aha, "If it were not for the tender mercies of the Holy One, blessed be he, 'and if they are overdriven for one day, all the flocks will die' in the time of Haman."

The event at hand now is identified with other moments in the history of Israel.

LXXXII:X.

1. A. "So Rachel died and she was buried on the way to Ephrath, [that is, Bethlehem, and Jacob set up a pillar upon her grave; it is the pillar of Rachel's tomb, which is there to this day. Israel journeyed on and pitched his tent beyond the tower of Eder]" (Gen. 35:16–21):

    B. Why did Jacob bury Rachel on the way to Ephrath?

    C. Jacob foresaw that the exiles would pass by there [en route to Babylonia].

    D. Therefore he buried her there, so that she should seek mercy for them: "A voice is heard in Ramah . . . Rachel weeping for her children . . . Thus says the Lord, 'Keep your voice from weeping . . . and there is hope for your future' " (Jer. 31:15–16).

The deeds of the patriarchs aim at the needs of Israel later on. The link between the lives of the patriarchs and the history of Israel forms a major theme in the exegetical repertoire before us. The life of Joseph serves for the same purpose, as in the following:

LXXXVII:VI.

1. A. "And although she spoke to Joseph [day after day, he would not listen to her, to lie with her or to be with her. But one day, when he went into the house to do his work and none of the men of the house was there in the house, she caught him by his garment, saying, 'Lie with me.' But he left his garment in her hand and fled and got out of the house]" (Gen. 39:10–13):

B. R. Yudan in the name of R. Benjamin bar Levi: "As to the sons of Levi, the trials affecting them were the same, and the greatness that they achieved was the same.

C. "The trials affecting them were the same: 'And although she spoke to Joseph [day after day.' 'Now it came to pass, when they spoke to him day by day' (Est. 3:4). [Mordecai, descended from Benjamin, was nagged every day.] 'He would not listen to her.' 'And he did not listen to them' (Est. 3:4).

D. "And the greatness that they achieved was the same: 'And Pharaoh took off his signet ring from his hand and put it upon Joseph's hand' (Gen. 41:42). 'And the king took off his ring, which he had taken from Haman and gave it to Mordecai' (Est. 8:2).

E. " 'And arrayed him in fine linen clothing and put a gold chain about his neck' (Gen. 41:42). 'And Mordecai went forth from the presence of the king in royal apparel of blue and white, and with a great crown of gold and with a robe of fine linen and purple' (Est. 8:15).

F. " 'And he made Joseph ride in the second chariot which he had' (Gen. 41:43). 'And cause Mordecai to ride on horseback through the street of the city' (Est. 6:9).

G. " 'And they cried before him, Abrech' (Gen. 41:43). 'And proclaimed before Mordecai, "Thus shall it be done to the man" ' (Est. 6:11)."

2. A. "He would not listen to her, to lie with her or to be with her":

B. "To lie with her" in this world, that he would not have children with her.

C. "Or to be with her" in the world to come.

3. A. "He would not listen to her, to lie with her or to be with her":

B. "To lie with her": even lying without sexual relations.

4. A. A noble lady asked R. Yose, "Is it possible that Joseph, at the age of seventeen, in his full vigor, could have done such a thing?"

B. He produced for her a copy of the book of Genesis. He began to read the story of Reuben and Judah. He said to her, "If these, who were adults and in their father's domain, were not protected by the Scripture [but were revealed by Scripture in all their lust], Joseph, who was a minor and on his own, all the more so [would have been revealed as lustful, had he done what the lady thought he had]."

The parallel drawn between Joseph and Benjamin-Mordecai permits the exegete to draw a parallel between the life of Joseph and the history of Israel. No. 2 expands on the base verse, and No. 3 presents an argument in favor of its authenticity, at the same time linking the present story to the two that have preceded.

LXXXVIII:I.

1. A. "Some time after this, the butler of the king of Egypt and his baker offended [Hebrew: sinned against] their lord the king of Egypt" (Gen. 40:1):

    B. "Deliver me from all my trangressions, make me not the reproach of the base" (Ps. 89:9):

    C. R. Hama bar Haninah said, "[Because they own this world,] the nations of the world ought not to have had among them sickly or weak people. Why are there sickly and weak people among them? It is so that they should not ridicule Israel, saying to them, 'Are you not a nation of sickly and weak people?'

    D. "This is on the count of the following verse: 'Make me not the reproach of the base.' "

    E. R. Samuel bar Nahman said, "[Because they own this world,] the nations of the world ought not to have had among them people who produce scabs. And why are there such people among them? It is so that they should not ridicule Israel, saying to them, 'Are you not a nation of lepers?'

    F. "This is on account of the following verse: '. . . make me not the reproach of the base.' "

2. A. Another interpretation: "Deliver me from all my transgressions, make me not the reproach of the base" (Ps. 89:9).

    B. This refers to Joseph.

    C. Since it is written, "And she called the men of her house" (Gen. 39:14), meaning that she put his name into everyone's mouth, the Holy One, blessed be he, said, "It is better that they turn against one another and not against that righteous man."

    D. Thus: "Some time after this, the butler of the king of Egypt and his baker offended [Hebrew: sinned against] their lord the king of Egypt" (Gen. 40:1).

The effect of the dual exegesis of the intersecting verse is to link Israel's experience to Joseph's, Nos. 1, 2 in order. The comment on the intersecting verse at No. 1 can readily stand on its own, but, joined to No. 2, illuminates the purpose of God in having Joseph thrown into prison and further comments on Israel's life among the nations. In all, this is a good example of what is achieved in the intersecting verse/base-verse construction. God of course governed Joseph's destiny, detail by detail, and as this becomes clear, the Jewish reader concludes that God's providence and benevolence continue to dictate what is to happen to Israel, even though that fact does not always prove self-evident. The personal history of the individual gives way to the national history of Israel:

XCVIII:IX.

1. A. "Binding his foal to the vine [and his ass's colt to the choice vine, he washes his garments in wine, and his vesture in the blood of grapes; his eyes shall be red with wine, and his teeth white with milk]" (Gen. 49:8–12):

    B. R. Judah, R. Nehemiah, and rabbis:

    C. R. Judah said, "In the case of a vine which produces poorly, they tie an ass to it. Thus: 'Binding his foal to the vine.'

    D. " 'And his ass's colt to the choice vine, he washes his garments in wine': in white wine.

    E. " 'And his vesture in the blood of grapes': in red wine."

    F. R. Nehemiah said, " 'Binding his foal to the vine': God binds to the vine, that is Israel, his city, namely, 'the city which I have chosen.'

    G. " 'And his ass's colt to the choice vine': the strong sons which are destined to arise from him."

    H. Rabbis said, " 'I am bound to the vine and the choice vine' [that is Israel].

    I. " 'Binding his foal to the vine and his ass's colt to the choice vine': when the one concerning whom it is written, 'Lowly and riding upon an ass, even upon a colt of the foal of an ass' (Zech. 9:9).

J. " 'He washes his garments in wine': for he will link together words of Torah.

K. " 'And his vesture in the blood of grapes': for he will explain their errors to them."

2. A. Said R. Hanin, "Israel does not require the learning of the King-Messiah in the age to come, as it is said, 'Unto him shall *the nations* seek' (Is. 11:1)—but not Israel.

B. "If so, why will the King-Messiah come? And what will he come to do? It is to gather together the exiles of Israel and to give them thirty religious duties: 'And I said to them, If you think good, give me my hire, and if not, forbear. So they weighed for my hire thirty pieces of silver' (Zech. 11:12)."

C. Rab said, "These refer to thirty heroes."

D. R. Yohanan said, "These refer to thirty religious duties."

E. They said to R. Yohanan, "Have you not accepted the view of Rab that the passage speaks only of the nations of the world?"

F. In the view of Rab, "And I said to them" speaks of Israel, and in the view of Israel, "And I said to them" speaks of the nations of the world.

G. In the view of Rab, when the Israelites have sufficient merit, the greater number of the thirty heroes are in the Land of Israel, and the lesser number in Babylonia, and when the Israelites do not have sufficient merit, the greater number is in Babylonia and the smaller number in the Land of Israel.

Judah reads the view in a simple way. Nehemiah makes it allude to Jerusalem. It is rabbis' view that is interesting, because they introduce the messianic theme and work it out in an unusual way. Now the Israelites will not require the Messiah to teach them the Torah. His job is only to reassemble Israel in the holy land. The secondary expansion reinforces rabbis' point.

XCIX:II.

1. A. "For the Lord God will do nothing unless he reveals his secret to his servants the prophets" (Amos 3:7).

B. Jacob linked two of his sons, corresponding to two of the monarchies, and Moses linked two of the tribes, corresponding to two of the monarchies.

C. Judah corresponds to the kingdom of Babylonia, for this is compared to a lion and that is compared to a lion. This is compared to a lion: "Judah is a lion's whelp" (Gen. 49:9), and so too Babylonia: "The first was like a lion" (Dan. 7:4).

D. Then by the hand of which of the tribes will the kingdom of Babylonia fall? It will be by the hand of Daniel, who comes from the tribe of Judah.

E. Benjamin corresponds to the kingdom of Media, for this is compared to a wolf and that is compared to a wolf. This is compared to a wolf: "Benjamin is a ravenous wolf, [in the morning devouring the prey, and at even dividing the spoil]." And that is compared to a wolf: "And behold, another beast, a second, like a wolf" (Dan. 7:5).

F. R. Hanina said, "The word for 'wolf' in the latter verse is written as 'bear.' It had been called a bear."

G. That is the view of R. Yohanan, for R. Yohanan said, " 'Wherefore a lion of the forest slays them' (Jer. 5:6) refers to Babylonia, and 'a wolf of the deserts spoils them' refers to Media."

H. [Reverting to E:] Then by the hand of which of the tribes will the kingdom of Media fall? It will be by the hand of Mordecai, who comes from the tribe of Benjamin.

I. Levi corresponds to the kingdom of Greece. This is the third tribe in order, and that is the third kingdom in order. This is written with a word that is made up of three letters, and that is written with a word which consists of three letters. This one sounds the horn and that one sounds the horn, this one wears turbans and that one wears helmets, this one wears pants and that one wears knee-cuts.

J. To be sure, this one is very populous, while that one is few in numbers. But the many came and fell into the hand of the few.

K. On account of merit deriving from what source did this take place? It is on account of the blessing that Moses bestowed: "Smiter through the loins of them that rise up against him" (Deut. 33:11).

L. Then by the hand of which of the tribes will the kingdom of Greece fall? It will be by the hand of sons of the Hasmoneans, who come from the tribe of Levi.

M. Joseph corresponds to the kingdom of Edom [Rome], for this one has horns and that one has horns. This one has horns: "His firstling bullock, majesty is his, and his horns are the horns of the wild ox" (Deut. 33:17). And that one has horns: "And concerning the ten horns that were on its head" (Dan. 7:20). This one avoided kept away from fornication while that one cleaved to fornication. This one paid respect for the honor owing to his father, while that one despised the honor owing to his father. Concerning this one it is written, "For I fear God" (Gen. 42:18), while in regard to that one it is written, "And he did not fear God" (Deut. 25:18). [So the correspondence in part is one of opposites.]

N. Then by the hand of which of the tribes will the kingdom of Edom fall? It will be by the hand of the anointed for war, who comes from the tribe of Joseph.

O. R. Phineas in the name of R. Samuel b. Nahman: "There is a tradition that Esau will fall only by the hand of the sons of Rachel: 'Surely the least of the flock shall drag them away' (Jer. 49:20). Why the least? Because they are the youngest of the tribes."

This impressive theory of Israel's history finds a place here only because of E. Yet the larger relevance—Jacob's predictions of the future—justifies including the composition.

By this point readers must find themselves altogether at home in the notion of the authorship of Genesis Rabbah that one should read the book of Genesis as if it portrayed the history of Israel and Rome. For that is the single obsession binding sages of the document at hand to common discourse with the text before them. Why Rome in the form it takes in Genesis Rabbah? And how come the obsessive character of sages disposition of the theme of Rome? Were their picture merely of Rome as tyrant and destroyer of the Temple, we should have no reason to link the text to the problems of the age of redaction and closure. But, as we have repeatedly observed, now it is Rome as Israel's brother, counterpart, and nemesis, Rome as the one thing standing in the way of Israel's, and the world's, ultimate salvation. So the stakes are different, and much higher. It is not a political Rome but a messianic Rome that is at issue: Rome as surrogate for Israel, Rome as obstacle to Israel. Why? It is because Rome now confronts Israel with a crisis, and, I argue, Genesis Rabbah constitutes a response to that crisis. Rome in the fourth century became Christian. Sages respond by facing that fact quite squarely and saying, "Indeed, it is as you say, a kind of Israel, an heir of Abraham as your texts explicitly claim. But we remain the sole legitimate Israel, the bearer of the birthright—we and not you. So you are our brother: Esau, Ishmael, Edom." And the rest follows.

Genesis Rabbah reached closure, people generally agree, toward the end of the fourth century. That century marks the beginning of the West as we have known it. Why so? Because in the fourth century, from the conversion of Constantine and over the next hundred years, the Roman empire became Christian—and with it, the West. So the fourth century marks the first century of the history of the West in that form in which the West would flourish for the rest of time, to our own day. Accordingly, we should not find surprising sages' recurrent references, in the reading of Genesis, to the struggle of two equal powers, Rome and Israel, Esau and Jacob, Ishmael and Isaac. The world-historical change, marking the confirmation in politics and power of the Christians' claim that Christ was king over all humanity, demanded from sages an appropriate, and, to Israel, persuasive, response.

By rereading the story of the beginnings, sages discovered the answer and the secret of the end. Rome claimed to be Israel, and, indeed, sages conceded, Rome shared the patrimony of Israel. That claim took the form of the Christians' appropriation of the Torah as "the Old Testament," so sages acknowledged a simple fact in acceding to the notion that, in some way, Rome too formed part of Israel. But it was the rejected part, the Ishmael, the Esau, not the Isaac, not the Jacob. The advent of Christian Rome precipitated the sustained, polemical, and, I think, rigorous and well-argued rereading of beginnings in light of the end. Rome then marked the conclusion of human history as Israel had known it. Beyond? The coming of the true Messiah, the redemption of Israel, the salvation of the world, the end of time. So the issues were not inconsiderable, and when the sages spoke of Esau/Rome, as they did so often, they confronted the life-or-death decision of the day.

LXXV:IX.

1. A. Someone else commenced discourse by citing this verse: "Do not grant, O Lord, the desires of the wicked, do not advance his evil plan" (Ps. 140:9).
   B. "Lord of all ages, do not give to the wicked Esau what his heart has devised against Jacob."
   C. What is the meaning of "Do not advance his evil plan"?
   D. He said before him, "Lord of the ages, make a bit for the mouth of the wicked Esau, so that he will not get full pleasure [from anything he does]." [The word for *evil plan* and for *bit* use the same consonants.]
   E. What sort of bit did the Holy One, blessed be he, make for Esau?
   F. Said R. Hama bar Haninah, "These are the barbarian nations, the Germans whom the Edomites fear."

Sages clearly followed the news of the day and drew their own conclusions from the Romans' political problems. Here again sages refer to contemporary considerations in interpreting the sense of Scripture.

LXXVI:VI.

1. A. " 'Deliver me, I pray you, from the hand of my brother, from the hand of Esau, for I fear him' ":
   B. "From the hand of my brother, who comes against me with the strength of Esau" [which was the sword] (Gen. 27:40).
   C. That is in line with this verse: "I considered the horns, and behold, there came up among them another horn, a little one" (Dan. 7:8).

D. This refers to Ben Neser [Odenathus of Palmyra].

E. "Before which three of the first horns were plucked up by the roots" (Dan. 7:8).

F. This refers to Macrinus, Carinus, and Cyriades.

G. "And behold, in this horn were eyes like the eyes of a man and a mouth speaking great things" (Dan. 7:8).

H. This speaks of the wicked realm, which imposes taxes on all the nations of the world.

I. Said R. Yohanan, "It is written, 'And as for the ten horns, out of this kingdom shall ten kings arise' (Dan. 7:24), that is, the ten sons of Esau.

J. " 'I considered the horns, and behold, there came up among them another horn, a little one,' meaning, the wicked realm.

K. " 'Before which three of the first horns were plucked up by the roots' speaks of the first three monarchies [Babylonia, Media, Greece].

L. " 'And behold, in this horn were eyes like the eyes of a man' alludes to the wicked realm, which looks enviously on someone's wealth, saying, 'Since, Mr. So-and-so has a lot of money, we shall elect him magistrate,' 'Since Mr. So-and-so has a lot of money, we shall elect him councillor.' "

2. A. " 'Lest he come and slay us all, the mothers with the children. But you did say, 'I will do you good and make your descendants as the sand of the sea, which cannot be numbered for multitude" ' " (Gen. 32:12):

B. "But you did say, 'You will not take the dam with the fledglings' " (Deut. 22:6).

C. Another matter: " 'Lest he come and slay us all, the mothers with the children. But you did say, "And whether it be cow or ewe, you shall not kill it and its young both in one day" ' " (Lev. 22:28).

The explicit allusion at No. 1 to Rome in the time of Odenathus is puzzling, because, of course, Odenathus at Palmyra was an independent chief, not ruler of Rome (!). The reading of Daniel has three Roman generals fall before Palmyra. Now what this has to do with the power of one's brother, the power of the sword, I take it, is simple. Jacob is made to refer to wanting to be saved from someone who exercises the sort of power that Esau exercises, namely, from Palmyra. The message to Israel is that Palmyra, no less than Rome, exercises a kind of power from which Israel is to be delivered, not power Israel is itself to aspire to wield. Then the sense of Yohanan's statement is that the cited verse speaks of Rome, not Palmyra, and that at issue is Rome as successor to the first three monarchies. So Yohanan reads Daniel in the way in which rabbis generally did, and in his view, there is no point of contact with our base-verse. It is a rather interesting construction therefore, in which a dispute on the meaning of Daniel has taken shape, only afterward to be brought into juxtaposition with our base-verse. The reason the compositor chose the completed statement of course is the opening allusion, but that alone. No. 2 goes over familiar ground, drawing up the setting of Jacob's address to call to God's attention the requirement of the Torah.

LXXXIII:II.

1. A. "These are the kings who reigned in the land of Edom before any king reigned over the Israelites: Bela the son of Beor reigned in Edom, the name of his city being Dinhabah" (Gen. 36:31–32):

    B. Said R. Aibu, "Before a king arose in Israel, kings existed in Edom: 'These are the kings who reigned in the land of Edom before any king reigned over the Israelites.' " [Freedman, p. 766, n. 4: "1 Kgs. 22:48 states, 'There was no king in Edom, a deputy was king.' This refers to the reign of Jehoshaphat. Subsequently in Jehoram's reign, Edom revolted and 'made a king over themselves' (2 Kgs. 8:20). Thus from Saul to Jehoshaphat, in which Israel had eight kings, Edom had no king but was ruled by a governor of Judah. Aibu observes that this was to balance the present period, during which Edom had eight kings while Israel had none. For that reason, Aibu employs the word for deputy when he wishes to say 'existed' thus indicating a reference to the verse in the book of Kings quoted above."]

    C. R. Yose bar Haninah said, "[Alluding to a mnemonic, with the first Hebrew letter for the word for kings, judges, chiefs, and princes:] When the one party [Edom] was ruled by kings, the other party [Israel] was ruled by judges, when one side was ruled by chiefs, the other side was ruled by princes."

D. Said R. Joshua b. Levi, "This one set up eight kings and that one set up eight kings. This one set up Bela, Jobab, Husham, Samlah, Shaul, Hadad, Baalhanan, and Hadar. The other side set up Saul, Ishbosheth, David Solomon, Rehoboam, Abijah, Asa, and Jehoshaphat.

E. "Then Nebuchadnezzar came and overturned both: 'That made the world as a wilderness and destroyed the cities thereof' (Is. 14:17).

F. "Evil-merodach came and exalted Jehoiakin, Ahasuerus came and exalted Haman."

The passage once more stresses the correspondence between Israel's and Edom's governments, respectively. The reciprocal character of their histories is then stated in a powerful way, with the further implication that, when the one rules, the other waits. So now Israel waits, but it will rule. The same point is made in what follows, but the expectation proves acute and immediate.

LXXXIII:IV.

3. A. "Magdiel and Iram: these are the chiefs of Edom, that is Esau, the father of Edom, according to their dwelling places in the land of their possession" (Gen. 36:42):

B. On the day on which Litrinus came to the throne, there appeared to R. Ammi in a dream this message: "Today Magdiel has come to the throne."

C. He said, "One more king is required for Edom [and then Israel's turn will come]."

4. A. Said R. Hanina of Sepphoris, "Why was he called Iram? For he is destined to amass [a word using the same letters] riches for the King-Messiah."

B. Said R. Levi, "There was the case of a ruler in Rome who wasted the treasuries of his father. Elijah of blessed memory appeared to him in a dream. He said to him, 'Your fathers collected treasures and you waste them.'

C. "He did not budge until he filled the treasuries again."

No. 3 presents once more the theme that Rome's rule will extend only for a foreordained and limited time, at which point the Messiah will come. No. 4 explains the meaning of the name Iram. The concluding statement also alleges that Israel's saints even now make possible whatever wise decisions Rome's rulers make. That forms an appropriate conclusion to the matter. Ending in the everyday world of the here and the now, we note that sages attribute to Israel's influence anything good that happens to Israel's brother, Rome. In our own day, even some of the children of Esau concede that point—but that has come about only after Esau murdered nearly a third of Jacob's sons and daughters.

7. Leviticus Rabbah

Leviticus Rabbah deals with a biblical book, not a Mishnah-trac-tate. But it approaches that book with a fresh plan, one in which exegesis does not dictate rhetoric, and in which amplification of an established text (whether Scripture or Mishnah) does not supply the underlying logic by which sentences are made to compose paragraphs, completed thoughts. The framers of Leviticus Rabbah treat topics, not particular verses. They make free-standing generalizations. They express cogent propositions through extended compositions, not episodic ideas. Earlier, things people wished to say were attached to predefined statements based on an existing text, constructed in accord with an organizing logic independent of the systematic expression of a single, well-framed idea. Now the authors so collect and arrange their materials that an abstract proposition emerges. That proposition is not expressed only or mainly through episodic restatements, assigned, as I said, to an order established by a base-text. Rather it emerges through a logic of its own. The framers of that composition undertook to offer propositions, declarative sentences (so to speak), in which, not through the exegesis of verses of Scripture in the order of Scripture but through an order dictated by their own sense of the logic of syllogistic composition, they would say what they had in mind. To begin with, they laid down their own topical program, related to, but essentially independent of, that of the book of Leviticus. Second, in expressing their ideas on these topics, they never undertook simply to cite a verse of Scripture and then to claim that that verse states precisely what they had in mind to begin with. Accordingly, through rather distinctive modes of expression, the framers said what they wished to say in their own way—just as had the authors of the Mishnah itself. True, in so doing, the composers of Leviticus Rabbah treated Scripture as had their predecessors. That is to say, to them as to those who had gone before, Scripture provided a rich treasury of facts.

When we listen to the framers of Leviticus Rabbah, we see how statements in the document at hand become intelligible not contingently, that is, on the strength of an established text, but a priori, that is, on the basis of a deeper logic of meaning and an independent principle of rhetorical intelligibility. As I said, Leviticus Rabbah is topical, not exegetical. Each of its thirty-seven *parashiyyot* pursues its given topic and develops points relevant to that topic. With Leviticus Rabbah rabbis take up the problem of saying what they wish to say not in an exegetical, but in a syllogistic and freely discursive logic and rhetoric. It follows that just as much as the Mishnah marks a radical break from all prior literature produced by Jews, so Leviticus Rabbah marks a stunning departure from all prior literature produced by a particular kind of Jews, namely, rabbis. Since these same rabbis defined Judaism as we have known it from their time to ours, we rightly turn to the book at hand for evidence about how the Scripture entered into, was absorbed by, and reached full status as the foundation document of the Judaism taking shape at just this time.

The paramount and dominant exegetical construction in Leviticus Rabbah is the base-verse/intersecting verse exegesis. In this construction, a verse of Leviticus is cited (hence: base-verse), and another verse, from such books as Job, Proverbs, Qohelet, or Psalms, is then cited. The latter, not the former, is subjected to detailed and systematic exegesis. But the exegetical exercise ends up by leading the intersecting verse back to the base-verse and reading the latter in terms of the former. In such an exercise, what in fact do we do? We read one thing in terms of something else. To begin with, it is the base-verse in terms of the intersecting verse. But it also is the intersecting verse in other terms as well—a multiple-layered construction of analogy and parable. The intersecting verse's elements always turn out to stand for, to signify, to speak of, something other than that to which they openly refer. Nothing says what it means. Everything important speaks metonymically, elliptically, parabolically, symbolically. All statements carry deeper meaning, which inheres in other statements altogether. The profound sense, then, of the base-verse emerges only through restatement within and through the intersecting verse—as if the base-verse spoke of things that, on the surface, we do not see at all.

Exegesis as we know it in Leviticus Rabbah (and not only there) consists in an exercise in analogical thinking—something is like something else, stands for, evokes, or symbolizes that which is quite outside itself. It may be the opposite of something else, in which case it conforms to the exact opposite of the rules that govern that something else. The reasoning is analogical or it is contrastive, and the fundamental logic is taxonomic. The taxonomy rests on those comparisons and contrasts we should call, as I said, metonymic and parabolic. In that case what lies on the surface misleads. What lies beneath or beyond the surface—there is the true reality, the world of truth and meaning. To revert to the issue of taxonomy, the traits that allow classification serve only for that purpose.

People who see things this way do not call a thing as it is. Self-evidently, they have become accustomed to perceiving more—or less—than is at hand. Perhaps that is a natural mode of thought for the Jews of this period (and not then alone), so long used to calling themselves God's first love, yet now seeing others with greater worldly reason claiming that same advantaged relationship. Not in mind only, but still more, in the politics of the world, the people that remembered its origins along with the very creation of the world and founding of humanity, that recalled how it alone served, and serves, the one and only God, for more than three hundred years had confronted a quite different existence. The radical disjuncture between the way things were and the way Scripture said things were supposed to be—and in actuality would some day become—surely imposed an unbearable tension. It was one thing for the slave born to slavery to endure. It was another for the free man sold into slavery to accept that same condition. The vanquished people, the nation that had lost its city and its temple, that had, moreoever, produced another nation from its midst to take over its Scripture and much else could not bear too much reality. That defeated people will then have found refuge in a mode of thought that trained vision to see things otherwise than as the eyes perceived them. Among the diverse ways by which the weak and subordinated accomodate to their circumstance, the one of iron-willed pretense in life is most likely to yield the mode of thought at hand: things never are, because they cannot be, what they seem.

Reading one thing in terms of something else, the builders of the document systematically adopted for themselves the reality of the Scripture, its history and doctrines. They transformed that history from a sequence of one-time events, leading from one place to some other, into an ever-present mythic world. No longer was there one Moses, one David, one set of happenings of a distinctive and never-to-be-repeated character. Now whatever happens, of which the thinkers propose to take account, must enter and be absorbed into that established and ubiquitous pattern and structure founded in Scripture. It is not that biblical history repeats itself. Rather, biblical history no longer constitutes history as a story of things that happened once, long ago, and pointed to some one moment in the future. Rather it becomes an account of things that happen every day—hence, an ever-present mythic world.

That, incidentally, is why they did not write history, an account of what was happening and what it meant. It was not that they did not recognize or appreciate important changes and trends reshaping their nation's life. They could not deny that reality. In their apocalyptic reading of the dietary and leprosy laws, they made explicit their close encounter with the history of the world as they knew it. But they had another mode of responding to history. It was to treat history as if it were already known and readily understood. Whatever happened had already happened. How so? Scripture dictated the contents of history, laying forth the structures of time, the rules that prevailed and were made known in events. Self-evidently, these same thinkers projected into Scripture's day the realities of their own, turning Moses and David into rabbis, for example. But this is how people think in that mythic, enchanted world in which, to begin with, reality blends with dream, and hope projects onto future and past alike how people want things to be.

We turn from the mode of thought to the message of the document for the age of its formulation, the fourth and early fifth centuries. The recurrent message may be stated in this way:

God loves Israel, so gave them the Torah, which defines their life and governs their welfare. Israel is alone in its category, so what is a virtue to Israel is a vice to the nations, life-giving to Israel, poison to the gentiles. True, Israel sins, but God forgives that sin, having punished the nation on account of it. Such a process has yet to come to an end, but it will culminate in Israel's complete regeneration. Meanwhile, Israel's assurance of God's love lies in the many expressions of special concern, for even the humblest and most ordinary aspects of the national life: the food the nation eats, the sexual practices by which it procreates. These life-sustaining, life-transmitting activities draw God's special interest, as a mark of his general love for Israel. Israel then is supposed to achieve its life in conformity with the marks of God's love. These indications moreover signify also the character of Israel's difficulty, namely, subordination to the nations in general, but to the fourth kingdom, Rome, in particular. Both food laws and skin diseases stand for the nations. There is yet another category of sin, also collective and generative of collective punishment, and that is social. The moral character of Israel's life, the treatment of people by one another, the practice of gossip and small-scale thuggery—these too draw down divine penalty. The nation's fate therefore corresponds to its moral condition. The moral condition, however, emerges not only from the current generation. Israel's richest hope lies in the merit of the ancestors, thus in the scriptural record of the merits attained by the founders of the nation, those who originally brought it into being and gave it life. The world to come upon the nation is so portrayed as to restate these same propositions. Merit overcomes sin, and doing religious duties or supererogatory acts of kindness will win merit for the nation that does them. Israel will be saved at the end of time, and the age, or world, to follow will be exactly the opposite of this one. Much that we find in the account of Israel's national life, worked out through the definition of the liminal relationships, recurs in slightly altered form in the picture of the world to come.

The one-time events of the generation of the flood, Sodom and Gomorrah, the patriarchs and the sojourn in Egypt, the exodus, the revelation of the Torah at Sinai, the golden calf, the Davidic monarchy and the building of the Temple, Sennacherib, Hezekiah, and the destruction of northern Israel, Nebuchadnezzar and the destruction of the Temple in 586, the life of Israel in Babylonian captivity, Daniel and his associates, Mordecai and Haman—these events occur over and over again. They turn out to serve as paradigms of sin and atonement, steadfastness and divine intervention, and equivalent lessons. We find, in fact, a fairly standard repertoire of scriptural heroes or villains, on the one side, and conventional lists of Israel's enemies and their actions and downfall, on the other. The boastful, for instance, include (VII:VI) the generation of the flood, Sodom and Gomorrah, Pharaoh, Sisera, Sennacherib, Nebuchadnezzar, the wicked empire (Rome)—contrasted to Israel, "despised and humble in this world." The four kingdoms recur again and again, always ending, of course, with Rome, with the repeated message that after Rome will come Israel. But Israel has to make this happen through its faith and submission to God's will. Lists of enemies ring the changes on Cain, the Sodomites, Pharaoh, Sennacherib, Nebuchadnezzar, Haman.

Accordingly, the mode of thought brought to bear upon the theme of history remains exactly the same as before: list-making, with data exhibiting similar taxonomic traits drawn together into lists based on common monothetic traits or definitions. These lists then through the power of repetition make a single enormous point or prove a social law of history. The catalogues of exemplary heroes and historical events serve a further purpose. They provide a model of how contemporary events are to be absorbed into the biblical paradigm. Since biblical events exemplify recurrent happenings, sin and redemption, forgiveness and atonement, they lose their one-time character. At the same time and in the same way, current events find a place within the ancient, but eternally present, paradigmatic scheme. So no new historical events, other than exemplary episodes in lives of heroes, demand narration because, through what is said about the past, what was happening in the times of the framers of Leviticus Rabbah would also come under consideration. This mode of dealing with biblical history and contemporary events produces two reciprocal effects. The first is the mythicization of biblical stories, their removal from the framework of ongoing, unique patterns of history and sequences of events and their transformation into accounts of things that happen all the time. The second is that contemporary events too lose all of their specificity and enter the paradigmatic framework of established mythic existence. So (1) the Scripture's myth happens every day, and (2) every day produces reenactment of the Scripture's myth.

In seeking the substance of the mythic being invoked by the exegetes at hand, who read the text as if it spoke about something else and the world as if it lived out the text, we uncover a simple fact. At the center of the pretense, that is, the as-if mentality of Leviticus Rabbah and its framers, we find a simple proposition. Israel is God's special love. That love is shown in a simple way. Israel's present condition of subordination derives from its own deeds. It follows that God cares, so Israel may look forward to redemption on God's part in response to Israel's own regeneration through repentance.

The message of Leviticus Rabbah attaches itself to the book of Leviticus, as if that book had come from prophecy and addressed the issue of salvation. But it came from the priesthood and spoke of sanctification. The paradoxical syllogism—the as-if reading, the opposite of how things seem—of the composers of Leviticus Rabbah therefore reaches simple formulation. In the very setting of sanctification we find the promise of salvation. In the topics of the cult and the priesthood we uncover the national and social issues of the moral life and redemptive hope of Israel. The repeated comparison and contrast of priesthood and prophecy, sanctification and salvation, turn out to produce a complement, which comes to most perfect union in the text at hand.

The basic mode of thought—denial of what is at hand in favor of a deeper reality-proves remarkably apt. The substance of thought confronts the crisis too.

Are we lost for good to the fourth empire, now-Christian Rome? No, we may yet be saved.

Has God rejected us forever? No, aided by the merit of the

patriarchs and matriarchs and of the Torah and religious duties, we gain God's love.

What must we do to be saved? We must do nothing, we must be something: sanctified.

That status we gain through keeping the rules that make Israel holy. So salvation is through sanctification, all embodied in Leviticus read as rules for the holy people.

The Messiah will come not because of what a pagan emperor does, nor, indeed, because of Jewish action either, but because of Israel's own moral condition. When Israel enters the right relationship with God, then God will respond to Israel's condition by restoring things to their proper balance. Israel cannot, but need not, so act as to force the coming of the Messiah. Israel can so attain the condition of sanctification, by forming a moral and holy community, that God's response will follow the established prophecy of Moses and the prophets. So the basic doctrine of Leviticus Rabbah is the metamorphosis of Leviticus. Instead of holy caste, we deal with holy people. Instead of holy place, we deal with holy community, in its holy Land. The deepest exchange between reality and inner vision, therefore, comes at the very surface: the rereading of Leviticus in terms of a different set of realities from those to which the book, on the surface, relates. No other biblical book would have served so well; it had to be Leviticus. Only through what the framers did on that particular book could they deliver their astonishing message and vision.

The complementary points of stress in Leviticus Rabbah—the age to come will come, but Israel must reform itself beforehand—address that context defined by Julian, on the one side, and by the new anti-Judaic Christian policy of the later fourth and fifth centuries, on the other. The repeated reference to Esau and Edom and how they mark the last monarchy before God's through Israel underlines the same point. These truly form the worst of the four kingdoms. But they also come at the end. If only we shape up, so will history. We therefore grasp an astonishing correspondence between how people are thinking, what they wish to say, and the literary context—rereading a particular book of Scripture in terms

of a set of values different from those expressed in that book—
in which they deliver their message. Given the mode of thought,
the crisis that demanded reflection, the message found congruent
to the crisis, we must find entirely logical the choice of Leviticus
and the treatment accorded to it. So the logic and the doctrine
prove remarkably to accord with the society and politics that
produced and received Leviticus Rabbah.

The particular passage we now consider concerns the fate of
Israel in the world, its place among the historical empires. The
message is that Israel's destiny lies in the hands of a loving God,
who cares about every detail of Israel's life, in the everyday and
in the historical planes as well. The food Israel eats or does not
eat stands, also, for the fate of Israel, the nation, and the biblical
rules about animals that are suitable or unsuitable convey histor-
ical-social laws about the destiny of the empires of the world.

XIII:V

1. A. Said R. Ishmael b. R. Nehemiah, "All the prophets foresaw
      what the pagan kingdoms would do [to Israel].
   B. "The first man foresaw what the pagan kingdoms would do [to
      Israel].
   C. "That is in line with the following verse of Scripture: 'A river
      flowed out of Eden [to the water the garden, and there it divided
      and became four rivers]' (Gen. 2:10). [The four rivers stand for
      the four kingdoms, Babylonia, Media, Greece, and Rome]."
2. A. R. Tanhuma said it, [and] R. Menahema [in the name of] R.
      Joshua b. Levi: "The Holy One, blessed be he, will give the cup
      of reeling to the nations of the world to drink in the world to
      come.
   B. "That is in line with the following verse of Scripture: 'A river
      flowed out of Eden' (Gen 2:10), the place from which justice
      [DYN] goes forth."
3. A. "[There it divided] and became four rivers" (Gen 2:10)—this
      refers to the four kingdoms.
   B. "The name of the first is Pishon (PSWN); [it is the one which
      flows around the whole land of Havilah, where there is gold;

and the gold of that land is good; bdellium and onyx stone are there]" (Gen. 2:11–12).

C. This refers to Babylonia, on account [of the reference to Babylonia in the following verse:] "And their [the Babylonians'] horsemen spread themselves (PSW)" (Hab. 1:8).

D. [It is further] on account of [Nebuchadnezzar's being] a dwarf, shorter than ordinary men by a handbreadth.

E. "[It is] the one which flows around the whole land of Havilah" (Gen. 2:11):

F. This [reference to the river's flowing around the whole land] speaks of Nebuchadnezzar, the wicked man, who came up and surrounded the entire Land of Israel, which places its hope in the Holy One, blessed be he.

G. That is in line with the following verse of Scripture: "Hope in God, for I shall again praise him" (Ps. 42:5).

H. "Where there is gold" (Gen. 2:11)—this refers to the words of Torah, "which are more to be desired than gold, more than much fine gold" (Ps. 19:11).

I. "And the gold of that land is good" (Gen. 2:12).

J. This teaches that there is no Torah like the Torah that is taught in the Land of Israel, and there is no wisdom like the wisdom that is taught in the Land of Israel.

K. Bdellium and onyx stone are there" (Gen. 2:12)—Scripture, Mishnah, Talmud, and lore.

4. A. "The name of the second river is Gihon; [it is the one which flows around the whole land of Cush]" (Gen. 2:13).

B. This refers to Media, which produced Haman, that wicked man, who spit out venom like a serpent.

C. It is on account of the verse: "On your belly will you go" (Gen. 3:14).

D. "It is the one which flows around the whole land of Cush" (Gen. 2:13).

E. [We know that this refers to Media, because it is said:] "Who rules from India to Cush" (Est. 1:1).

5. A. "And the name of the third river is Tigris (HDQL), [which flows east of Assyria]" (Gen. 2:14).

B. This refers to Greece [Syria], which was sharp (HD) and speedy (QL) in making its decrees, saying to Israel, "Write on the horn of an ox that you have no portion in the God of Israel."

C. "Which flows east (QDMT) of Assyria" (Gen. 2:14).

D. Said R. Huna, "In three aspects the kingdom of Greece was in advance (QDMH) of the present evil kingdom [Rome]: in respect to ship-building, the arrangement of camp vigils, and language."

E. Said R. Huna, "Any and every kingdom may be called 'Assyria' (ashur), on account of all of their making themselves powerful at Israel's expense."

F. Said R. Yose b. R. Hanina, "Any and every kingdom may be called Nineveh (NNWH), on account of their adorning (NWY) themselves at Israel's expense."

G. Said R. Yose b. R. Hanina, "Any and every kingdom may be called Egypt (MSRYM), on account of their oppressing (MSY-RYM) Israel."

6. A. "And the fourth river is the Euphrates (PRT)" (Gen. 2:14).

B. This refers to Edom [Rome], since it was fruitful (PRT), and multiplied through the prayer of the elder [Isaac at Gen. 27:39].

C. Another interpretation: It was because it was fruitful and multiplied, and so cramped the world.

D. Another explanation: Because it was fruitful and multiplied and cramped his son.

E. Another explanation: Because it was fruitful and multiplied and cramped his house.

F. Another explanation: "Parat"—because in the end, "I am going to exact a penalty from it."

G. That is in line with the following verse of Scripture: "I have trodden (PWRH) the winepress alone" (Is. 63:3).

7. A. [Gen. R. 42:2:] Abraham foresaw what the evil kingdoms would do [to Israel].

B. "[As the sun was going down,] a deep sleep fell on Abraham; and lo, a dread and great darkness fell upon him]" (Gen. 15:12).

C. "Dread" ('YMH) refers to Babylonia, on account of the statement, "Then Nebuchadnezzer was full of fury (HMH)" (Dan. 3:19).

D. "Darkness" refers to Media, which brought darkness to Israel through its decrees: "to destroy, to slay, and to wipe out all the Jews" (Est. 7:4).

E. "Great"refers to Greece.

F. Said R. Judah b. R. Simon, "The verse teaches that the kingdom of Greece set up one hundred twenty-seven governors, one hundred and twenty-seven hyparchs, and one hundred twenty-seven commanders."

G. And rabbis say, "They were sixty in each category."

H. R. Berekhiah and R. Hanan in support of this position taken by rabbis: " 'Who led you through the great terrible wilderness, with its fiery serpents and scorpions and thirsty ground where there was no water]' (Deut. 8:15).

I. "Just as the scorpion produces eggs by sixties, so the kingdom of Greece would set up its administration in groups of sixty."

J. "Fell on him" (Gen. 15:12).

K. This refers to Edom, on account of the following verse: "The earth quakes at the noise of their [Edom's] fall" (Jer. 49:21).

L. There are those who reverse matters.

M. "Fear" refers to Edom, on account of the following verse: "And this I saw, a fourth beast, fearful, and terrible" (Dan. 7:7).

N. "Darkness" refers to Greece, which brought gloom through its decrees. For they said to Israel, "Write on the horn of an ox that you have no portion in the God of Israel."

O. "Great" refers to Media, on account of the verse: "King Ahasuerus made Haman [the Median] great" (Est. 3:1).

P. "Fell on him" refers to Babylonia, on account of the following verse: "Fallen, fallen is Babylonia" (Is. 21:9).

8. A. Daniel foresaw what the evil kingdoms would do [to Israel].

B. Daniel said, "I saw in my vision by night, and behold, the four winds of heaven were stirring up the great sea. And four great beasts came up out of the sea, [different from one another. The first was like a lion and had eagles' wings. Then as I looked, its wings were plucked off . . . And behold, another beast, a second one, like a bear . . . After this I looked, and lo, another, like a leopard . . . After this I saw in the night visions, and behold, a fourth beast, terrible and dreadful and exceedingly strong; and it had great iron teeth]" (Dan. 7:3–7).

C. If you enjoy sufficient merit, it will emerge from the sea, but if not, it will come out of the forest.

D. The animal that comes up from the sea is not violent, but the one that comes up out of the forest is violent.

E. Along these same lines: "The boar out of the wood ravages it" (Ps. 80:14).

F. If you enjoy sufficient merit, it will come from the river, and if not, from the forest.

G. The animal that comes up from the river is not violent, but the one that comes up out of the forest is violent.

H. "Different from one another" (Dan. 7:3).

I. Differing from [hating] one another.

J. This teaches that every nation that rules in the world hates Israel and reduces them to slavery.

K. "The first was like a lion [and had eagles' wings]" (Dan. 7:4).

L. This refers to Babylonia.

M. Jeremiah saw [Babylonia] as a lion. Then he went and saw it as an eagle.

N. He saw it as a lion: "A lion has come up from his thicket" (Jer. 4:7).

O. And [as an eagle:] "Behold, he shall come up and swoop down as the eagle" (Jer. 49:22).

P. People said to Daniel, "What do you see?"

Q. He said to them, "I see the face like that of a lion and wings like those of an eagle: 'The first was like a lion and had eagles' wings. Then, as I looked, its wings were plucked off, and it was lifted up from the ground [and made to stand upon two feet like a man and the heart of a man was given to it]' " (Dan. 7:4).

R. R. Eleazar and R. Ishmael b. R. Nehemiah:

S. R. Eleazar said, "While the entire lion was smitten, its heart was not smitten.

T. "That is in line with the following statement: 'And the heart of a man was given to it' (Dan. 7:4)."

U. And R. Ishmael b. R. Nehemiah said, "Even its heart was smitten, for it is written, 'Let his heart be changed from a man's' " (Dan. 4:17).

X. "And behold, another beast, a second one, like a bear. [It was raised up one side; it had three ribs in its mouth between its teeth, and it was told, Arise, devour much flesh]" (Dan. 7:5).

Y. This refers to Media.

Z. Said R. Yohanan, "It is like a bear."

AA. It is written, "similar to a wolf" (DB); thus, "And a wolf was there."

BB. That is in accord with the view of R. Yohanan, for R. Yohanan said, "Therefore a lion out of the forest [slays them]' (Jer. 5:6)—this refers to Babylonia.

CC. " 'A wolf of the deserts spoils them' (Jer. 5:6) refers to Media.

DD. " 'A leopard watches over their cities' (Jer. 5:6) refers to Greece.

EE. " 'Whoever goes out from them will be savaged' (Jer. 5:6) refers to Edom.

FF. "Why so? 'Because their transgressions are many, and their backslidings still more' (Jer. 5:6)."

GG. "After this, I looked, and lo, another, like a leopard [with four wings of a bird on its back; and the beast had four heads; and dominion was given to it]" (Dan. 7:6).

HH. This [leopard] refers to Greece, which persisted impudently in making harsh decrees, saying to Israel, "Write on the horn of an ox that you have no share in the God of Israel."

II. "After this I saw in the night visions, and behold, a fourth beast, terrible and dreadful and exceedingly strong; [and it had great iron teeth; it devoured and broke in pieces and stamped the residue with its feet. It was different from all the beasts that were before it; and it had ten horns]" (Dan. 7:7).

JJ. This refers to Edom [Rome].

KK. Daniel saw the first three visions on one night, and this one he saw on another night. Now why was that the case?

LL. R. Yohanan and R. Simeon b. Laqish:

MM. R. Yohanan said, "It is because the fourth beast weighed as much as the first three."

NN. And R. Simeon b. Laqish said, "It outweighed them."

OO. R. Yohanan objected to R. Simeon b. Laqish, " 'Prophesy, therefore, son of man, clap your hands [and let the sword come down twice; yea, thrice. The sword for those to be slain; it is the sword for the great slaughter, which encompasses them]' (Ez. 21:14–15). [So the single sword of Rome weighs against the three others]."

PP. And R. Simeon b. Laqish, how does he interpret the same passage? He notes that [the threefold sword] is doubled (Ez. 21:14), [thus outweighs the three swords, equally twice their strength].

9. A. Moses foresaw what the evil kingdoms would do [to Israel].

B. "The camel, rock badger, and hare" (Deut. 14:7). [Compare: "Nevertheless, among those that chew the cud or part the hoof, you shall not eat these: the camel, because it chews the cud but does not part the hoof, is unclean to you. The rock badger, because it chews the cud but does not part the hoof, is unclean to you. And the hare, because it chews the cud but does not part the hoof, is unclean to you, and the pig, because it parts the hoof and is cloven-footed, but does not chew the cud, is unclean to you" (Lev. 11:4–8).]

C. The camel (GML) refers to Babylonia, [in line with the following verse of Scripture: "O daughter of Babylonia, you who are to be devastated!] Happy will be he who requites (GML) you, with what you have done to us" (Ps. 147:8).

D. "The rock badger" (Deut. 14:7)—this refers to Media.

E. Rabbis and R. Judah b. R. Simon.

F. Rabbis say, "Just as the rock badger exhibits traits of uncleanness and traits of cleanness, so the kingdom of Media produced both a righteous man and a wicked one."

G. Said R. Judah b. R. Simon, "The last Darius was Esther's son. He was clean on his mother's side and unclean on his father's side."

H. "The hare" (Deut. 14:7)—this refers to Greece. The mother of King Ptolemy was named "Hare" [in Greek: lagos].

I. "The pig" (Deut 14:7)—this refers to Edom [Rome].

J. Moses made mention of the first three in a single vese and the final one in a verse by itself [(Deut. 14:7, 8)]. Why so?

K. R. Yohanan and R. Simeon b. Laqish.

L. R. Yohanan said, "It is because [the pig] is equivalent to the other three."

M. And R. Simeon b. Laqish said, "It is because it outweighs them."

N. R. Yohanan objected to R. Simeon b. Laqish, " 'Prophesy, therefore, son of man, clap your hands [and let the sword come down twice, yea thrice]' (Ez. 21:14)."

O. And how does R. Simeon b. Laqish interpret the same passage? He notes that [the threefold sword] is doubled (Ez. 21:14).

10. A. [Gen. R. 65:1:] R. Phineas and R. Hilqiah in the name of R. Simon: "Among all the prophets, only two of them revealed [the true evil of Rome], Assaf and Moses.

B. "Assaf said, 'The pig out of the wood ravages it' (Ps. 80:14).

C. "Moses said, 'And the pig, [because it parts the hoof and is cloven-footed but does not chew the cud]' (Lev. 11:7).

D. "Why is [Rome] compared to a pig?

E. "It is to teach you the following: Just as, when a pig crouches and produces its hooves, it is as if to say, 'See how I am clean [since I have a cloven hoof],' so this evil kingdom takes pride, seizes by violence, and steals, and then gives the appearance of establishing a tribunal for justice."

F. There was the case of a ruler in Caesarea, who put thieves, adulterers, and sorcerers to death, while at the same time telling his counselor, "That same man [I] did all these three things on a single night."

11. A. Another interpretation: "The camel" (Lev. 11:4).

B. This refers to Babylonia.

C. "Because it chews the cud [but does not part the hoof]" (Lev. 11:4).

D. For it brings forth praises [with its throat] of the Holy One, blessed be he. [The Hebrew words for *chew the cud*—bring up cud—are now understood to mean "give praise." GRH is connected with GRWN, throat, hence, "bring forth [sounds of praise through] the throat."

E. R. Berekhiah and R. Helbo in the name of R. Ishmael b. R. Nahman: "Whatever [praise of God] David [in writing a psalm] treated singly [item by item], that wicked man [Nebuchadnezzar] lumped together in a single verse.

F. " 'Now I, Nebuchadnezzar, praise and extol and honor the King of heaven, for all his works are right and his ways are just, and those who walk in pride he is able to abase' (Dan. 4:37).

G. " 'Praise'—'O Jerusalem, praise the Lord' (Ps. 147:12).

H. " 'Extol'—'I shall extol you, O Lord, for you have brought me low' (Ps. 30:2).

I. " 'Honor the king of heaven'—'The Lord reigns, let the peoples tremble! He sits enthroned upon the cherubim, let the earth quake' (Ps. 99:1).

J. " 'For all his works are right'—'For the sake of thy steadfast love and thy faithfulness' (Ps. 115:1).

K. " 'And his ways are just'—'He will judge the peoples with equity' (Ps. 96:10).

L. " 'And those who walk in pride'—'The Lord reigns, he is robed in majesty, the Lord is robed, he is girded with strength' (Ps. 93:1).

M. " 'He is able to abase'—'All the horns of the wicked he will cut off' (Ps. 75:11))."

N. "The rock badger" (Lev. 11:5)—this refers to Media.

O. "For it chews the cud"—for it gives praise to the Holy One, blessed be he: "Thus says Cyrus, king of Persia, 'All the kingdoms of the earth has the Lord, the God of the heaven, given me' " (Ezra 1:2).

P. "The hare"—this refers to Greece.

Q. "For it chews the cud"—for it gives praise to the Holy One, blessed be he.

R. Alexander the Macedonian, when he saw Simeon the Righteous, said, "Blessed be the God of Simeon the Righteous."

S. "The pig" (Lev. 11:7)—this refers to Edom.

T. "For it does not chew the cud"—for it does not give praise to the Holy One, blessed be he.

U. And it is not enough that it does not give praise, but it blasphemes and swears violently, saying, "Whom do I have in heaven, and with you I want nothing on earth" (Ps. 73:25).

12. A. Another interpretation [of GRH, cud, now with reference to GR, stranger:]

B. "The camel" (Lev. 11:4)—this refers to Babylonia.

C. "For it chews the cud" [now: brings up the stranger]—for it exalts righteous men: "And Daniel was in the gate of the king" (Dan. 2:49).

D. "The rock badger" (Lev. 11:5)—this refers to Media.

E. "For it brings up the stranger"—for it exalts righteous men: "Mordecai sat at the gate of the king" (Est. 2:19).

F. "The hare" (Lev. 11:6)—this refers to Greece.

G. "For it brings up the stranger"—for it exalts the righteous.

H. When Alexander of Macedonia saw Simeon the Righteous, he would rise up on his feet. They said to him, "Can't you see the Jew, that you stand up before this Jew?"

I. He said to them, "When I go forth to battle, I see something like this man's visage and I conquer."

J.   "The pig" (Lev. 11:7)—this refers to Rome.

K.   "But it does not bring up the stranger"—for it does not exalt the righteous.

L.   And it is not enough that it does not exalt them, but it kills them.

M.   That is in line with the following verse of Scripture: "I was angry with my people, I profaned my heritage; I gave them into your hand, you showed them no mercy; on the aged you made your yoke exceedingly heavy" (Is. 47:6).

N.   This refers to R. Aqiba and his colleagues.

13. A.   Another interpretation [now treating "bring up the cud" (GR) as "bring along in its train" (GRR)]:

B.   "The camel" (Lev. 11:4)—this refers to Babylonia.

C.   "Which brings along in its train"—for it brought along another kingdom after it.

D.   "The rock badger" (Lev. 11:5)—this refers to Media.

E.   "Which brings along in its train"—for it brought along another kingdom after it.

F.   "The hare" (Lev. 11:6)—this refers to Greece.

G.   "Which brings along in its train"—for it brought along another kingdom after it.

H.   "The pig" (Lev. 11:7)—this refers to Rome.

I.   "Which does not bring along in its train"—for it did not bring along another kingdom after it.

J.   And why is it then called "pig" (HZYR)? For it restores (MHZRT) the crown to the one who truly should have it [namely, Israel, whose dominion will begin when the rule of Rome ends].

K.   That is in line with the following verse of Scripture: "And saviors will come up on Mount Zion to judge the Mountain of Esau [Rome], and the kingdom will then belong to the Lord" (Ob. 1:21).

To stand back and consider this vast apocalyptic vision of Israel's history, we first review the message of the construction as a whole. This comes in two parts, first, the explicit, then the· implicit. As to the former, the first claim is that God had told the prophets what would happen to Israel at the hands of the pagan kingdoms, Babylonia, Media, Greece, Rome. These are further represented by Nebuchadnezzar, Haman, Alexander for Greece, Edom or Esau, interchangeably, for Rome. The same vision came from Adam, Abraham, Daniel and Moses. The same policy toward Israel—oppression, destruction, enslavement, alienation from the true God—emerged from all four.

How does Rome stand out? First, it was made fruitful through the prayer of Isaac in behalf of Esau. Second, Edom is represented by the fourth and final beast. Rome is related through Esau, as Bayblonia, Media, and Greece are not. The fourth beast was seen in a vision separate from the first three. It was worst of all and outweighed the rest. In the apocalypticizing of the animals of Leviticus 11:4–8/Deuteronomy 14:7, the camel, rock badger, hare, and pig, the pig, standing for Rome, again emerges as different from the others and more threatening than the rest. Just as the pig pretends to be a clean beast by showing the cloven hoof, but in fact is an unclean one, so Rome pretends to be just but in fact governs by thuggery. Edom does not pretend to praise God but only blasphemes. It does not exalt the righteous but kills them. These symbols concede nothing to Christian monotheism and biblicism. Of greatest importance, while all the other beasts bring further ones in their wake, the pig does not: "It does not bring another kingdom after it." It will restore the crown to the one who will truly deserve it, Israel. Esau will be judged by Zion, so Obadiah 1:21. Now how has the symbolization delivered an implicit message? It is in the treatment of Rome as distinct, but essentially equivalent to the former kingdoms. This seems to me a stunning way of saying that the now-Christian empire in no way requires differentiation from its pagan predecessors. Nothing has changed, except matters have gotten worse. Beyond Rome, standing in a straight line with the others, lies the true shift in history, the rule of Israel and the cessation of the dominion of the (pagan) nations. To conclude, Leviticus Rabbah came to closure, it is generally agreed, around 400–450 C.E., that is, approximately a century after the Roman Empire in the east had begun to become Christian, and half a century after the last attempt to rebuild the Temple in Jerusalem had failed—a tumultuous age indeed. Accordingly, we have had the chance to see how distinctive and striking are the ways in which, in the text at hand, the symbols of animals that stand for the four successive empires of humanity and point towards the messianic time, serve for the framers' message.

8. The Bavli

The issue of process, we recall, concerns the relationship of the two components of the one whole Torah of Moses, our rabbi. We ask how the propositions of the oral Torah were supposed to relate to the authority of the written Torah. By the end of the composition of those components of the oral Torah that would be complete in ancient times—from the Mishnah through the Bavli—the consensus had been reached that statements in the oral Torah could be shown to derive from, to rest upon the authority of, the written Torah. Hence a systematic effort to locate warrant or proof in the written Torah for propositions first surfacing in the oral Torah would follow. This brings us to the matter of proposition. What required proof, in particular, was that the coming resurrection of the dead was a fact that derived from Scripture, the written Torah.

The topical issue focussed attention on teleology: the meaning and end of the life of Israel. This may be divided into two distinct propositions. One—important in the Mishnah—concerned the sanctification of Israel in the natural world, corresponding to the pattern of holiness of the supernatural world above. The purpose and stress of the Mishnah's system of Israel's life—its worldview, its way of life, its doctrine of Israel—then centered upon the matter of sanctification. The other proposition on the goal and purpose of all things produced the doctrine of salvation of the nation, the division of time into this age as against the coming age. We may therefore contrast two distinct, if correlated, teleological theories, the one symmetrical to nature and pointing toward supernature, the other resting on history and aiming at the end of time, the one teleology lacking all eschatological or historical compo-

nent, the other utterly eschatological in its definition, the ones-
peaking of the individual and his or her resurrection after death,
the other addressing the nation and its coming redemption after
history.

The Bavli, coming at the end of the line, joins the two issues
around which I have organized this anthology, process and proposition. The principal interest of the Bavli's authorship, in their
amplification of Mishnah-tractate Sanhedrin Chapter Ten, is in
proofs, from Scripture, of the resurrection of the dead. The part
of the rather protracted chapter devoted to Mishnah-tractate Sanhedrin Chapter Ten, which is Bavli Sanhedrin Chapter Eleven,
pursues that question of process. The topic of the chapter, we
know full well, concerns salvation: a share in the world to come.

We shall follow that discussion as it treats Mishnah-tractate Sanhedrin paragraphs 10:1–2, numbered by the Bavli's editors as
Chapter Eleven. Because of the length of the chapter as a whole,
we limit our review to that one matter. But our abstract provides
a full and encyclopedic picture of the doctrine of salvation that
would characterize the Judaism of the dual Torah emerging from
antiquity and flourishing down to our own day. It is a fitting point
on which to conclude this anthology.

11:1–2

    A. *All Israelites have a share in the world to come,*

    B. *as it is said, "your people also shall be all righteous,
they shall inherit the land forever; the branch of my
planting, the work of my hands, that I may be glorified" (Is. 60:21).*

    C. *And these are the ones who have no portion in the
world to come:*

    D. *He who says, the resurrection of the dead is a teaching
which does not derive from the Torah, and the Torah
does not come from Heaven; and an Epicurean.*

    E. *R. Aqiba says, "Also: He who reads in heretical
books,*

F. *"and he who whispers over a wound and says, 'I will put none of the diseases upon you which I have put on the Egyptians, for I am the Lord who heals you' (Ex. 15:26)."*

G. *Abba Saul says, "Also: He who pronounces the divine Name as it is spelled out."*

M. 11:1

A. *Three kings and four ordinary folk have no portion in the world to come.*

B. *Three kings: Jeroboam, Ahab, and Manasseh.*

C. *R. Judah says, "Manasseh has a portion in the world to come,*

D. *"since it is said, 'And he prayed to him and he was entreated of him and heard his supplication and brought him again to Jerusalem into his kingdom' (2 Chr. 33:13)."*

E. *They said to him, "To his kingdom he brought him back, but to the life of the world to come he did not bring him back."*

F. *Four ordinary folk: Balaam, Doeg, Ahitophel, and Gehazi.*

M. 11:2

I.

A. Why all this [that is, why deny the world to come to those listed]?

B. On Tannaite authority [it was stated], "Such a one denied the resurrection of the dead, therefore he will not have a portion in the resurrection of the dead.

C. "For all the measures [meted out by] the Holy One, blessed be he, are in accord with the principle of measure for measure."

D. For R. Samuel bar Nahmani said R. Jonathan said, "How do we know that all the measures [meted out by] the Holy One, blessed be he, accord with the principle of measure for measure?

E. "As it is written, 'Then Elisha said, Hear you the word of the Lord. Thus says the Lord, Tomorrow about this time shall a measure of fine flour be sold for a shekel, and two measures of barley for a shekel in the gates of Samaria' (2 Kgs. 7:1).

F. "And it is written, 'Then a lord on whose hand the king leaned answered the man of God and said, Behold, if the Lord made windows in heaven, might this thing be? And he said, Behold, you shall see it with your eyes, but shall not eat thereof' (2 Kgs. 7:2).

G. [90B] "And it is written, 'And so it fell unto him; for the people trod him in the gate and he died' " (2 Kgs. 7:20).

H. But perhaps it was Elisha's curse that made it happen to him, for R. Judah said Rab said, "The curse of a sage, even for nothing, will come about"?

I. If so, Scripture should have said, "They trod upon him and he died." Why say, "They trod upon him in the gate"?

J. It was that on account of matters pertaining to [the sale of wheat and barley at] the gate [which he had denied, that he died].

II.
A. How, on the basis of the Torah, do we know about the resurrection of the dead?

B. As it is said, "And you shall give thereof the Lord's heave-offering to Aaron the priest" (Num. 18:28).

C. And will Aaron live forever? And is it not the case that he did not even get to enter the Land of Israel, from the produce of which heave-offering is given?

D. Rather, this teaches that he is destined once more to live, and the Israelites will give him heave-offering.

E. On the basis of this verse, therefore, we see that the resurrection of the dead is a teaching of the Torah.

III.
A. A Tannaite authority of the house of R. Ishmael [taught], " '. . . to Aaron . . ., 'like Aaron.' [That is to say,] just as Aaron was in the status of an associate [who ate his produce in a state of cultic cleanness even when not in the Temple], so his sons must be in the status of associates."

B. Said R. Samuel bar Nahmani said R. Jonathan, "How on the basis of Scripture do we know that people do not give heave-offering to a priest who is in the status of an ordinary person [and not an associate]?

C. "As it is said, 'Moreover he commanded the people who lived in Jerusalem to give the portion of the Levites, that they might hold fast to the Torah of the Lord' (2 Chr. 31:4).

D. "Whoever holds fast to the Torah of the Lord has a portion, and whoever does not hold fast to the Torah of the Lord has no portion."

E. Said R. Aha bar Ada said R. Judah, "Whoever hands over heave-offering to a priest who is in the status of an ordinary person is as if he throws it in front of a lion.

F. "Just as, in the case of a lion, it is a matter of doubt whether he will tear at the prey and eat it or not do so,

G. "so in the case of a priest who is in the status of an ordinary person, it is a matter of doubt whether he will eat it in a condition of cultic cleanness or eat it in a condition of cultic uncleanness."

H. R. Yohanan said, "[If one gives it to an improper priest], he also causes him to die, for it is said, 'And . . . die therefore if they profane it' " Lev. 22:9)."

I. The Tannaite authority of the house of R. Eliezer B. Jacob [taught], "One also gets him involved in the sin of guilt [of various kinds], for it is written, 'Or suffer them to bear the iniquity of trespass when they eat their holy things' (Lev. 22:16)."

IV.

A. It has been taught on Tannaite authority:

B. R. Simai says, "How on the basis of the Torah do we know about the resurrection of the dead?

C. "As it is said, 'And I also have established my covenant with [the patriarchs] to give them the land of Canaan' (Ex. 6:4).

D. " 'With you' is not stated, but rather, 'with them,' indicating on the basis of the Torah that there is the resurrection of the dead."

V.

A. Minim asked Rabban Gamaliel, "How do we know that the Holy One, blessed be he, will resurrect the dead?"

B. He said to them, "It is proved from the Torah, from the Prophets, and from the Writings." But they did not accept his proofs.

C. "From the Torah: for it is written, 'And the Lord said to Moses, Behold, you shall sleep with your fathers and rise up' (Deut. 31:16)."

D. They said to him, "But perhaps the sense of the passage is, 'And the people will rise up' (Deut. 31:16)?"

E. "From the Prophets: as it is written, 'Thy dead men shall live, together with my dead body they shall arise. Awake and sing, you that live in the dust, for your dew is as the dew of herbs, and the earth shall cast out its dead' (Is. 26:19)."

F. "But perhaps that refers to the dead whom Ezekiel raised up."

G. "From the Writings, as it is written, 'And the roof of your mouth, like the best wine of my beloved, that goes down sweetly, causing the lips of those who are asleep to speak' (Song 7:9)."

H. "But perhaps this means that the dead will move their lips?"

I. That would accord with the view of R. Yohanan.

J. For R. Yohanan said in the name of R. Simeon b. Yehosedeq, "Any authority in whose name a law is stated in this world moves his lips in the grave,

K. "as it is said, 'Causing the lips of those that are asleep to speak.' "

L. [The minim would not concur in Gamaliel's view] until he cited for them the following verse: " 'Which the Lord swore to your fathers to give to them' (Deut. 11:21)—to them and not to you, so proving from the Torah that the dead will live."

M. And there are those who say that it was the following verse that he cited to them: " 'But you who cleaved to the Lord you God are alive, everyone of you this day' (Deut. 4:4). Just as on this day all of you are alive, so in the world to come all of you will live."

VI.

A. Romans asked R. Joshua b. Hananiah, "How do we know that the Holy One will bring the dead to life and also that he knows what is going to happen in the future?"

B. He said to them, "Both propositions derive from the following verse of Scripture:

C. "As it is said, 'And the Lord said to Moses, Behold you shall sleep with you fathers and rise up again, and this people shall go awhoring . . .' (Deut 31:16)."

D. "But perhaps the sense is, '[The people] will rise up and go awhoring'?

E. He said to them, "Then you have gained half of the matter, that God knows what is going to happen in the future."

VII.

A. It has also been stated on Amoraic authority:

B. Said R. Yohanan in the name of R. Simeon b. Yohai, "How do we know that the Holy One, blessed be he, will bring the dead to life and knows what is going to happen in the future?

C. "As it is said, 'Behold, you shall sleep with you fathers, and . . . rise again . . .' (Deut. 31:16)."

VIII.

A. It has been taught on Tannaite authority:

B. Said R. Eliezer b. R. Yose, "In this matter I proved false the books of the minim.

C. "For they would say, 'The principle of the resurrection of the dead does not derive from the Torah.'

D. "I said to them, 'You have forged your Torah and have gained nothing on that account.

E. " 'For you say, "The principle of the resurrection of the dead does not derive from the Torah." '

F. "Lo, Scripture says, '[Because he has despised the Lord of the Lord . . .] that soul shall be cut off completely, his iniquity shall be upon him' (Num. 15:31).

G. " ' "Shall be utterly cut off . . .," in this world, in which case, at what point will ". . . his iniquity be upon him . . ."?

H. " 'Will it not be in the world to come?' "

I. Said R. Pappa to Abayye, "And might one not have replied to them that the words 'utterly cut off . . .,' signify the two worlds [this and the next]?"

J. [He said to him,] "They would have answered, 'The Torah speaks in human language [and the doubling of the verb carries no meaning beyond its normal sense].' "

IX.

A. This accords with the following Tannaite dispute:

B. " 'That soul shall be utterly cut off'—'shall be cut off'—in this world, 'utterly'—in the world to come," the words of R. Aqiba.

C. Said R. Ishmael to him, "And has it not been said, 'He reproaches the Lord, and that soul shall be cut off' (Num. 15:31). Does this mean that there are three worlds?

D. "Rather: '. . . It will be cut off . . .,' in this world, '. . . utterly . . .,' in the world to come, and 'utterly cut off . . .,' indicates that the Torah speaks in ordinary human language."

E. Whether from the view of R. Ishmael or of R. Aqiba, what is the meaning of the phrase, "His iniquity shall be upon him"?

F. It accords with that which has been taught on Tannaite authority:

G. Is it possible that that is the case even if he repented?

H. Scripture states, "His iniquity shall be upon him."

I. I have made the statement at hand only for a case in which "his iniquity is yet upon him" [but not if he repented].

X.

A. Queen Cleopatra asked R. Meir, saying, "I know that the dead will live, for it is written, 'And [the righteous] shall blossom forth out of your city like the grass of the earth' (Ps. 72:16).

B. "But when they rise, will they rise naked or in their clothing?"

C. He said to her, "It is an argument a fortiori based on the grain of wheat.

D. "Now if a grain of wheat, which is buried naked, comes forth in many garments, the righteous, who are buried in their garments, all the more so [will rise in many garments]!"

XI.   A. Caesar said to Rabban Gamaliel, "You maintain that the dead will live. But they are dust, and can the dust live?"

B. [91A] His daughter said to him, "Allow me to answer him.

C. "There are two potters in our town, one who works with water, the other who works with clay. Which is the more impressive?"

D. He said ot her, "The one who works with water."

E. She said to him, "If he works with water, will he not create even more out of clay?"

XII.   A. A Tannaite authority of the house of R. Ishmael [taught], "[Resurrection] is a matter of an argument *a fortiori* based on the case of a glass utensil.

B. "Now if glassware, which is the work of the breath of a mortal man, when broken, can be repaired,

C. "a mortal man, who is made by the breath of the Holy One, blessed be he, how much the more so [that he can be repaired, in the resurrection of the dead]."

XIII.   A. A min [heretic] said to R. Ammi, "You say that the dead will live. But they are dust, and will the dust live?"

B. He said to him, "I shall draw a parable for you. To what may the matter be compared?

C. "It may be compared to the case of a mortal king, who said to his staff, 'Go and build a great palace for me, in a place in which there is no water or dirt [for bricks].'

D. "They went and built it, but after a while it collapsed.

E. "He said to them, 'Go and rebuild it in a place in which there are dirt and water [for bricks].'

F. "They said to him, 'We cannot do so.'

G. "He became angry with them and said to them, 'In a place in which there is neither water nor dirt you were able to build, and now in a place in which there are water and dirt, how much the more so [should you be able to build it]!'

H. "And if you [the min] do not believe it, go to a valley and look at a rat, which today is half-flesh and half-dirt and tomorrow will turn into a creeping thing, made all of flesh. Will you say that it takes much time? Then go up to a mountain and see that today there is only one snail, but tomorrow it will rain and the whole of it will be filled with snails."

XIV.

A. A min said to Gebiha, son of Pesisa, [a hunchback,] "Woe for you! You are guilty! For you say that the dead will live. Those who are alive die, and will those who are dead live?"

B. He said to him, "Woe for you! You are guilty! For you say that the dead will not live. [Now if we] who were not [alive before birth] now live, will not those who do live all the more so [live again]?"

C. He said to him, "Have you then called me guilty? If I stood up, I could kick you and straighten out your hump."

D. He said to him, "If you could do that, you would be a physician, a specialist who collects enormous fees."

XV.

A. Our rabbis have taught on Tannaite authority:

B. On the twenty-four of Nisan the tax-farmers were dismissed from Judea and Jerusalem.

C. When the Africans came to trial with Israel before Alexander of Macedonia, they said to him, "The land of Canaan belongs to us, for it is written, 'The land of Canaan, with the coasts thereof' (Num. 34:2), and Canaan was the father of these men."

D. Said Gebiha, son of Pasisa, to sages, "Give me permission, and I shall go and defend the case with them before Alexander of Macedonia. If they should win out over me, say, 'You won over a perfectly common person of our group,' and if I should win out over them, say to them, 'It is the Torah of Moses that overcame you.' "

E. They gave him permission, and he went and engaged in debate with them. He said to them, "From whence do you bring proof?"

F. They said to him, "From the Torah."

G. He said to them, "I too shall bring you proof only from the Torah, for it is said, 'And he said, Cursed be Canaan, a servant of servants shall he be to his brothers' (Gen. 9:25).

H. "Now if a slave acquires property, for whom does he acquire it? And to whom is the property assigned?

I. "And not only so, but it is quite a number of years since you have served us."

J. Said King Alexander to them, "Give him an answer."

K. They said to him, "Give us a span of three days' time." He gave them time.

L. They searched and did not find an answer. They forthwith fled, leaving their fields fully sown and their vineyards laden with fruit, and that year was the Sabbatical Year. [So the Israelites could enjoy the produce in a time in which they most needed it.]

XVI.

A. There was another time, [and] the Egyptians came to lay claim against Israel before Alexander of Macedonia. They said to him, "Lo, Scripture says, 'And the Lord gave the people favor in the sight of the Egyptians, and they lent them gold and precious stones' (Ex. 12:36). Give us back the silver and gold that you took from us."

B. Said Gebiha, son of Pasisa, to sages, "Give me permission, and I shall go and defend the case with them before Alexander of Macedonia. If they should win out over me, say, 'You won over a perfectly common person of our group,' and if I should win out over them, say to them, 'It is the Torah of Moses, our master, that overcame you.' "

C. They gave him permission, and he went and engaged in debate with them. He said to them, "From whence do you bring proof?"

D. They said to him, "From the Torah."

E. He said to them, "I too shall bring you proof only from the Torah, for it is said, 'Now the sojourning of the children of Israel, who dwelt in Egypt, was four hundred and thirty years' (Ex. 12:40).

F. "Now pay us the salary of six hundred thousand people whom you enslaved in Egypt for four hundred and thirty years."

G. Said Alexander of Macedonia to them, "Give him an answer."

H. They said to him, "Give us time, a span of three days."

I. He gave them time. They searched and found no answer. They forthwith fled, leaving their fields sown and their vineyards laden with fruit, and that year was the Sabbatical Year.

XVII.

A. There was another time, [and] the children of Ishmael and the children of Keturah came to trial with the Israelites before Alexander of Macedonia. They said to him, "The land of Canaan belongs to us as well as to you, for it is written, 'Now these are the generations of Ishmael, son of Abraham' (Gen. 25:12), and it is written, 'And these are the generations of Isaac, Abraham's son' (Gen. 25:19). [Both Ishmael and Isaac have an equal claim on the land, hence so too their descendants]."

B. Said Gebiha, son of Pasisa, to sages, "Give me permission, and I shall go and defend the case with them before Alexander of Macedonia. If they should win out over me, say, 'You won over a perfectly common person of our group,' and if I should win out over them, say to them, 'It is the Torah of Moses, our master, that overcame you.' "

C. They gave him permission, and he went and engaged in debate with them. He said to them, "From whence do you bring proof?"

D. They said to him, "From the Torah."

E. He said to them, "I too shall bring you proof only from the Torah, for it is said, 'And Abraham gave all that he had to Isaac. But to the sons of the concubines which Abraham had Abraham gave gifts' (Gen. 25:5–6).

F. "In the case of a father who gave a bequest to his sons while he was yet alive and sent them away from one another, does any one of them have a claim on the other? [Certainly not.]"

G. What were the gifts [that he gave]?

H. Said R. Jeremiah bar Abba, "This teaches that he gave them [the power of utilizing the divine] Name [for] unclean [purposes]."

XVIII.

A. Antoninus said to Rabbi, "The body and the soul both can exempt themselves from judgment.

B. "How so? The body will say, 'The soul is the one that has sinned, for from the day that it left me, lo, I am left like a silent stone in the grave.'

C. "And the soul will say, 'The body is the one that sinned. For from the day that I left it, lo, I have been flying about in the air like a bird.' "

D. He said to him, "I shall draw a parable for you. To what may the matter be likened? To the case of a mortal king who had a lovely orchard, and in it were [91B] luscious figs. He set in it two watchmen, one crippled and one blind.

E. "Said the cripple to the blind man, 'There are luscious figs that I see in the orchard. Come and carry me, and let us get some to eat. The cripple rode on the blind man and they got the figs and ate them. After a while the king said to them, 'Where are the luscious figs?'

F. "Said the cripple, 'Do I have feet to go to them?'

G. "Said the blind man, 'Do I have eyes to see?'

H. "What did the king do? He had the cripple climb onto the blind man, and he inflicted judgment on them as one.

I. "So the Holy One, blessed be he, brings the soul and places it back in the body and judges them as one, as it is said, 'He shall call to the heavens from above and to the earth, that he may judge his people' (Ps. 50:4).

J. " 'He shall to call to the heavens from above'—this is the soul.

K. " 'And to the earth, that he may judge his people'—this is the body."

XIX.

A. Said to Antoninus to Rabbi. "Why does the sun rise in the east and set in the west?"

B. He said to him, "If thing were opposite, you would still ask me the same thing!"

C. He said to him, "This is what I meant to ask you: Why does it set in the west?"

D. He said, "To give a greeting to its maker, as it is written, 'And the host of the heavens make obeisance to you' (Neh. 9:6) . . ."

E. He said to him, "Then let it go halfway through the firmament, pay its respects, and then ascend from there [eastward]."

XX.

A. Said Antoninus to Rabbi, "At what point is the soul placed in man? Is it at the moment that it is decreed [that the person shall be born] or when the embryo is formed?"

B. He said to him, "From the moment when it is formed."

C. He said to him, "Is it possible that a piece of flesh should keep for three days of it is not salted and not become rotten?

D. "Rather, it should be from the time at which it is decreed [that the person should come into being."

E. Said Rabbi, "This is something that Antoninus taught me, and a verse of Scripture supports his view, for it is said, 'And your decree has preserved my soul' (Job 10:12)."

XXI.

A. And Antoninus said to Rabbi, "At what point does the impulse to do evil take hold of a man? Is it from the moment of creation or from the moment of parturition?"

B. He said to him, "It is from the moment of creation."

C. He said to him, "If so, the fetus will kick its mother's womb and escape. Rather, it is from the moment of parturition."

D. Said Rabbi, "This is something that Antoninus taught me, and a verse of Scripture supports his view, for it is said, 'At the door [of the womb] sin lies in wait' (Gen. 4:7)."

XXII.   A. R. Simeon b. Laqish contrasted [these two verses]: "It is written, 'I will gather them . . . with the blind and the lame, the woman with child and her that trail travails with child together' (Jer. 31:8), and it is written, 'Then shall the lame man leap as a hart and the tongue of the dumb sing, for in the wilderness shall waters break out and streams in the desert' (Is. 35:6). How so [will the dead both retain their defects and also be healed]?

    B. "They will rise [from the grave] bearing their defects and then be healed."

XXIII.   A. Ulla contrasted [these two verses]: "It is written, 'He will destroy death forever and the Lord God will wipe away tears from all faces' (Is. 25:9), and it is written, 'For the child shall die a hundred years old . . . there shall no more thence an infant of days' (Is. 65:20).

    B. "There is no contradiction. The one speaks of Israel, the other of idolators."

    C. But what do idolators want there [Freedman, p. 612, n. 9: in the reestablished state after the resurrection]?

    D. It is to those concerning whom it is written, "And strangers shall stand and feed your flocks, and the sons of the alien shall be your plowmen and your vinedressers" (Is. 61:5).

XXIV.   A. R. Hisda contracted [these two verses]: "It is written, 'Then the moon shall be confounded and the sun ashamed, when the Lord of hosts shall reign' (Is. 24:23), and it is written, 'Moreover the light of the moon shall be as the light of seven days' (Is 30:26).

    B. "There is no contradiction. The one refers to the days of the Messiah, the other to the world to come."

    C. And in the view of Samuel, who has said, "There is no difference between the world to come and the days of the Messiah, except the end of the subjugation of the exilic communities of Israel"?

    D. There still is no contradiction. The one speaks of the camp of the righteous, the other the camp of the Presence of God.

XXV.   A. Raba contrasted [these two verses]: "It is written, 'I kill and I make alive' (Deut. 32:39) and it is written, 'I wound and I heal' (Deut. 32:39). [Freedman, p. 613, n. 4, 5: The former implies that one is resurrected just as he was at death, thus with blemishes, and the other implies that at the resurrection all wounds are healed].

B. "Said the Holy One, blessed be he, 'What I kill I bring to life,' and then, 'What I have wounded I heal.' "

XXVI.   A. Our rabbis have taught on Tannaite authority: "I kill and I make alive" (Deut. 32:39).

B. Is it possible to suppose that there is death for one person and life for the other, just as the world is accustomed [now]?

C. Scripture says, "I wound and I heal" (Deut. 32:39).

D. Just as wounding and healing happen to one person, so death and then resurrection happen to one person.

E. From this fact we derive an answer to those who say, "There is no evidence of the resurrection of the dead based on the teachings of the Torah."

XXVII. A. It has been taught on Tannaite authority:

B. R. Meir says, "How on the basis of the Torah do we know about the resurrection of the dead?

C. "As it is said, 'Then shall Moses and the children of Israel sing this song to the Lord' (Ex. 15:1).

D. "What is said is not 'sang' but 'will sing,' on the basis of which there is proof from the Torah of the resurrection of the dead.

E. "Along these same lines: 'Then shall Joshua build an altar to the Lord God of Israel' (Josh. 8:30).

F. "What is said is not 'built' but 'will build,' on the basis of which there is proof from the Torah of the resurrection of the dead."

G. Then what about this verse: "Then will Solomon build a high place for Chemosh, abomination of Moab" (1 Kgs. 11:7)? Does it mean that he will build it? Rather, the Scripture treats him as though he had built it [even though he had merely thought about doing so].

XXVIII. A. Said R. Joshua b. Levi. "How on the basis of Scripture may we prove the resurrection of the dead?

B. "As it is said, 'Blessed are those who dwell in your house, they shall ever praise you, selah' (Ps. 84:5).

C. "What is said is not 'praised you' but 'shall praise you,' on the basis of which there is proof from the Torah of the resurrection of the dead."

D. And R. Joshua b. Levi said, "Whoever recites the song [of praise] in this world will have the merit of saying it in the world to come,

E. "as it is said, 'Happy are those who dwell in you house, they shall ever praise you, selah' (Ps. 84:5)."

F. Said R. Hiyya b. Abba said R. Yohanan, "On what basis do we know about the resurrection of the dead from Scripture?

G. "As it says, 'Your watchman shall lift up the voice, with the voice together they shall sing (Is. 52:8).'

H. "What is said is not 'sang' but 'will sing' on the basis of which there is proof from the Torah of the resurrection of the dead."

I. Said R. Yohanan, "In the future all the prophets will sing in unison, as it is written, 'Your watchman shall lift up the voice, with the voice together they shall sing (Is. 57:8).'"

XXX.   A. Said R. Judah said Rab, "Whoever withholds a teaching of law from a disciple is as if he steals the inheritance of his fathers from him.

B. "For it is said, 'Moses commanded us Torah, even the inheritance of the congregation of Jacob' (Deut. 33:4).

C. "It is an inheritance destined for all Israel from the six days of creation."

D. Said R. Hana bar Bizna said R. Simeon the Pious, "Whoever withholds a teaching of law from a disciple is cursed even by the fetuses in their mothers' womb, as it is said, 'He who withholds grain [92A] will be cursed by the embryo' (Prov. 11:26), for the word at hand can only mean 'embryo,' as it is written, 'And one embryo shall be stronger than the other people' (Gen. 25:23) [referring to Jacob and Esau in the womb].

E. "And the cited word can only mean 'cursing,' as it is written, 'How shall I curse whom God has not cursed?' (Num. 23:8).

F. "And the word for grain speaks only of 'the Torah,' as it is written, 'Nourish yourselves with grain lest he be angry' (Ps. 2:12)."

G. Ulla bar Ishmael say, "They pierce him like a sieve, for here it is written, 'The people will pierce him,' (Prov. 11:26), and the word means pierce in the verse, 'And he pierced a hole in the lid of it' (2 Kgs. 12:10)."

H. And Abayye said, "He will be like a fuller's trough [so perforated as a drainage plank]."

I. And if he does teach a law, what is his reward?

J. Said Raba said R. Sheshet, "He will merit blessing like those that came to Joseph, as it is said, 'But blessing shall be upon the head of the one who sells' (Prov. 11:26).

K. "And the one who sells speaks only of Joseph, as it is said, 'And Joseph was the governor over the land, and he was the one who sells to all the people of the land' (Gen. 47:6)."

XXXI.   A. Said R. Sheshet, "Whoever teaches Torah in this world will have the merit of teaching it in the world to come,

B. "as it is said, 'And he who waters shall water again too, (Prov. 11:25)."

XXXII. A. Said Raba, "How on the basis of the Torah do we find evidence for the resurrection of the dead?

B. "As it is said, 'Let Reuben live and not die' (Deut. 33:6).

C. " 'Let Reuben live' in this world, and 'not die', in the world to come."

D. Rabina said, "Proof derives from here: 'And many of them that sleep in the dust of the earth shall awake, some to everlasting life, and some to shame and everlasting contempt.' (Dan. 12:2)."

E. R. Ashi said, "Proof derives from here: 'But go your way till the end be, for you shall rest and stand in your lot at the end of days' (Dan. 12:13)."

XXXIII.

A. Said R. Eleazar, "Every authority who leads the community serenely will have the merit of leading them in the world to come, as it is said, 'For he who has mercy on them shall lead them, even by springs of water shall he guide them' (Is. 49:10)."

B. And said R. Eleazar, "Great is knowledge, for it is set between two names [lit. letters] [of God], as it is written, 'For a God of knowledge is the Lord' (1 Sam. 2:3)."

C. And said R. Eleazar, "Great is the sanctuary, for it is set between two names [of God], as it is written, 'You have made for yourself, O Lord, a sanctuary, O Lord, your hands have established it' (Ex. 15:17)."

D. To this view R. Ada Qarhinaah objected, "Then how about the following: Great is vengeance, for it is set between two names [of God], as it is written, 'O God of vengeance, O Lord, O God of vengeance, appear' (Ps. 94:1)."

E. He said to him, "In context, that is quite so, in line with what Ulla said."

F. For Ulla said, "What purpose is served by these two references to 'appear'? One speaks of the measure of good, the other, the measure of punishment."

G. And said R. Eleazar, "In the case of any man who has knowledge it is as if the house of the sanctuary had been built in his own time, for this [knowledge] is set between two names of [God], and that [the Temple] likewise is set between two names of [God]."

H. And said R. Eleazar, "Any man in whom there is knowledge in the end will be rich, for it is said, 'And by knowledge shall the chambers be filled with all precious and pleasant riches' (Prov 24:4)."

I. And said R. Eleazar, "It is forbidden to have pity on any man in whom there is no knowledge, as it is said, 'For it is a people of no understanding; therefore he that made them will not have mercy upon them, and he that formed them will show them no favor' (Is. 27:11)."

J. And said R. Eleazar, "Whoever gives his bread to someone who does not have knowledge in the end will be afflicted with sufferings, for it is said, 'They who eat your bread have laid a wound under you, there is no understanding in him' (Obad. 1:7), and the word for 'wound' can mean only suffering, as it is written, 'When Ephraim saw his sickness and Judah his suffering' [using the same word] (Hos. 5:13)."

K. And said R. Eleazar, "Any man who has no knowledge in the end will go into exile, as it is said, 'Therefore my people have gone into exile, because they have no knowledge' (Is. 5:13)."

L. And said R. Eleazar, "Any house in which words of Torah are not heard by night will be eaten up by fire, as it is said, 'All darkness is hid in his secret places; a fire not blown shall consume him; he grudges him that is left in his tabernacle' (Job 20:26).

M. "The word for 'grudges' means only a disciple of a sage, as it is written, 'And in those left [using the same root] whom the Lord shall call' (Joel 3:5). [Freedman, p. 616, n. 12: The first part of the verse, 'all darkness is hid . . .,' is interpreted as, his secret places are not illumined by the study of the law; the last part, 'he grudges . . .,' as, he looks with disfavor upon any student who enters his house for a meal]."

N. And said R. Eleazar, "Whoever does not give a benefit to disciples of sages from his property will see no blessing ever, as it is said, 'There is none who remains to eat it, therefore shall he not hope for prosperity' (Job 20:21).

O. "The word for 'remain' refers only to a disciple of a sage, as it is written, 'And in those left whom the Lord shall call' (Joel 3:5)."

P. And said R. Eleazar, "Anyone who does not leave a piece of bread on his table will never see a sign of blessing, as it is said, 'There be none of his food left, therefore shall he not hope for his prosperity' (Job 20:21)."

Q. But has not R. Eleazar said, "Whoever leaves pieces of bread on his table is as if he worships an idol, as it is said, 'That prepare a table for God and that furnish the drink offering to Meni' (Is 65:11)"?

R. There is no contradiction, in the one case [the latter] a complete loaf is left alongside, and in the other case [the former], no complete loaf is left [with the crumbs].

S. And said R. Eleazar, "Whoever goes back on what he has said is as if he worships an idol.

T. "Here it is written, 'And I seem to him as a deceiver' (Ge. 27:12), and elsewhere it is written, 'They [idols] are vanity and the work of deceivers' (Jer. 10:15)."

U. And said R. Eleazar, "Whoever stares at a woman's sexual parts will find that his 'bow' is emptied out, as it is said, 'Shame shall empty your bow [of strength]' (Hab. 3:9)."

V. And said R. Eleazar, "One should always accept [things] and so endure."

W. Said R. Zira, "We too also have learned on Tannaite authority:

X. *"As to a room without windows, people are not to open windows for it to examine whether or not it is afflicted with a plague sign [M. Neg. 2:3].* [Thus the possible signs will be missed because of the obscurity of the room. Likewise humility protects one's life.]"

Y. That makes the case.

XXXIV.

A. Said R. Tabi said R. Josiah, "What is the meaning of this verse of Scripture: 'The grave and the barren womb and the earth that is not filled by water' (Prov. 30:16)?

B. "What has the grave to do with the womb?

C. "It is to say to you, just as the womb takes in and gives forth, so Sheol takes in and gives forth.

D. "And is it not an argument *a fortiori?* If in the case of the womb, in which they insert [something] in secret, the womb brings forth in loud cries, Sheol, into which [bodies] are placed with loud cries, is it not reasonable to suppose that from the grave people will be brought forth with great cries?

E. "On the basis of this argument there is an answer to those who say that the doctrine of the resurrection of the dead does not derive from the Torah."

XXXV.

A. A Tannaite authority of the house of Elishah [taught], "The righteous whom the Holy One, blessed be he, is going to resurrect will not revert to dust,

B. "for it is said, 'And it shall come to pass that he that is left in Zion and he that remains in Jerusalem shall be called holy, even everyone that is written among the living in Jerusalem' (Is. 4:3).

C. "Just as the Holy One lives forever, so they shall live forever.

D. [92B] "And if you want to ask, as to those years in which the Holy One, blessed be he, will renew his world, as it is said, 'And the Lord alone shall be exalted in that day' (Is. 2:11), during that time what will the righteous do?

E. "The answer is that the Holy One, blessed be he, will make them wings like eagles, and they will flutter above the water, as it is said, 'Therefore will not fear, when the earth be moved and the mountains be carried in the midst of the sea' (Ps. 44:3).

F. "And if you should say that they will have pain [in all this], Scripture says, 'But those who wait upon the Lord shall renew their strength, they shall mount up with wings as eagles, they shall run and not be weary, they shall walk and not be faint' (Is. 40:31)."

G. And should we derive [the opposite view] from the dead whom Ezekiel resurrected?

H. He accords with the view of him who said that, in truth, it was really a parable.

I. For it has been taught on Tannaite authority:

J. R. Eliezer says, "The dead whom Ezekiel resurrected stood on their feet, recited a song, and then died."

K. What song did they recite?

L. "The Lord kills in righteousness and revives in mercy" (1 Sam. 2:6).

M. R. Joshua says, "They recited this song, 'The Lord kills and makes live, he brings down to the grave and brings up' (1 Sam. 2:6)."

N. R. Judah says, "It was true it was a parable."

O. Said to him R. Nehemiah, "If it was true, then why a parable? And if a parable, why true? But in truth it was a parable."

P. R. Eliezer, son of R. Yose the Galilean, says, "The dead whom Ezekiel resurrected went up to the Land of Israel and got married and produced sons and daughters."

Q. R. Judah b. Betera stood up and said, "I am one of their grandsons, and theses are the phylacteries that father's father left me from them."

R. And who were the dead whom Ezekiel resurrected?

S. Said Rab, "They were the Ephraimites who reckoned the end of time and erred, as it is said, 'And the sons of Ephraim, Shuthelah and Bared his son and Tahath his son and Eladah his son and Tahath his son. And Zabad his son and Shuthelah his son and Ezzer and Elead, whom the men of Gath that were born in the land slew' (1 Chr. 7:20–21). And it is written, 'And Ephraim their father mourned many days and his brethren came to comfort him' (1 Chr. 7:22)."

T. And Samuel said, "They were those who denied the resurrection of the dead, as it is said, 'Then he said to me, Son of man, these bones are the whole house of Israel; behold, they say, Our bones are dried and our hope is lost, we are cut off for our parts' (Ez. 37:11)."

U. Said R. Jeremiah, "These were the men who had not a drop of religious duties to their credit, as it is written, 'O you dry bones, hear the word of the Lord' (Ez. 37:4)."

V. R. Isaac Nappaha said, "They were the men who had covered the sanctuary entirely with abominations and creeping things, as it is said, 'So I went in and saw, and behold, every form of creeping things and abominable beasts and all the idols of the house of Israel, portrayed upon the wall round about' (Ez. 8:10).

W. "While [in the case of the dry bones] it is written, 'And caused me to pass by them round about' (Ez. 37:2). [Freedman, p. 620, n. 1: The identification is based on the use of 'round about' in both narratives. In his view even those who in their despair surrender themselves to abominable worship are not excluded from the bliss of resurrection.]"

X. R. Yohanan said, "They were the dead in the valley of Dura."

Y. And said R. Yohanan, "From the river Eshel to Rabbath is the valley of Dura. For when Nebuchadnezzar, that wicked man, exiled Israel, there were young men who outshone the sun in their beauty. Chaldean women would see them and reach orgasm [from the mere gaze]. They told their husbands and their husbands told the king. The king ordered them killed. Still, the wives would reach orgasm [merely from laying eyes on the corpses]. The king gave an order and they trampled [the corpses beyond all recognition]."

XXXVI. A. Our rabbis have taught on Tannaite authority:

B. When Nebuchadnezzar, the wicked man, cast Hananiah, Mishael, and Azariah, into the fiery furnace, the Holy One, blessed be he, said to Ezekiel, "Go and raise the dead in the valley of Dura."

C. When he had raised them, the bones came and smacked that wicked man in his face. He said, "What are these things?"

D. They said to him, "The friend of these is raising the dead in the valley of Dura."

E. He then said, " 'How great are his signs, and how mighty his wonders. His kingdom is an everlasting kingdom, and his dominion is from generation to generation' (Dan. 3:23)."

F. Said R. Isaac, "May liquid gold pour into the mouth of that wicked man.

G. "For had not an angel come and slapped his mouth shut, he would have attempted to shame [by the excellence of his composition] all the songs and praises that David had recited in the book of Psalms."

XXXVII. A. Our rabbis have taught on Tannaite authority:

B. Six miracles were done on that day, and these are they:

C. The furnace floated, the furnace split open, the foundations crumbled, the image was turned over on its face, the four kings were burned up, and Ezekiel raised the dead in the valley of Dura.

D. And all of the others were a matter of tradition, but the [miracle of the] four kings is indicated in a verse of Scripture: "Then Nebuchadnezzar the king sent to gather together the princes, the governors, and the captains, the judges, the treasurers, the counselors, the sheriffs, and all the rulers of the provinces [to come to the dedication of the image]" (Dan. 3:2),

E. and it is written, "There are certain Jews . . ." (Dan. 3:2),

F. and also: "And the princes, governors, and captains, and the king's counselors, being gathered together, saw these men, upon whom the fire had no power" (Dan. 3:27).

XXXVIII.   A. A Tannaite authority of the house of R. Eliezer b. Jacob [taught], "Even in time of danger a person should not pretend that he does not hold his high office.

B. "For it is said, 'Then these men were bound in their coats, their hose, and their other garments' (Dan. 3:21). [Freedman, p. 621, n. 8: These were garments specially worn by men in their exalted position, and they did not doff them though cast into the furnace.]"

XXXIX.   A. Said R. Yohanan, "[93A] The righteous are greater than ministering angels.

B. "For it is said, 'He answered and said, Lo, I see four men loose, walking in the midst of the fire, and they are not hurt, and the form of the fourth is like the son of God' (Dan. 3:25) [Freedman, p. 621, n. 9: Thus the angel is mentioned last, as being least esteemed]."

XL.   A. Said R. Tanhum bar Hanilai, "When Hananiah, Mishael, and Azariah went out of the fiery furnace, all the nations of the world came and slapped the enemies of Israel [that is, Israel] on their faces.

B. "They said to them, 'You have a god such as this, and yet you bow down to an idol!'

C. "Forthwith they said this verse, 'O Lord, righteousness belongs to you, but to us shamefacedness, as at this day' (Dan. 9:7)."

XLI.   A. Said R. Samuel bar Nahmani said R. Jonathan, "What is the meaning of the verse of Scripture, 'I said, I will go up to the palm tree, I will take hold of the boughs thereof' (Song 7:9)?

B. "I said I will go up to the palm tree' refers to Israel.

C. "But now 'I grasped' only one bough, namely, Hananiah, Mishael, and Azariah."

XLII.   A. And said R. Yohanan, "What is the meaning of the verse of Scripture, 'I saw by night, and behold a man riding upon a red horse, and he stood among the myrtle trees that were in the bottom' (Zech. 1:8)?

B. "What is the meaning of, 'I saw by night'?

C. "The Holy One blessed be he, sought to turn the entire world into night.

D. "And behold, a man riding'—'man' refers only to the Holy One, blessed be he, as it is said, 'The Lord is a man of war, the Lord is his name' (Ex. 15:3).

E. " 'On a red horse'—the Holy One, blessed be he, sought to turn the entire world to blood.

F. "When, however, he saw Hananiah, Mishael, and Azariah, he cooled off, as it is said, 'And he stood among the myrtle trees that were in the deep.'

G. "The word for 'myrtle trees' speaks only of the righteous as it is written, 'And he brought up the myrtle' (Est. 2:7) [another name of Esther].

H. "And the word for 'deep' speaks only of Babylonia, as it is said, 'That says to the deep, be dry, and I will dry up your rivers' (Is. 44:27) [Freedman, p. 622, n. 11: To Babylon, situated in a hollow].

I. "Forthwith, those who were filled with [red] anger turned pale, and those who were red turned white [in serenity]."

J. Said R. Pappa, "Those proves that a white horse in a dream is a good thing."

XLIII.   A. The rabbis [Hananiah, Mishael, and Azariah]—where did they go?

B. Said Rab, "They died through the working of the evil eye."

C. And Samuel said, "They drowned in spit."

D. And R. Yohanan, said, "They went up to the land of Israel, got married, and produced sons and daughters."

E. This accords with a Tannaite dispute on the same issue:

F. R. Eliezer says, "They died through the working of the evil eye."

G. R. Joshua says, "They drowned in spit."

H. And sages say, "They went up to the land of Israel, got married, and produced sons and daughters, as it is said, 'Hear now, Joshua, the high priest, and your fellows who sit before you, for they are men wondered at' (Zech. 3:8).

I. "Who are men who are wondered at? One must say, This refers to Hananiah, Mishael, and Azariah."

J. And where did Daniel go?

K. Said Rab, "To dig a large wall at Tiberias."

L. And Samuel said, "To buy fodder."

M. R. Yohanan said, "To buy pigs in Alexandria, Egypt."

N. Can this be true?

O. And have we not learned in the Mishnah:

P. *Todos the physician said, "A cow or a pig does not leave Alexandria, Egypt, out of which they do not cut its womb, so that it will not breed" [M. San. 4:4].*

Q. He brought little ones, to which they gave no thought.

XLIV. A. Our rabbis have taught on Tannaite authority:

B. There were three who were involved in that scheme [to keep Daniel out of the furnace]: the Holy One, blessed be he, Daniel, and Nebuchadnezzar.

C. The Holy One, blessed be he, said, "Let Daniel leave here, so that people should not say that they were saved on account of Daniel's merit [and not on their own merit]."

D. Daniel said, "Let me get out of here, so that through me the verse will not be carried out, 'The graven images of their gods you shall burn with fire' (Dan. 7:25). [They may make a god of me.]"

E. Nebuchadnezzar said, "Let Daniel get out of here, lest people say that [the king] has burned up his god [Daniel] in fire."

F. And how do we know that [Nebuchadnezzar] worshiped [Daniel]?

G. As it is written, "Then the king Nebuchadnezzar fell upon his face and worshiped Daniel" (Dan. 2:46).

XLV. A. "Thus says the Lord of hosts, the God of Israel, of Ahab, son of Kolaiah, and of Zedekiah, son of Maaseiah, who prophesy a lie to you in my name" (Jer. 29:21).

B. And it is written, "And of them shall be taken up a curse by all the captivity of Judah who are in Babylonia, saying, The Lord make you like Zedekiah and like Ahab, whom the king of Babylonia roasted in fire" (Jer. 29:22).

C. What is said is not "whom he burned in fire" but "whom he roasted in fire."

D. Said R. Yohanan in the name of R. Simeon b. Yohai, "This teaches that he turned them into popcorn."

XLVI. A. "Because they have committed villainy in Israel and have committed adultery with their neighbors' wives" (Jer. 29:23):

B. What did they do?

C. They went to Nebuchadnezzar's daughter. Ahab said to her, "Thus said the Lord, 'Give yourself to Zedekiah.' "

D. And Zedekiah said, "Thus said the Lord, 'Give yourself to Ahab.' "

E. She went and told her father. He said to her, "The god of these men hates lewdness. When they come to you, send them to me."

F. When they came to her, she sent them to her father. He said to them, "Who said this to you?"

G. They said, "The Holy One, blessed be he."

H. "But lo, I asked Hananiah, Mishael, and Azariah, and they said to me, 'It is forbidden.' "

I. They said to him, "We too are prophets like them. To them the message was not given, to us [God] gave the message."

J. He said to him, "I want to test you in the same manner I tested Hananiah, Mishael, and Azariah."

K. They said to him, "They were three, and we are two."

L. He said to them, "Choose anyone you like to go with you."

M. They said to him, "Joshua, the high priest." They were thinking, "Joshua, whose merit is great, will protect us."

N. They seized them and tossed them into the fire. They were roasted. As to Joshua, the high priest, his clothing was singed.

O. For it is said, "And he showed me Joshua, the high priest, standing before the angel of the Lord" (Zech. 3:1), and it is written, "And the Lord said to Satan, the Lord rebuke you, O Satan" (Zech. 3:2).

P. [Nebuchadnezzar] said to [Joshua], "I know that you are righteous. But what is the reason that the fire had any power whatsoever over you? Over Hananiah, Mishael, and Azariah the fire had no power at all."

Q. He said to him, "They were three, and I am only one."

R. He said to him, "Lo, Abraham was only one."

S. "But there were no wicked men with him, and the fire was not given power to burn him, while in my case, I was joined with wicked men, so the fire had the power to burn me."

T. This is in line with what people say, "If there are two dry brands and one wet one, the dry ones kindle the wet one."

U. Why was he punished in this way?

V. Said R. Pappa, "Because his sons had married wives who were not fit for marriage into the priesthood and he did not object, as it is said, 'Now Joshua was clothed with filthy clothing' (Zech. 3:3).

W. "Now was it Joshua's way to dress in filthy garments? Rather this teaches that his sons had married women who were not worthy to marry into the priesthood, and he did not object."

XLVII. A. Said R. Tanhum, "In Sepphoris, Bar Qappara interpreted the following verse: 'These six [grains] of barley gave he to me' (Ruth 3:17).

B. "What are the six of barley? If we should say that they were actually six of barley, was it the way of Boaz to give out a gift of only six barley grains?

C. "[93B] Rather it must have been six seahs of barley?

D. "And is it the way of a woman to carry six seahs?

E. "Rather, this formed an omen to her that six sons are destined to come forth from her, each of whom would receive six blessings, and these are they: David, the Messiah, Daniel, Hananiah, Mishael, and Azariah.

F. "David, as it is written, 'Then answered one of the servants and said, Behold I have seen the son of Jesse, the Bethlehemite, who is cunning in playing and a mighty, valiant man, and a man of war, and understanding in matters, and a handsome man, and the Lord is with him' (1 Sam. 16:18). [Freedman, p. 626, n. 1: The six epithets, viz., cunning in playing, mighty, valiant, etc., are regarded as blessings applicable to each of the six persons mentioned]."

G. And said R. Judah said Rab, "The entire verse was stated by Doeg only as vicious gossip.

H. " 'Cunning in playing'—skillful in asking questions;

I. " 'a mighty valiant man'—skillful in answering them;

J. " 'a man of war'—skillful in the battle of Torah-learning;

K. " 'understanding in matters'—understanding in learning one thing from another;

L. " 'and a comely person'—who argues for his position with considerable reasons;

M. " 'and the Lord is with him'—the law everywhere follows his opinion.

N. " 'And in all regards,' he said to him, 'my son Jonathan is his equal.'

O. "When he said, 'The Lord is with him'—something which did not apply to himself—he was humbled and envied him.

P. "For of Saul it is written, 'And wherever he turned about, he vexed them' (1 Sam. 14:47), while of David it is written, 'And wherever he turned about he prospered.' "

Q. How do we know that this was Doeg?

R. It is written here, "Then one of the servants answered," meaning, "one who was distinguished from the other young men," and there it is written, "Now a man of the servants of Saul was there that day, detained before the Lord, and his name was Doeg, an Edomite, head herdmen that belonged to Saul" (1 Sam. 21:8). [Freedman, p. 626, n. 8: Thus "a man" that is, "one distinguished" is the epithet applied to Doeg.]

S. [Reverting to Bar Qappara's statement:] "The Messiah, as it is written, 'And the spirit of the Lord shall rest upon him, the spirit of wisdom and understanding, the spirit of counsel and might, the spirit of knowledge of the fear of the Lord, and shall make him of quick understanding in the fear of the Lord' (Is. 11:2–3)."

T. And R. Alexandri said, "The use of the words 'for quick understanding' indicates that he loaded him down with good deeds and suffering as a mill [which uses the same letters] is loaded down."

U. [Explaining the same word, now with reference to the formation of the letters of the word to mean "smell,"] said Raba, "[The Messiah] smells and judges, for it is written, 'And he shall judge not after the sight of his eyes nor reprove after the hearing of his ears, yet with righteousness shall he judge the poor' (Ex. 11:3–4)."

V. Bar Koziba ruled for two and a half years. He said to rabbis, "I am the Messiah."

W. They said to him, "In the case of the Messiah it is written that he smells a man and judges. Let us see whether you can smell a man and judge."

X. When they saw that he could not smell a man and judge, they killed him.

Y. [Reverting again to Bar Qappara's statement:] "Daniel, Hananiah, Mishael, and Azariah, as it is written, 'In whom there was no blemish, but well favored, skillful in all wisdom, and cunning in knowledge, understanding science, and such as had ability in them to stand in the king's palace, and whom they might teach the learning and the tongue of the Chaldeans' (Dan. 1:4)."

Z. What is the meaning of, "In whom there was no blemish" (Dan. 1:4)?

AA. Said R. Hama bar Hanina, "Even the scar made by bleeding was not on them."

BB. What is the meaning of, "And such as had ability in them to stand in the king's palace" (Dan. 1:3)?

CC. Said R. Hama in the name of R. Hanina, "This teaches us that they restrained themselves from laughing and chatting, from sleeping, and they held themselves in when they had to attend to the call of nature, on account of the reverence owing to the king."

XLVIII. A. "Now among these were of the children of Judah, Daniel, Hananiah, Mishael, and Azariah" (Dan. 1:6):

B. Said R. Eleazar, "All of them came from the children of Judah."

C. And R. Samuel bar Nahmani said, "Daniel came from the children of Judah, but Hananiah, Mishael, and Azariah came from the other tribes."

XLIX. A. "And of your sons which shall issue from you, which you shall beget, shall they take away, and they shall be eunuchs in the palace of the king of Babylonia" (2 Kgs. 20:18):

B. What are these "eunuchs"?

C. Rab said, "Literally, eunuchs."

D. And R. Hanina said, "The sense is that idolatry was castrated [i.e. made sterile] in their time."

E. In the view of him who has said that idolatry was castrated in their time, that is in line with the verse of Scripture, "And there is no hurt in them" (Dan. 3:25).

F. But in the view of him who says that "eunuch" is in its literal sense, what is the meaning of, "And there is no hurt in them" (Dan. 3:25) [since they had been castrated]?

G. It is that the fire did them no injury.

H. But has it not been written, "Nor the smell of fire had passed on them" (Dan. 3:27)?

I. There was neither injury nor the smell of fire.

J. In the view of him who has said that idolatry was made a eunuch in their time, that is in line with the following verse: "For thus says the Lord to the eunuchs who keep my Sabbaths" (Is. 56:4).

K. But in the view of him who says that eunuch is in its literal sense, would Scripture dwell on what is embarrassing to the righteous?

L. Among the group were both sorts [actual eunuchs, as well as those in whose day were idols sterilized].

M. Now there is no difficulty for the view of him who says that they were literally eunuchs in the following verse: "Even to them will I give in my house and within my walls a place and a name better than of sons and of daughters" (Is. 56:5).

N. But in the view of the one who says that the sense is that in their day idolatry was made a eunuch, what is the sense of the statement, "Better than of sons and of daughters"?

O. Said R. Nahman bar Isaac, "Better than the sons whom they had already had and who had died."

P. What is the meaning of the statement, "I shall give them an everlasting name, that shall not be cut off" (Is. 56:5)?

Q. Said R. Tanhum, "Bar Qappara interpreted the matter in Sepphoris: 'This refers to the book of Daniel, which is called by his name.' "

L.

A. Now since whatever concerns Ezra was stated by Nehemiah b. Hachlia, what is the reason that the book was not called by his name?

B. Said R. Jeremiah bar Abba, "It is because he took pride in himself, as it is written, 'Think up on me for good, my God' (Neh. 5:19)."

C. David also made such a statement, "Remember me, Lord, with the favor that you bear for your people, visit me with your salvation" (Ps. 106:4).

D. It was supplication that David sought.

E. R. Joseph said, "It was because [Nehemiah] had spoken disparagingly about his predecessors, as it is said, 'But the former governors who had been before me were chargeable unto the people and had taken of them bread and wine, beside forty shekels of silver' (Neh. 5:15).

F. "Furthermore, he spoke in this way even of Daniel, who was greater than he was."

G. And how do we know that Daniel was greater than he was?

H. As it is written, "And I Daniel alone saw the vision, for the men that were with me did not see the vision, but a great quaking fell upon them, so that they fled to hide themselves" (Dan. 10:7).

I. "For the men that were with me did not see the vision" (Dan. 10:7):

J. Who were they?

K. R. Jeremiah (some say, R. Hiyya b. Abba) said, "They were Haggai, Zechariah, and Malachi [94A]."

L. They were greater than he, and he was greater than they.

M. They were greater than he, for they were prophets, and he was not a prophet.

N. And he was greater than they, for he saw a vision and they did not see a vision.

O. And since they did not see it, what is the reason that they were frightened?

P. Even though they did not see it, their star saw it.

Q. Said Rabina, "That yields the conclusion that one who is afraid even though he saw nothing is so because his star saw something.

R. "What is his remedy?"

S. "Let him jump four cubits from where he is standing."

T. "Or let him recite the *Shema*.

U. "But if he is standing in an unclean place, let him say, 'The butcher's goat is fatter than I am.' "

LI.

A. "Of the increase of his government and peace there shall be no end" (Is. 9:6):

B. R. Tanhum said, "In Sepphoris, Bar Qappara expounded this verse as follows:

C. " 'On what account is every M in the middle of a word open, but the one in the word *increase* is closed?

D. " 'The Holy One, blessed be he, proposed to make Hezekiah Messiah, and Sennacherib into Gog and Magog.

E. " 'The attribute of justice said before the Holy One, blessed be he, "Lord of the world, Now if David, king of Israel, who recited how many songs and praises before you, you did not make Messiah, Hezekiah, for whom you have done all these miracles, and who did not recite a song before you, surely should not be made Messiah."

F. " 'On what account the M was closed?'

G. " 'Forthwith, the earth went and said before him, "Lord of the world, I shall say a song before you in the place of this righteous man, so you make him Messiah."

H. " 'The earth went and said a song before him, as it is said, "From the uttermost part of the earth we have heard songs, even glory to the righteous" (Is. 24:16).

I. " 'Said the prince of the world before him, "Lord of the world, [The earth] has carried out your wish in behalf of this righteous man."

J. " 'An echo went forth and said, "It is my secret, it is my secret" (Ps. 24:16).

K. " 'Said the prophet, "Woe is me, woe is me" (Is. 24:16). How long?'

L. "How dealt treacherously, yes, the treacherous dealers have dealt very treacherously" (Is. 24:16).

M. And said Raba, and some say, R. Isaac, "Until spoilers come, and those who spoil spoilers."

LII. A. "The burden of Dumah. He calls to me out of Seir, Watchman, what of the night? Watchman, what of the night?" (Is. 21:11):

B. Said R. Yohanan, "That angel who is appointed over the souls is named Dumah. All the souls gathered to Dumah, and said to him, 'Watchman, what of the night? Watchman, what of the night?' (Is. 21:11).

C. "Said the watchman, 'The morning comes and also the night, if you will inquire, inquire, return, come' (Is. 21:11)."

LIII. A. A Tannaite authority in the name of R. Pappias [said], "It was a shame for Hezekiah and his associates that they did not recite a song, until the earth opened and said a song, as it is said, 'From the uttermost part of the earth have we heard songs, even glory to the righteous' (Is. 24:16)."

B. Along these same lines you may say, "And Jethro said, Blessed be the Lord who has delivered you" (Ex. 18:10).

C. A Tannaite authority in the name of R. Pappias said, "It was a shame for Moses and the six hundred thousand, that they did not say, 'Blessed . . .,' until Jethro came and said, 'Blessed is the Lord.' "

LIV. A. "And Jethro rejoiced" (Ex. 18:9):

B. Rab and Samuel—

C. Rab said, "It was that he passed a sharp knife across his flesh [circumcizing himself]."

D. And Samuel said, "All his flesh became goose-pimples [because of the destruction of the Egyptians]."

E. Said Rab, "That is in line with what people say, 'As to a proselyte, up to the tenth generation do not insult an Aramaean [since he retains his former loyalty, as Jethro did to the Egyptians].' "

LV. A. "Therefore shall the Lord, the Lord of hosts, send among his fat ones leanness" (Is. 10:16):

B. What is "among his fat ones leanness"?

C. Said the Holy One, blessed be he, "Let Hezekiah come, who has eight names, and exact punishment from Sennacherib, who has eight names."

D. As to Hezekiah, it is written, "For unto us a child is born, unto us a son is given, and the government shall be upon his shoulder, and his name shall be called wonderful, counselor, mighty, judge, everlasting, father, prince, and peace" (Is. 9:5).

E. And there is yet the name "Hezekiah" too?

F. [Hezekiah] means "Whom God has strengthened."

G. Another matter: it is Hezekiah, for he strengthened Israel for their father in heaven.

H. As to Senacherib, it is written, "Tiglath-pileser" (2 Kgs. 15:29), "Pilneser" (1 Chr. 5:26), "Shalmeneser" (2 Kgs. 17:3), "Pul" (2 Kgs. 15:29), "Sargon" (Is. 20:1), "Asnapper" (Ezra 4:10), "Rabba" (Ezra 4:10), and "Yaqqira" (Ezra 4:10).

I. And there is yet the name "Sennacherib" too.

J. It bears the sense that his conversation is contentious.

K. Another matter: He talked and babbled against the Most High.

L. [Referring to Ezra 4:10], said R. Yohanan, "On what account did that wicked man have the merit of being called 'the great and noble Asnapper' (Ezra 4:10)?

M. "Because he did not speak critically of the land of Israel, as it is said, 'Until I come and take you away to a land like your own land' (2 Kgs. 18:32)."

N. Rab and Samuel: One said he was a shrewd king, and the other said he was a foolish king.

O. In the view of him who said that he was a shrewd king, if he had said, "A land that is better than yours," they would have said to him, "You are lying to us."

P. In the view of him who said that he was a foolish king, if [the land to which they would be exiled was no better than their own], then what value was there [in their agreeing to go].

Q. Where did he exile them?

R. Mar Zutra said, "To Africa."

S. R. Hanina said, "To the mountains of Salug."

T. But [for its part], the Israelites spoke critically about the land of Israel. When they came to Shush, they said, "This is the same as our land."

U. When they got to Elmin, they said, "It is like the house of eternities [Jerusalem]."

V. When they go to Shush Tere, they said, "This is twice as good."

LVI.   A. "And beneath his glory shall he kindle a burning like the burning of a fire" (Is. 10:16):

B. Said R. Yohanan, "Under his glory, but not actually his glory."

C. That is in line with how R. Yohanan called his clothing "Those who do me honor."

D. R. Eleazar said, "Under his glory' literally, just as is the burning of the sons of Aaron.

E. "Just as in that case it was a burning of the soul while the body endured, so here there is a burning of the soul while the body remained intact."

LVII.   A. A Tannaite authority in the name of R. Joshua b. Qorhah taught, "Since Pharaoh blasphemed personally, the Holy One, blessed be he, exacted punishment from him personally.

B. "Since Sennacherib blasphemed [94B] through a messenger, the Holy One, blessed be he, exacted punishment from him through a messenger.

C. "In the case of Pharaoh, it is written, 'Who is the Lord, that I should obey his voice' (Ex. 5:2).

D. "The Holy One, blessed be he, exacted punishment from him personally, as it is written, 'And the Lord overthrough the Egyptians in the midst of the sea' (Ex. 14:27), and it also is written, 'You did walk through the sea with your horses' (Hab. 3:15).

E. "In the case of Sennacherib, it is written, 'By your messengers you have reproached the Lord' (2 Kgs. 19:23), so the Holy One, blessed be he, exacted punishment from him through a messenger, as it is written, 'And the angel of the Lord went out and smote in the camp of the Assyrians a hundred fourscore and five thousand' (2 Kgs. 19:23)."

LVIII.

A. R. Hanina b. Pappa contrasted two verses: "It is written, 'I will enter the height of his border' (Is. 37:24), and it is further written, 'I will enter into the lodgings of his borders' (2 Kgs. 19:23).

B. "Said that wicked man, 'First I shall destroy the lower dwelling, and afterward I shall destroy the upper dwelling.' "

LIX.

A. Said R. Joshua b. Levi, "What is the meaning of the verse of Scripture, 'Am I now come up without the Lord against this place to destroy it? The Lord said to me, Go up against this land and destroy it' (2 Kgs. 18:25).

B. "What is the sense of the passage?

C. "He had heard the prophet, who had said, 'Since this people refuses the waters of Shiloah that go softly and rejoice in Rezina and Ramaliah's son, [now therefore behold the Lord brings up upon them the waters of the river, strong and many, even the king of Assyria and all his glory, and he shall come up over all his channels and go over all his banks]' (Is. 8:6). [Freedman, p. 635, n. 3: This was understood by Sennacherib as an order to possess Jerusalem.]"

D. Said R. Joseph, "Were it not for the following rendering of this verse of Scripture, I should not have understood what it meant: 'Because this people is tired of the rule of the house of David, which rules them mildly, like the waters of Shiloah, which flow gently, and have preferred Razin and the son of Ramaliah.' "

LX.

A. Said R. Yohanan, "What is the meaning of this verse: 'The curse of the Lord is in the house of the wicked, but he blesses the habitation of the just' (Prov. 3:33)?

B. " 'The curse of the Lord is in the house of the wicked' refers to Pekah, son of Ramaliah, who would eat forty seahs of pigeons for dessert.

C. " 'But he blesses the habitation of the just' refers to Hezekiah, king of Judea, who would eat a litra of vegetables for a whole meal."

LXI. A. "Now therefore behold, the Lord brings up upon them the waters of the river, strong and many, even the king of Assyria and all his glory" (Is. 8:7).

B. And it is written, "And he shall pass through Judea, he shall overflow and go over, he shall reach even to the neck" (Is. 8:8).

C. Then why was [Sennacherib] punished?

D. The prophet prophesied about the ten tribes, but [Sennacherib] gave mind to the whole of Jerusalem.

E. The prophet came to him and said to him, " 'For the wearied is not for the oppressor' (Is. 8:23)."

F. Said R. Eleazar b. R. Berekhiah, "The people that is weary because of its devotion to Torah-study will not be given into the power of the one that oppresses it."

LXII. A. What is the meaning of this verse: "When aforetime the land of Zebulun and the land of Naphtali lightened its burden, but in later times it was made heavy by the way of the sea, beyond Jordan, in Galilee of the nations" (Is. 8:23)?

B. It was not like the early generations, who made the yoke of the Torah light for themselves, but the later generations, who made the yoke of the Torah heavy for themselves.

C. And these were worthy that a miracle should be done for them, just as was done for those who passed through the sea and trampled over the Jordan.

D. If Sennacherib should repent, well and good, but if not, I shall make him into dung among the nations [a play on the latters GLL, the word for Galilee and dung].

LXIII. A. "After these things, and the truth thereof, Sennacherib, king of Assyria, came and entered Judea and encamped against the fortified cities and thought to win them for himself" (2 Chr. 32:1):

B. Such a recompense [to Hezekiah] for such a gift? [Freedman, p. 636, n. 9: The previous verse relates that Hezekiah turned earnestly to the service of God. Was then Sennacherib's invasion his just reward?]

C. What is the sense of, "After these things and the truth thereof" (2 Chr. 32:1)?

D. Said Rabina, "After the Holy One, blessed be he, went and took an oath, saying 'If I say to Hezekiah that I am going to bring Sennacherib and hand him over to you, he will say to me, "I don't want him and I don't want his terror either." ' "

E. "So the Holy One, blessed be he, went ahead and took an oath ahead of time that he would bring him, as it is said, 'The Lord of hosts has sworn, saying, Surely as I have thought, so shall it come to pass, and as I have purposed, so shall it stand, that I will break the Assyrian in my land and upon my mountains tread him under foot; then shall his yoke depart from off them, and his burden depart from off their shoulders' (Is. 14:24–25)."

F. Said R. Yohanan, "Said the Holy One, blessed be he, 'Let Sennacherib and his company come and serve as a crib for Hezekiah and his company.' "

LXIV.

A. "And it shall come to pass in that day that his burden shall be taken away from off your shoulders and his yoke from off your neck, and the yoke shall be destroyed because of the oil" (Is. 10:27):

B. Said R. Isaac Nappaha, "The yoke of Sennacherib will be destroyed because of the oil of Hezekiah, which he would kindle in the synagogues and schoolhouses.

C. "What did [Hezekiah] do? He affixed a sword at the door of the schoolhouse and said, 'Whoever does not take up study of the Torah will be pierced by this sword.'

D. "They searched from Dan to Beer Sheba and found no ignoramus, from Gabbath to Antipatris and found no boy or girl, no man or woman, not expert in the laws of uncleanness and cleanness.

E. "Concerning that generation Scripture says, 'And it shall come to pass in that day that a man shall nourish a young cow and two sheep' (Is. 7:21), and it says,

'And it shall come to pass on that day that every place shall be, where there were a thousand vines at a thousand silverlings, it shall even be for briers and thorns' (Is. 7:23).

F. "Even though 'a thousand vines are worth a thousand pieces of silver,' yet it shall be 'for briers and thorns.' "

LXV.

A. "And your spoil shall be gathered like the gathering of a caterpillar" (Is. 33:4):

B. Said the prophet to Israel, "Gather your spoil."

C. They said to him, "Is it for individual spoil or for sharing?"

D. He said to them, " 'Like the gathering of a caterpillar' (Is. 33:4): Just as in the gathering of a caterpillar it is each one for himself, so in your spoil it is each one for himself."

E. They said to him, "And is not the money of the ten tribes mixed up with it?"

F. He said to them, " 'As the watering of pools does he water it' (Is. 33:4): Just as pools of water serve to raise up a human being from a state of uncleanness to a state of cleanness, so the money that has belonged to Israelites, once it has fallen into the hands of idolators, forthwith imparts cleanness. [Freedman, p. 638, n. 5: When the Israelites have abandoned all hope of the return thereof other Jews may take it.]"

LXVI.

A. Said R. Huna, "That wicked man [Sennacherib] made ten marches that day,

B. "as it is said, 'He is come to Aiath, he is passed at Migron, at Michmash he has laid up his carriages, they are gone over the passage, they have taken up their lodgings at Geba, Ramah is afraid, Gibeah of Saul is fled, Lift up your voice, O daughter of Gallim, cause it to be heard to Laish, O poor Anathoth, Madmenah is removed, the inhabitants of Gebim gather themselves to flee' (Is. 10:28–31)."

C. But they are more than that?

D. [Huna responded,] "Lift up your voice, O daughter of Gallim," was said by the prophet to the congregation of Israel [as follows]:

E. " 'Lift up your voice, O daughter of Gallim'—daughter of Abraham, Isaac, and Jacob, who carried out religious duties like the waves of the ocean [in number].

F. " 'Cause it to be heard to Laish'—from this one do not fear, but fear the wicked Nebuchadnezzar, who is compared to a lion.

G. "For it is written, 'The lion is come up from his thicket' (Jer. 4:7)."

H. What is [95A] the sense of "O poor Anathoth" (Is. 10:31)?

I. Jeremiah b. Hilkiah is destined to come up from Anathoth and to prophesy, as it is written, "The words of Jeremiah, son of Hilkiah, of the priest who were in Anathoth in the land of Benjamin" (Jer. 1:1).

J. But is there any parallel? There [Nebuchadnezzar] is called a lion, but what is written here is *laish* [another word for lion].

K. Said R. Yohanan, "A lion is called six things: *ari* (Jer. 4:7), *kefir* (Gen. 49:9), *labi* (Gen. 39:9), *laish* (Judges 14:5), *shahal* (Ps. 91:13), and *shahaz* (Job 28:8)."

L. If so, they are fewer [than ten]?

M. "They are gone over" [and] "the passage" and up to two [more].

LXVII.

A. What is the meaning of the statement, "As yet shall be halt at Nob that day" (Is. 10:32)?

B. Said R. Huna, "That day alone remained [for the punishment of] the sin committed at Nob [Sam. 22:17–19]. [Freedman, p. 639, n. 9: When the priests of Nob were massacred. God set a term for punishment, of which that day was the last.]

C. "The Chaldean [soothsayers] said to him, 'If you go now, you will overpower it, and if not, you will not overpower it.'

D. "A journey that should require ten days required only one day.

E. "When they got to Jerusalem, they piled up mattresses so that, when he climbed up and took up his position on the top one, he could see Jerusalem. When he saw it, it looked tiny in his eyes. He said, 'Is this really the city of Jerusalem, on account of which I moved all my troops and came up and conquered the entire province? Is it not smaller and weaker than all of the cities of the peoples that by my power I have already conquered?!'

F. "He went and got up and shook his head and waved his hand backward and forward, with contempt, toward the mountain of the house of the sanctuary in Zion and toward the courts of Jerusalem."

G. "They said, 'Let us raise a hand against it right now.'

H. "He said to them, 'You are tired. Tomorrow each one of your bring me a stone and we shall stone it [Freedman, following Jastrow].'

I. "Forthwith: 'And it came to pass that night that the angel of the Lord went out and smote in the camp of the Assyrians a hundred fourscore and five thousand, and when they arose early in the morning, behold they were all dead corpses' (2 Kgs. 19:35)."

J. Said R. Pappa, "That is in line with what people say: 'Justice delayed is justice denied.'"

LXVIII. A. "And Ishbi-be-nob, who was of the sons of the giant, the weight of whose spear weighed three hundred shekels of brass in weight, being girded with a new sword, thought to have slain David" (2 Sam. 21:16):

B. What is the sense of "Ishbi-benob"?

C. Said R. Judah said Rab, "It was a man [ish] who came on account of the matter of [the sin committed at] Nob.

D. "Said the Holy One, blessed be he, to David, 'How long will the sin committed [against Nob] be concealed in your hand? On your account, Nob was put to death, the city of priests, on your account, Doeg the Edomite was sent into exile; on your account, Saul and his three sons were killed.

E. "'Do you want you descendents to be wiped out, or do you want to be handed over into the power of an enemy?'

F. "He said to him, 'Lord of the world, It is better that I be handed over to an enemy but that my descendents not be wiped out.' "

G. One day, when he went out to Sekhor Bizzae [Freedman, p. 640, n. 7: literally: "your seed to cease"], Satan appeared to him in the form of a deer. He shot an arrow at it, and the arrow did not reach [the deer]. It drew him until he came to the land of the Philistines. When Ishbi-benob saw him, he said, "This is the one who killed Goliath, my brother."

H. He bound him, doubled him up, and threw him under an olive press. A miracle was done for [David], in that the earth underneath him became soft. This is in line with the following verse of Scripture: "You have enlarged my steps under me, that my feet did not slip" (Ps. 18:37).

I. That day was the eve of the Sabbath [Friday]. Abishai ben Zeruiah [David's nephew] was washing his head in four casks of water. He saw stains of blood [in the water].

J. Some say a dove came and slapped its wings before him.

K. He said, "The congregation of Israel is compared to a dove, for it is said, 'You are as the wings of a dove covered with silver' (Ps. 68:14). This then bears the inference that David, king of Israel, is in trouble."

L. He came to his house and did not find him. He said, "We have learned in the Mishnah: *People are not to ride on his horse or sit on his throne or hand his sceptre [M. San. 2:5].*

M. "What is the rule about a time of crisis?"

N. He came and asked at the schoolhouse. They said to him, "In a time of crisis it is all right."

O. He mounted his mule and rode off and the earth crumbled up [to make the journey quick]. While he was riding along, he saw Orpah, mother of [Ishbi-benob] who was spinning. When she saw him, she broke off the spindle. He threw it at her head and killed her.

P. When Ishbi-benob saw him, he said, "Now there are two against me, and they will kill me."

Q. He threw David up and stuck his spear [into the ground], saying, "Let him fall on it and be killed."

R. [Abishai] shouted the Name [of God], so David was suspended between heaven and earth.

S. But why should David himself not have said it?

T. Because one who is bound cannot free himself from his chains.

U. He said to him, "What do you want here?"

V. He said to him, "This is what the Holy One, blessed be he, has said to me, and this is what I said to him."

W. He said to him, "Take back your prayer. May your son's son sell wax, but may you not suffer."

X. He said to him, "If so, help me."

Y. That is in accord with what is written, "But Abishai, son of Zeruiah, helped him" (2 Sam. 21:17).

Z. Said R. Judah said Rab, "He helped him, in prayer."

AA. Abishai pronounced the Name and brought [David] down.

BB. He pursued the two of them. When they came to Kubi, they said, "Let us stand against him."

CC. When they came to Bethre, they said, "Will two whelps kill a lion?"

DD. They said to him, "Go find Orpah, your mother, in the grave."

EE. When they mentioned the name of his mother to him, he grew weak, and they killed him.

FF. So it is written, "Then the men of David swore to him, saying, You shall no more go out with us to battle, that you not put out the light of Israel" (2 Sam. 21:17).

LXIX.   A. Our rabbis have taught on Tannaite authority:

B. For three did the earth fold up [to make their journey quicker]: Eliezer, Abraham's servant, Jacob our father, and Abishai b. Zeruiah.

C. As to Abishai, son of Zeruiah, it is as we have just said.

D. As to Eliezer, Abraham's servant, it is written, "And I came this day to the well" (Gen. 24:42), meaning that that very day he had set out.

E. As to Jacob, our father, [95B] as it is written, "And Jacob went out from Beer Sheba and went to Haran" (Gen. 28:10), and it is said, "And he lighted upon a certain place and tarried there all night, because the sun had set" (Gen. 28:11).

F. When he got to Haran, he said, "Is it possible that I have passed through a place in which my ancestors have prayed, and I did not say a prayer there?"

G. He wanted to go back. As soon as the thought of going back had entered his mind, the earth folded up for him. Forthwith: "He lighted upon a place" (Gen. 28:11).

H. Another matter: "Lighting upon . . ." refers only to praying, as it is written, "Therefore do not pray for this people or lift up a cry or prayer for them nor make intercession [using the same root] to me" (Jer. 7:16).

I. "And he tarried there all night, because the sun had set" (Gen. 28:10):

J. After he had prayed, he wanted to go back. Said the Holy One, blessed be he, "This righteous man has come to the house of my dwelling. Should he go forth without spending the night?"

K. Forthwith the sun set. That is in line with what is written, "And as he passed over Penuel, the sun rose for him" (Gen. 32:32).

L. And did it rise only for him? And did not it not rise for the entire world?

M. "But," said R. Isaac, "Since the sun had set [too soon] on his account, it also rose on his account."

LXX.   A. And how do we know that the seed of David ceased [cf. LXVIII.E]?

B. As it is written, "And when Athaliah, mother of Ahaziah, saw that her son was dead, she rose and destroyed all the royal seed" (2 Kgs. 11:1).

C. And lo, Joash remained. Also Abiathar remained, for it is written, "And one of the sons of Ahimelech, son of Ahitub, named Abiathar, escaped" (1 Sam. 22:20).

D. Said R. Judah said Rab, "If Abiathar were not left to Ahimelech, son of Ahitub, neither shred nor remnant of the seed of David would have survived."

LXXI.

A. Said R. Judah said Rab, "The wicked Sennacherib came against them with forty-five thousand men, sons of kings seated on golden chariots, with their concubines and whores, and with eighty thousand mighty soldiers, garbed in coats of mail, and sixty thousand swordsmen running before him, and the rest cavalry.

B. And so they came against Abraham, and in the age to come so they will come with Gog and Magog.

C. On Tannaite authority it was taught: The length of his camp was four hundred parasangs, and the breadth of his horses, neck to neck, was forty parasangs, and the total of his army was two million six hundred thousand less one.

D. Abayye asked, "Does this mean less one myriad or one thousand?"

E. The question stands.

LXXII.

A. It was taught on Tannaite authority:

B. The first ones crossed by swimming, as it is said, "He shall overflow and go over" (Is. 8:8).

C. The middle ones crossed standing up, as it is said, "He shall reach even to the neck" (Is. 8:8).

D. The last group brought up the dirt [of the river] with their feet and so found no water in the river to drink, so that they had to bring them water from some other place, which they drank, as it is said, "I have digged and drunk water" (Is. 37:25).

E. [How could the army have been so large,] for is it not written, "Then the angel of the Lord went forth and smote in the camp of the Assyrians a hundred and fourscore and five thousand, and when they arose early in the morning, behold, they were all dead corpses" (Is. 37:36)?

F. Said R. Abbahu, "Those were the heads of the troops."

G. Said R. Ashi, "Read the text closely with the same result; for it is written, '[Therefore shall the Lord . . . send] among his fat ones leanness [i.e. the cream of the crop].' "

H. Said Rabina, "Read the text closely with the same result; for it is written, 'And the Lord sent an angel, which cut off all the men of valor, and the leaders and the princes in the camp of the king of Assyria. So he returned with shamefacedness to his own land, and when he entered into the house of his god, they that came forth of his own bowels slew him there with the sword' (2 Chr. 32:21)."

I. This proves [that the reference is only to the leaders (Freedman, p. 644, n. 6)].

LXXIII.

A. How did [the angel] smite [the army]?

B. R. Eliezer says, "He hit them with his hand, as it is said, 'And Israel saw the great hand' (Ex. 14:31), that was destined to exact punishment of Sennacherib."

C. R. Joshua says, "He hit them with a finger, as it is said, 'Then the magicians said to Pharaoh, This is the finger of God' (Ex. 8:14), that finger that was destined to exact punishment of Sennacherib."

D. R. Eleazar, son of R. Yose the Galilean, says, "Said the Holy One, blessed be he, to Gabriel, 'Is your sickle sharpened?'

E. "He said before him, 'Lord of the world, it has been ready and sharpened since the six days of creation, as it is said, "For they fled from the swords, from the sharpened sword" (Is. 21:15).' "

F. R. Simeon b. Yohai says, "That season was the time for the ripening of the produce. Said the Holy One, blessed be he, to Gabriel, When you go forth to ripen the produce, attack them, as it is said, 'As he passes, he shall take you, for morning by morning shall he pass by, by day and by night, and it shall be a sheer terror to understand the report' (Is. 28:19)."

G. Said R. Pappa, "This is in line with what people say: 'As you pass by, reveal yourself to your enemy' [and so take revenge whenever you have the chance]."

H. Others say, "He blew into their noses and they died, as it is said, 'And he shall also blow upon them, and they shall wither' (Is. 40:24)."

I. R. Jeremiah b. Abba said, "He clapped his hands at them and they died, as it is written, 'I will also smite my hands together and I will cause my fury to rest' (Ez. 21:22)."

J. R. Isaac Nappaha said, "He opened their eyes for them and they heard a song of the living creatures [of the heaven] and they died, as it is written, 'At your exaltation the people were scattered' (Is. 33:3)."

LXXIV.

A. How many [of Sennacherib's army] remained?

B. Rab said, "Ten, as it is said, 'And the rest of the trees of his forest shall be few, that a child may write them' (Is. 10:19).

C. "What is the letter representing a number that a child can write? The one that stands for ten."

D. Samuel said, "Nine, as it is written, 'Yet gleaning grapes shall be left in it, as the shaking of an olive tree, two and three berries in the top of the uppermost bough, four and five in the utmost fruitful branches thereof' (Is. 17:6)." [Freedman, p. 645, n. 12: This is rendered: "just as after the shaking of an olive tree there may remain two olives here and three there, so shall there be left of the arm army four here and five there—nine in all."]

E. R. Joshua b. Levi said, "Fourteen, as it is written, 'Two, three . . ., four, five' (Is. 17:6)."

F. R. Yohanan said, "Five: Sennacherib, his two sons, Nebuchadnezzar, and Nebuzaradan.

G. "Nebuzaradan['s survival is] a tradition.

H. "Nebuchadnezzar, as it is written, 'And the form of the fourth is like an angel of God' (Dan. 3:25).

I. "If he had not seen [an angel], how would he have known?

J. "Sennacherib and his two sons, as it is written, 'And it came to pass, as he was worshiping in the house of Nisroch his god, that Adrammelech and Sharezer, his sons, smote him with the sword' (2 Kgs. 19:37)."

LXXV.   A. Said R. Abbahu, "Were it not that a verse of Scripture is explicitly spelled out, it would not have been possible to say it:

B. "For it is written, 'In the same day shall the Lord shave with a razor that is hired, namely, by the riverside, by the king of Assyria, the head and the hair of the feet, and it shall consume the beard' (Is. 7:20).

C. "The Holy One, blessed be he, came and appeared before [Sennacherib] as an old man. He said to him, 'When you go against the kings of east and west, whose sons you brought and saw killed, what will you say to them?'

D. "He said to him, 'This man [I] was also fearful on that account.'

E. "He said to him, 'What should we do?'

F. "He said to him, 'Go [96A] and change your appearance.'

G. " 'How shall I change?'

H. "He said to him, 'Go and bring me a razor, and I shall shave you.'

I. " 'Where shall I get it?'

J. "He said to him, 'Go to that house and bring it from there.'

K. "He went and found it. Ministering angels came and appeared to him in the form of men, grinding palm nuts.'

L. "He said to them, 'Give me the razor.'

M. "They said to him, 'Grind a cask of palm nuts, and we shall give it to you.'

N. "He ground a cask of palm nuts, and they gave the razor to him.

O. "It got dark before he came back. [God] said to [Sennacherib], 'Go and bring fire.'

P. "He went and brought fire. While he was blowing on it, the fire caught his beard, so [God] shaved his head as well as his beard. [Freedman, p. 646, n. 8: Thus he was shaved with a razor hired by his own work, a work which is done 'by the riverside,' 'grinding,' the water providing power for the mill.]"

Q. They said, "This is in line with what is written: 'And it shall also consume the beard' (Is. 7:20)."

R. Said R. Pappa, "This is in line with what people say: 'If you are singeing an Aramaean's hair and it suits him, light a fire to his beard, so you will not suffer his mockery.' "

S. [Reverting to the tale of Abbahu:] "He went and found a plank from Noah's ark. He said, 'This must be the great god who saved Noah from the flood.'

T. "He said, 'If that man [I] goes and is victorious, he will offer his two sons before you.'

U. "His sons heard and killed him. That is in line with the verse of Scripture, 'And it came to pass, as he was worshiping in the house of Nisroch his god, that Adrammelech and Sharezer his sons smote him with the sword' (2 Kgs. 19:37)."

LXXVI. A. "And he fought against them, he and his servants, by night, and smote them" (Gen. 14:15):

B. Said R. Yohanan, "That angel who was assigned to Abraham was named 'Night,' as it is said, '[Let the day perish wherein I was born] and the Night which said, There is a man-child conceived' (Job 3:3). [Freedman, p. 647, n. 4: The verse, Gen. 14:15, is translated, 'and Night fought on their behalf, he and his . . . .']"

C. R. Isaac Nappaha ["the smith"] said, "It did for him the deeds that are done by night, as it is said, 'They fought from heaven, the stars in their courses fought against Sisera' (Judges 5:20)."

D. R. Simeon b. Laqish said, "What the smith [Yohanan] has said is better than what the son of the smith [Isaac] has said."

E. "And he pursued them to Dan" (Gen. 14:14):

F. Said R. Yohanan, "When that righteous man came to Dan, he grew weak. He foresaw that the children of his children were destined to commit acts of idolatry in Dan, as it is said, 'And he set the one in Beth El, and the other he put in Dan' (1 Kgs. 12:29).

G. "And also that wicked man [Nebuchadnezzar] did not grow strong until he reached Dan, as it is said, 'From Dan the snorting of his horse was heard' (Jer. 8:16)."

LXXVII.   A. Said R. Zira, "Even though R. Judah b. Beterah sent word from Nisibis, 'Pay heed to an elder who has forgotten his learning through no fault of his own and to cut the jugular veins [in slaughtering a beast], in accord with the view of R. Judah,

B. " 'and take heed of the sons of the ordinary folk, for from them [too] will Torah go forth,'

C. "for such a matter as the following we may convey matters to them [and not refrain from teaching this lesson:]

D. " ' "You are righteous, Lord, when I please with you, yet let me talk to thee of your judgments, wherefore does the way of the wicked prosper? Wherefore are all they happy who deal very treacherously? You have planted them, yes, they have taken root, they grow, yes, they bring forth fruit" (Jer. 12:1–2).

E. " 'What did he answer him? "If you have run with the footmen and they have tired you, then how can you contend with the horses? And if in a land of peace, in which you trust, they have wearied you, how will you do in the prideful swelling of the Jordan?" (Jer. 12:5)

F. " 'The matter may be compared to the case of a man who said, "I can run in a marsh three parasangs before horses." He happened upon a man on foot and ran before him for only three mils on dry land, and he got tired.

G. " 'He said to him, "Now if matters are this way when you run before a man on foot, all the more so [will you be unable to run] before horses! And if matters are this way for three mils, how much the more so in three parasangs! And if matters are this way in dry land, how much the more so in a marsh!"

H. " ' "So it is with you. If on account of the reward for taking four steps [explained later, J–Y] that I paid that

wicked man, which he took in running on account of
my honor, you are amazed, when I pay the reward
owing to Abraham, Isaac, and Jacob, who ran before
me like horses, how much the more so [will you be
amazed]!"

I. " 'This is in line with the following verse of Scripture:
"My heart within me is broken because of the prophets, all my bones shake, I am like a drunken man, and
like a man whose wine has overcome, because of the
Lord and because of the words of his holiness" (Jer.
23:9).' "

J. As to the reference to the four steps [taken by the
wicked man in honor of God], what is its meaning?

K. It is in accord with that which is written: "At that
time Merodach-baladan, son of Baladan, king of Babylonia, sent letters and a present to Hezekiah [for he
had heard that he had been sick and recovered]" (Is.
39:1).

L. And merely because Hezekiah was sick and got better,
did he sent him letters and a present?!

M. Yes, so as "to inquire of the wonder that was done in
the land" (2 Chr. 32:31).

N. For R. Yohanan said, "That day on which Ahaz died
was only two hours long, and on the day on which
Hezekiah got sick and got better, the Holy One,
blessed be he, gave back the other ten hours.

O. "For it is written, 'Behold I will bring again the
shadow of the degrees which is gone down in the sun
dial of Ahaz, ten degrees backward. So the sun returned ten degrees, by which degrees it was gone
down' (Is. 38:8). [Freedman, p. 649, nn. 5–6: The sun
had set ten hours too soon, to allow no time for funeral eulogies. This was in order to make atonement
for his sins, for the disgrace of being deprived of the
usual funeral honors expiates one's misdeeds. The return of the ten degrees to which Isaiah refers is as-
sumed to mean a prolongation of the day by ten
hours, light having healing powers.]

P. "[Merodach-baladan] said to [his staff], 'What is going
on?'

Q. "They said to him, 'Hezekiah got sick and got better.'

R. "He said, 'Is there such a great man in the world, and should I now want to greet him?'

S. "He wrote him, 'Peace to King Hezekiah, peace to the city of Jerusalem, peace to the great God!'

T. "Nebuchadnezzar was the scribe of Baladan. At that time he was not there. When he came, he said to him, 'What did you write?'

U. "They said to him, 'This is what we wrote.'

V. "He said to him, 'You called him "the great God" and yet you mentioned him last?'

W. "He said, 'Rather, this is how you should write: "Peace to the great God, peace to the city of Jerusalem, peace to King Hezekiah." '

X. "They said to him, 'Let the one who has read the letter serve as the messenger.'

Y. "He ran after [the messenger] [thus in honor of God]. But when he had run four steps, Gabriel came and froze him in place."

Z. Said R. Yohanan, "Had Gabriel not come and kept him standing in place, there would have been no remedy for (the enemies of) Israel." [Freedman, p. 650, n. 3: The learned children of the ordinary folk should thus be informed that the honor paid to them is due to the slight merit of their fathers, as in this case.]

LXXVIII. A. What is the meaning of the fact that [Merodach-] Baladan is called "the son of Baladan"?

B. They say: Baladan was king, and his appearance changed into that of a dog, so his son sat on the throne.

C. When he would sign a document, he would write his name and the name of his father, "King Baladan."

D. This is the sense of that which is written: "A son honors his father, and a servant his master" (Mal. 1:6).

E. "A son honors his father" (Mal. 1:6) refers to what we have just said.

F. As to "A servant his master" (Mal. 1:6)?

G. It is in line with that which is written: "Now in the fifth month, on the tenth day of the month, the nineteenth year of Nebuchadnezzar, king of Babylonia, came Nebuzaradan, captain of the guard, and stood before the king of Babylonia in Jerusalem. And he burned the house of the Lord and the house of the king" (Jer. 52:12–13).

H. [96B] But did Nebuchadnezzar go up to Jerusalem? Has it not been written, "They carried him up to the King of Babylonia, to Riblah" (Jer. 52:9)? "And," said R. Abbahu, "that town is the same as Antioch."

I. R. Hisda and R. Isaac b. Abudimi: One said, "His picture was engraved on [Nebuzaradan's] chariot."

J. The other said, "He was so much in awe of him that it was as though he were standing before him."

LXXIX.   A. Said Raba, "It was bearing three hundred mules loaded with iron axes that could break iron that Nebuchadnezzar sent Nebuzaradan. All of them broke on one gate of Jerusalem, as it is said, 'And now they attack its gate together; with axes and hammers they hit it' (Ps. 74:6).

B. "He wanted to go back. He said, 'I am afraid that they might do to me as they did to Sennacherib.'

C. "A voice came forth: 'Leaper son of a leaper, leap, Nebuzaradan! The time has come for the sanctuary to be destroyed and the palace burned.'

D. "Left to him was only a single axe. He went and hit it with its head, and the gate opened, as it is said, 'A man was famous according as he had lifted up axes upon thick trees' (Ps. 74:5).

E. "He continued with the killing until he reached the Temple. He set fire to it. The Temple sought to rise up [to heaven], but from heaven it was pushed down, as it is said, 'The Lord has trodden down the virgin daughter of Judah as in a winepress' (Lam. 1:15).

F. "He was elated, but an echo came and said, 'You have killed a dead people, you have burned a burned Temple, you have crushed already ground corn, as it is said, 'Take the millstones and grind meal, uncover your locks, make the leg bare, uncover the thigh, pass over the rivers' (Is. 47:2).

G. "What is said is not 'wheat' but 'ground meal.'"

H. [Nebuzaradan] saw the blood of Zechariah boiling. He said to them, "What is this?"

I. They said to him, 'It is the blood of the sacrifices, that has been poured out."

J. He said to them, "Come and let us bring [animal blood to make a comparison to see whether they are alike or not alike]." He slaughtered an animal and the blood was not like [that which was boiling].

K. He said to them, "Explain it to me, and if not, I shall comb your flesh with iron combs."

L. They said to him, "This one was a priest and a prophet, and he prophesied to Israel concerning the destruction of Jerusalem, so they killed him."

M. He said to them, "I shall be the one to appease him." He brought rabbis and killed them over him, but [the blood] did not come to rest. He brought school children and killed them over him, but still the blood did not come to rest. He brought the blossoms of the priesthood and killed them over him, and still the blood did not come to rest, until he had killed over him ninety-four myriads, and still his blood did not rest.

N. He drew near [the blood] and said, "Zechariah, Zechariah, I have destroyed the best of them. Do you want me to kill them all?"

O. Forthwith the blood came to rest.

P. He gave thought to repentance, saying, "Now if they, who killed only a single person, were treated in such a way, that man [I]—what will come of him?"

Q. He fled, sent his instructions to his household [giving over his property to his family], and then converted [to Judaism].

LXXX.   A. Our rabbis have taught on Tannaite authority:

B. Naaman was a resident proselyte.

C. Nebuzaradan was a righteous proselyte.

D. Grandsons of Sisera studied Torah in Jerusalem.

E. Grandsons of Sennacherib taught Torah in public.

F. And who were they? Shemaiah and Abtalion.

G. Grandsons of Haman studied Torah in Bene Beraq.

H. And so too grandsons of that wicked man [Nebuchadnezzar] did the Holy One, blessed be he, want to bring under the wings of the Presence of God.

I. Said the ministering angels before the Holy One, blessed be he, "Lord of the world, will you bring under the wings of your Presence him who destroyed your house and burned your Temple?"

J. For it is written, "We should have healed Babylonia, but she is not healed" (Jer. 21:9).

K. Said Ulla, "This speaks of Nebuchadnezzar."

L. Said R. Samuel b. Nahmani, "This refers to the 'canals of Babylonia' (Ps. 137:1), which flow among the palm trees of Babylonia."

LXXXI.   A. Said Ulla, "Ammon and Moab were bad neighbors of Jerusalem.

B. "When they heard the prophets prophesying the destruction of Jerusalem, they sent word to Nebuchadnezzar, 'Go out and come here.'

C. "He said, 'I am afraid that they will do to me what they did to those who came before me.'

D. "They sent to him, ' "For the man is not at home" (Prov. 7:19), and "man" can refer only to the Holy One, blessed be he, as it is said, "The Lord is a man of war" (Ex. 15:3).'

E. "He replied, 'He is nearby and he will come.'

F. "They sent to him, ' "He has gone on a far journey" (Prov. 7:19).'

G. "He sent to them, 'There are righteous men there, who will pray for mercy and bring him back.'

H. "They sent to him, ' "He has taken a bag of money with him" (Prov. 7:20), and "money" refers only to the righteous, as it is said, "So I bought her to me for fifteen pieces of silver and for a homer of barley and a half-homer of barley" (Hos. 3:2).'

I. "He sent word to them, 'The wicked may repent and pray for mercy and bring him back.'

J. "They sent to him, 'He has already set a time for them, as it is said, "And he will come home at the day appointed" (Prov. 7:20), and "day appointed" can refer only to time, as it is said, "In the time appointed on our solemn feast day" (Ps. 81:1,3).'

K. "He sent word to them, 'It is winter, and I cannot make the trip because of the snow and rain.'

L. "They sent to him, 'Come through the mountains [if need be]. For it is said, "Send you a messenger to the ruler of the earth [that he may come] by way of the rocks to the wilderness to the mountain of the daughter of Zion" (Is. 16:1).'

M. "He sent to them, 'If I come, I shall not have a place in which to make camp.'

N. "They sent word to him, 'Their cemeteries are superior to your palaces, as it is written, "At that time, says the Lord, they shall bring out the bones of the king of Judea and the bones of his princes and the bones of the priests and the bones of the prophets and the bones of the inhabitants of Jerusalem, out of their graves. And they shall spread them before the sun and the moon and all the host of heaven, whom they have loved and whom they have served and after whom they have walked" (Jer. 8:1–2).' [Freedman, p. 654, n. 1: The great burial vaults will be cleared out to give shelter to Nebuchadnezzar's army.]"

LXXXII. A. Said R. Nahman to R. Isaac, "Have you heard when the son of 'the fallen one' will come?"

B. He said to him, "Who is the son of 'the fallen one'?"

C. He said to him, "It is the Messiah."

D. "Do you call the Messiah 'the son of the fallen one'?"

E. He said to him, "Yes, for it is written, 'On that day I will raise up [97A] the tabernacle of David, the fallen one' (Amos 9:11)."

F. He said to him, "This is what R. Yohanan said, 'The generation to which the son of David will come will be one in which disciples of sages grow fewer,

G. " 'and, as to the others, their eyes will wear out through suffering and sighing,

H. " 'and troubles will be many, and laws harsh, forever renewing themselves so that the new one will hasten onward before the old one has come to an end.' "

LXXXIII.   A. Our rabbis have taught on Tannaite authority:

B. The seven-year cycle in which the son of David will come:

C. As to the first one, the following verse of Scripture will be fulfilled: "And I will cause it to rain upon one city and not upon another" (Amos 4:7).

D. As to the second year, the arrows of famine will be sent forth.

E. As to the third, there will be a great famine, in which men, women, and children will die, pious men and wonder-workers alike, and the Torah will be forgotten by those that study it.

F. As to the fourth year, there will be plenty which is no plenty.

G. As to the fifth year, there will be great prosperity, and people will eat, drink, and rejoice, and the Torah will be restored to those that study it.

H. As to the sixth year, there will be rumors.

I. As to the seventh year, there will be wars.

J. As to the end of the seventh year [the eighth year], the son of David will come.

K. Said R. Joseph, "Lo, how many septennates have passed like that one, and yet he has not come."

L. Said Abayye, "Were there rumors in the sixth year and wars in the seventh year?

M. "And furthermore, did they come in the right order?"

LXXXIV.   A. It has been taught on Tannaite authority:

B. R. Judah says, *"In the generation in which the son of David will come, the gathering place will be for prostitution, Galilee will be laid waste, Gablan will be made desolate, and the men of the frontier will go about from town to town, and none will take pity on them; and the wisdom of scribes will putrefy; and those who fear sin will be rejected; and the truth will be herded away [M. Sot. 9:15AA–GG].*

C. "For it is said, 'And the truth will be herded away' (Is. 59:15)."

D. What is the meaning of the statement, "The truth will be herded away" (Is. 59:15)?

E. Said members of the house of Rab, "This teaches that it will be divided into herds and herds, each going its way."

F. What is the meaning [of the concluding passage of the same verse], "And he who departs from evil makes himself a prey" (Is. 59:15)?

G. Said members of the house of R. Shila, "Whoever departs from evil will be treated as a fool [using the same letters as those for "prey"] by other people."

LXXXV. A. Said Raba, "To begin with I had supposed that there is no truth in the world. One of the rabbis, R. Tabut by name (and some say, R. Tabyomi by name), who would not go back on his word even though people gave him all the treasures of the world, said to me that one time he happened to come to a place called Truth.

B. "It was a place in which people would not go back on their word, and in which no person died before his day.

C. "He took a woman of theirs as wife and had two sons from her.

D. "One day his wife was sitting and shampooing her hair. Her neighbor came and knocked on the door. Thinking that it would be improper [to say what his wife was doing], he said to her, 'She is not here.'

E. "His two sons died.

F. "The people of the place came to him and said to him, 'What is going on?'

G. "He said to them, 'This is what happened.'

H. "They said to him, 'By your leave, please go away from our place, so as not to encite Satan against these men [us].' "

LXXXVI. A. It has been taught on Tannaite authority:

B. *R. Nehorai says, "In the generation in which the son of David will come, children will shame elders, and elders will stand up before children. 'The daughter rises up against the mother, and the daughter-in-law against her mother-in-law' (Mic. 7:6). The face of the generation is the face of a dog, and a son is not ashamed before his father" [M. Sot. 9:15HH–KK].*

LXXXVII. A. It has been taught on Tannaite authority:

B. *R. Nehemiah says, "In the generation in which the son of David will come, presumption increases, and dearth increases, and the vine gives its fruit and wine at great cost. The government turns to heresy, and there is no reproof" [M. Sot. 9:15W–Z].*

C. That statement supports the view of R. Isaac.

D. For R. Isaac said, "The son of David will come only when the entire kingdom has turned to heresy."

E. Said Raba, "What is the text of Scripture that makes that point?

F. " 'It is all turned white, he is clean' (Lev. 13:13). [Freedman, p. 656, n. 5: When all are heretics, it is a sign that the world is about to be purified by the advent of the Messiah.]"

LXXXVIII. A. Our rabbis have taught on Tannaite authority:

B. "For the Lord shall judge his people and repent himself of his servants, when he sees that their power has gone, and there is none shut up or left" (Deut. 32:36).

C. The son of David will come only when traitors are many.

D. Another matter: Only when disciples are few.

E. Another matter: Only when a penny will not be found in anyone's pocket.

F. Another matter: Only when people will have given up hope of redemption, as it is said, "There is none shut up or left" (Deut. 32:36), as it were, when there is none [God being absent] who supports and helps Israel.

G. That accords with the statement of R. Zira, who, when he would find rabbis involved in [figuring out when the Messiah would come], would say to them, 'By your leave, I ask you not to put it off.

H. " 'For we have learned on Tannaite authority: "Three things come on the spur of the moment, and these are they: the Messiah, a lost object, and a scorpion." ' "

LXXXIX. A. Said R. Qattina, "The world will exist for six thousand years and be destroyed for one thousand,

B. "as it is said, 'And the Lord alone shall be exalted in that day' (Is. 2:11)."

C. Abayye said, "It will be desolate for two thousand years, as it is said, 'After two days will he revive us, in the third day, he will raise us up and we shall live in his sight' (Hos. 6:2)."

D. It has been taught on Tannaite authority in accord with the view of R. Qattina:

E. Just as at the advent of the Sabbatical Year the world will lie fallow for one out of seven years,

F. so it is with the world. A thousand years will the world lie fallow out of seven thousand years,

G. as it is said, "And the Lord alone shall be exalted in that day" (Is. 2:11), and Scripture says, "A Psalm and song for the Sabbath Day" (Ps. 92:1)—a day that is wholly the Sabbath.

H. And Scripture says, "For a thousand years in your sight are but as yesterday when they are past" (Ps. 90:4). [A day for a thousand years.]

XC.   A. A Tannaite authority of the house of Elijah [said], "For six thousand years the world will exist.

B. "For two thousand it will be desolate, two thousand years [will be the time of] Torah, and two thousand years will be the days of the Messiah,

C. "[97B] but on account of our numerous sins what has been lost [of those years, in which the Messiah should have come but has not come] has been lost."

XCI.   A. Said Elijah to R. Sala the Pious, "The world will last for no fewer than eighty-five Jubilees [of fifty years each], and the son of David will come in the last one."

B. He said to him, "Will it be in the first or the last year of the last Jubilee?"

C. He said to him, "I do not know."

D. "Will it come at the end or not come at the end of the fiftieth year?"

E. He said to him, "I do not know."

F. R. Ashi said, "This is what he said to him: 'Up to that time, do not look for his coming, but from that time onward, do look for his coming.' "

XCII. A. R. Hanan, son of Tahalipa, sent to R. Joseph, "I came across a man who had in hand a scroll, written in Assyrian [block] letters in the holy language.

B. "I said to him, 'Where did you get this?'

C. "He said to me, 'I was employed in the Roman armies, and I found it in the Roman archives.'

D. "In the scroll it is written that after four thousand two hundred ninety-two years from the creation of the world, the world will be an orphan.

E. "[As to the years to follow] in some there will be wars of the great dragons, and in some, wars of Gog and Magog, and the rest will be the days of the Messiah.

F. "And the Holy One, blessed be he, will renew his world only after seven thousand years."

G. R. Aha, son of Raba, said, " 'After five thousand years' is what is to be repeated."

XCIII. A. It has been taught on Tannaite authority:

B. R. Nathan says, "This verse of Scripture pierces to the depth:

C. " 'For the vision is yet for an appointed time, but at the end it shall speak and not lie; though he tarry, wait for him; because it will surely come, it will not tarry' (Hab. 2:3)."

D. This is not in accord with our rabbis, who interpreted, "Until a time and times and the dividing of time" (Dan. 7:25).

E. Nor does it accord with R. Simlai, who would interpret, "You feed them with the bread of tears and give them tears to drink a third time" (Ps. 80:6).

F. Nor does it accord with R. Aqiba, who would interpret the verse, "Yet once, it is a little while, and I will shake the heavens and the earth" (Hag. 2:6).

G. Rather, the first kingdom will last for seventy years, the second kingdom for fifty-two years, and the kingdom of Ben Koziba will be for two and a half years.

XCIV. A. What is the meaning of the verse, "But at the end it shall speak and not lie" (Hab. 2:3)?

B. Said R. Samuel bar Nahmani said R. Johathan, "[Freedman, p. 659, n. 5: Reading the verse as, 'He will blast him who calculates the end,'] blasted be the bones of those who calculate the end [when the Messiah will come].

C. "For they might say, 'Since the end has come and he has not come, he will not come.'

D. "Rather, wait for him, as it is said, 'Though he tarry, wait for him' (Hab. 2:3).

E. "Should you say that we shall wait, but he may not wait, Scripture responds, 'And therefore will the Lord wait, that he may be gracious to you, and therefore will he be exalted, that he may have mercy upon you' (Is. 30:18).

F. "Then, since we are waiting and he is waiting, what is holding things up?

G. "It is the attribute of justice that is holding things up.

H. "But if the attribute of justice is holding things up, why should we wait?

I. "It is so as to receive the reward for our patience, as it is written, 'Blessed are all those who wait for him' (Is. 30:9)."

XCV. A. Said Abayye, "There are in the world never fewer than thirty-six righteous men, who look upon the face of the Presence of God every day, for it is said, 'Happy are those who wait for him' (Is. 30:18), and the numerical value of the letters in the word 'for him' is thirty-six."

B. Is this so? And did not Raba say, "The row of the righteous before the Holy One, blessed be he, is made up of eighteen thousand, as it is said, 'There shall be eighteen thousand round about' (Ez. 48:35)"?

C. There is no contradiction between the two views. The former number refers to those few who see him through a bright mirror, the latter number refers to those many who see him only through a dirty mirror.

D. And are they so numerous?

E. And did not Hezekiah said R. Jeremiah said in the name of R. Simeon b. Yohai, "I have myself seen the inhabitants of the upper world, and they are only a few. If they are a thousand, my son and I are among their number. If they are only a hundred, my son and I are among their number. If they are only two, they are only my son and I.'

F. There is still no contradiction. The larger number speaks of those who go inside only with permission, the smaller number those who go inside even without permission.

XCVI.

A. Said Rab, "All of the ends have passed, and the matter now depends only on repentance and good deeds."

B. And Samuel said, "It is sufficient for a mourner to remain firm in his mourning."

C. This accords with the following dispute among Tannaite authorities:

D. R. Eliezer says, "If the Israelites repent, they will be redeemed, and if not, they will not be redeemed."

E. Said R. Joshua to him, "If they do not repent, will they not be redeemed?!

F. "Rather, the Holy One, blessed be he, will raise up for them a king whose decrees will be as harsh as those of Haman, and the Israelites will repent, and [God] will restore them to a good path]."

G. A further Tannaite version:

H. R. Eliezer says, "If the Israelites repent, they will be redeemed, as it is said, 'Return, backsliding children, and I will heal your backslidings' (Jer. 3:22)."

I. Said to him R. Joshua, "And is it not written, 'You have sold yourselves for nought, and you shall be redeemed without money' (Is. 52:3)?

J. " 'You have sold yourselves for nought'—for idolatry.

K. " 'But you shall be redeemed without money'—with neither repentance nor doing good deeds."

L. Said to him R. Eliezer, "But is it not written, 'Return to me and I shall return to you' (Mal. 3:7)?"

M. Said to him R. Joshua, "But is it not written, 'For I am master over you, and I will take you, one from a city and two from a family and I will bring you to Zion' (Jer. 3:14)?"

N. Said to him R. Eliezer, "But it is written, 'In returning and rest you shall be saved' (Is. 30:5)."

O. Said R. Joshua to R. Eliezer, "But is it not written, 'Thus says the Lord, the redeemer of Israel, and his holy one, to whom man despises, to him whom the nations abhor, to a servant of rulers, [98A] kings shall see and arise, princes also shall worship' (Is. 49:7)?"

P. Said to him R. Eliezer, "But is it not written, 'If you will return, O Israel, says the Lord, return to me' (Jer. 4:1)?"

Q. Said to him R. Joshua, "But it is written elsewhere, 'And I heard the man clothed in linen, which was upon the waters of the river, when he held up his right hand and his left hand to heaven and swore by him who lives forever that it shall be for a year, two years, and half a year and when he shall have accomplished scattering the power of the holy people, all these things shall be finished' (Dan. 12:7)."

R. And R. Eliezer shut up.

XCVII. A. And said R. Abba, "You have no indication of the end more openly stated than the following, as it is said: 'But you, O Mountains of Israel, shall shoot forth your branches and yield your fruit to my people, Israel, for they are at hand to come' (Ez. 36:8)."

B. R. Eliezer says, "Also the following, as it is said: 'For before these days there was no hire for man, nor any hire for beast neither was there any peace to him that went out or came in because of the affliction' (Zech. 8:10)."

C. What is the meaning of the phrase, "Neither was there any peace to him that went out or came in because of the affliction"?

D. Rab said, "Even to disciples of sages, concerning whom peace is written in Scripture, as it is written, 'Great peace shall they have who love your Torah' (Ps. 119:165)."

E. "Neither was there any peace . . . because of the affliction" (Zech. 8:10):

F. And Samuel said, "Until all prices will be equal."

XCVIII. A. Said R. Hanina, "The son of David will come only when a fish will be sought for a sick person and not be found, as it is said, 'Then I will make their waters deep and cause their rivers to run like oil' (Ez. 32:14), and it is written, 'In that day I will cause the horn of the house of Israel to sprout forth' (Ez. 29:21)."

B. Said R. Hama bar Hanina, "The son of David will come only when the rule over Israel by the least of the kingdoms will come to an end, as it is said, 'He shall both cut off the springs with pruning books and take away and cut down the branches' (Is. 18:5), and further: 'In that time shall the present be brought to the Lord of hosts of a people that is scattered and peeled' (Is. 18:7)."

C. Said Zeiri said R. Hanina, "The son of David will come only when arrogant people will no longer be [found] in Israel, as it is said, 'For then I will take away out of the midst of you those who rejoice in your pride' (Zeph. 8:11), followed by: 'I will also leave in the midst of you an afflicted and poor people, and they shall take refuge in the name of the Lord' (Zeph. 3:12)."

D. Said R. Simlai in the name of R. Eliezer b. R. Simeon, "The son of David will come only when all judges and rulers come to an end in Israel, as it is said, 'And I will turn my hand upon you and purely purge away your dross and take away all your sin, and I will restore your judges as at the first' (Is. 1:25–26)."

XCIX. A. Said Ulla, "Jerusalem will be redeemed only through righteousness, as it is written, 'Zion shall be redeemed with judgment and her converts with righteousness' (Is. 1:27)."

B. Said R. Pappa, "If the arrogant end [in Israel], the Magi will end [in Iran], if the judges end [in Israel], the rulers of thousands will come to an end [in Iran].

C. "If the arrogant end [in Israel], the magi will end [in Iran], as it is written, 'And I will purely purge away your haughty ones and take away all your sin' (Is. 1:25).

D. "If judges end [in Israel], the rulers of thousands will come to an end [in Iran], as it is written, 'The Lord has taken away your judgments, he has cast out your enemy' (Zeph. 3:15)."

C. A. Said R. Yohanan, "If you see a generation growing less and less, hope for him, as it is said, 'And the afflicted people will you save' (2 Sam. 22:28)."

B. Said R. Yohanan, "If you see a generation over which many troubles flow like a river, hope for him, as it is written, 'When the enemy shall come in like a flood, the spirit of the Lord shall lift up a standard against him' (Is. 59:19), followed by: 'And the redeemer shall come to Zion' (Is. 59:20)."

C. And said R. Yohanan, "The son of David will come to a generation that is either entirely righteous or entirely wicked.

D. "A generation that is entirely righteous, as it is written, 'Your people also shall be all righteous, they shall inherit the land for ever' (Is. 60:21),

E. "or a generation that is entirely wicked, as it is written, 'And he saw that there was no man and wondered that there was no intercessor' (Is. 59:16), and it is written, 'For my own sake, even for my own sake I will do it' (Is. 60:22)."

CI. A. Said R. Alexandri, "R. Joshua b. Levi contrasted verses as follows:

B. " 'It is written, "In its time [will the Messiah come]," and it is also written, "I [the Lord] will hasten it."

C. [" 'What is the meaning of the contrast?]

D. " 'If [the Israelites] have merit, I will hasten it, if they do not, [the Messiah] will come in due course.

E. " 'It is written, "And behold, one like the son of man came with the clouds of heaven" (Dan. 7:13, and it is written, "Behold your king comes to you . . . lowly and riding upon an ass" (Zech. 9:7). [What is the meaning of the contrast?]

F. " 'If [the Israelites] have merit, it will be "with the clouds of heaven" (Dan. 7:13), and if they do not have merit, it will be "lowly and riding upon an ass" (Zech. 98:7).' "

CII. A. Said King Shapur to Samuel, "You say that the Messiah will come on an ass [which is a humble way]. Come and I shall send him a white horse that I have."

B. He said to him, "Do you have one of many colors?"

CIII. A. R. Joshua b. Levi found Elijah standing at the door of the burial vault of R. Simeon b. Yohai. He said to him, "Am I going to come to the world to come?"

B. He said to him, "If this master wants."

C. Said R. Joshua b. Levi, "Two did I see, but a third voice did I hear."

D. He said to him, "When is the Messiah coming?"

E. He said to him, "Go and ask him."

F. "And where is he sitting?"

G. "At the gate of the city."

H. "And what are the marks that indicate who he is?"

I. "He is sitting among the poor who suffer illness, and all of them untie and tie their bandages all together, but he unties them and ties them one by one. He is thinking, 'Perhaps I may be wanted, and I do not want to be held up.' "

J. He went to him, saying to him, "Peace be unto you, my master and teacher."

K. He said to him, "Peace be unto you, son of Levi."

L. He said to him, "When is the master coming?"

M. He said to him, "Today."

N. He went back to Elijah, who said to him, "What did he tell you?"

O. He said to him, " 'Peace be unto you, son of Levi.' "

P. He said to him, "He [thereby] promised you and your father the world to come."

Q. He said to him, "But he lied to me. For he said to me, 'I am coming today,' but he did not come."

R. He said to him, "This is what he said to you, " 'Today, if you will obey his voice" (Ps. 95:7).' "

CIV.

A. His disciples asked R. Yose b. Qisma, "When is the son of David coming?"

B. He said to them, "I am afraid [to answer], lest you ask an omen from me [that my answer is right]."

C. They said to him, "We shall not ask for an omen from you." He said to them, "When this gate falls and is rebuilt, falls and is rebuilt, and falls a third time. They will not suffice to rebuild it before the son of David will come."

D. They said to him, "Our master, give us an omen."

E. He said to them, "But did you not say to me that you would not ask for an omen from me?"

F. They said to him, "Even so."

G. He said to them, "Then let the waters of the grotto of Banias turn to blood," and they turned to blood.

H. When he died, he said to them, "Dig my bier deep into the ground, [98B] for there is not a palm tree in Babylonia on which a Persian horse has not been tied, nor is there a bier in the land of Israel from which a Median horse will not eat straw."

CV.

A. Said Rab, "The son of David will come only when the monarchy [of Rome] will spread over Israel for nine months,

B. "as it is said, 'Therefore will he give them up, until the time that she who travails has brought forth; then the remnant of his brethren shall return to the children of Israel' (Mic. 5:2)."

CVI.

A. Said Ulla, "Let him come, but may I not see him."

B. Said Rabba, "Let him come, but may I not see him."

C. R. Joseph said, "May he come, and may I have the merit of sitting in the shade of the dung of his ass."

D. Said Abayye to Rabbah, "What is the reason [that some do not wish to see the coming of the Messiah]? Is it because of the turmoil of the Messiah?

E. "And has it not been taught on Tannaite authority:

F. "His disciples asked R. Eliezer, 'What should someone do to save himself from the turmoil of the Messiah?'

G. "[He replied to them], 'Let him engage in study of the Torah and acts of loving-kindness.'

H. "And lo, the master [at hand] practices Torah-study and acts of loving-kindness. [So why not want to see him?]"

I. He said to him, "Perhaps he fears sin will cause [him to suffer], in line with what R. Jacob bar Idi said."

J. For R. Jacob bar Idi contrasted two verses of Scripture, as follows: "It is written, 'And behold, I am with you and will keep you wherever you go' (Gen. 28:15), and another verse states, 'Then Jacob was greatly afraid' (Gen. 32:8).

K. "[Why the contrast between God's promise and Jacob's fear?] Jacob feared [and thought to himself,] 'Sin which I have done may cause [punishment for me instead].' "

L. That accords with what has been taught on Tannaite authority:

M. "Till your people pass over, O Lord, till your people pass over, that you have acquired" (Ex. 15:16).

N. "Till your people pass over" refers to the first entry into the land [in Joshua's time].

O. "Till your people pass over, that you have acquired" refers to the second entry into the land [in the time of Ezra and Nehemiah. Thus a miracle was promised not only on the first occasion, but also on the second. But it did not happen the second time around. Why not?]

P. On the basis of this statement, sages have said, "The Israelites were worthy of having a miracle performed for them in the time of Ezra also, just as it had been performed for them in the time of Joshua b. Nun, but sin caused the miracle to be withheld."

CVII.

A. So said R. Yohanan, "Let his come, but let me not see him."

B. Said R. Simeon b. Laqish to him, "What is the scriptural basis for the view? Shall we say that it is because it is written, 'As if a man fled from a lion and a bear met him, or went into the house and leaned his hand on the wall and a serpent bit him' (Amos 5:19)?

C. "Come and I shall show you an example of such a case in this world.

D. "When a man goes out to the field and bailiff meets him, it is like one whom a lion meets. He goes into town and a tax collector meets him, it is like one whom a bear meets.

E. "He goes into his house and finds his sons and daughters suffering from hunger, it is like one whom a snake bit.

F. "Rather, it is because it is written, 'Ask you now and see whether a man travails with child? Why do I see every man with his hands on his loins, as women in travail, and all faces are turned into paleness?' (Jer. 30:6)."

G. What is the sense of, "Why do I see every man . . ."?

H. Said Raba bar Isaac said Rab, "It speaks of him to whom all [manly] power belongs [God]."

I. And what is the sense of "all faces are turned into paleness"?

J. Said R. Yohanan, "[It speaks of God's] heavenly family and his earthly family, at the moment at which God says, 'These are the creation of my hands, and those are the creation of my hands. How shall I destroy these [gentiles] on account of [what they have done to] those [Israelites]? [Freedman, p. 667, n. 2: to avenge the wrongs suffered by the Jews. Because the suffering would be so great that even the Almighty would lament it, Yohanan desired to be spared the Messiah's coming.]"

K. Said R. Pappa, "This is in line with what people say: 'The ox runs and falls, so the horse is put in its stall.' [Freedman, p. 667, n. 3: Then it is hard to get the horse out. So the Israelites, having fallen, were replaced in power by the gentiles, but on their recovery, it will be difficult to remove the gentiles from their position without inflicting much suffering.]"

CVIII.

A. Said R. Giddal said Rab, "The Israelites are going to eat [and not starve] in the years of the Messiah."

B. Said R. Joseph, "That is self-evident. If not, then who will eat? Joe and Mo?! [Text: Hiliq and Bileq?]"

C. [The statement at hand] serves to exclude the view of R. Hillel, who has said, "There will be no further Messiah for Israel, for they already consumed him in the time of Hezekiah."

CIX.

A. Said Rab, "The world was created only for David."

B. And Samuel said, "For Moses."

C. And R. Yohanan said, "For the Messiah."

D. What is his name?

E. The house of R. Shila said, "His name is Shiloh, as it is said, 'Until Shiloh come' (Gen. 49:10)."

F. Members of the house of R. Yannai say, "His name is Yinnon, for it is written, 'His name shall endure forever, before the sun was, his name is Yinnon' (Ps. 72:17)."

G. Members of the house of R. Haninah said, "It is Haninah, as it is said, 'Where I will not give you Haninah' (Jer. 16:13)."

H. Others say, "His name is Menahem, son of Hezekiah, for it is written, 'Because Menahem that would relieve my soul, is far' (Lam. 1:16)."

I. Rabbis said, "His name is 'the leper of the school house,' as it is written, 'Surely he has borne our griefs and carried our sorrows, yet we did esteem him a leper, smitten of God and afflicted' (Is. 53:4)."

CX. A. Said R. Nahman, "If he is among the living, he is such as I, as it is said, 'And their nobles shall be of themselves and their governors shall proceed from the midst of them' (Jer. 30:21)."

B. Said Rab, "If he is among the living, he is such as our Holy Rabbi [Judah the Patriarch], and if he is among the dead, he is such as Daniel, the most desirable man."

C. Said R. Judah said Rab, "The Holy One, blessed be he, is destined to raise up for [Israel] another David, as it is said, 'But they shall serve the Lord their God and David their king, whom I will raise up for them' (Jer. 30:9).

D. " 'Raised up' is not what is said, but rather, 'will raise up.' "

E. Said R. Pappa to Abayye, "But lo, it is written, 'And my servant David shall be their prince forever' (Ez. 37:25) [with the title for prince standing for less than the title for king]."

F. [He said to him,] "It is like a king and a viceroy [the second David being king]."

CXI. A. R. Simlai interpreted the following verse: "What is the meaning of that which is written, 'Woe to you who desire the day of the Lord! To what end is it for you? The day of the Lord is darkness and not light' (Amos 5:18)?

B. "The matter may be compared to the case of the cock and the bat who were waiting for light.

C. "The cock said to the bat, 'I am waiting for the light, for the light belongs to me, but what do you need light for [99A]?' "

D. That is in line with what a min said to R. Abbahu, "When is the Messiah coming?"

E. He said to him, "When darkness covers those men."

F. He said to him, "You are cursing me."

G. He said to him, "I am merely citing a verse of Scripture: 'For behold, the darkness shall cover the earth, and great darkness the people, but the Lord shall shine upon you, and his glory shall be seen upon you' (Is. 60:2)."

CXII.   A. It has been taught on Tannaite authority:

B. R. Eliezer says, "The days of the Messiah will last forty years, as it is said, 'Forty years long shall I take hold of the generation' (Ps. 95:10)."

C. R. Eliezer b. Azariah says, "Seventy years, as it is said, 'And it shall come to pass in that day that Tyre shall be forgotten seventy years, according to the days of one king' (Is. 23:15).

D. "Now what would be a one [and singular] king? We must say that it is the Messiah."

E. Rabbi says, "Three generations, as it is said, 'They shall fear you with the sun and before the moon, a generation and generations' (Ps. 72:5)."

CXIII.   A. R. Hillel says, "Israel will have no Messiah, for they consumed him in the time of Hezekiah."

B. Said R. Joseph, "May R. Hillel's master forgive him. When did Hezekiah live? It was in the time of the first Temple. But Zechariah prophesied in the second Temple's time and said, 'Rejoice greatly, O daughter of Zion, shout, O daughter of Jerusalem, behold your king comes to you; he is just and has salvation; lowly and riding upon an ass and upon a colt the foal of an ass' (Zech. 9:9)."

CXIV.   A. A further teaching on Tannaite authority:

B. R. Eliezer says, "The days of the Messiah will last for forty years. Here it is written, 'And he afflicted you and made you hunger and fed you with manna' (Deut. 8:3), and elsewhere: 'Make us glad according to the

days [forty years in the wilderness] in which you have
afflicted us' (Ps. 90:15)."

C. R. Dosa says, "Four hundred years. Here it is written,
'And they shall serve them and they shall afflict them
four hundred years' (Gen. 15:13), and elsewhere:
'Make us glad according to the days wherein you have
afflicted us' (Ps. 90:15)."

D. Rabbi says, "Three hundred and sixty-five years, according to the number of days in the solar year, as it
is said, 'For the day of vengeance is in my heart and
the year of my redemption has come' (Is. 63:4)."

E. What is the meaning of "the day of vengeance is in
my heart" (Is. 63:4)?

F. Said R. Yohanan, "I have revealed it to my heart, but
I have not revealed it to my limbs."

G. R. Simeon b. Laqish said, "To my heart I have revealed it, to the ministering angels I have not revealed
it."

H. Abimi, son of R. Abbahu, stated on Tannaite authority, "The days of the Messiah for Israel will be
seven thousand years, as it is said, 'And as the bride-
groom rejoices over the bride [a week], so shall your
God rejoice over you' (Is. 62:5)."

I. Said R. Judah said Samuel, "The days of the Messiah
are the same as the days that have passed from the day
of the creation of the world even to now, as it is said,
'As the days of heaven upon earth' (Deut. 11:21)."

J. R. Nahman bar Isaac said, "As the days from Noah
to now, as it is said, 'For this is as the waters of Noah,
which are mine, so I have sworn it' (Is. 54:9)."

CXV.　A. Said R. Hiyya bar Abba said R. Yohanan, "All of the
prophets prophesied only concerning the days of the
Messiah.

B. "But as to the world to come [thereafter]: 'Eye has
not seen, O Lord, beside you, what he has prepared
for him who waits for him' (Is. 64:3)."

C. That statement differs from the view of Samuel.

D. For said Samuel, "There is no difference between this
world and the days of the Messiah except for [Israel's]
subjugation to the rule of the empires alone."

E. And said R. Hiyya bar Abba said R. Yohanan, "All of the prophets prophesied only concerning those who repent, but as to the perfectly righteous people [who have never sinned to begin with]: 'Eye has not seen, O God, beside you, what he has prepared for him who waits for him' (Is. 54:3)."

F. That statement differs from the view of R. Abbahu.

G. For, said R. Abbahu, "In the place in which those who repent stand, the righteous cannot stand, for it is said, 'Peace, peace to him who is far off and to him that is near' (Is. 57:19).

H. " 'To begin with, he was 'far off,' and then he repented and so became 'near.'

I. "What is the sense of 'far off? Originally far off [a sinner], and what is the sense of 'near'? Originally near and still near. [Freedman, p. 671, n. 3: Thus he assigns a higher rank to the repentant sinner than to the completely righteous.]"

J. R. Yohanan said, " 'To the one who was distant' because he was far from sin, and 'near' in that he was near sin but distanced himself from it."

K. And said R. Hiyya bar Abba said R. Yohanan, "All of the prophets prophesied only concerning him who marries his daughter off to a disciple of sages, conducts business to the advantage of a disciple of a sage, and benefits a disciple of a sage from his wealth.

L. "But as to disciples of sages themselves: 'Eye has not seen, O God beside you' (Is. 64:3)."

M. What is the meaning of the phrase, "Eye has not seen"?

N. Said R. Joshua b. Levi, "This refers to wine that has been kept in the grapes from the six days of creation."

O. R. Simeon b. Laqish said, "This refers to Eden, which no eye has ever seen.

P. "And if you should say, 'Then where did Adam dwell?' the answer is, in the garden.

Q. "And if you should say, 'But it was the Garden that was Eden,' Scripture says, 'And a river issued from Eden to water the garden' (Gen. 2:10)."

CXVI.

A. *And he who says, "The Torah does not come from heaven"* [M. 11:1D]:

B. Our rabbis have taught on Tannaite authority:

C. "Because he has despised the word of the Lord and broken his commandment, that soul shall utterly be cut off" (Num. 15:31):

D. This refers to one who says, "The Torah does not come from heaven."

E. Another matter:

F. "Because he has despised the word of the Lord": This refers to an Epicurean.

G. Another matter:

H. "Because he has despised the word of the Lord": This refers to one who is without shame in interpreting the Torah.

I. "And broken his commandment": This refers to one who removes the mark fleshly arks of the covenant.

J. "That soul shatter utterly be cut off": "Be cut off"—in this world. "Utterly"—in the world to come.

K. On the basis of this exegesis, said R. Eliezer the Modite, *"He who treats Holy Things as secular, he who despises the appointed times, he who humiliates his companion in public, he who removes the signs of the covenant of Abraham, our father, and he who exposes aspects of the Torah not in accord with the law, even though he has in hand learning in Torah and good deeds, will have no share in the world to come"* [M. Abot 3:11].

L. A further teaching on Tannaite authority:

M. "Because he has despised the word of the Lord" (Num. 14:31): This refers to one who says, "The Torah does not come from heaven."

N. And even if he had said, "The entire Torah comes from heaven, except for this one verse, which the Holy One, blessed be he, did not say, but which Moses said on his own," such a one falls under the verse, "Because he has despised the word of the Lord" (Num. 15:31).

O. And even if he had said, "The entire Torah comes from heaven, except for one minor point, an argument a fortiori, an argument based on analogy," such a one falls under the verse, "Because he has despised the way of the Lord" (Num. 15:31).

CXVII.

A. It has been taught on Tannaite authority:

B. R. Meir would say, "He who studies the Torah but does not teach it falls under the verse, 'Because he has despised the word of the Lord' (Num. 15:31)."

C. R. Nathan says, "Whoever does not pay close attention to the Mishnah."

D. R. Nehorai says, "Whoever has the possibility of taking up the study of the Torah and does not do so."

E. R. Ishmael says, "This refers to one who worships an idol."

F. What provides the implication that such a one is subject to discussion here?

G. It accords with what the Tannaite authority of the house of R. Ishmael [said], " 'Because he has despised the word of the Lord' (Num. 15:31) refers to one who despises the statement that was made to Moses at Sinai: 'I am the Lord your God. You shall have no other gods before me' (Ex. 20:2–3)."

CXVIII.

A. **R. Joshua b. Qorhah says, "Whoever studies the Torah and does not review it is like a man who sows seed but does not harvest it."**

B. **R. Joshua says, "Whoever learns the Torah and forgets it is like a woman who bears and buries."**

C. **R. Aqiba says, "[99B] A song is in me, a song always" [T. Ah. 16:8H–I].**

D. Said R. Isaac b. Abudimi, "What is the pertinent prooftext? As it is said, 'He who labors labors for himself, for his mouth craves it of him' (Prov. 16:26).

E. "He labors in one place, and the Torah labors for him in a different place."

CXIX.

A. Said R. Eleazar, "Every man was born to work, as it is said, 'For man is born to work' (Job 5:7).

B. "I do not now whether it is for work done with the mouth that he is created, or whether it is for labor done through physical work that he was created.

C. "When Scripture says, 'For his mouth craves it of him' (Prov. 16:26), one has to conclude that it is for work done with the mouth that he was created.

D. "Yet I still do not know whether it was to labor in the Torah or to labor in some sort of other conversation.

E. "When Scripture says, 'This book of the Torah shall not depart out of your mouth' (Josh. 1:8), one must conclude that it is for labor in the Torah that he is created."

F. That is in line with what Raba said, "All bodies serve to bear burdens. Happy are those who have the merit of bearing the burden of the Torah."

CXX. A. "Whoever commits adultery with a woman lacks understanding" (Prov. 6:32):

B. Said R. Simeon b. Laqish, "This refers to one who studies the Torah at occasional intervals.

C. "For it is said, 'For it is a pleasant thing if you keep them within you, they shall withal be fitted in your lips' (Prov. 22:18). [Freedman, p. 673, n. 11: One can keep the Torah only if its words are fitted always on his lips, not at rare intervals only.]"

CXXI. A. Our rabbis have taught on Tannaite authority:

B. "But the soul that does anything presumptuously" (Num. 15:30):

C. This refers to Manasseh, son of Hezekiah, who would go into session and interpret tales seeking flaws in them, saying, "Did Moses have nothing better to do than to write such verses as 'And Lotan's sister was Timna' (Gen. 36:22); 'and Timna was concubine to Eliphaz' (Gen. 36:12); 'and Reuben went in the days of the wheat harvest and found mandrakes in the field' (Gen. 30:14)?"

D. An echo came forth and said to him, " 'You sit and speak against your brother; you slander your own mother's son. These things you have done, and I keep silence; you thought that I was altogether such a one as a yourself, but I will reprove you and set them in order before your eyes' (Ps. 50:20–21)."

E. Concerning him it is spelled out in tradition: "Woe to them who draw iniquity with cords of vanity and sin as it were with a cart rope" (Is. 5:18).

F. What is the sense of "and sin as it were with a cart rope"?

G. Said R. Assi, "The inclincation to do evil to begin with is like a spider's thread and ends up like a cart rope."

H. In any event, what is the meaning of, "And Lotan's sister was Timna" (Gen. 36:22)?

I. She was a princess, as it is written, "Duke Lotan, Duke Timna," and "duke" refers to a kid who has not yet got his crown.

J. She had wanted to convert to Judaism. She came to Abraham, Isaac, and Jacob, and they did not accept her. She went and became the concubine to Eliphaz, son of Esau, saying, "It is better to be a handmaiden to this nation and not a noble woman to any other nation."

K. From her descended Amalak, who distressed Israel.

L. What is the reason? It was because they should not have put her off [but should have accepted her].

M. "And Reuben went in the days of the wheat harvest [and found mandrakes in the field]" (Gen. 36:12):

N. Said Raba, son of R. Isaac, said Rab, "On the basis of this verse, we learn that righteous folk do not lay hands on what is stolen."

O. "And found mandrakes in the field" (Gen. 36:12):

P. What are these?

Q. Said Rab, "Mandrakes."

R. Said Levi, "Violets."

S. Said R. Jonathan, "Mandrake flowers."

CXXII. A. Said R. Alexandri, "Whoever is occupied in study of the Torah for the sake of heaven brings peace to the family above and to the family below,

B. "as it is said, 'Or let him take hold of my strength that he may make peace with me, and he shall make peace with me' (Is. 27:5)."

C. Rab said, "It is as if he built the palace above and the one below, as it is said, 'And I have put my words in your mouth and I have covered you in the shadow of my hand, that I may plant the heavens and lay the foundations of the earth, and say to Zion, You are my people' (Is. 51:16)."

D. R. Yohanan said, "Also he shields the world, as it is said, 'And I have covered you in the shadow of my hand' (Is. 51:16)."

E. Levi said, "Also he draws the redemption nearer, as it is said, 'And say to Zion, you are my people' (Is. 51:16)."

CXXIII. A. Said R. Simeon b. Laqish, "Whoever teaches Torah to the son of his neighbor is credited by Scripture as if he had made him,

B. "as it is said, 'And the souls which they had made in Haran' (Gen. 12:5)."

C. R. Eleazar said, "It is as though he had made the words of Torah, as it is said, 'Therefore keep the words of this covenant and make them' (Deut. 29:9)."

D. Raba said, "It is as though he had made himself, as it is said, 'And make them' (Deut. 29:9).

E. "Do not read 'them' but 'yourselves.' "

CXXIV. A. Said R. Abbahu, "Whoever makes his neighbor carry out a religious duty is credited by Scripture as if he himself had done it, as it is said, 'The Lord said to Moses, Take . . . your rod, with which you hit the river' (Ex. 17:5).

B. "But did Moses hit the river? It was Aaron who hit the river.

C. "Rather, this shows, whoever makes his neighbor carry out a religious duty is credited by Scripture as if he himself had done it."

CXXV. A. *An Epicurean [M. 11:1D]:*

B. Both Rab and R. Hanina say, "This refers to one who humiliates disciples of sages."

C. Both R. Yohanan and R. Joshua b. Levi say, "It is one who humiliates his fellow before a disciple of a sage."

D. Now from the viewpoint of him who says it is one who humiliates his fellow before a sage, it would also encompass a disciple of a sage himself, who *exposes aspects of the Torah not in accord with the law [M. Abot 3:11]* [acts impudently against the Torah (Freedman)].

E. But in the view of him who says that an Epicurean is one who humiliates a disciple of a sage himself, then what sort of person would fall into the category of one *who exposes aspects of the Torah not in accord with the law* [M. Abot 3:11]?

F. It would be someone of the sort of Manasseh b. Hezekiah.

G. There are those who repeat on Tannaite authority the dispute at hand in conjunction with the latter, rather than the former category, as follows:

H. *One who exposes aspects of the Torah [not in accord with the law]* [M. Abot 3:11]:

I. Rab and R. Hanina say, "It is one who humiliates a disciple of sages."

J. R. Yohanan and R. Joshua b. Levi say, "It is one who humiliates his fellow before a disciple of a sage."

K. Now from the viewpoint of him who says it is one who humiliates a disciple of a sage himself, then one who reveals aspects of the Torah, one who humiliates his fellow before a disciple of a sage, would be an Epicurean.

L. But from the viewpoint of him who says that it is one who humiliates his fellow before a disciple of a sage, with one who reveals aspects of the Torah [in an improper way] as an Epicurean, then who would fall into that latter category?

M. Said R. Joseph, "It would, for example, be those who say, 'What good are the rabbis for us? It is for their own benefit that they study Scripture. It is for their own benefit that they repeat Mishnah-teachings.' "

N. Said Abayye to him, "That too falls into the category of one who reveals aspects of the Torah in an improper way, for it is written, 'Thus says the Lord, But for my covenant [studied] day and night, I had not appointed the ordinances of heaven and earth' (Jer. 33:25). [Freedman, p. 676, n. 3: The world endures only because the Torah—my covenant'—is studied. To deny the utility of scholars therefore is to express disbelief of what is asserted in the Torah.]"

O. Said R. Nahman bar Isaac, "The proof derives as well from the following, as it is said, 'Then I will spare all the place for their sakes' (Gen. 18:26)."

P. Rather, it is one who for example was sitting before his master, and the topic of discussion moved to another subject, and he said, "This is what we said on the subject," rather than, "Master, you have said [on that topic]."

Q. Raba said, "It would, for example, be like the members of the house of Benjamin, the physician, who say, 'What good are rabbis to us? They have never [100A] permitted us to eat a raven or forbidden us to eat a dove [but are limited to what the Torah itself states]."

R. When people of the house of Benjamin brought Raba a problem involving the validity of a beast that had been slaughtered and that may not have been able to survive, if he found a reason to permit the matter, he would say to them, "See, I do permit the raven to you."

S. When he found a reason to prohibit it, he would say to them, "See, I do forbid the dove to you."

T. R. Pappa said, "It would be such as one who said, 'O, these rabbis!' "

U. R. Pappa forgot himself and said, 'O these rabbis!" He sat and fasted.

CXXVI. A. Levi bar Samuel and R. Huna bar Hiyya were fixing the mantles of the Torah scrolls of the house of R. Judah. When they got to the scroll of Esther, they said, "Lo, this scroll of Esther does not have to have a mantle at all."

B. He said to them, "This sort of talk also appears to be Epicureanism."

CXXVII.

A. R. Nahman said, "It is one who refers to his master by his name."

B. For R. Yohanan said, "On what account was Gehazi punished? Because he called his master by name,

C. "as it is said, 'My lord, O king, this is the woman, and this is her son whom Elisha restored to life' (2 Kgs. 8:5)."

CXXVIII.

A. R. Jeremiah was in session before R. Zira and said, "The Holy One, blessed be he, by which there will be many kinds of delicious produce, as it is said, 'And by the river upon that bank thereof on this side and on that side, shall grow all trees for meat, whose leaf shall not fade, neither shall the fruit thereof be consumed; it shall bring forth new fruit, according to his months, because their waters they issued out of the sanctuary, and the fruit therefore shall be for meat, and the leaf thereof for medicine' (Ez. 47:12)."

B. "Said to him a certain old man, 'Well said, and so did R. Yohanan say.' "

C. Said R. Jeremiah to R. Zira, "Behavior of this sort [condescension to the master] likewise appears to be Epicureanism."

D. He said to him, "But this represented a mere support for your position.

E. "But if you have heard any tradition, this is the tradition that you heard:

F. "R. Yohanan was in session and interpreting Scripture as follows: 'The Holy One, blessed be he, is destined to bring forth precious stones and jewels which are thirty cubits long and thirty cubits high, and engrave on them an engraving ten by twenty cubits, and he will set them up as the gates of Jerusalem, for it is written, "And I will make your windows of agates and your gates of carbuncles" (Is. 54:12).'

G. " 'A disciple ridiculed him, saying, "Now if we do not find jewels the size of a dove's egg, are we going to find any that big?"

H. " 'After some time he took a sea voyage, and he saw ministering angels cutting previous stones and jewels. He said to them, "As to these, what are they for?"

I. " 'They said to him, "The Holy One, blessed be he, is destined to set them up as the gates of Jerusalem."

J. " 'When he came back, he found R. Yohanan in session and expounding Scripture. He said to him, "Rabbi, indeed give your exposition, for it is appropriate that you should expound Scripture. Exactly as you said, so I myself saw."

K. " 'He said to him, "Empty head! Had you not seen, would you not have believed me! You are one who ridicules teachings of sages." He set his eye on him and turned him into a hill of bones.' "

L. An objection was raised [to the teaching of Yohanan]:

M. "And I will make you go upright" (Lev. 26:13).

N. R. Meir says, "It is the height of two hundred cubits, twice the height of Adam."

O. R. Judah says, "A hundred cubits, the length of the Temple and its walls, as it is written, 'That our sons may be as plants grown up in their youth, that our daughters may be as corner stones, fashioned after the similitude of the Temple' (Ps. 144:12)."

P. What R. Yohanan meant was [Freedman]: the ventilation-windows. [These would be ten by twenty, but the gates themselves would be much taller (Freedman, p. 678, n. 7)].

Q. What is the meaning of the phrase, "And the leaf thereof is for medicine" (Ez. 47:12)?

R. R. Isaac bar. Abodimi and R. Hisda: One said, "It is to open up the upper mouth [and help the dumb to speak]."

S. One said, "It is to open the lower mouth [and heal the barrenness of a barren woman]."

T. It has been taught on Tannaite authority:

U. Hezekiah said, "It is to open the mouth of the dumb."

V. Bar Qappara said, "It is to open the mouth of the barren women."

W. R. Yohanan said, "It serves as medicine, literally."

X. What is the meaning of the statement, "Medicine"?

Y. R. Samual bar Nahmani said, "It is to improve the appearance of masters of mouths [disciples]."

CXXIX. A. R. Judah b. R. Simon interpreted, "Whoever blackens his face [in fasting] on account of teachings of Torah in this world will find that the Holy One, blessed be he, polishes his luster in the world to come.

B. "For it is said, 'His countenance shall be as the Lebanon, excellent as the cedars' (Song 5:15)."

C. R. Tanhum bar Hanilai said, "Whoever starves himself for words of Torah in this world will the Holy One, blessed be he, feed to satisfaction in the world to come,

D. "as it is said, 'They shall be abundantly satisfied with the fatness of your house, and you shall make them drink of the river of your pleasures' (Ps. 36:9)."

E. When R. Dimi came, he said, "The Holy One, blessed be he, is destined to give to every righteous person his full pack-load, as it is said, 'Blessed be the Lord, day by day, who loads us with benefits, even the God of our salvation, selah' (Ps. 68:20)."

F. Said Abayye to him, "And is it possible to say so? Is it not said, 'Who has measured the waters in the hollow of his hand and measured out heaven with the span' (Is. 40:12)?"

G. He said to him, "What is the reason that you are not at home in matters of lore? They say in the West in the name of Raba bar Mari, 'The Holy One, blessed be he, is destined to give each righteous person three hundred and ten worlds, as it is said, "That I may cause those who love me to inherit substance and I will fill their treasures," (Prov. 8:21), and the numerical value of the word for substance is three hundred ten.' "

CXXX. A. It has been taught on Tannaite authority:

B. R. Meir says, *"By the same measure by which a man metes out, do they mete out to him [M. Sot. 1:7A],*

C. "For it is written, 'By measure in sending her away thou dost contend with her.' " (Is. 27:8).

D. Said R. Judah, "And can one say so? If a person gives a handful [to charity] to a poor man in this world, will the Holy One, blessed be he, give him a handful [of his, so much larger hand], in the world to come?

E. "And has it not been written, 'And meted out heaven with a span' (Is. 40:12)?"

F. [Meir replied] "But do you not say so? Which measure is greater? That of goodness or that of punishment? [100B]

G. "With regard to the measure of goodness it is written, 'And he commanded the clouds from above, and opened the doors of heaven and rained down manna upon them to eat' (Ps. 78:23–24).

H. "With regard to the measure of punishment it is written, 'And the windows of heaven were opened' (Gen. 7:11) [Freedman, p. 680, n. 5: 'Doors' implies a greater opening than windows; God metes out reward more fully than punishment.]

I. "In respect to the measure even of punishment it is written, 'And they shall go forth and look upon the carcasses of the men who have transgresed against me, for their worm shall not die, neither shall their fire be quenched, and they shall be a horror to all flesh' (Is. 66:24).

J. "But is it not so that if a person put his finger into a fire in this world, he will be burned right away?

K. "But just as the Holy One, blessed be he, gives the wicked the power to receive their punishment, so the Holy One, blessed be he, gives the righteous the power to receive the goodness that is coming to them."

CXXXI.

A. *R. Aqiba says, "Also: He who reads in heretical books . . ." [M. 11:1E]:*

B. It was taught on Tannaite authority: That is the books of the minim.

CXXXII.

A. R. Joseph said, "It is also forbidden to read in the book of Ben Sira."

B. Said to him Abayye, "What is the reason for that view?

C. "Should I say that it is because it is written in it, 'Do not skin the fish, even from the ear, so that you will not go and bruise it, but roast it in the fire and eat two loaves with it'?

D. "In point of fact in the explicit view of Scripture it is also said, 'You shall not destroy the trees thereof' (Deut. 20:19). [Freedman, p. 681, nn. 1–2: A fish is fit for consumption even if baked or roasted with its skin and therefore it is wasteful to remove it. Likewise, one must not wantonly destroy what is fit for use].

E. "And if it is a matter of exegesis [and not the literal sense], then the saying teaches us proper conduct, namely, that one should not have sexual relations in an unnatural way.

F. "Rather, might it be because it is written in it, 'A daughter is a worthless treasure for her father. For concern for her, he cannot sleep by night. In her childhood, it is lest she be seduced; in her girlhood, it is lest she play the whore; in her maturity, it is lest she not wed; once she is wed it is lest she not have sons. In her old age it is lest she practice witchcraft'?

G. "But rabbis have also made the same statement: 'The world cannot exist without males and without females. Happy is he whose children are males, and woe is him whose children are females.'

H. "Rather, might it be because it is written in [Ben Sira]: 'Do not admit despair into your heart, for despair has killed many men'?

I. "Lo, Solomon made the same statement; 'Anxiety in the heart of man makes him stoop' (Prov. 12:25)."

J. R. Ammi and R. Assi: One said, "Let him banish it from his mind.'

K. The other said, "Let him tell it to others."

L. [Reverting to Abayye's inquiry:] "Rather might it be because it is written in [Ben Sira]: 'Keep large numbers of people away from your house, and do not let just anyone into your house'?

M. "Lo, Rabbi also made that statement.

N. "For it has been taught on Tannaite authority:

O. "Rabbi says, 'A person should never admit a great many friends into his house, as it is said, 'A man who has many friends brings evil upon himself' (Prov. 18:24).'

P. "Rather, it is because it is written in it: 'A man with a thin beard is wise, a man with a thick beard is a fool; one who blows forth his beard is not thirsty. One who says, "What is there to eat with my bread"—take the bread away from him. [He too is not hungry.] He who parts his beard will overpower the world [being very clever.]' [This foolish statement, in point of fact, forms the basis for Joseph's judgment.]"

Q. Said R. Joseph, "But the excellent statement in the book [of Ben Sira] we do expound.

R. "[For example:] 'A good woman is a good gift, who will be put into the bosom of a God-fearing man. A bad woman is a plague for her husband. What is his remedy? Let him drive her from his house and be healed from what is plaguing him.

S. " 'A lovely wife—happy is her husband. The number of his days is doubled.

T. " 'Keep your eyes from a woman of charm, lest you be taken in her trap. Do not turn to her husband to drink wine with him, or strong drink, for through the looks of a beautiful woman many have been slain, and numerous are those who have been slain by her.

U. " 'Many are the blows with which a peddler is smitten [for dealing with women]. Those who make it a habit of committing fornication are like a spark that lights the ember. "As a cage is full of birds, so are their houses full of deceit" ' (Jer. 5:27).

V. " 'Keep large numbers of people away from your house, and do not let just anybody into your house.

W. " 'Let many people ask how you are, but reveal your secret to one out of a thousand. From her who lies in your house keep protected the opening of your mouth.

X. " 'Do not worry about tomorrow's sorrow, "For you do not know what a day may bring forth" (Prov.

27:1). Perhaps tomorrow you will no longer exist and it will turn out that you will worry about a world that is not yours.' "

Y. " 'All the days of the poor are evil" (Prov. 15:15): Ben Sira said, "So too his nights. His roof is the lowest in town, his vineyard on the topmost mountain. Rain flows from other roofs onto his and from his vineyard onto other vineyards."

CXXXIII.   A. Said R. Zira said Rab, "What is the meaning of the verse of Scripture, 'All the days of the afflicted are evil' (Prov. 15:15)?

B. "This refers to masters of Talmud.

C. " 'But he that is of a good heart has a continuous banquet' (Prov. 15:15)? This refers to masters of the Mishnah."

D. Raba said, "Matters are just the opposite."

E. And that is in line with what R. Mesharshia said in the name of Raba, "What is the meaning of the verse of Scripture: 'Whoever removes stones shall be hurt with them' (Qoh. 10:9)?

F. "This refers to masters of the Mishnah.

G. " 'But he who cleaves wood shall be warmed by it' (Qoh. 10:9)?

H. "This refers to masters of Talmud."

I. R. Hanina says, " 'All of the days of the afflicted are evil' (Prov. 15:15) refers to a man who has a bad wife.

J. " 'But he that is of a good heart has a continuous banquet' (Prov. 15:15) refers to a man who has a good wife.

K. R. Yannai says, " 'All the days of the afflicted are evil' (Prov. 15:15) refers to one who is fastidious.

L. " 'But he that is of a good heart has a continuous banquet' (Prov. 15:15) refers to one who is easy to please."

M. R. Yohanan said, " 'All the days of the afflicted are evil' (Prov. 15:15) refers to a merciful person.

N. " 'But he that is of a good heart has a continuous banquet' (Prov. 15:15) refers to someone who is cruel by nature [so nothing bothers him]."

O. R. Joshua b. Levi said, " 'All the days of the afflicted are evil' (Prov. 15:15) refers to [101A] someone who is worrisome.

P. " 'But he that is of a good heart has a continuous banquet' (Prov. 15:15) refers to one who is serene."

Q. R. Joshua b. Levi said, " 'All the days of the afflicted are evil' (Prov. 15:1)—but are there [not] Sabbaths and festival days [on which the afflicted gets some pleasure]?"

R. The matter accords with what Samuel said. For Samuel said, "The change in diet [for festival meals] is the beginning of stomach ache."

CXXXIV. A. Our rabbis have taught on Tannaite authority:

B. **He who recites a verse of the Song of Songs and turns it into a kind of love song, and he who recites a verse in a banquet hall not at the proper time [but in a time of carousal] bring evil into the world [cf. T. San. 12:10A].**

C. For the Torah puts on sack cloth and stands before the Holy One, blessed be he, and says before him, "Lord of the world, your children have treated me like a harp which scoffers play."

D. He then says to her, "My daughter, when they eat and drink, what should keep them busy?"

E. She will say to him, "Lord of the world, if they are masters of Scripture, let them keep busy with the Torah, Prophets, and Writings; if they are masters of the Mishnah, let them keep busy with the Mishnah, law and lore; and if they are masters of the Talmud, let them keep busy on Passover with the laws of the Passover, with the laws of Pentecost on Pentecost, and with the laws of the Festival [of Tabernacles] on the Festival."

F. R. Simeon b. Eleazar gave testimony in the name of R. Simeon b. Hanania, "Whoever recites a verse of Scripture at the proper time brings good to the world,

G. "as it is said, 'And a word spoken in season, how good is it' (Prov. 15:23)."

CXXXV. A. And he who whispers over a wound [M. 1:1F]:

B. Said R. Yohanan, "That is the rule if one spits over the wound, for people may not make mention of the Name of heaven over spit."

CXXXVI. A. It has been stated on Amoraic authority:

B. Rab said, "Even 'When the plague of leprosy' (Lev. 13:1) [may not be recited]."

CXXXVII. A. Our rabbis have taught on Tannaite authority:

B. People may annoint and massage the intestines on the Sabbath, and whisper to snakes and scorpions on the Sabbath, and place utensils on the eyes on the Sabbath.

C. Said Rabban Simeon b. Gamaliel, "Under what circumstances? In the case of a utensil that may be carried, [on the Sabbath], but in the case of a utensil that may not be carried, it is forbidden."

D. And a question may not be addressed on a matter having to do with demons on the Sabbath.

E. R. Yose says, "Even on a weekday it is forbidden to do so."

F. Said R. Huna, "The decided law accords with the view of R. Yose.

G. "And R. Yose made that statement only on account of the danger involved in doing so."

H. This is illustrated by the case of R. Isaac bar Joseph, who got stuck in a cedar tree, and a miracle was done for him, so that the cedar tree split open and spit him out. [Freedman, p. 685, n. 5: He consulted a demon, which turned itself into a tree and swallowed him; it was ony through a miracle that he escaped.]

CXXXVIII. A. Our rabbis have taught on Tannaite authority:

B. People may annoint and massage the intestines on the Sabbath, so long as one not do so as he does on a weekday.

C. How then should one do it?

D. R. Hama, son of R. Hanini, said, "One puts on some oil and then massages."

E. R. Yohanan said, "One puts on oil and massages simultancously."

CXXXIX. A. Our rabbis have taught on Tannaite authority:

B. As to the spirits of oil or eggs it is permitted to address questions to them, except that they prove unreliable.

C. People whisper over oil that is in a utensil but not over oil that is held in the hand.

D. Therefore people apply oil by hand and not out of a utensil.

CXL.

A. R. Isaac bar Samuel bar Marta happened to stay at a certain inn. They brought him oil in a utensil, and he anointed himself.

B. He broke out in blisters all over his face.

C. He went to a market place, and a certain woman saw him and said to him, "The blast of Hamath do I see here."

D. She did something for him, and he was healed.

CXLI.

A. Said R. Abba to Rabba bar Mari, "It is written, 'I will put none of these diseases upon you, which I have brought upon the Egyptians, for I am the Lord who heals you' (Ex. 15:26).

B. "But if he does not place those diseases, what need is there for healing anyhow?"

C. He said to him, "This is what R. Yohanan said, 'This verse of Scripture provides its own interpretation, since it is said, "And he said, If you will diligently obey the voice of the Lord your God" (Ex. 15:16). "If you obey, I shall not place those diseases upon you, and if you will not obey, I will do so."

D. " 'Yet even so: "I am the Lord who heals you" (Ex. 15:26).' "

CXLII.

A. Said Rabbah bar bar Hanah, "When R. Eliezer fell ill, his disciples came in to call on him.

B. "He said to them, 'There is great anger in the world [to account for my sickness].'

C. "They began to cry, but R. Aqiba began to laugh. They said to him 'Why are you laughing?'

D. "He said to them, 'Why are you crying?'

E. "They said to him, 'Is it possible that, when a scroll of the Torah [such as Eliezer] is afflicted with disease, we should not cry?'

F. "He said to them, 'For that reason I am laughing. So long as I observed that, as to my master, his wine did not turn to vinegar, his flax was not smitten, his oil did not putrefy, and his honey did not become rancid,

G. " 'I thought to myself, "Perhaps, God forbid, my master has received his reward in this world." But now that I see my master in distress, I rejoice [knowing that he will receive his full reward in the world to come.]'

H. "[Eliezer] said to him, 'Aqiba, have I left out anything at all from the whole of the Torah?'

I. "He said to him, '[Indeed so, for] you have taught us, our master, "For there is not a just man upon earth, who does good and does not sin" (Qoh. 7:20).' "

CXLIII.

A. Our rabbis have taught on Tannaite authority:

B. When R. Eliezer fell ill, four elders came to call on him: R. Tarfon, R. Joshua, R. Eleazar b. Azariah, and R. Aqiba.

C. R. Tarfon responded first and said, "You are better for Israel than a drop of rain, for a drop of rain is good for this world, but my master is good for this world and the world to come."

D. R. Joshua responded and said, "You are better for Israel than the orb of the sun, for the orb of the sun serves for this world, but my master serves for this world and the world to come."

E. R. Eleazar b. Azariah responded and said, "You are better for Israel than a father and a mother, for a father and a mother are for this world, but my master is for this world and the world to come."

F. R. Aqiba responded and said, "Suffering is precious."

G. He said to them, "Prop me up so that I may hear the statement of Aqiba, my disciple, who has said, 'Suffering is precious.' "

H. He said to him, "Aqiba, how do you know?"

I. He said to him, "I interpret a verse of Scripture: 'Manasseh was twelve years old when he began to reign, and he reigned fifty five years in Jerusalem . . . and he did what was evil in the sight of the Lord' (2 Kgs. 21:1–2).

J. "And it is written [101B], 'These are the proverbs of Solomon, which the men of Hezekiah, king of Judah, copied out' (Prov. 25:1).

K. "Now is it possible that Hezekiah, king of Judah, taught the Torah to the entire world, but to his son, Manasseh, he did not teach the Torah? [Obviously not!]

L. "But out of all the trouble that [his father] took with him, and with all the labor that he poured into him, nothing brought him back to the good way except for suffering.

M. "For it is said, 'And the Lord spoke to Manasseh and to his people, but they would not hearken to him. Therefore the Lord brought upon them the captains of the host of the king of Assyria, who took Manasseh among the thorns and bound him with chains and carried him to Babylonia' (2 Chr. 33:10–11).

N. "And it is written, 'And when he was in affliction, he sought the Lord his God and humbled himself greatly before the God of his fathers. And he prayed to him and he was entreated of him and heard his supplication and brought him again to Jerusalem to his kingdom, and Manasseh knew that the Lord is God' (2 Chr. 33:12–13).

O. "So you learn that suffering is precious."

CXLIV. A. Our rabbis have taught on Tannaite authority:

B. Three came with a self-serving plea, and these are they: Cain, Esau, and Manasseh.

C. Cain, as it is written, "Is my sin too great to be forgiven?" (Gen. 4:13).

D. He said before him, "Lord of the world, Is my sin any greater than that of the six hundred thousand who are destined to sin before you? And yet you will forgive them!"

E. Esau, as it is written, "Have you but one blessing, my father?" (Gen. 27:38).

F. Manasseh: To begin with he called upon many gods and in the end he called upon the God of his fathers.

CXLV.

A. Abba Saul says, "Also: he who pronounces the divine Name as it is spelled out" [M. 11:1G].

B. On Tannaite authority [it was stated]:

C. That is the rule in the provinces, and [when it is] in blasphemous language.

CXLVI.

A. *Three kings and four ordinary folk [have no portion in the world to come. Three kings: Jeroboam, Ahab, and Manasseh] [M. 11:2A–B]:*

B. Our rabbis have taught on Tannaite authority:

C. "Jeroboam": for he treated the people as his sexual object.

D. Another matter: "Jeroboam": for he made strife in the people.

E. Another matter: "Jeroboam": for he brought strife between the people of Israel and their father in heaven.

F. Son of Nebat, a son who saw [a vision] but did not see [its meaning].

CXLVII.

A. On Tannaite [authority it was stated]:

B. Nebat is the same as Micah and Sheba son of Bichri.

C. Nebat: Because he saw a vision but did not see [its meaning].

D. Micah: Because he was [Freedman]: crushed in the building. [Freedman, pp. 688–689, n. 11: According to legend, when the Israelites in Egypt did not complete their tale of bricks, their children were built into the walls instead. On Moses' complaining thereof to God, He answered him that He was thus weeding out the destined wicked. As proof, he was empowered to save Micah, who had already been built into it, but only to become an idolator on his reaching manhood. Rashi also gives an alternative rendering: he became impoverished through building—presumably his idolatrous shrine.]

E. But what was his real name: It was Sheba, son of Bichri.

CXLVIII.

A. Our rabbis have taught on Tannaite authority:

B. There were three who saw [a vision] but did not see [its meaning], and these are they: Nabat, Ahitophel, and Pharaoh's astrologers.

C. Nabat saw fire coming forth from his penis. He thought that [it meant that] he would rule, but that was not the case. It was that Jeroboam would come forth from him [who would rule].

D. Ahitophel saw *saraat* spread over him and over his penis. He thought it meant that he would be king, and that was not the case. It was Sheba, his daughter, from whom Solomon would come forth.

E. The astrologers of Pharaoh: In line with what R. Hama, son of R. Hanina, said, "What is the meaning of the verse of Scripture, 'These are the waters of rebellion, because they strove' (Num. 20:13)?

F. "These are the waters which the astrologers of Pharaoh foresaw, and about which erred.

G. "They saw that the savior of Israel would be smitten because of water. So [Pharaoh] decreed, 'Every son that is born you shall cast into the river' (Ex. 1:22).

H. "But they did not know that it was on account of the water of rebellion that he would be smitten."

CXLIX. A. And how do we know that [Jeroboam] will not come into the world to come?

B. As it is written, "And this thing became sin to the house of Jeroboam, even to cut it off and to destroy it from off the face of the earth" (1 Kgs. 13:34).

C. "To cut it off" in this world.

D. "And to destroy it" in the world to come.

CL. A. Said R. Yohanan, "On what account did Jeroboam have the merit to rule?

B. "Because he reproved Solomon.

C. "And on what account was he punished?

D. "Because he reproved him publicly.

E. "So it is said, 'And this was the cause that the lifted up his hand against the king: Solomon built Millo and repaired the breaches of the city of David his father' (1 Kgs. 11:27).

F. "He said to him, 'David your father made breaches in the wall so that the Israelites might come up for the pilgrim-festivals, but you have filled them in so as to collect a tax for the daughter of Pharaoh.' "

G. And what is the meaning of the phrase, "That he lifted up his hand against the king"(1 Kgs. 11:27)?

H. Said R. Nahman, "Because he took off his phylacteries in his presence."

CLI.

A. Said R. Nahman, "The arrogance that characterized Jeroboam is what drove him out of the world.

B. "For it is said, 'Now Jeroboam said in his heart, Now shall the kingdom return to the house of David. If this people go up to sacrifice in the house of the Lord at Jerusalem, then shall the heart of this people turn to their Lord, even to Rehoboam, king of Judah, and they shall kill me and go again to Rehoboam, king of Judah' (1 Kgs. 12:27–28).

C. "He said, 'We have a tradition that no one may sit down in the Temple courtyard except kings of the house of Judah alone. When the people see that Rehoboam is sitting down and I am standing, they will think that he is king, and I am merely a servant.

D. " 'But if I sit down, I shall be in the position of rebelling against the monarchy, and they will kill me and follow him.' "

E. "Forthwith: 'Wherefore the king took counsel and made two calves of gold and said to them, It is too much for you to go up to Jerusalem. Behold your gods O Israel, who brought you up out of the land of Egypt, and he put one in Beth El and the other the put in Dan' (1 Kgs. 12:28)."

F. What is the meaning of the phrase, "The king took counsel"?

G. Said R. Judah, "That he sat a wicked person next to a righteous person. He said to them, 'Will you sign everything that I do?'

H. "They said to him, 'Yes.'

I. "He said to them, 'I want to be king.'

J. "They said to him, 'Yes.'

K. "He said to them, 'Will you do whatever I say?'

L. "They said to him, 'Yes.' "

M. " 'Even to worship an idol?'

N. "The righteous one said to him, 'God forbid.'

O. "The wicked one said to the righteous one, 'Do you think that a person such as Jeroboam would really worship an idol? Rather, what he wants to do is to test us to see whether or not we shall accept his word [102A].' "

P. "Even Ahijah the Shilonite made a mistake and signed, for Jehu was a very righteous man, as it is said, 'And the Lord said to Jehu, Because you have done well in executing what is right in my eyes and have done to the house of Ahab according to all that was in my heart, your children of the fourth generation shall sit upon the throne of Israel' (2 Kgs. 10:30).

Q. "But it is written, 'But Jehu took no heed to walk in the law of the Lord God of Israel with all his heart, for he did not depart from the sins of Jeroboam, which he had made Israel to sin' (2 Kgs. 10:31)."

R. What caused it?

S. Said Abayye, "A covenant made orally, as it is said, 'And Jehu gathered all the people together and said to them, Ahab served Baal a little but Jehu shall serve him much' (2 Kgs. 10:18). [Freedman, p. 691, n. 5: These words, though spoken guilefully, had to be fulfilled.]"

T. Raba said, "He saw the signature of Ahijah the Shilonite, and he erred on that account."

CLII.   A. It is written, "And the revolters are profound to make slaughter, though I have been a rebuke of all of them" (Hos. 5:2):

B. Said R. Yohanan, "Said the Holy One, blessed be he, 'They have gone deeper than I did. I said, "Whoever does not go up to Jerusalem for the Festival transgresses an affirmative requirement," but they have said, "Whoever does go up to Jerusalem for the festival will be stabbed with a sword." ' "

CLIII.

A. "And it came to pass at that time, when Jeroboam went out of Jerusalem, that the prophet Ahijah the Shilonite found him in the way, and he had clad himself with a new garment" (1 Kgs. 11:20):

B. It was taught on Tannaite authority in the name of R. Yose, "It was a time designated for punishment. [Freedman, p. 691, n. 9: On that occasion Ahijah prophesied the division of the kingdom as a punishment for Solomon's backsliding.]"

C. "In the time of their visitation they shall perish" (Jer. 51:18):

D. It was taught on Tannaite authority in the name of R. Yose, "A time designated for punishment."

E. "In an acceptable time I have heard you" (Is. 49:8):

F. It was taught on Tannaite authority in the name of R. Yose, "A time designated for good."

G. "Nevertheless in the day when I visit, I will visit their sin upon them: (Ex. 32:34):

H. It was taught on Tannaite authority in the name of R. Yose, "A time designated for punishment."

I. "And it came to pass at that time that Judah went down from his brethren" (Gen. 38:1):

J. It was taught on Tannaite authority in the name of R. Yose, "A time designated for punishment."

K. "And Rehoboam went to Shechem, for all Israel were come to Shechem to make him king" (1 Kgs. 12:1):

L. It was taught on Tannaite authority in the name of R. Yose, "A time designated for punishment. In Shechem men raped Dinah, in Shechem his brothers sold Joseph, in Shechem the kingdom of David was divided."

CLIV.

A. "Now it came to pass at that time that Jeroboam went out of Jerusalem" (1 Kgs. 11:29):

B. Said R. Hanina bar Pappa, "He went out of the realm of Jerusalem."

CLV.

A. "And the prophet Ahijah the Shilonite found him in the way, and he clad himself with a new garment, and the two were alone in the field" (1 Kgs. 11:29):

B. What is this "new garment"?

C. Said R. Nahman, "It was as with a new garment: just as a new garment has no sort of blemish, so the Torah-learning of Jeroboam had no sort of flaw."

D. Another matter. "A new garment":

E. It was that they said things so new that no ear had ever heard them.

F. "And the two were alone in the field" (1 Kgs. 11:29): What is the meaning of this statement?

G. Said R. Judah said Rab, "It is that all the disciples of sages were as grass of the field before them [and of no account]."

H. And there is he who says, "It is that the reasons for the rulings of the Torah were revealed to them in the open as in a field."

CLVI.   A. "Therefore shall you give parting gifts to Moresheth-gath, the houses of Achzib shall be a lie to the kings of Israel" (Mic. 1:14):

B. Said R. Hanina bar Pappa, "An echo came forth and said to them, 'He who killed the Philistine and gave you possession of Gath—to his sons you will give parting gifts.' "

C. "Therefore the houses of Achzib shall be a lie to the kings of Israel" (Mich. 1:14) [Freedman, p. 693, n. 2: "Since you deal treacherously with the house of David, preferring the rule of the kings of Israel, therefore you shall be delivered into the hands of the heathen, whose religion is false."]

CLVII.   A. Said R. Hinnena bar Pappa, "Whoever derives benefit from this world without reciting a blessing is as if he steals from the Holy One, blessed be he, and the community of Israel.

B. "For it is said, 'Who robs from his father or his mother and says, It is no transgression, is the companion of a destroyer' (Prov. 28:24).

C. " 'His father' is only the Holy One, blessed be he, as it is said, 'Is not [God] your father, who has bought you' (Deut. 32:6), and 'his mother' can mean only the congregation of Israel, as it is said, 'My son, hear the instruction of your father and do not forsake the Torah of your mother' (Prov. 1:8)."

D. "What is the sense of "He is the companion of a destroyer" (Prov. 28:24)?

E. "He is companion of Jeroboam, son of Nebat, who destroyed Israel for their father in heaven."

CLVIII. A. "And Jeroboam drove Israel from following the Lord and made them sin a great sin" (2 Kgs. 17:21):

B. Said R. Hanin, "It was like two sticks that rebound from one another."

CLIX. A. "[These are the words which Moses spoke to all Israel in the wilderness] and Di Zahab" (Deut. 1:1):

B. Said a member of the house of R. Yannai, "Moses said before the Holy One, blessed be he, 'Lord of the world, on account of the silver and gold which you showered on Israel until they said, "Enough," they were caused to make for themselves gods of gold.'

C. "It is comparable to the case of a lion, who does not tear and roar on account of what is in a basket containing straw, but because of what is in a basket of meat."

D. Said R. Oshaia, "Up to the time of Jeroboam, the Israelites would suck from a single calf [sinning on account of only one], but from that time on, it was from two or three calves."

E. Said R. Isaac, "You do not have any sort of punishment that comes upon the world in which is contained at least one twenty-fourth of part of the overweight of a litra of the first calf.

F. "For it is written, 'Nevertheless in the day when I visit, I will visit their sin upon them' (Ex. 32:34)."

G. Said R. Hanina, "After twenty-four generations this verse of Scripture will be exacted: 'He cried also in my ears with a loud voice, saying, Cause the visitations of the city to draw near, even every man with his destroying weapon in his hand' (Ez. 9:1)." [Freedman, p. 694, n. 4: The use of "visitations" suggests that this was the fulfillment of the doom threatened in Ex. 32:34. There were twenty-four generations from that of the wilderness, when the calf was made, to that of Zedekiah, in whose reign the state was overthrown and Judah was deported to Babylonia.]

CLX. A. "After this thing Jeroboam did not turn from his evil way" (1 Kgs. 13:33):

B. What is the sense of 'after'?

C. Said R. Abba, "After the Holy One, blessed be he, seized Jeroboam by his garment and said to him, 'Repent, and you and the son of Jesse and I shall walk about in the Garden of Eden.'

D. "He said to him, 'He who will be at the head?'

E. " 'The son of Jesse will be at the head.'

F. " 'If so, I don't want it.' "

CLXI. A. R. Abbahu would regularly give a public interpretation of the three kings [of M. 11:2A]. He fell ill and undertook not to give such an address [since he thought the illness was punishment for speaking about the king's sins].

B. When [102B] he got better, he reversed himself and gave an address. They said to him, "You undertook not to speak about them."

C. He said to them, "Did they repent, that I should repent!"

CLXII. A. At the house of R. Ashi, [the group] arose [from studying] at the teaching of the three kings. He said, "Tomorrow we shall open discourse with the topic of 'our colleagues' [M. 11:2, that is, the three kings, all of whom were held to be disciples of sages."]

B. Manasseh came and appeared in a dream: "Do you call us 'your colleague' and 'your father's colleague'? [If you are as good as we are, then tell me] from what part of the bread do you take the piece for reciting the blessing, 'Who brings forth bread from the earth'?"

C. He said to him, "I don't know."

D. He said to him, "If you have not learned from what part of the bread do you take a piece for reciting the blessing, 'Who brings forth bread from the earth,' how can you call us 'your colleague'?"

E. He said to him, "Teach me. Tomorrow I shall expound the matter in your name in the class session."

F. He said to him, "One takes the part that is baked into a crust [and not the dough on the inside]."

G. He said to him, "If you are so wise, then what is the reason that you worshiped an idol?"

H. He said to him, "If you had been there, you would have picked up the hem of your garment and run after me."

I. The next day he said to the rabbis, "Let us begin with our teacher."

CLXIII. A. The name of 'Ahab' signifies that he was a brother to heaven (ah) but father of idolatry (ab).

B. "He was brother to heaven, as it is written, 'A brother is born for trouble' (Prov. 17:17).

C. "He was father to idolatry, as it is written, 'As a father loves his children' (Ps. 103:13)."

CLXIV. A. "And it came to pass, that it was a light thing for him to walk in the sins of Jeroboam, the son of Nebat" (1 Kgs. 16:31):

B. Said R. Yohanan, "The lightest [sins] committed by Ahab were as the most severe ones that were committed by Jeroboam.

C. "And on what account did Scripture blame Jeroboam? It was because he was the beginning of the corruption."

CLXV. A. "Yes, their altars are as heaps in the furrows of the fields" (Hos. 12:12):

B. Said R. Yohanan, "You have no furrow in the whole of the land of Israel in which Ahab did not set up an idol and bow down to it."

CLXVI. A. And how do we know that [Ahab] will not enter the world to come?

B. As it is written, "And I will cut off from Ahab him who pisses against the wall, him that is shut up and forsaken in Israel" (1 Kgs. 21:21).

C. "Shut up" in this world.

D. "Forsaken" in the world to come.

CLXVII. A. Said R. Yohanan, "On what account did Omri merit the monarchy? Because he added a single town to the land of Israel, as it is written, 'And he bought the hill Samaria of Shemer for two talents of silver and built on the hill and called the name of the city which he built after the name of Shemer, owner of the hill, Samaria' (1 Kgs. 16:24)."

B. Said R. Yohanan, "On what account did Ahab merit ruling for twenty-two years? Because he honored the Torah, which was given with twenty-two letters [of the Hebrew alphabet], as it is said, 'And he sent messages to Ahab, king of Israel, to the city, and said to him, Thus says Hen-hadad, Your silver and your gold is mine, your wives also and your children, even the goodliest are mine . . . Yet will I send my servants to you tomorrow at this time and they shall search your house, and the houses of your servants, and it shall be, that whatsoever is pleasant in your eyes they shall put in their hand and take it away . . . Therefore he said to the messengers of Ben-hadad, Tell my lord the king, all that you send for to your servants at the first I will do, but this thing I may not do' (1 Kgs. 20:3, 6, 9)."

C. "What is the meaning of 'whatsoever is pleasant in your eyes'? Is it not a scroll of the Torah?"

D. But could it not be an idol?

E. "Let it not enter your mind, for it is written, 'And all the leaders and all the people said to him, Do not listen to him or consent' (1 Kgs. 20:8) [the elders being sages]."

F. And perhaps they were elders [who were identified with] the shame [of the idol itself]?

G. Is it not written, "And the saying pleased Absalom well and all the elders of Israel" (2 Sam. 17:4)? On this passage, said R. Joseph, "They were elders [associated with] the shame."

H. "In that passage, it is not written, 'And all the people,' while here it is written, 'And all the people.' It is not possible that among them were no righteous men, for it is written, 'Yet have I left seven thousand in Israel, all the knees which have not bowed to Baal and every mouth which has not kissed him' (1 Kgs. 19:18)."

CLXVIII.   A. Said R. Nahman, "Ahab was right in the middle [between wickedness and righteousness], as it is said, 'And the Lord said, Who shall persuade Ahab, that he may go up and fall at Ramoth-Gildean? And one said in this manner, and one said in that manner' (1 Kgs. 22:20). [Freedman, p. 697, n. 1: This shows that it was a difficult matter to lure him to his fate, and that must have been because his righteousness equaled his guilt.]"

B. To this proposition R. Joseph objected, "We speak of one concerning whom it is written, 'But there was none like Ahab, who sold himself to work wickedness in the sight of the Lord, whom Jezebel his wife stirred up' (1 Kgs. 21:25),

C. "on which passage it was repeated on Tannaite authority, 'Every day she would weigh out gold shekels for idolatry,' and can you say that he was right in the middle?

D. "Rather, Ahab was generous with his money, and because he gave benefit to disciples of sages out of his property, half of his sins were forgiven."

CLXIX.   A. "And there came forth the spirit and stood before the Lord and said, I will persuade him. And the Lord said to him, With what? And he said, I will go forth and will be a lying spirit in the mouth of his prophets. And he said, You shall persuade him and also prevail. Go forth and do so" (1 Kgs. 22:21–23):

B. What spirit was it?

C. Said R. Yohanan, "It was the spirit of Naboth the Jezreelite."

D. What is meant by "go forth"?

E. Said Rabina, "Go forth from my precincts, as it is written, 'He who lies will not tarry in my sight' (Ps.101:7)."

F. Said R. Pappa, "This is in line with what people say, 'He who exacts vengeance destroys his house.' "

CLXX.   A. "And Ahab made a grove, and Ahab did more to provoke the Lord God of Israel to anger than all of the kings of Israel that were before him" (1 Kgs. 16:33):

   B. Said R. Yohanan, "It was that he wrote on the gates of Samaria, 'Ahab has denied the God of Israel.' Therefore he has no portion in the God of Israel."

CLXXI.   A. "And he sought Ahaziah, and they caught him for he hid in Samaria" (2 Chr. 22:9):

   B. Said R. Levi, "He was blotting out the mentions of the divine name [in the Torah] and writing in their place the names of idols."

CLXXII.   A. Manasseh—[Based on the root for the word "forget"] for he forgot the Lord.

   B. Another explanation: Manasseh—for he made Israel forget their father in heaven.

   C. And how do we know that he will not come to the world to come?

   D. As it is written, "Manasseh was twelve years old when he began to reign, and he reigned fifty-five years in Jerusalem, . . . and he made a grove as did Ahab, king of Israel" (2 Kgs. 21:2–3).

   E. Just as Ahab has no share in the world to come, so Manasseh has no share in the world to come.

CLXXIII.   A. *R. Judah says, "Manasseh has a portion in the world to come, since it is said, 'And he prayed to him and he was entreated of him . . .' (2 Chr. 33:13)" [M. 11:2C–D]:*

   B. Said R. Yohanan, "Both authorities [who dispute the fate of Manasseh] interpret the same verse of Scripture, as it is said, 'And I will cause to be removed to all the kingdoms of the earth, because of Manasseh, son of Hezekiah, king of Judah' (Jer. 15:4).

   C. "One authority takes the view that it is 'on account of Manasseh,' who repented, while they did not repent.

   D. "The other authority takes the view [103A] that it is 'because of Manasseh,' who did not repent."

CLXXIV.   A. Said R. Yohanan, "Whoever maintains that Manasseh has no share in the world to come weakens the hands of those who repent."

B. For a Tannaite authority repeated before R. Yohanan, "Manasseh repented for thirty-three years, as it is written, 'Manasseh was twelve years old when he began to reign, and he reigned fifty-five years in Jerusalem and he made a grove as did Ahab, king of Israel' (2 Kgs. 21:2–3).

C. "How long did Ahab rule? Twenty-two years. How long did Manasseh rule? Fifty-five years. Take away twenty-two years, and you are left with thirty-three."

CLXXV.   A. Said R. Yohanan in the name of R. Simeon b. Yohai, "What is the meaning of the verse of Scripture, 'And he prayed to him and an opening was made for him' (2 Chr. 33:13)?

B. "It should say,'and he was entreated of him'!

C. "It teaches that the Holy One, blessed be he, made a kind of cave for him in the firmament, so as to receive him in repentance, despite the [contrary will of] the attribute of justice."

D. And said R. Yohanan in the name of R. Simeon b. Yohai, "What is the meaning of the verse of Scripture, 'In the beginning of the reign of Jehoiakim, son of Josiah, king of Judah' (Jer. 26:1)?

E. "And it is written, 'In the beginning of the reign of Zedekiah, king of Judah' (Jer. 28:1).

F. "And is it the case that, up to that time there were no kings?

G. "Rather, the Holy One, blessed be he, planned to return the world to [its beginning condition of] chaos and formlessness on account of Jehoiakim. When, however, he took a close look at his generation, his anger subsided.

H. "[Along these same lines], the Holy One, blessed be he, planned to return the world to chaos and formlessness on account of the generation of Zedekiah. But when he took a close look at Zedekiah, his anger subsided."

I. But with regard to Zedekiah, also, it is written, "And he did that which was evil in the sight of God" (2 Kgs. 24:19)?

J. He could have stopped others but did not do so.

K. And said R. Yohanan in the name of R. Simeon b. Yohai, "What is the meaning of the verse of Scripture, 'If a wise man contends with a foolish man, whether rage or laughter, there is no satisfaction' (Prov. 29:9)?

L. "Said the Holy One, blessed be he, 'I was angry with Ahaz and I handed him over to the kings of Damascus and he sacrificed and offered incense to their gods, as it is said, 'For he sacrificed to the gods of Damascus who smote him, and he said, Because the gods of the kings of Syria help them, therefore will I sacrifice to them that they may help me. But they were the ruin of him and of all Israel' (2 Chr. 28:23).

M. "I smiled upon Amaziah and delivered the kings of Edom into his power, so he brought their gods and bowed down to them, as it is said, "Now it came to pass, after Amaziah was come from the slaughter of the Edomites, that he brought the gods of the children of Seir and set them up to be his gods and bowed down himself before them and burned incense to them" (2 Chr. 25:14).' "

N. Said R. Pappa, "This is in line with what people say: 'Weep for the one who does not know, laugh for the one who does not know. Woe to him who does not know the difference between good and bad.' "

O. "And all the princes of the king of Babylonia came in and sat in the middle gate" (Jer. 39:3):

P. Said R. Yohanan in the name of R. Simeon b. Yohai, "It was the place in which laws were mediated."

Q. Said R. Pappa, "That is in line with what people say: 'In the place in which the master hangs up his sword, the shepherd hangs up his pitcher.' [Freedman, p. 700, n. 3: Where the Jews decided upon their laws, there Nebuchadnezzer issued his decrees.]"

CLXXVI. A. Said R. Hisda said R. Jeremiah bar Abba, "What is the meaning of the following verse: 'I went by the field of the slothful and by the vineyard of the man void of understanding. And lo, it was all grown over with thorns and nettles had covered the face thereof, and the stone wall thereof was broken down' (Prov. 24:30–31)?

B. " 'I went by the field of the slothful'—this speaks of Ahaz.

C. " 'And by the vineyard of the man void of understanding'—this speaks of Manasseh.

D. " 'And lo, it was all grown over with thorns'—this refers to Amon.

E. " 'And nettles had covered the face thereof—this refers to Jehoiakim.

F. " 'And the stone wall thereof was broken down'—this refers to Zedekiah, in whose time the Temple was destroyed."

G. And said R. Hisda said R. Jeremiah bar Abba, "There are four categories who will not receive the face of the Presence of God:

H. "The categories of scoffers, flatterers, liars, and slanderers.

I. "The category of scoffers, as it is written, 'He has stretched out his hand against scorners' (Hos. 7:5).

J. "The category of flatterers, as it is written, 'He who speaks lies shall not be established in my sight' (Job 13:16).

K. "The category of liars, as it is written, 'He who speaks lies shall not be established in my sight' (Ps. 101:7).

L. "The category of slanderers, as it is written, 'For you are not a God who has pleasure in wickedness; evil will not dwell with you' (Ps. 5:5). 'You are righteous, O Lord, and evil will not dwell in your house' [Ps. 5 addresses slander.]"

M. And said R. Hisda said R. Jeremiah bar Abba, "What is the meaning of the verse, 'There shall not evil befall you, neither shall any plague come near your dwelling' (Ps. 91:10)?

N. "There shall not evil befall you' means that the evil impulse will not rule over you.

O. "Neither shall any plague come near your dwelling' means that, when you come home from a trip, you will never find that your wife is in doubt as to whether or not she is menstruating."

P. "Another matter: 'There shall not evil befall you' means that bad dreams and fantasies will never frighten you.

Q. " 'Neither shall any plague come near your dwelling' means that you will not have a son or a disciple who in public burns his food [that is, teaches something heretical].

R. "Up to this point is the blessing that his father had given him.

S. "From this point forward comes the blessing that his mother had given to him: 'For he shall give his angels charge over you, to keep you in all your ways. They shall bear you in their hands . . . You shall tread upon the lion and the adder' (Ps. 91:10).

T. "Up to this point is the blessing that his mother gave him.

U. "From this point onward comes the blessing that heaven gave him:

V. "[103B] Because he has set his love upon me, therefore will I deliver him. I will set him on high, because he has known my name. He shall call upon me, and I will answer him. I will be with him in trouble. I will deliver him and honor him. With long life will I satisfy him and show him my salvation' (Ps. 91:14–16)."

CLXXVII. A. Said R. Simeon b. Laqish, "What is the meaning of the following verse of Scripture: 'And from the wicked their light is withheld, and the high arm shall be broken' (Job 38:15)?

B. "Why is the letter *ayin* in the word for wicked suspended [in the text, being written above the level of the line, making it read 'poor,' rather than 'wicked' (Freedman, p. 701, n. 10)]?

C. "When a person becomes poor below, he is made poor above [Freedman, p. 701, n. 11: Where one earns the disapproval of man, it is proof that he has earned the disapproval of God too.]"

D. Then the letter should not be written at all?

E. R. Yohanan and R. Eleazar: One said, "It is because of the honor owing to David."

F. The other said, "It is because the honor owing to Nehemiah B. Hachaliah. [Freedman, p. 702, n. 1: Both had many enemies yet were truly righeous men.]"

CLXXVIII. A. Our rabbis have taught on Tannaite authority:

B. Manasseh would teach the book of Leviticus from fifty-five viewpoints, corresponding to the years of his reign.

C. Ahab did so in eighty-five ways.

D. Jeroboam did so in a hundred and three ways.

CLXXIX. A. It has been taught on Tannaite authority:

B. R. Meir would say, "Absalom has no share in the world to come,

C. "as it is said, 'And they smote Absalom and slew him' (2 Sam. 18:15).

D. "They smote him' in this world.

E. "And they slew him' in the world to come."

CLXXX. A. It has been taught on Tannaite authority:

B. R. Simeon b. Eleazar says in the name of R. Meir, "Ahaz, Ahaziah, and all the kings of Israel concerning whom it is written, 'And he did what was evil in the sight of the Lord' will not live or be judged [in the world to come]."

CLXXXI. A. "Moreover Manasseh shed much innocent blood, until he had filled Jerusalem from one end to another, beside his sin wherewith he made Judah to sin, in doing that which was evil in the sight of the Lord" (2 Kgs. 21:16):

B. Here [in Babylonia] it is explained that he killed Isaiah, [and that is the sin at hand].

C. In the West they say that it was that he made an idol as heavy as a thousand men, and every day it killed them all.

D. In accord with whose position is the following statement made by Rabbab b. b. Hana: "The soul of a righteous man is balanced against the whole world"?

E. In accord with whom? With the position of him who has said that he had killed Isaiah.

CLXXXII.   A. [It is written,] "And he set the graven image" (2 Chr. 33:7), and it is stated, "And the graves and the graven images which he had set up" (2 Chr. 33:19). [Was there one image or were there many?]

B. Said R. Yohanan, "In the beginning he made one face for it, and in the end he made four faces for it, so that the Presence of God should see it and become angry.

C. "Ahaz set up in the upper chamber, as it is written, 'And the altars that were on top of the upper chamber of Ahaz' (2 Kgs. 23:13).

D. "Manasseh set it in the Temple, as it is written, 'And he set up a graven image of the graven image of the grove that he had made in the house, of which the Lord said to David and to Solomon his son, In this house and in Jerusalem which I have chosen out of all tribes of Israel will I put my name for ever' (2 Kgs. 21:7).

E. "Amon put it into the Holy of Holies, as it is said, 'For the bed is shorter than that a man can stretch himself on it, and the covering narrower than that he can wrap himself in it' (Is. 28:20)."

F. What is the sense of, "For the bed is shorter than that one can stretch himself on it"?

G. Said R. Samuel bar Nahmani said R. Jonathan, "This bed is too short for two neighbors to rule over it at one time."

H. What is the sense of "And the covering is narrower"?

I. Said R. Samuel bar Nahmani, "When R. Jonathan would reach this verse of Scripture, he would cry. 'He of whom it is written, "He gathers the waters of the sea together as a heap" (Ps. 33:7)—should a molten statue rival him!' "

CLXXXIII.   A. Ahaz annulled the sacrificial service and sealed the Torah, for it is said, "Bind up the testimony, seal the Torah among my disciples" (Is. 8:16).

B. Manasseh blotted out the mentions of the divine Name and destroyed the altar.

C. Amon burned the Torah and let spiderwebs cover the altar.

D. Ahaz permitted consanguineous marriages.

E. Manasseh had sexual relations with his sister.

F. Amon had sexual relations with his mother, as it is said, "For Amon sinned very much" (2 Chr. 33:23).

G. R. Yohanan and R. Eleazar: one said that he burned the Torah.

H. The other said that he had sexual relations with his mother.

I. His mother said to him, "Do you have any pleasure from the place from which you came forth?"

J. He said to her, "Am I doing anything except to spite my creator?"

K. When Jehoiakim came, he said, "The ones who came before me really did not know how to anger him. Do we need him for anything more than his light? We have pure gold, which we use [for light], so let him take away his light."

L. They said to him, "But do not silver and gold belong to him, as it is written, 'Mine is the silver, and mine is the gold, saith the Lord of hosts' (Hag. 2:8)?"

M. He said to them, "He has already given them to us, as it is said, 'The heavens are the Lord's, and the earth he has given to the children of men' (Ps. 115:16)."

CLXXXIV. A. Said Raba to Rabbah bar Mari, "On what account did they not count Jehoiakim [among those who do not get the world to come]?

B. "For it is written of him, 'And the remaining words of Jehoiakim and the abomination which he wrought and that which was found upon him' (2 Chr. 36:8)."

C. What is the sense of "That which was found upon him" (2 Chr. 36:8)?

D. R. Yohanan and R. Eleazar: One said that he engraved the name of his idol on his penis.

E. The other said that he engraved the name of heaven on his penis.

F. [Rabbah b. Mari] said to him, "As to the matter of kings, I have not heard any answer. But as to ordinary people, I have heard an answer.

G. "Why did they count Micah? Because he made his bread available to travelers, for it is said, 'Every traveler turned to the Levites.' "

H. "And he shall pad through the sea with affliction and shall smite the waves in the sea" (Zech. 10:11)."

I. Said R. Yohanan, "This speaks of the idol of Micah."

J. It has been taught on Tannaite authority:

K. R. Nathan says, "From Hareb to Shiloah is three mils, and the smoke of the pile and the smoke of the image of Micah mixed together. The ministering angels wanted to drive [Micah] off. The Holy One, blessed be he, said to them, 'Leave him alone, for his bread is made available to travelers.' "

L. And for the same matter those involved in the matter of the concubine at Gibeah [Judges 19] were punished.

M. Said the Holy One, blessed be he, "On account of the honor owing to me you did not protest, and on account of the honor owing to a mortal you protested."

CLXXXV. A. Said R. Yohanan in the name of R. Yose b. Qisma, "Great is a mouthful of food, for it set a distance between two families and Israel,

B. "as it is written, '[An Ammonite or Moabite shall not enter the congregation of the Lord] . . . because they did not meet you with bread and water in the way when you came forth from Egypt' (Deut. 33:4–5)."

C. And R. Yohanan on his own said, "It creates distance among those who are close; it draws near those who are afar; it blinds the eye [of God] from the wicked; it makes the Presence of God rest even on the prophets of Baal, and it makes an unwitting offense appear to be deliberate [if it is performed in connection with care of the wayfarer]."

D. [Now to spell out the foregoing:] "It creates distance among those who are close":

E. [Proof derives] from [104A] the case of Ammon and Moab.

F. "It draws near those who are afar":

G. [Proof derives] from the case of Jethro.

H. For said R. Yohanan, "As a reward for saying, 'Call him that he may eat bread' (Ex. 2:20), [Jethro]'s descendants had the merit of going taking seats [as authorities] in the chamber of the hewn stones, it is said, 'And the family of the scribes which dwell at Jabez, the Tirathites, the Shimeathites, and Suchathites. These are the Kenites that came of Hemath, the father of the house of Rechan' (1 Chr. 2:55).

I. "And elsewhere it is written, 'And the children of the Kenite, Moses' father-in-law, went up out of the city of palm trees with the children of Judah into the wilderness of Judah, which lies in the south of Arab, and they went and dwelt among the people' (Judges 1:16). [Freedman, p. 705, n. 10: This shows that the Kenites were descended from Jethro and they sat in the hall of hewn stones as scribes and sanhedrin.]"

J. "It blinds the eye [of God] from the wicked":

K. [Proof derives] from the case of Micah.

L. "It makes the Presence of God rest even on the prophets of Baal":

M. [Proof derives] from the friend of Iddo, the prophet, for it is written, "And it came to pass, as they sat at the table, that the word of the Lord came to the prophet that brought him back" (1 Kgs. 13:20). [Freedman, p. 706, n. 2: He was a prophet of Baal, yet God's word came to him as a reward for his hospitality.]

N. "And it makes an unwitting offense appear to be deliberate":

O. [Proof derives] from what R. Judah said Rab, said, "Had Jonathan only brought David two loaves of bread, Nob, the city of priests, would not have been put to death, Doeg the Edomite would not have been troubled, and Saul and his three sons would not have been killed. [Freedman, p. 706, n. 4: For had he provided him with food, he would not have taken any from Ahimelech. Thus all this happened, though Jonathan's initial offense was due to an oversight.]"

CLXXXVI. A. Why did they not list Ahaz [at M. 11:2]?

B. Said R. Jeremiah bar Abba, "Because he was positioned between two righteous men, between Jotham and Hezekiah."

C. R. Joseph said, "Because he had the capacity to be ashamed on account of Isaiah, as it is said, 'Then said the Lord to Isaiah, Go forth now to meet Ahaz, you and Shear-jashub your son, at the end of the conduit of the upper pool in the highway of the field of the fuller's trough' (Is. 7:3)."

D. What is the source of "fuller's trough"?

E. Some say, "He hid his face [using the same consonants] and fled."

F. Some say, "He dragged a fuller's trough [the meaning of the word in general] on his head and fled."

CLXXXVII. A. Why did they not list Amon [at M. 11:2]?

B. On account of the honor owing to Josiah.

C. In that case, they also should not have listed Manasseh, on account of the honor owing to Hezekiah.

D. The son imparts merit to the father, but the father does not give any merit to the son, for it is written, "Neither is there any one who can deliver out of my hand" (Deut. 32:39).

E. Abraham cannot save Ishmael. Isaac cannot save Esau.

F. If you go that far, then Ahaz also was omitted from the list on account of the honor owing to Hezekiah.

CLXXXVIII. A. And on that account did they not list Jehoiakim?

B. It is on account of what R. Hiyya b. R. Abuyyah said.

C. For R. Hiyya b. R. Abuyyah said, "It was written on the skull of Jehoiakim, 'This and yet another.' "

D. The grandfather of R. Perida found a skull tossed at the gates of Jerusalem, on which was written, "This and yet another."

E. He buried it, but it did not stay buried, and he buried it again but it did not stay buried.

F. He said, "It must be the skull of Jehoiakim, for it is written in that connection, 'He shall be buried with the burial of an ass, drawn and cast forth beyond the gates of Jerusalem' (Jer. 22:19)."

G. He said, "Still, he was a king, and it is not proper to treat him lightly."

H. He wrapped the skull in silk and put it in a closet. His wife saw it. She thought, "This is [the bone of] his first wife, whom he has not forgotten."

I. She lit the oven and burned it up, and that is the meaning of what is written, "This and yet another." [Freedman, p. 707, n. 2: These indignities made sufficient atonement for him that he should share in the future world.]

CLXXXIX. A. It has been taught on Tannaite authority:

B. R. Simeon b. Eleazar said, "On account of [Hezekiah's] statement, 'And I have done that which was good in your sight,' (2 Kgs. 20:3), [he had further to ask,] 'What shall be the sign [that the Lord will heal me]' (2 Kgs. 20:9)?"

C. "On account of the statement, 'What shall be the sign' (2 Kgs. 20:9), gentiles ate at his table.

D. "On account of gentiles' eating at his table, [2 Kgs. 20:17–18), he made his children go into exile."

E. That statement supports what Hezekiah said.

F. For Hezekiah said, "Whoever invites an idolator into his house and serves him [as host] causes his children to go into exile, as it is said, 'And of your sons who will issue from you, which you shall beget, shall they take away; and they shall be eunuchs in the palace of the king of Babylonia' (2 Kgs. 20:18)."

G. "And Hezekiah was happy about them and showed them the treasure house, the silver and gold, spices and precious ointment" (Is. 39:2).

H. Said Rab, "What is the sense of 'his treasure house'? It means, his wife, who served them drinks."

I. Samuel said, "His treasury is what he showed them."

J. R. Yohanan said, "His weapons, which had the capacity to consume other weapons, is what he showed them."

CXC. A. "How does the city sit solitary" (Lam. 1:1):

B. Said Rabbah said R. Yohanan, "On what account were the Israelites smitten with the word 'how' [that begins the dirge]? [Since the numerical value of the letters of the word equals thirty-six], it is because they violated the thirty-six rules in the Torah that are penalized by extirpation."

C. Said R. Yohanan, "Why were they smitten [with a dirge that is] alphabetical?

D. "Because they violated the Torah, which is given through the alphabet. [Freedman, p. 708, n. 6: Its words are formed from the alphabet.]"

CXCI. A. "Sit solitary" (Lam. 1:1):

B. Said Rabbah said R. Yohanan, "Said the Holy One, blessed be he, 'I said, "Israel then shall dwell in safety alone, the foundation of Jacob shall be upon a land of corn and wine, also his heavens shall drop down dew" (Deut. 33:28) [so that sitting solitary was supposed to be a blessing (Freedman, p. 708, n. 8)], but now, where they dwell will be alone.' "

CXCII. A. "The city that was full of people" (Lam. 1:1):

B. Said Rabbah said R. Yohanan, "For they used to marry off a minor girl to an adult male, or an adult woman to a minor boy, so that they should have many children. [But two minors would not marry.]"

CXCIII. A. "She is become as a widow" (Lam. 1:1):

B. Said R. Judah said Rab, "Like a widow, but not actually a widow, but like a woman whose husband has gone overseas and plans to return to her."

CXCIV. A. "She was great among the nations and princess among the provinces" (Lam. 1:1):

B. Said R. Rabbah said R. Yohanan, "Everywhere they go they become princes of their masters."

CXCV. A. Our rabbis have taught on Tannaite authority:

B. There is the case of two men who were captured on Mount Carmel. The kidnapper was walking behind them. [104B] One of them said to his fellow, "The camel that is walking before us is blind in one eye, it is carrying two skins, one of wine and one of oil, and of the two men that are leading it, one is an Israelite and the other is a gentile."

C. The kidnapper said to them, "Stiff-necked people, how do you know?"

D. They said to him, "As to the camel, it is eating from the grass before it on the side on which it can see, but on the side on which it cannot see, it is not eating.

E. "And it is carrying two skins, one of wine and one of oil. The one of wine drips and the drippings are absorbed in the ground, while the one of oil drips, and the drippings remain on the surface.

F. "And as the two men who are leading it, one is a gentile and one is an Israelite. The gentile relieves himself right on the road, while the Israelite turns to the side [of the road]."

G. The man ran after them and found that things were just as they had said. He came and kissed them on their head and brought them to his house. He made a great banquet for them and danced before them, saying, "Blessed is he who chose the seed of Abraham and gave part of his wisdom to them, and wherever they go they become the princes over their masters."

H. He sent them away and went home in peace.

CXCVI.

A. "She weeps, yes, she weeps in the night" (Lam. 1:2):

B. Why these two acts of weeping?

C. Said Rabbah said R. Yohanan, "One is for the first Temple and the other is for the second Temple."

D. "At night":

E. On account of things done in the night, as it is said, "And all the congregation lifted up their voice and cried, and the people wept that night [at the spies' false report]" (Num. 14:1).

F. Said Rabbah said R. Yohanan, "That was the ninth of Ab. Said the Holy One, blessed be he, to Israel, 'You have wept tears for nothing. I now shall set up for you weeping for generations to come.' "

G. Another interpretation of "At night":

H. Whoever cries at night will find that his voice is heard.

I. Another interpretation of "At night":

J. Whoever cries at night finds that the stars and planets will cry with him.

K. Another interpretation of "At night":

L. Whoever cries at night finds that whoever hears his voice will cry along with him.

M. That was the case of a woman in the neighborhood of Rabban Gamaliel, whose child died. She was weeping by night on account of the child. Rabban Gamaliel heard her voice and cried with her, until his eyelashes fell out. The next day, his disciples recognized what had happened and removed the woman from his neighborhood.

CXCVII. A. "And her tears are on her cheeks" (Lam. 1:2):

B. Said Rabbah said R. Yohanan, "It is like a woman who weeps for the husband of her youth, as it is said, "Lamentation like a virgin girded with sackcloth for the husband of her youth' (Joel 1:8)."

CXCVIII. A. "Her adversaries are the chief" (Lam. 1:5):

B. Said Rabbah said R. Yohanan, "Whoever persecutes Israel becomes head,

C. "as it is said, 'Nevertheless, there shall be no weariness for her that oppressed her. In the former time he brought into contempt the land of Zebulun and the land of Naphtali, but in the latter time he has made it glorious, by way of the sea, beyond Jordan, the circuit of the nations' (Is. 8:23)."

D. Said Rabbah said R. Yohanan, "Whoever oppresses Israel does not get tired."

CXCIX. A. "May it not happen to you, all passersby" (Lam. 1:12):

B. Said Rabbah said R. Yohanan, "On this basis we find in the Torah support for saying [when reciting woes], 'May it not happen to you.' "

CC. A. "All passersby" (Lam. 1:12):

B. Said R. Amram said Rab, "They have turned me into one of those who transgress the law.

C. "For in respect to Sodom, it is written, 'And the Lord rained upon Sodom [and upon Gomorrah] brimstone and fire' (Gen. 19:24). But in respect to Jerusalem it is written. 'From above he has sent fire against my bones and it prevails against them' (Lam. 1:13).

[Freedman, p. 711, n. 4: Thus Jerusalem was treated as Sodom and Gomorrah.]"

D. "For the iniquity of the daughter of my people is greater than the sin of Sodom" (Lam. 4:6):

E. And is any sort of favoritism shown in such a matter [since Jerusalem was left standing, Sodom was wiped out]?

F. Said Rabbah said R. Yohanan, "[Not at all, in fact] there was a further measure [of punishment] directed against Jerusalem but not against Sodom.

G. "For with respect to Sodom, it is written, 'Behold, this was the iniquity of your sister, Sodom, pride, fullness of bread, and abundance of idleness was in her and in her daughters, neither did she strengthen the hand of the poor and the needy' (Ez. 16:49).

H. "With respect to Jerusalem, by contrast it is written, 'The hands of merciful women have boiled their own children' (Lam. 4:10). [Freedman, p. 711, n. 8: Jerusalem suffered extreme hunger, which Sodom never did, and this fact counterbalanced her being spared total destruction.]"

CCI.

A. "The Lord has trodden under foot all my mighty men in the midst of me" (Lam. 1:15):

B. This is like a man who says to his fellow, "This coin has been invalidated."

C. "All your enemies have opened their mouths against you" (Lam. 2:16):

D. Said Rabbah said R. Yohanan, "On what account does the letter P come before the letter *ayin* [in the order of verses in the chapter of Lamentation, while in the alphabet, the ayin comes before the P]?

E. "It is on account of the spies, who said with their mouths [and the word for mouth begins with a P] what their eyes had not seen [and the word for eye begins with an *ayin*.]"

CCII.

A. "They eat my people as they eat bread and do not call upon the Lord" (Ps. 14:4):

B. Said Rabbah said R. Yohanan, "Whoever eats the bread of Israelites tastes the flavor of bread, and who does not eat the bread of Israelites does not taste the flavor of bread."

CCIII.   A. "They do not call upon the Lord" (Ps. 14:4):

B. Rab said, "This refers to judges."

C. And Samuel said, "This refers to those who teach children."

CCIV.   A. Who counted [the kings and commoners of M. 11:2A]?

B. Said R. Ashi, "The men of the great assembly counted them."

CCV.   A. Said R. Judah said Rab, "They wanted to count yet another [namely, Solomon], but an apparition of his father's face came and prostrated himself before them. But they paid no attention to him. A fire came down from heaven and licked around their chairs, but they did not pay attention. An echo come forth and as said to them, 'Do you see a man diligent in his business? He shall stand before kings, he shall not stand before mean men' (Prov. 22:29).

B. "[God speaks:] 'He who gave precedence to my house over his house, and not only so, but built my house over a span of seven years, while building his own house over a span of thirteen years—he shall stand before kings, he shall not stand before mean men.' "

C. "But they paid no attention to that either.

D. "An echo came forth, saying, 'Should it be according to your mind? He will recompense it, whether you refuse or whether you choose, and not I' (Job 34:33)."

CCVI.   A. Those who interpret signs [symbolically] would say, "All of them [listed at M. 11:2] will enter the world to come, as it is said, "Gilead is mine, Manasseh is mine, Ephraim also is the strength of my head, Judah is my lawgiver, Moab is my washpot, over Edom will I cast my shoe, Philistia, you triumph because of me' (Ps. 60:9–10):

B. " 'Gideon is mine' speaks of Ahab, who fell at Ramoth-gilead.

C. " 'Manasseh'—literally.

D. " 'Ephraim also is the strength of my head' speaks of Jeroboam, who comes from Ephraim.

E. " 'Judah is my lawgiver' refers to Ahitophel, [105A] who comes from Judah.

F. " 'Moab is my washpot' refers to Gehazi, who was smitten on account of matters having to with washing.

G. " 'Over Edom will I cast my shoe' refers to Doeg the Edomite.

H. " 'Philistia, you triumph because of me': The ministering angels said before the Holy One, blessed be he, 'Lord of the world, if David should come, who killed the Philistine, and who gave Gath to them as an inheritence, what are you going to do to him?'

I. "He said to them, 'It is my task to make them friends of one another.' "

CCVII. A. "Why is this people of Jerusalem slidden back by a perpetual backsliding?" (Jer. 8:5):

B. Said Rab, "The community of Israel answered the prophet with a lasting reply [a play on the words for backsliding and answer, using the same root].

C. "The prophet said to Israel, 'Return in repentence. Your fathers who sinned—where are they now?'

D. "They said to him, 'And your prophets, who did not sin, where are they now? For it is said, "Your fathers, where are they? and the prophets, do they live forever" (Zech. 1:5)?'

E. "He said to them, 'They repented and confessed as it is said, "But my words and my statutes, which I commanded my servants the prophets, did they not take hold of your fathers? And they returned and said, Like as the Lord of hosts thought to do unto us, according to our ways and according to our doings, so has he dealt with us" (Zech. 1:6).' "

F. Samuel said, "Ten men came and sat before him. He said to them, 'Return in repentance.'

G. "They said to him, 'If a master has sold his slave, or a husband has divorced his wife, does one party have any further claim upon the other? [Surely not.] Freed-

man, p. 714, n. 3: Since God has sold us to Nebuchadnezzar, he has no further claim upon us, and we
have no cause to repent. This in Samuel's view was
the victorious answer.]

H. "Said the Holy One, blessed be he, to the prophet,
'Go and say to them, "Thus says the Lord, where is
the bill of your mother's divorcement, whom I have
put away? Or which of my creditors is it to whom I
have sold you? Behold for your iniquities you have
sold yourselves, and for your transgressions is your
mother put away" ' (Is. 50:1)."

I. And this is in line with what R. Simeon b. Laqish
said, "What is the meaning of what is written, 'David
my servant [and] Nebuchadnezzar my servant' (Jer.
43:10)?

J. "It is perfectly clear before him who spoke and
brought the world into being that the Israelites were
going to say this, and therefore the Holy One, blessed
be he, went ahead and called him 'his servant.' [Why
so?] If a slave acquires property, to whom does the
slave belong, and to whom does the property belong?
[Freedman, p. 714, n. 7: Even if God had sold them
to Nebuchadnezzar, they still belong to God.]' "

CCVIII.   A. "And that which comes into your mind shall not be
at all, that you say, We will be as the heathen, as the
families of the countries, to serve wood and stone. As
I live, says the Lord God, surely with a mighty hand
and with an outstretched arm, and with fury poured
out, will I rule over you" (Ez. 20:32–33):

B. Said R. Nahman, "Even with such anger may the All-
Merciful rage against us, so long as he redeems us."

CCIX.   A. "For he chastizes him to discretion and his God
teaches him" (Is. 28:26):

B. Said Rabbah bar Hanah, "Said the prophet to Israel,
'Return in repentence.'

C. "They said to him, 'We cannot do so. The impulse to
do evil rules over us.'

D. "He said to them, 'Reign in your desire.'

E. "They said to him, 'Let his God teach us.' "

CCX.

A. *Four ordinary folk: Balaam, Doeg, Ahitophel, and Gehazi [M. 11:2F]:*

B. [The name] Balaam [means] not with [the rest of] the people [using the same consonants], [who will inherit the world to come].

C. Another interpretation: Balaam, because he devoured the people.

D. "Son of Beor" means that he had sexual relations with a cow [a play on the consonants of the word for Beor].

CCXI.

A. It was taught on Tannaite authority:

B. Beor, Cushan-rishathaim, and Laban, the Syrian, are one and the same person.

C. Beor: because he had sexual relations with a cow.

D. Cushan-rishathaim [two acts of wickedness], for he committed two acts of wickedness against Israel, one in the time of Jacob and one in the time of the Judges.

E. But what was his real name? It was Laban the Aramaean.

CCXII.

A. It is written, "The son of Beor" (Num. 22:50), but it also is written, "His son was Beor" (Num. 24:3).

B. Said R. Yohanan, "His father was his son as to prophecy."

CCXIII.

A. Balaam is the one who will not come to the word to come. Lo, others will come.

B. In accord with whose view is the Mishnah-passage at hand?

C. It represents the view of R. Joshua.

D. For it has been taught on Tannaite authority:

E. **[In Tosefta's version:] R. Eliezer says, "None of the gentiles has a portion in the world to come,**

F. **"as it is said, 'The wicked shall return to sheol, all the gentiles who forget God' (Ps. 9:18).**

G. **" 'The wicked shall return to Sheol'—these are the wicked Israelites.**

H. **" 'And all the gentiles who forget God'—these are the nations."**

I. **Said to him R. Joshua, "If it had been written, 'The wicked shall return to Sheol—all the gen-**

tiles' and then said nothing further, I should have maintained as you do.

J. "Now, that it is in fact written, 'All the gentiles who forget God,' it indicates that there also are righteous people among the nations of the world who have a portion in the world to come" [T. San. 13:2E–J].

K. And that wicked man [Balaam] also gave a sign concerning his own fate, when he said, "Let me die the death of the righteous" (Num. 23:10).

L. [He said,] "If my soul dies the death of the righteous, may my future be like his, and if not, 'Then behold I go to my people' (Num. 24:14)."

CCXIV. A. "And the elders of Moab and the elders of Midian departed" (Num. 22:7):

B. It was taught on Tannaite authority:

C. There was never peace between Midian and Moab. The matter may be compared to two dogs who were in a kennel, barking at one another.

D. A wolf came and attacked one. The other said, "If I do not help him today, he will kill him, and tomorrow he will come against me."

E. So the two dogs went and killed the wolf.

F. Said R. Pappa, "This is in line with what people say: 'The weasel and the cat can make a banquet on the fat of the unlucky.'"

CCXV. A. "And the princess of Moab abode with Balaam" (Num. 22:8):

B. And as to the princess of Midian, where had they gone?

C. When he said to them, "Lodge here this night and I will bring you word again [as the Lord shall speak to me]," (Num. 22:8), they said, "Does any father hate his son? [No chance!]"

CCXVI. A. Said R. Nahman, "Hutzbah, even against heaven, serves some good. To begin with, it is written, 'You shall not go with them' (Num. 22:12), and then it is said, 'Rise up and go with them' (Num. 22:20)."

B. Said R. Sheshet, "Hutzbah is dominion without a crown.

C. "For it is written, 'And I am this day weak, though anointed king, and these men, the sons of Zeruiah, be too hard for me' (2 Sam. 3:39). [Freedman, p. 717, n. 1: Thus their boldness and impudence outweighed sovereignty.]"

CCXVII.   A. Said R. Yohanan, "Balaam had one crippled foot, for it is written, 'And he walked haltingly' (Num. 23:3).

B. "Samson had two crippled feet, as it is said, 'An adder in the path that bites the horses' heels' (Gen. 49:17). [Freedman, p. 717, n. 3: This was a prophecy of Samson. 'An adder in the path' is taken to mean that he would have to slither along like an adder, being lame in both feet.]

C. "Balaam was blind in one eye, as it is said, 'Whose eye is open' (Num. 24:3).

D. "He practiced enchantment with his penis.

E. "Here it is written, 'Falling but having his eyes open' (Num. 24:3), and elsewhere: 'And Haman was fallen on the bed whereon Esther was' (Est. 7:8)."

F. It has been stated on Amoraic authority:

G. Mar Zutra said, "He practiced enchantment with his penis."

H. Mar, son of Rabina, said, "He had sexual relations with his ass."

I. As to the view that he practiced enchantment with his penis it is as we have just now stated.

J. As to the view that he had sexual relations with his ass:

K. Here it is written, "He bowed, he lay down as a lion and as a great lion" (Num. 24:9), and elsewhere it is written, "At her feet [105B] he bowed, he fell" (Jud. 5:27)."

CCXVIII.   A. "He knows the mind of the Most High" (Num. 24:16):

B. Now if he did not know the mind of his own beast, how could he have known the mind of the Most High?

C. What is the case of the mind of his beast?

D. People said to him, "What is the reason that you did not ride on your horse?"

E. He said to them, "I put it out to graze in fresh pasture."

F. [The ass] said to him, "Am I not your ass" (Num. 22:30). [That shows he rode an ass, not a horse.]

G. "[You are] merely for carrying loads."

H. "Upon whom you rode" (Num. 22:30).

I. "It was a happenstance."

J. "Ever since I was yours, until this day" (Num. 22:30).

K. [The ass continued,] "And not only so, but I serve you for sexual relations by night."

L. Here it is written, "Did I ever do so to you" (Num. 22:30) and elsewhere it is written, "Let her serve as his companion." [The same word is used, proving that sexual relations took place as with David and the maiden in his old age.]

M. Then what is the meaning of the statement, "He knows the mind of the Most High" (Num. 24:16)?

N. He knew how to tell the exact time at which the Holy One, blessed be he, was angry.

O. That is in line with what the prophet said to Israel, "O my people, remember now what Balak, king of Moab, consulted, and what Balaam the son of Beor answered him from Shittim to Gilgal, that you may know the righteousness of the Lord" (Mic. 6:5).

P. What is the meaning of the statement, "That you may know the righteousness of the Lord" (Mic. 6:5)?

Q. Said the Holy One, blessed be he, to Israel, "Know that I have done many acts of charity with you, that I did not get angry with you in the time of the wicked Balaam.

R. "For if I had become angry during all those days, there would not remain out of (the enemies of) Israel a shred or a remnant."

S. That is in line with what Balaam said to Balak, "How shall I curse one whom God has not cursed? Or shall I rage, when the Lord has not raged?" (Num. 23:8).

T. This teaches that for all those days the Lord had not been angry.

U. But: "God is angry every day" (Ps. 7:12).

V. And how long does his anger last? It is a moment, for it is said, "For his anger endures but a moment, but his favor is life" (Ps. 30:5).

W. If you wish, I shall propose, "Come, my people, enter into your chambers and shut your doors about you, hide yourself as it were for a brief moment, until the indignation be past" (Is. 26:20).

X. When is he angry? It is in the first three hours [of the day], when the comb of the cock is white.

Y. But it is white all the time?

Z. All the other time it has red streaks, but when God is angry, there are no red streaks in it.

CCXIX.   A. There was a *min* [heretic] living in the neighborhood of R. Joshua b. Levi, who bothered him a great deal. One day he took a chicken and tied it up at the foot of his bed and sat down. He said, "When that moment comes [at which God is angry], I shall curse him."

B. When that moment came, he was dozing. He said, "What this teaches is that it is improper [to curse,] for it is written, 'Also to punish is not good for the righteous' (Prov. 17:26)—even in the case of a min."

CCXX.   A. A Tannaite authority in the name of R. Meir [said], "When the sun shines and the kings put their crowns on their heads and bow down to the sun, forthwith he is angry."

CCXXI.   A. "And Balaam rose up in the morning and saddled his ass" (Num. 22:21):

B. A Tannaite authority taught in the name of R. Simeon b. Eleazar, "That love annuls the order of proprieties [we learn] from the case of Abraham.

C. "For it is written, 'And Abraham rose up early in the morning and saddled his ass' (Gen. 22:3) [not waiting for the servant to do so].

D. "And that hatred annuls the order of proprieties [we learn] from the case of Balaam.

E. "For it is said, 'And Balaam rose up early in the morning and saddled his ass' (Num. 22:21)."

CCXXII.   A. Said R. Judah said Rab, "Under all circumstances a person should engage in study of Torah and practice of religious duties, even if it is not for their own sake, for out of doing these things not for their own sake one will come to do them for their own sake."

B. For as a reward for the fifty-two offerings that Balak offered, he had the merit that Ruth should come forth from him.

C. Said R. Yose bar Huna, "Ruth was the daughter of Egion, grandson of Balak, king of Moab."

CCXXIII.   A. Said Raba to Rabbah bar Mari, "It is written, '[And moreover the king's servants came to bless our lord king David, saying] God make the name of Solomon better than your name, and make his throne greater than your throne' (1 Kgs. 1:47).

B. "Now is this appropriate to speak in such a way to a king?"

C. He said to him, "What they meant is, 'as good as . . . .' [Freedman, p. 720, n. 2: 'God make the name of Solomon illustrious even as the nature of your own and make his throne great according to the character of your throne.']

D. "For if you do not say this, then [take account of the following:] 'Blessed above women shall be Jael, the wife of Heber the Kenite, be, blessed shall she be above women in the tent' (Jud. 5:24).

E. "Now who are the women in the tent? They are Sarah, Rebecca, Rachel, and Leah.

F. "Is it appropriate to speak in such a way? Rather, what is meant is 'as good as . . .,' and here too the sense is, 'as good as . . .' "

G. That statement differs from what R. Yose bar Honi said.

H. For R. Yose bar Honi said, "One may envy anybody except for his son and his disciple.

I. "One learns the fact about one's son from the case of Solomon.

J. "And as to the case of one's disciple, if you wish, I shall propose, 'Let a double quantity of your spirit be upon me' (2 Kgs. 2:9).

K. "Or if you wish, I shall derive proof from the following: 'And he laid his hands upon him and gave him a charge' (Num. 27:23)."

CCXXIV. A. "And the Lord put a thing in the mouth of Balaam" (Num. 23:5):

B. R. Eleazar says, "It was an angel."

C. R. Jonathan said, "It was a hook."

CCXXV. A. Said R. Yohanan, "From the blessing said by that wicked man, you learn what he had in his heart.

B. "He wanted to say that they should not have synagogues and school houses: 'How goodly are your tents, O Jacob' (Num. 24:5).

C. "[He wanted to say that] the Presence of God should not dwell on them: 'And your tabernacles, O Israel' (Num. 24:5).

D. "[He wanted to say] that their kingdom should not last [thus, to the contrary]: 'As the valleys are they spread forth' (Num. 24:6);

E. "that they should have no olives and vineyards: 'As the trees of aloes which the Lord has planted' (Num. 24:6);

F. "that their kings should not be tall: 'And as cedar trees beside the waters' (Num. 24:6);

G. "that they should not have a king succeed his father as king: "He shall pour the water out of his buckets' (Num. 24:6);

H. "that their kingdom should not rule over others: 'And his seed shall be in many waters' (Num. 24:6);

I. "that their kingdom should not be strong: 'And his king shall be higher than Agag' (Num. 24:6);

J. "that their kingdom not be fearful: 'And his kingdom shall be exalted' (Num. 24:6)."

K. Said R. Abba b. Kahana, "All of them were [ultimately] turned into a curse, except for the one on the synagogues and school houses, as it is said, 'But the Lord your God turned the curse into a blessing for you, because the Lord your God loved you' (Deut. 23:6).

L. "The curse'—not the [other] curses . . ."

CCXXVI.   A. Said R. Samuel bar Nahmani said R. Jonathan, "What
               is the meaning of the verse of Scripture: 'Faithful are
               the wounds of a friend, but the kisses of an enemy
               are deceitful' (Prov. 27:6)?

           B. "Better was the curse with which Ahijah the Shilonite
               cursed the Israelites than the blessing with which the
               wicked Balaam blessed them.

           C. "Ahijah the Shilonite cursed the Israelites by reference
               to a reed, as it is said, "For the Lord shall smite Israel
               as a reed is shaken in the water' (1 Kgs. 14:15).

           D. "Just as a reed stands in a place in which there is water,
               so its stem [106A] is renewed and its roots abundant,
               so that, even if all the winds in the world come and
               blow against it, they cannot move it from its place,
               but it goes on swaying with them. When the winds
               fall silent, the reed stands in its place. [So is Israel].

           E. "But the wicked Balaam blessed them by reference to
               a cedar tree [at 24:6].

           F. "Just as a cedar tree does not stand in a place in which
               there is water, so its roots are few, and its truck is not
               renewed, so that while, even if all the winds in the
               world come and blow against it, they will not move
               it from its place, when the south wind blows against
               it, it uproots it right away and turns it on its face, [so
               is Israel].

           G. "And not only so, but the reed has the merit that from
               it a quill is taken for the writing of scrolls of the To-
               rah, Prophets, and Writings."

CCXXVII.   A. "And he looked on the Kenite and took up his par-
               able" (Num. 24:21A):

           B. Said Balaam to Jethro the Kenite, "Were you not with
               us in that conspiracy [of Pharaoh, Ex. 1:22]? [Of
               course you were.] Then who gave you a seat among
               the mighty men of the earth [in the sanhedrin]?"

           C. This is in line with what R. Hiyya bar Abba said R.
               Simai said, "Three participated in that conspiracy [of
               Ex. 1:22, to destroy the Israelites in the river], Ba-
               laam, Job, and Jethro.

           D. "Balaam, who gave the advice, was slain. Job, who
               kept silent, was judged through suffering. Jethro, who

fled, had the merit that some of his sons' sons would go into session [as judges] in the Hewn-Stone Chamber,

E. "as it is said, 'And the families of scribes which dwelt at Jabez, the Tirahites, the Shemathites, the Sucathites. These are the Kenites that came of Hammath, the father of the house of Rehab' (2 Chr. 2:55). And it is written, 'And the children of the Kenite, Moses' father-in-law . . .' (Jud. 1:16)."

CCXXVIII. A. "And he took up his parable and said, Alas, who shall live when God does this" (Num. 24:23):

B. Said R. Yohanan, "Woe to the nation who is at hand when the Holy One, blessed be he, effects the redemption of his children!

C. "Who would want to throw his garment between a lion and a lioness when they are having sexual relations?"

CCXXIX. A. "And ships shall come from the coast of Chittim" (Num. 24:24):

B. Said Rab, "[Legions will come] from the coast of Chittim" [cf. Freedman, p. 722, n. 12].

C. "And they shall afflict Assyria and they shall afflict Eber" (Num. 24:24):

D. Up to Assyria they shall kill, from that point they shall enslave.

CCXXX. A. "And now, behold, I go to my people; come and I shall advise you what this people shall do to your people in the end of days" (Num. 24:24):

B. Rather than saying, "This people to your people," it should say, "Your people to this people." [Freedman, p. 723, n. 4: He advised the Moabites to ensnare Israel through uncharity. Thus he was referring to an action by the former to the latter, while Scripture suggests otherwise.]

C. Said R. Abba, "It is like a man who curses himself but assigns the curse to others. [Scripture alludes to Israel but refers to Moab.]

D. "[Balaam] said to [Balak], 'The God of these people hates fornication, and they lust after linen [clothing, which rich people wear]. Come and I shall give you advice: Make tents and set whores in them, an old one outside and a girl inside. Let them sell linen garments to them.'

E. "He made tents for them from the snowy mountain to Beth Hajeshimoth [north to south] and put whores in them, old women outside, young women inside.

F. "When an Israelite was eating and drinking and carousing and going out for walks in the market, the old lady would say to him, 'Don't you want some linen clothes?'

G. "The old lady would offer them at true value, and the girl would offer them at less.

H. "This would happen two or three times, and then [the young one] would say to him, 'Lo, you are at home here. Sit down and make a choice for yourself.' Gourds of Ammonite wine would be set near her. (At this point the wine of gentiles had not yet been forbidden to Israelites.) She would say to him, 'Do you want to drink a cup of wine?'

I. "When he had drunk a cup of wine, he would become inflamed. He said to her, 'Submit to me.' She would then take her god from her bosom and say to him, 'Worship this.'

J. "He would say to her, 'Am I not a Jew?'

K. "She would say to him, 'What difference does it make to you? Do they ask anything more from you than that you bare yourself?' But he did not know that that was how this idol was served.

L. " 'And not only so, but I shall not let you do so until you deny the Torah of Moses, your master!'

M. "As it is said, 'They went in to Baal-peor and separated themselves unto that shame, and their abominations were according as they loved' (Hos. 9:10)."

CCXXXI.　A. "And Israel dwelt in Shittim" (Num. 25:1):

B. R. Eliezer says, "The name of the place actually was Shittim."

C. R. Joshua says, "It was so called because when there they did deeds of idiocy (STWT)."

D. "And they called the people to the sacrifice of their gods" (Num. 25:2):

E. R. Eliezer says, "They met them naked."

F. R. Joshua says, "They all had involuntary seminal emissions."

G. What is the meaning of Rephidim [Ex. 17:8: "Then came Amalek and fought with Israel in Rephidim"]?

H. R. Eliezer says, "It was actually called Rephidim."

I. R. Joshua says, "It was a place in which they weakened their [ties to] the teachings of the Torah, as it is written, 'The fathers shall not look back to their children for feebleness of hands' (Jer. 47:3)."

CCXXXII. A. R. Yohanan said, "Any passage in which the word, 'And he abode' appears, it means suffering.

B. "So: 'And Israel abode in Shittim, and the people began to commit whoredom with the daughters of Moab' (Num. 23:1).

C. " 'And Jacob dwelt in the land where his father was a stranger, in the land of Canaan' (Gen. 37:1). 'And Joseph brought to his father their evil report' (Gen. 37:3).

D. "And Israel dwelt in the land of Egypt, in the country of Goshen' (Gen. 47:27), 'And the time drew near that Israel must die' (Gen. 47:29).

E. " 'And Judah and Israel dwelt safely, every man under his vine and under his fig tree' (1 Kgs. 5:5). 'And the Lord stirred up an adversary to Solomon, Hadad the Edomite; he was the king's seed in Edom' (1 Kgs. 11:14)."

CCXXXIII. A. "And they slew the kings of Midian, beside the rest of them that were slain . . . Balaam also, the son of Beor, they slew with the sword" (Num. 31:8):

B. What was he doing there anyhow?

C. Said R. Yohanan, "He went to collect a salary on account of the twenty-four thousand Israelites whom he had brought down' [Cf. Num. 25:1–9]."

D. Mar Zutra b. Tobiah said Rab said, "That is in line with what people say: 'When the camel went to ask for horns, the ears that he had they cut off him.' "

CCXXXIV. A. "Balaam also, the son of Beor, the soothsayer, [did the children of Israel slay with the sword]" (Josh. 13:22):

B. A soothsayer? He was a prophet!

C. Said R. Yohanan, "At first he was a prophet, but in the end, a mere soothsayer."

D. Said R. Pappa, "This is in line with what people say: "She who came from princes and rulers played the whore with a carpenter.' "

CCXXXV. A. [106B] "Did the children of Israel slay with the sword, among thoses who were slain by them" (Josh. 13:22).

B. Said Rab, "They inflicted upon him all four forms of execution: stoning, burning, decapitation, and strangulation."

CCXXXVI. A. A min said to R. Hanina, "Have you heard how old Balaam was?"

B. He said to him, "It is not written out explicitly. But since it is written, 'Bloody and deceitful men shall not live out half their days' (Ps. 55:24), he would have been thirty-three or thirty-four years old."

C. He said to him, "You have spoken well. I saw the notebook of Balaam, in which it is written, "Balaam, the lame, was thirty-three years old when Phineas, the brigand, killed him.' "

CCXXXVII. A. Said Mar, son of Rabina, to his son, "In regard to all of those [listed as not having a share in the world to come], you should take up the verses relating to them and expound them only in the case of the wicked Balaam.

B. "In his case, in whatever way one can expound the relevant passages [to his detriment], you do so."

CCXXXVIII. A. It is written, "Doeg" (1 Sam. 21:8) [meaning, "anxious" (Freedman, p. 276, n. 1)] and it is written, "Doeeg" (1 Sam. 22:18) [with letters indicating "woe" being inserted (Freedman, ad loc.)].

B. Said R. Yohanan, "To begin with, the Holy One, blessed be he, sits and worries lest such a son one go forth to bad ways. After he has gone forth to bad ways, he says, 'Woe that this one has gone forth!' "

CCXXXIX. A. Said R. Isaac, "What is the meaning of the verse of Scripture, "Why do you boast yourself in mischief, O mighty man? The goodness of God endures forever' (Ps. 52:3)?

B. "Said the Holy One, blessed be he, to Doeg, 'Are you not a hero in Torah-learning! Why do you boast in mischief? Is not the love of God spread over you all day long?' "

C. And said R. Isaac, "What is the meaning of the verse of Scripture, 'But to the wicked God says, What have you to do to declare my statutes?' (Ps. 50:16)?

D. "So the Holy One, blessed be he, said to the wicked Doeg, 'What have you to do to declare my statutes? When you come to the passages that deal with murderers and slanderers, what have you to say about them!' "

CCXL. A. "Or that you take my covenant in your mouth?" (Ps. 50:16):

B. Said R. Ammi, "The Torah-knowledge of Doeg comes only from the lips and beyond [but not inside his heart]."

CCXLI. A. Said R. Isaac, "What is the meaning of the verse of Scripture, 'The righteous also shall see and fear and shall laugh at him' (Ps. 52:8)?

B. "To begin with they shall fear [the wicked], but in the end they shall laugh at him."

C. And said R. Isaac, "What is the meaning of the verse of Scripture: 'He has swallowed down riches and he shall vomit them up again, the God shall cast them out of his belly' (Job 20:15)?

D. "Said David before the Holy One, blessed be he, 'Lord of the world, let Doeg die.'

E. "He said to him, ' "He has swallowed down riches, and he shall vomit them up again" (Job. 20:15).'

F. "He said to him, ' "Let God cast them out of his belly" (Job. 20:15).' "

G. And said R. Isaac, "What is the meaning of the verse of Scripture: 'God shall likewise destroy you forever' (Ps. 52:7)?

H. "Said the Holy One, blessed be he, to David, 'Should I bring Doeg to the world to come?'

I. "He said to him, ' "God shall likewise destroy you forever" (Ps. 52:7).' "

J. "What is the meaning of the verse: 'He shall take you away and pluck you out of the tent and root you out of the land of the living, selah' (Ps. 52:7)?

K. "Said the Holy One, blessed be he, 'Let a tradition in the schoolhouse be repeated in his name.'

L. "He said to him, ' "He shall take you away and pluck you out of the tent" (Ps. 52:7).'

M. " 'Then let his children be rabbis.'

N. " ' "And your root out of the land of the living, se-lah!" ' "

O. And said R. Isaac, "What is the meaning of the verse of Scripture: 'Where is he who counted, where is he who weighed? Where is he who counted the towers' (Is. 33:18)?

P. " 'Where is he who counted all the letters in the To-rah? Where is he who weighed all of the arguments *a fortiori* in the Torah?'

Q. " 'Where is he who counted the towers'—who counted the three hundred decided laws that concern the 'tower that flies in the air' [that is, the laws governing the status of the contents of a closed cabinet not standing on the ground]."

CCXLII.   A. Said R. Ammi, "Four hundred questions did Doeg and Ahitophel raise concerning the 'tower flying in the air,' and they could not answer any one of them."

B. Said Raba, "Is there any recognition of the achievement of raising questions? In the time of R. Judah, all of their repetition of Mishnah-teachings concerned the civil laws [of Baba Qamma, Baba Mesia, and Baba Batra], while, for our part, we repeat the Mishnah-traditions even dealing with tractrate Uqsin [a rather peripheral topic].

C. "When for his part R. Judah came to the law, '*A woman who pickles vegetables in a pot* [M. Toh. 2:1], or some say, '*Olives which were pickled with their leaves are insusceptible to uncleanness'* (M. Uqs. 2:1], he would say, 'I see here all the points of reflection of Rab and Samuel.

D. "But we repeat the tractate of Uqsin at thirteen sessions [having much more to say about it].

E. "When R. Judah merely removed his shoes [in preparation for a fast], it would rain.

F. "When we cry out [in supplication], no one pays any attention to us.

G. "But the Holy One, blessed be he, demands the heart, as it is written, 'But the Lord looks on the heart' (1 Sam. 16:7)."

CCXLIII.   A. Said R. Mesharsheya, "Doeg and Ahitophel did not know how to reason concerning traditions."

B. Objected Mar Zutra, "Can it be the case that one concerning whom it is written, 'Where is he who counted, where is he who weighed, where is he who counted the towers?' (Is. 33:18) should not be able to reason concerning traditions?

C. "But it never turned out that traditions [in their names] were stated in accord with the decided law, for it is written, 'The secret of the Lord is with those who fear him' (Ps. 25:14)."

CCXLIV.   A. Said R. Ammi, "Doeg did not die before he forgot his learning, as it is said, 'He shall die without instruction, and in the greatness of his folly he shall go astray' (Prov. 5:23)."

B. Rab said, "He was afflicted with *saraat,* for it is said, 'You have destroyed all them who go awhoring from you' (Ps. 73:27), and elsewhere it is written, 'And if it not be redeemed within the span of a full year, then the house shall be established finally [to him who bought it]' (Lev. 25:30).

C. "[The word indicated as 'finally' and the word for 'destroyed' use the same letters]. And we have learned in the Mishnah: *The only difference between one who is definitely afflicted with saraat and one who is shut away for observation is in respect to letting the hair grow long and tearing the garment* [M. Meg. 1:7],

[Freedman, p. 729, n. 6: which shows that the term at hand is used to indicate someone is afflicted with saraat. Hence the first of the two verses is to be rendered, 'You have smitten with defininte leprosy all those who go awhoring from you.']"

CCXLV.

A. Said R. Yohanan, "Three injurious angels were designated for Doeg: one to make him forget his learning, one to burn his soul, and one to scatter his dust among the synagogues and schoolhouses."

B. And said R. Yohanan, "Doeg and Ahitophel never saw one another. Doeg lived in the time of Saul, and Ahitophel in the time of David.

C. And said R. Yohanan, "Doeg and Ahitophel did not live out half their days."

D. It has been taught on Tannaite authority along these same lines:

E. "Bloody and deceitful men shall not live out half their days" (Ps. 55:24):

F. Doeg lived only for thirty-four years, Ahitophel for thirty-three.

G. And said R. Yohanan, "At the outset David called Ahitophel his master, at the end he called him his friend, and finally he called him his disciple.

H. "At the beginning he called him his master: 'But it was you, a man my equal, my guide, and my acquaintance' (Ps. 55:14).

I. "Then his companion: 'We took sweet counsel together and walked into the house of God in company' (Ps. 55:15).

J. "Finally, his disciple: 'Yea, my own familiar friend, in whom I trusted [107A], who ate my bread, has lifted his heel against me' (Ps. 56:10). [Freedman, p. 729, no. 10: This is understood to refer to Ahitophel, and eating bread is a metaphor for 'who learned of my teaching.']"

CCXLVI.

A. Said R. Judah said Rab, "One should never put himself to the test, for lo, David, king of Israel, put himself to the test and he stumbled.

B. "He said before him, 'Lord of the world, on what account do people say, "God of Abraham, God of Isaac, and God of Jacob," but they do not say, "God of David"?'

C. "He said to him, 'They endured a test for me, while you have not endured a test for me.'

D. "He said before him, 'Lord of the world, here I am. Test me.'

E. "For it is said, 'Examine me, O Lord, and try me' (Ps. 26:1).

F. "He said to him, 'I shall test you, and I shall do for you something that I did not do for them. I did not inform them [what I was doing], while I shall tell you what I am going to do. I shall try you with a matter having to do with sexual relations.'

G. "Forthwith: 'And it came to pass in an eventide that David arose from off his bed' (2 Sam. 11:2)."

H. Said R. Judah, "He turned his habit of having sexual relations by night into one of having sexual relations by day.

I. "He lost sight of the following law:

J. " 'There is in man a small organ, which makes him feel hungry when he is sated and makes him feel sated when he is hungry.' "

K. "And he walked on the roof of the king's palace, and from the roof he saw a woman washing herself, and the woman was very beautiful to look upon" (2 Sam. 11:2):

L. Bath Sheba was shampooing her hair behind a screen. Satan came to [David] and appeared to him in the form of a bird. He shot an arrow at [the screen] and broke it down, so that she stood out in the open, and he saw her.

M. Forthwith: "And David sent and inquired after the woman. And one said, Is not this Bath Sheba, the daughter of Eliam, the wife of Uriah the Hittite? And David sent messengers and took her, and she came to him, and he lay with her; for she was purified from her uncleanness; and she returned to her house" (2 Sam. 11:2–3).

N. That is in line with what is written: "You have tried my heart, you have visited me in the night, you have tried me and shall find nothing: I am purposed that my mouth shall not transgress" (Ps. 17:3).

O. He said, "Would that a bridle had fallen into my mouth, that I had not said what I said!"

CCXLVII.

A. Raba interpreted Scripture, asking, "What is the meaning of the following verse: 'To the chief musician, a Psalm of David. In the Lord I put my trust, how do you say to my soul, Flee as a bird to your mountain?' (Ps. 11:1)?

B. "Said David before the Holy One, blessed be he, 'Lord of the world, Forgive me for that sin, so that people should not say, "The mountain that is among you [that is, your king] has been driven off by a bird." ' "

C. Raba interpreted Scripture, asking, "What is the meaning of the following verse: 'Against you, you alone, have I sinned, and done this evil in your sight, that you might be justified when you speak and be clear when you judge' (Ps. 11:1)?

D. "Said David before the Holy One, blessed be he, 'Lord of the world. It is perfectly clear to you that if I had wanted to overcome my impulse to do evil, I should have done so. But I had in mind that people not say, "The slave has conquered the Master [God, and should then be included as 'God of David']." ' "

E. Raba interpreted Scripture, asking, "What is the meaning of the following verse: 'For I am ready to halt and my sorrow is continually before me' (Ps. 38:18)?

F. "Bath Sheba, daughter of Eliam, was designated for David from the six days of creation, but she came to him through anguish."

G. And so did a Tannaite authority of the house of R. Ishmael ach], "Bath Sheba, daughter of Eliam, was designated for David, but he 'ate' her while she was yet unripe."

H. Raba interpreted Scripture, asking, "What is the meaning of the following verse: 'But in my adversity they rejoiced and gathered themselves together, yes, the abjects gathered themselves together against me and I did not know it, they tore me and did not cease' (Ps. 35:15)?

I. "Said David before the Holy One, blessed be he, 'Lord of the world, it is perfectly clear to you that if they had torn my flesh, my blood would not have flowed [because I was so embarassed].

J. " 'Not only so, but when they take up the four modes of execution inflicted by a court, they interrupt their Mishnah-study and say to me, "David, he who has sexual relations with a married woman—how is he put to death?"

K. " 'I say to them, "He who has sexual relations with a married woman is put to death through strangulation, but he has a share in the world to come, while he who humiliates his fellow in public has no share in the world to come." ' "

CCXLVIII. A. Said R. Judah said Rab, "Even when David was sick, he carried out the eighteen acts of sexual relations that were owing to his [eighteen] wives, as it is written, 'I am weary with my groaning, all night I make my bed swim, I water my couch with my tears' (Ps. 6:7)."

B. And said R. Judah said Rab, "David wanted to worship idols, as it is said, 'And it happened that when David came to the head, where he worshiped God' (2 Sam. 15:32), and 'head' only means idols, as it is written, 'This image's head was of fine gold' (Dan. 2:32).

C. " 'Behold, Hushai, the Archite came to meet him with his coat rent and earth upon his head' (2 Sam. 15:32):

D. "He said to David, 'Are people to say that a king such as you has worshiped idols?'

E. "He said to him, 'Will the son of a king such as me kill him? It is better that such a king as me worship an idol and not profane the Name of heaven in public.'

F. "He said, 'Why then did you marry a woman captured in battle? [Freedman, p. 732, n. 7: Absalom's mother, Maachah, the daughter of Talmai, king of Geshur, was a war captive.]"

G. "He said to him, 'As to a woman captured in battle, the All-Merciful has permitted marrying her.'

H. "He said to him, 'You did not correctly interpret the meaning of the proximity of two verses. For it is written, "If a man has stubborn and rebellious son" (Deut. 21:18).

I. " '[The proximity teaches that] whoever marries a woman captured in battle will have a stubborn and rebellious son.' "

CCXLIX.   A. R. Dosetai of Biri interpreted Scripture, "To what may David be likened? To a gentile merchant.

B. "Said David before the Holy One, blessed be he, 'Lord of the world, 'Who can understand his errors?" (Ps. 19:13).'

C. "He said to him, 'They are remitted for you.'

D. " ' "Cleanse me of hidden faults" (Ps. 19:13).'

E. " 'They are remitted to you.'

F. " ' "Keep back your servant also from presumptuous sins" (Ps. 19:13).'

G. " 'They are remitted to you.'

H. " ' "Let them not have dominion over me, then I shall be upright" (Ps. 19:13), so that the rabbis will not hold me up as an example.'

I. " 'They are remitted to you.'

J. " ' "And I shall be innocent of great transgression" (Ps. 19:13), so that they will not write down my ruin.'

K. "He said to him, 'That is not possible. Now if the Y that I took away from the name of Sarah [changing it from Sarai to Sarah] stood crying for so many years until Joshua came and I added the Y [removed from Sarah's name] to his name, as it is said, "And Moses called Oshea, the son of Nun, Jehoshua" (Num. 13:16), how much the more will a complete passage of Scripture [cry out if I remove that passage from its rightful place]!' "

CCL.   A. "And I shall be innocent from great transgression: (Ps. 19:13):

B. He said before him, "Lord of the world, forgive me for the whole of that sin [as though I had never done it]."

C. He said to him, "Solomon, your son, even now is destined to say in his wisdom, 'Can a man take fire in his bosom, and his clothes not be burned? Can one go upon hot coals, and his feet not be burned? So he who goes in to his neighbor's wife, whoever touches her shall not be innocent' (Prov. 6:27–29)."

D. He said to him, "Will I be so deeply troubled?"

E. He said to him, "Accept suffering [as atonement]."

F. He accepted the suffering.

CCLI.

A. Said R. Judah said Rab, "For six months David was afflicted with *saraat,* and the Presence of God left him, and the sanhedrin abandoned him.

B. "He was afflicted with *saraat,* as it is written, 'Purge me with hyssop and I shall be clean, wash me and I shall be whiter than snow' (Ps. 51:9).

C. "The Presence of God left him, as it is written, 'Restore to me the joy of your salvation and uphold me with your free spirit' (Ps. 51:14).

D. "The Sanhedrin abandoned him, as it is written, 'Let those who fear you turn to me and those who have known your testimonies' (Ps. 119:79).

E. "How do we know that this lasted for six months? As it is written, 'And the days that David ruled over Israel were forty years: [107B] Seven years he reigned in Hebron, and thirty-three he reigned in Jerusalem' (1 Kgs. 2:11).

F. "Elsewhere it is written, 'In Hebron he reigned over Judah seven years and six months' (2 Sam. 5:5).

G. "So the six months were not taken into account. Accordingly, he was afflicted with *saraat* [for such a one is regarded as a corpse].

H. "He said before him, 'Lord of the world, forgive me for that sin.'

I. " 'It is forgiven to you.'

J. " ' "Then show me a token for good, that they who hate me may see it and be ashamed, because you, Lord, have helped me and comforted me" (Ps. 86:17).'

K. "He said to him, 'While you are alive, I shall not reveal [the fact that you are forgiven], but I shall reveal it in the lifetime of your son, Solomon.'

L. "When Solomon had built the house of the sanctuary, he tried to bring the ark into the house of the Holy of Holies. The gates cleaved to one another. He recited twenty-four prayers [Freedman, p. 734, n. 4: in 2 Chr. 6, words for prayer, supplication, and hymn occur twenty-four times], but was not answered.

M. "He said, 'Lift up your head, O you gates, and be lifted up, you everlasting doors, and the King of glory shall come in. Who is this King of glory? The Lord strong and might, the Lord mighty in battle' (Ps. 24:7ff.).

N. "And it is further said, 'Lift up your heads, O you gates even lift them up, you everlasting doors' (Ps. 24:7).

O. "But he was not answered.

P. "When he said, 'Lord God, turn not away the face of your anointed, remember the mercies of David, your servant' (2 Chr. 6:42), forthwith he was answered.

Q. "At that moment the faces of David's enemies turned as black as the bottom of a pot, for all Israel knew that the Holy One, blessed be he, had forgiven him for that sin."

CCLII.   A. *Gehazi [M. 11:2F]:*

B. As it is written, "And Elisha came to Damascus" (2 Kgs. 8:7).

C. Where was he traveling [when he came to Damascus]?

D. Said R. Yohanan, "He went to bring Gehazi back in repentence, but he did not repent.

E. "He said to him, 'Repent.'

F. "He said to him, 'This is the tradition that I have received from you: "Whoever has both sinned and caused others to sin will never have sufficient means to do penitence." ' "

G. What had he done?

H. Some say, "He hung a lodestone on the sin[ful statue built by] Jeroboam and suspended it between heaven and earth."

I. Others say, "He carved on it the Name of God, so that it would say, 'I [am the Lord your God] . . . You shall not have [other gods . . .]' (Ex. 20:1–2)."

J. Still others say, "He drove rabbis away from his presence, as it is said, 'And the sons of the prophets said to Elisha, "See now the place where we swell before you is too small for us' " (2 Kgs. 6:1). The sense then is that up to that time, it was not too small."

CCLIII.

A. Our rabbis have taught on Tannaite authority:

B. Under all circumstances the left hand should push away and the right hand should draw near,

C. not in the manner of Elisha, who drove away Gehazi with both hands.

D. What is the case with Gehazi?

E. As it is written, "And Naaman said, 'Be pleased to accept two talents' " (2 Kgs. 5:23).

F. And it is written, "But he said to him, 'Did I not go with you in spirit when the man turned from his chariot to meet you? Was it a time to accept money and garments, olive orchards and vineyards, sheep and oxen, menservants and maidservants' " (2 Kgs. 5:26).

G. But did he receive all these things? He got only silver and garments.

H. Said R. Isaac, "At that moment Elisha was occupied with the study of the list of eight dead creeping things" (M. Shab. 14:1, Lev. 11:29FF.].

I. Naaman, head of the army of the king of Syria, was afflicted with *saraat*. A young girl who had been taken captive from the land of Israel said to him, "If you go to Elisha, he will heal you."

J. When he got there, he said to him, "Go, immerse in the Jordan."

K. He said to him, "You are making fun of me!"

L. Those who were with him said to him, "Go, try it, what difference does it make to you?"

M. He went and immersed in the Jordan and was healed.

N. He came and brought him everything that he had, but [Elisha] would not take it. Gehazi took leave of Elisha and went and took what he took and hid it.

O. When he came back, Elisha saw the marks of *saraat,* as they blossomed all over his head.

P. "He said to Gehazi, 'Wicked one! The time has come to receive the reward for the eight dead creeping things: "Therefore the leprosy of Naaman shall cleave to you and to your descendants forever" (2 Kgs. 8:27).' "

CCLIV. A. "Now there were four men who were lepers [at the entrance to the gate]" (2 Kgs. 7:3):

B. R. Yohanan said, "This refers to Gehazi and his three sons."

C. It has been taught on Tannaite authority:

D. R. Simeon b. Eleazar says, "Also in one's natural impulse, as to a child or a woman, one should push away with the left hand and draw near with the right hand." [Freedman, p. 736, n. 2: The uncensored edition continues: What of R. Joshua b. Perahiah?—When King Yannai slew our Rabbis, R. Joshua b. Perahiah (and Jesus) fled to Alexandria of Egypt. On the resumption of peace, Simeon b. Shetach sent to him: "From me, (Jerusalem) the holy city, to thee, Alexandria of Egypt (my sister). My husband dwelleth within thee and I am desolate." He arose, went, and found himself in a certain inn, where great honor was shown him. "How beautiful is this Acsania?" (The word denotes both inn and innkeeper, R. Joshua used it in the first sense; the answer assumes the second to be meant.) Thereupon (Jesus) observed, "Rabbi, her eyes are narrow." "Wretch," he rebuked him, "dost thou thus engage thyself." He sounded four hundred trumpets and excommunicated him. He (Jesus) came before him many times pleading. "Receive me!" But he would pay no heed to him. One day he (R. Joshua) was reciting the

Shema, when Jesus came before him. He intended to receive him and made a sign to him. He (Jesus) thinking that it was to repel him, went, put up a brick, and worshiped it. "Repent," said he (R. Joshua) to him. He replied, "I have thus learned from thee: He who sins and causes others to sin is not afforded the means of repentance.' And a Master has said, 'Jesus the Nazarene practiced magic and led Israel astray."]

CCLV.
A. Our rabbis have taught on Tannaite authority:

B. Elisha bore three illnesses,

C. one because he brought the she-bears against the children, one because he pushed Gehazi away with both hands, and one on account of which he died.

D. For it is said, "Now Elisha had fallen sick of the ailment of which he died" (2 Kgs. 13:14).

CCLVI.
A. Until Abraham there was no such thing as [the sign of] old age. Whoever saw Abraham thought, "This is Isaac." Whoever saw Isaac thought, "This is Abraham."

B. Abraham prayed for mercy so that he might have [signs of] old age, as it is said, "And Abraham was old, and well stricken in age" (Gen. 24:1).

C. Until the time of Jacob there was no such thing as illness, so he prayed for mercy and illness came about, as it is written, "And someone told Joseph, behold, your father is sick: (Gen. 48:1).

D. Until the time of Elisha, no one who was sick ever got well. Elisha came along and prayed for mercy and got well, as it is written, "Now Elisha had fallen sick of the illness of which he died" (2 Kgs. 13:14) [Freedman: This shows that he had been sick on previous occasions too, but recovered.]

The important question at hand is self-evident: how has the compositor of this tractate of monstrous proportions arranged the materials at hand? The answer to the question is equally self-evident: he has laid out available materials, available in large blocks indeed, in accord with (1) the thematic program of the Mishnah, and (2) the further principles of agglutination and conglomeration dictated by the materials at hand. In each major unit (signified in what follows by a Roman numeral), he has taken up a fact—a topic, and allegation—of the Mishnah. Once he has dealt with that fact, he then drew upon materials that supplied a secondary expansion of it, and made use, further, of entire blocks of materials already arranged and joined together on the basis of principles of organization other than those deriving from Mishnah-exegesis. That, in a single statement, accounts for the arrangement of everything at hand. Let us proceed to test the thesis just now announced by reviewing an outline of the units of the immense construction at hand.

I. The life of the world to come: when and why is it denied [M. 11:1A–D]

A. Those who do not believe in it did not get it: I

B. How on the basis of the Torah do we know that there will be resurrection of the dead: II–X

C. Disputes with pagans on the resurrection of the dead: XI–XIV (Tradental construction based on Gebihah: XIV–XVII)

D. Other disputes with pagan sages: XVIII–XXI

E. Verses on the resurrection of the dead: XXII–XXV, XXVII–XXXV (Tradental construction based on Deut. 32:39: XXV–XXVI)

II. Examples in Scripture of the Resurrection of the Dead

A. Daniel's case: Hananiah, Mishael, and Azariah: XXXVI–XLIV, XLVII–XLIX (Further materials on Nebuchadnezzer: XLV–XLVI) (Tradental continuation of XLIX:L)

III. Messianic Passages of Scripture. Sennacherib, Nebuchadnezzar

A. Isaiah and Hezekiah: LI–LXVII, LXXI–LXXXI

B. David: LXVIII–LXX

We see, therefore, that the entire construction devotes itself to the exposition of the Mishnah. Two units, one on the resurrection of the dead, the other on Messianic crises in Israelite history, complement unit I. Units I, IV–X, systematically work their way through the Mishnah's statements. Units II and III treat the resurrection of the dead, on the one hand, and the coming of the Messiah, on the other. Certainly any effort to expound the theme of the life of the world to come would have to deal with these other two topics, and, what the compositor has done is simply place into the correct context-namely, M. 11:1A–B—the available materials on these other two components of the principal congeries of ideas at hand. That is, once we take up the world to come, we deal also with the resurrection and the coming the the Messiah. Then, as is clear, the compositor simply proceeded on his way, generally defining the Mishnah's terms, often also greatly expanding on the themes introduced by the Mishnah. So the construction as a whole, seemingly vast and formless, turns out to follow rather simple rules of composition and organization.

For Further Reference

This anthology, while free standing and meant to be read on its own, provides a summary of principal ideas of, as well as a selection of translations made by, the author, in a number of prior books. Each of those books provides an extensive bibliography on its subject. The more important items are as follows:

A Life of Yohanan ben Zakaai. Leiden, 1962: Brill. Awarded the Abraham Berliner Prize in Jewish History, Jewish Theological Seminary of America, 1962. Second edition, completely revised, 1970. Japanese translation: Yamamoto Shoten Publishing House, Tokyo. Expected in 1988.

Aphrahat and Judaism. The Christian Jewish Argument in Fourth Century Iran. Leiden, 1971: Brill.

The Rabbinic Traditions about the Pharisees before 70. Leiden, 1971: Brill. I–III.

The Tosefta. Translated from the Hebrew. N.Y., 1977–1986: Ktav. I–VI.

The Talmud of the Land of Israel. A Preliminary Translation and Explanation. Chicago: The University of Chicago Press: 1982–1989.

Judaism and Scripture: The Evidence of Leviticus Rabbah. Chicago, 1985: The University of Chicago Press.

Genesis Rabbah. The Judaic Commentary on Genesis. A New American Translation. Atlanta, 1985: Scholars Press for Brown Judaic Studies.

Sifra. The Judaic Commentary on Leviticus. A New Translation. The Leper. Leviticus 13:1–14:57. Chico, 1985: Scholars Press for Brown Judaic Studies. Based on the translation of *Sifra Parashiyyot Negaim* and *Mesora* in *A History of the Mishnaic Law of Purities. VI. Negaim. Sifra*. [With a section by Roger Brooks.]

Sifré to Numbers. An American Translation. I. 1–58 Atlanta, 1986: Scholars Press for Brown Judaic Studies.

Sifré to Numbers. An American Translation. II. 59–115. Atlanta, 1986: Scholars Press for Brown Judaic Studies. [III. *116–161:* William Scott Green].

Sifré to Deuteronomy. An American Translation (Atlanta, 1987: Scholars Press for Brown Judaic Studies) I–II.

A History of the Mishnaic Law of Purities. Leiden, 1977: Brill. XXI. *The Redaction and Formulation of the Order of Purities in the Mishnah and Tosefta.* And XXII. *The Mishnaic System of Uncleanness. Its Context and History.*

A History of the Mishnaic Law of Holy Things. Leiden, 1979: Brill. VI. *The Mishnaic System of Sacrifice and Sanctuary.*

A History of the Mishnaic Law of Women. Leiden, 1980: Brill. V. *The Mishnaic System of Women.*

A History of the Mishnaic Law of Appointed Times. Leiden, 1981: Brill. V. *The Mishnaic System of Appointed Times.*

A History of the Mishnaic Law of Damages. Leiden, 1985: Brill. V. *The Mishnaic System of Damages.*

The Integrity of Leviticus Rabbah. The Problem of the Autonomy of a Rabbinic Document. Chico, 1985: Scholars Press for Brown Judaic Studies.

Comparative Midrash: The Plan and Program of Genesis Rabbah and Leviticus Rabbah. Atlanta, 1986: Scholars Press for Brown Judaic Studies.

Judaism. The Evidence of the Mishnah. Chicago, 1981: University of Chicago Press. Paperback edition: 1984. *Choice,* "Outstanding Academic Book List," 1982–83. Second printing, 1985. Hebrew translation: Tel Aviv, 1986: Sifriat Poalim. Italian translation: Casale Monferrato, 1987: Editrice Marietti.

Judaism in Society: The Evidence of the Yerushalmi. Toward the Natural History of a Religion. Chicago, 1983: The University of Chicago Press. *Choice,* "Outstanding Academic Book List," 1984–1985.

Judaism: The Classical Statement. The Evidence of the Bavli. Chicago, 1986: University of Chicago Press. *Choice,* "Outstanding Academic Book List," 1987.

Ancient Israel after Catastrophe. The Religious World-View of the Mishnah. The Richard Lectures for 1982. Charlottesville, 1983: The University Press of Virginia.

The Foundations of Judaism. Method, Teleology. Doctrine. Philadelphia, 1983–85: Fortress Press. I–III. I. *Midrash in Context. Exegesis in Formative Judaism.* II. *Messiah in Context. Israel's History and Destiny in Formative Judaism.* Italian translation: Casale Monferrato, 1988: Editrice Marietti. III. *Torah: From Scroll to Symbol in Formative Judaism.*

The Oral Torah. The Sacred Books of Judaism. An Introduction. San Francisco, 1985: Harper & Row.

Vanquished Nation, Broken Spirit. The Virtues of the Heart in Formative Judaism. New York, 1986: Cambridge University Press.

Judaisms and their Messiahs in the beginning of Christianity. New York, 1986: Cambridge University Press. [Edited with William Scott Green, and Ernest S. Frerichs.]

Judaism in the Matrix of Christianity. Philadelphia, 1986: Fortress Press.

Judaism and Christianity in the Age of Constantine. The Initial Confrontation. Chicago, 1987: University of Chicago Press.

The Death and Birth of Judaism. The Impact of Christianity, Secularism, and the Holocaust on Jewish Faith. New York, 1987: Basic Books.

Method and Meaning in Ancient Judaism. Missoula, 1979: Scholars Press for Brown Judaic Studies. Second printing, 1983.

Method and Meaning in Ancient Judaism. Second Series. Chico, 1980: Scholars Press for Brown Judaic Studies.

Method and Meaning in Ancient Judaism. Third Series. Chico, 1980: Scholars Press for Brown Judaic Studies.

Ancient Judaism. Disputes and Debates. Chico, 1984: Scholars Press for Brown Judaic Studies.

The Pharisees. Rabbinic Perspectives. New York, 1985: Ktav Publishing House.

The Jews in Talmudic Babylonia. A Political History. New York, 1986: Ktav.

Judaism, Christianity, and Zoroastrianism in Talmudic Babylonia. New York, 1986: Ktav.

Early Rabbinic Judaism. Historical Studies in Religion, Literature, and Art. Leiden, 1975: Brill.

From Politics to Piety. The Emergence of Pharisaic Judaism. Englewood Cliffs, 1973: Prentice-Hall. Second printing, New York, 1978: Ktav. Japanese translation: Tokyo, 1985: Kyo Bun Kwan.

Editor: *Contemporary Judaic Fellowship. In Theory and in Practice.* New York, 1972: Ktav.

Invitation to the Talmud. A Teaching Book. New York, 1973: Harper & Row. Second printing, 1974. Paperback edition, 1975. Reprinted: 1982. Second edition, completely revised, San Francisco, 1984: Harper & Row. Japanese translation: Tokyo, 1988: Yamamoto Shoten.

First Century Judaism in Crisis. Yohanan ben Zakkai and the Renaissance of Torah. Nashville, 1975: Abingdon. Second Printing, New York, 1981: Ktav.

Torah from Our Sages: Pirke Avot. A New American Translation and Explanation. Chappaqua, 1983: Rossel.

Our Sages, Gods, and Israel. An Anthology of the Yerushalmi. Chappaqua, 1984: Rossel. 1985 selection, Jewish Book Club.

Judaism in the Beginning of Christianity. Philadelphia, 1983: Fortress. British edition, London, 1984: SPCK. German translation, Stuttgart, 1988: Calwerverlag. Dutch translation, Kampen, 1986: J. H. Kok. French translation: Paris, 1986: Editions du Cerf. 1986. Norwegian: Trondheim, 1987: Relieff. Japanese, expected in Tokyo, 1989: Kyo Bun Kwan.

Genesis and Judaism: The Perspective of Genesis Rabbah. An Analytical Anthology. Atlanta, 1986. Scholars and Press for Brown Judaic Studies.

Judaism: The First Two Centuries. Abbreviated version of *Judaism: The Evidence of the Mishnah* Chicago, 1988: University of Chicago Press.

General Index

Index to Biblical and Talmudic References

2 Mishnah